T0323491

Making Commons Dynamic

With an emphasis on the challenges of sustaining the commons across local to global scales, *Making Commons Dynamic* examines the empirical basis of theorising the concepts of commonisation and decommonisation as a way to understand commons as a process and offers analytical directions for policy and practice that can potentially help maintain commons as commons in the future.

Focusing on commonisation–decommonisation as an analytical framework useful to examine and respond to changes in the commons, the chapter contributions explore how natural resources are commonised and decommonised through the influence of multi-level internal and external drivers, and their implications for commons governance across disparate geographical and temporal contexts. It draws from a large number of geographically diverse empirical cases – 20 countries in North, South, and Central America and South- and South-East Asia. They involve a wide range of commons – related to fisheries, forests, grazing, wetlands, coastal-marine, rivers and dams, aquaculture, wildlife, tourism, groundwater, surface freshwater, mountains, small islands, social movements, and climate.

The book is a transdisciplinary endeavour with contributions by scholars from geography, history, sociology, anthropology, political studies, planning, human ecology, cultural and applied ecology, environmental and development studies, environmental science and technology, public policy, Indigenous/tribal studies, Latin American and Asian studies, and environmental change and governance, and authors representing the commons community, NGOs, and policy. Contributors include academics, community members, NGOs, practitioners, and policymakers. Therefore, commonisation–decommonisation lessons drawn from these chapters are well suited for contributing to the practice, policy, and theory of the commons, both locally and globally.

Prateep Kumar Nayak is Associate Professor and Associate Director of Graduate Studies in the School of Environment, Enterprise and Development, Faculty of Environment, University of Waterloo, Canada.

Routledge Studies in Environment, Culture, and Society

Series editors: Bernhard Glaeser and Heike Egner

This series opens up a forum for advances in environmental studies relating to society and its social, cultural, and economic underpinnings. The underlying assumption guiding this series is that there is an important, and so far little-explored, interaction between societal as well as cultural givens and the ways in which societies both create and respond to environmental issues. As such, this series encourages the exploration of the links between prevalent practices, beliefs, and values, as differentially manifested in diverse societies, and the distinct ways in which those societies confront the environment.

Trading Environments
Frontiers, Commercial Knowledge, and Environmental Transformation, 1750–1990
Edited by Gordon M. Winder and Andreas Dix

Transdisciplinary Research and Sustainability
Collaboration, Innovation and Transformation
Edited by Martina Padmanabhan

Global Change in Marine Systems
Integrating Natural, Social and Governing Responses
Edited by Patrice Guillotreau, Alida Bundy and Ian Perry

In Pursuit of Healthy Environments
Historical Cases on the Environment-Health Nexus
Edited by Esa Ruuskanen and Heini Hakosalo

Making Commons Dynamic
Understanding Change Through Commonisation and Decommonisation
Edited by Prateep Kumar Nayak

For more information, please visit: www.routledge.com/Routledge-Studies-in-Environment-Culture-and-Society/book-series/RSECS

Making Commons Dynamic

Understanding Change Through Commonisation and Decommonisation

Edited by Prateep Kumar Nayak

LONDON AND NEW YORK

First published 2021
by Routledge
2 Park Square, Milton Park, Abingdon, Oxon OX14 4RN

and by Routledge
52 Vanderbilt Avenue, New York, NY 10017

Routledge is an imprint of the Taylor & Francis Group, an informa business

British Library Cataloguing-in-Publication Data
A catalogue record for this book is available from the British Library

Library of Congress Cataloging-in-Publication Data
A catalog record has been requested for this book

ISBN: 978-0-367-13800-4 (hbk)
ISBN: 978-0-429-02863-2 (ebk)

Typeset in Times New Roman
by Newgen Publishing UK

Access the Support Material: www.routledge.com/9780367138004

This work is dedicated to all those millions of commoners, in every corner of this world, who tirelessly work to maintain their commons as commons for the future generations.

Contents

PART V
Closing 309

Illustrations

Figures

Tables

Box

Note on editor

Prateep Kumar Nayak is Associate Professor and Associate Director of Graduate Studies in the School of Environment, Enterprise and Development, Faculty of Environment, University of Waterloo, Canada. Prateep's academic background is in political science, environmental studies, and international development. He does interdisciplinary work with an active interest in combining social and ecological perspectives. Prateep's research focuses on the understanding of complex human–environment connections (or disconnections) with particular attention to change, its drivers, their influence and possible ways to deal with them. His main research interests include commons, environmental governance, social–ecological system resilience, environmental justice, and political ecology. In the past, Prateep worked as a development professional in India on issues around community-based governance of land, water, and forests commons, focusing specifically at the interface of research, implementation, and public policy. Prateep is a lead author for IPBES Global Assessment of Sustainable use of Wild Species and a member of the Human Dimensions Working Group, Integrated Marine Biosphere Research (IMBeR). Prateep was the co-chair of the 2015 Biennial Conference International Association for the Study of the Commons. He is a past Trudeau Scholar, a Harvard University Fellow in Sustainability Science, and a recipient of Canada's Governor General Academic Gold Medal. Prateep is also the Project Director of Vulnerability to Viability (V2V) Global Partnership for building strong small-scale fisheries.

Note on contributors

Evan J. Andrews is a PhD candidate at the University of Waterloo's School of Environment, Resources and Sustainability, where he holds a Joseph-Armand Bombardier Canada Doctoral Scholarship. He specialises in human behaviour and governance in inland and coastal fisheries and contributes broadly to transdisciplinary research and practice in the field of sustainability science. In addition, Mr. Andrews is an early career research leader in the policy sciences field, and currently serves as the Vice President of the Society of Policy Scientists.

Derek Armitage is a professor in the School of Environment, Resources and Sustainability, University of Waterloo, Canada. His academic background is in geography, environmental studies, and international development. Prior to academia, Derek worked as a consultant on a variety of projects for Environment Canada, Fisheries and Oceans Canada, the GEF (World Bank), ADB, and IADB, and before that, as a CUSO volunteer in Tanzania. He is a Senior Fellow, Earth Systems Governance project, Adjunct Professor, Natural Resources Institute (University of Manitoba), and past Working Group Leader, Oceans Management Research Network (Canada). Derek also serves as an editor for the journals *Ecology and Society* and *Conservation Letters*.

Xavier Basurto is an associate professor at the Marine Lab of the Nicholas School of the Environment at Duke University. He has formal training in public policy, anthropology, and biology. His research program on the commons has mostly focused on the communities of the Gulf of California in Mexico where he has been studying the governance of coastal marine resources since 1999.

Fikret Berkes is a professor emeritus in the Natural Resources Institute, University of Manitoba, Canada. Berkes is an applied ecologist by background and works at the interface of natural and social sciences. He joined the University of Manitoba in 1991 as the Director of NRI, a position he occupied until 1996. He has served as the president of the International

Association for the Study of Common Property (1996–1998) and as the leader of a number of research groups. He has devoted most of his professional life to investigating the relations between societies and their resources, and to examining the conditions under which the "tragedy of the commons" may be avoided. He works on theoretical and practical aspects of community-based management, co-management, and traditional knowledge. His publications include the books *Sacred Ecology* (2008), *Breaking Ice* (2005), *Navigating Social-Ecological Systems* (2003), and *Managing Small-Scale Fisheries* (2001). See his list of publications and downloadable PDFs elsewhere on this web site. Dr. Berkes holds a Tier I Canada Research Chair (2002) and the title of Distinguished Professor (2003).

Jessica Blythe is an assistant professor of Environmental Sustainability at Brock University. Her research interests include climate change adaptation, equitable ocean governance, and transformations to sustainability.

Carlos Cowan Ros has a doctorate in Sciences (UFRRJ, Brazil), and master's in Rural Development (UFRGS, Brazil) and Agronomic Engineering (UBA, Argentina). Carlos is a researcher at the Centre for Urban and Rural Studies of the National Scientific and Technical Research Council (CONICET), and Director of the Specialization in Rural Development at the University of Buenos Aires. His research focuses on the themes of peasants, Indigenous peoples, public policies, and rural development.

Ana Carolina Esteves Dias is an interdisciplinary researcher working on coastal governance. She is currently pursuing her PhD at the University of Waterloo, Canada. She also holds a bachelor's degree in Biology and a master's in Human Ecology from the University of Campinas, Brazil. Ana's research explores and creates ways to improve coastal governance, integrating coastal conservation and community wellbeing. Her main areas of expertise and interest include marine protected areas, governance fit, social wellbeing, ecosystem services, community-based conservation. Ana is a co-founder of the Socio-ecological Co-creation Network for Latin America (RESACA), which explores and develops co-creation methodologies from the transdisciplinary dialogue between art, science, politics, and society to respond to social–ecological challenges. She is a member of the Environmental Change and Governance Group (ECGG), Research and outreach group on Conservation and Management of the Commons (CGCommons), the Community-based Research Network (CCRN), and a past Institutional Fellow at the Brazilian National Institute for Space Research.

Patricia Dorn has a BSc in Geography from Kiel (Germany) and an interdisciplinary master's in Sustainability Studies from Vienna, Austria. Her research focuses on sacred ecology and marine governance. She previously worked with the German Development Cooperation in South-East Asia, and currently she is working with the Indo-German Biodiversity Programme in New Delhi.

Sherman Farhad is currently finishing her first postdoctoral fellowship at the Environmental Sustainability Research Centre at Brock University (Canada) to start her new post-doc at University of Cordoba (Spain). She holds a PhD in Environment and Society from Universidad Pablo de Olavide (Spain). Sherman is interested in human–environment relationships from complex systems perspective. Her research focuses on environmental governance (specially on commons governance, ecosystem services governance, and water governance), social–ecological resilience, and sustainability transformations. She is particularly interested in how societies perceive, interpret, and deal with environmental changes and uncertainties, and how diverse stakeholders (resource users, government actors, and researchers) can co-manage natural resources and co-create knowledge for sustainability transformation. Her empirical work has been based in rural Spain and rural Iran, and most recently in Canada.

Eranga Kokila Galappaththi is a PhD candidate from McGill University. His present research with Dr. James Ford focuses on climate change adaptation in the Canadian Arctic and Sri Lanka. Eranga graduated from the University of Manitoba with an MSc, focusing on community-based shrimp aquaculture with Dr. Fikret Berkes. Eranga also holds an MBA from the University of Peradeniya and a BSc from Ocean University. His research interests include resilience and complex human–environment systems, vulnerability and adaptation to climate change, and the theoretical elements of the commons, with an emphasis on community-based management, (adaptive) co-management, and indigenous knowledge.

Iroshani Madu Galappaththi is a doctoral student in the School of Environment, Resources and Sustainability at the University of Waterloo, Canada, and a member of the Environmental Change and Governance Research Group. Madu's research interests broadly include understanding human–environment interactions from a governance perspective. Her past research focused on participatory approaches to resource governance involving small-scale shrimp farming communities in coastal Sri Lanka. Madu's ongoing thesis research examines the governance and institutional context of dried fish value chains in India and Sri Lanka with attention to gender relations.

Alejandro García Lozano is from Caracas, Venezuela, but grew up in Miami, Florida. He is currently a Nexus Postdoctoral Fellow in Sustainable Oceans at Arizona State University and Conservation International, working to assess the prevalence of human rights abuses in global fisheries. In 2020, he earned a PhD in Marine Science and Conservation from Duke University.

His doctoral research investigated the historical and political dimensions of cooperativism in Mexican small-scale fisheries. His research examines how different sets of actors navigate or shape institutional arrangements, engage in collective action, and employ diverse discursive and material practices to influence policies and negotiate access to resources.

Gustavo García-López is an assistant professor at the Graduate School of Planning, University of Puerto Rico–Rio Piedras. Previously, he was a Marie Curie postdoctoral researcher at the Institute of Environmental Science and Technology (ICTA), Autonomous University of Barcelona, in the European Network of Political Ecology (ENTITLE) project. His interests focus on the political dimensions of collective action in environmental movements, and community-based and multi-level environmental governance, with particular attention to forests, water, and urban green and public spaces. He has carried out fieldwork research in the United States, Mexico, and Puerto Rico.

C. Emdad Haque is Professor at the Natural Resources Institute of the University of Manitoba, Canada. He has authored/co-authored more than 120 refereed articles and has written/edited 15 monographs, including *Disaster Risk and Vulnerability: Mitigation through Mobilizing Communities and Partnerships* (with D. Etkin; 2013) and *Mitigation of Natural Hazards and Disasters: International Perspectives* (2005). Dr. Haque is the recipient of the 1998 Brandon University Senate Award for Excellence in Research. He was also awarded the Visiting Research Fellowship by the Queen Elizabeth House of the University of Oxford, UK, in 1996–1997, and the Fulbright Research Chair by the Fulbright Foundation in 2008. His has published in *World Development, Society and Nature, Human Ecology, Environmental Hazards, Environmental Management, PLOS*, and *International Health.* His current research interests include development and conservation, population displacement and resettlement, risk assessment, disaster and emergency management, impact assessment, public policy assessment, and integrated resource management and sustainable development.

Craig Johnson is Professor of Political Science at the University of Guelph in Canada. He holds a PhD in International Development from the London School of Economics (2000), and has taught at the London School of Economics, the School of Oriental and African Studies, University College London, and the University of Oxford. He is the author of *Arresting Development: The Power of Knowledge for Social Change* (2009), co-editor of *Policy Windows and Livelihood Futures: Prospects for Poverty Reduction in Rural India* (2006), and co-editor of *The Urban Climate Challenge: Rethinking the Role of Cities in the Global Climate Regime* (2015 and 2017). His latest book is *The Power of Cities in Global Climate*

Politics, which will be published with the Pagrave/MacMillan Pivot Series on Cities and the Global Politics of the Environment in 2017.

Shah Raees Khan is the founder of Envirolead Canada and serves as an advisor since 2014. Dr. Khan has been actively involved in providing research-based scientific support for a numerous and diversified environmental projects for Oil & Gas and development sector. His expertise is in socio-ecological studies, impact studies, biophysical assessments, environmental monitoring, risk assessment, resource management, and compliance with regulatory guidelines. His interests are to explore the issues of governance of mountain resources and the impacts on ecosystem services and promote reconciliation between livelihoods and conservation. He is a member of Eco Canada, member of the International Association for the Study of Common Property (IASC) and has contributed papers to its biennial conferences.

Daniel Klooster is Professor of Environmental Studies at the University of Redlands. His research addresses community forestry as a sustainable development strategy in Mexico at scales ranging from common property land tenure rules to trans-national institutions such as the Forest Stewardship Council's forest certification and, most recently, to the trans-border communities built by the indigenous Mexicans who migrate to the United States from forest-owning communities, which is his current research project. Through interviews with members of Mexican indigenous communities in their home territories and with migrants from those same communities living in the United States, his research project aims to clarify two main questions regarding the implications of Mexican rural out-migration for community land-management capabilities and choices: does out-migration undermine the viability of local commons management institutions and do the trans-border re-connections between sending communities and their expatriate community members mitigate these effects?

Gabriela Lichtenstein received her PhD in Behavioral Ecology from the University of Cambridge and worked a post-doc at the Department of Geography, University of Buenos Aires. She currently holds a research position at the National Scientific and Technical Research Council (CONICET) in Argentina, lectures at University of Buenos Aires and UNSAM, and is affiliated with the National Institute for Anthropology and Latin American Thought (INAPL). Gabriela chaired UICN's SSC South American Camelid Specialist Group from 2007 to 2014. She has 20 years of experience of studying the socio-economic impacts of wild South American camelid use in Andean countries including the distribution of benefits, local participation, and the link between conservation and poverty alleviation. Her interest in articulating research results with policy has led her to collaborate with CITES, FWS, the Vicuña Convention, national and local management authorities. She is one of the lead authors for the IPBES Sustainable Use of Wild Species Global Assessment.

Yolanda Lopez-Maldonado is a human ecologist and geographer specialised in freshwater resources. She is interested in complex systems analysis and groundwater modelling along with community-based conservation and women's involvement in natural resource management. Yolanda is a successful Indigenous researcher and practitioner with extensive experience in freshwater issues, Indigenous and traditional peoples, human-environmental systems, community-based conservation, participative action-research, systems analysis, and transdisciplinary approaches. She has been awarded the Young Research Scholar at the International Institute for Applied Systems Analysis (2015), Austria, and the Beijer Institute, The Royal Swedish Academy of Sciences (2016–2019), Stockholm, Sweden. Yolanda is a member of the Specialist Group on the Cultural and Spiritual Values of Protected Areas, IUCN World Commission on Protected Areas, and the Ramsar Culture Network. She is also involved in human/water rights (as a Delegate for the Global Forum on Indigenous Issues Rights, United Nations) and groundwater conservation arenas (e.g. well and sinkhole clean-up activities, stakeholder workshops, underwater exploration). In her home country, Mexico, Yolanda is working towards solutions by combining natural and social sciences with traditional ecological knowledge, which respects Indigenous knowledge. Yolanda is also an Indigenous environmental defender engaged in peaceful action to protect environmental rights of Indigenous People.

Prateep Kumar Nayak is Associate Professor and Associate Director of Graduate Studies in the School of Environment, Enterprise and Development, Faculty of Environment, University of Waterloo, Canada. His academic background is in political science, environmental studies, and international development. He does interdisciplinary work with an active interest in combining social and ecological perspectives. Prateep's research focuses on the understanding of complex human–environment connections (or disconnections) with particular attention to change, its drivers, their influence, and possible ways to deal with them. His main research interests include commons, environmental governance, social-ecological system resilience, environmental justice, and political ecology. In the past, Prateep worked as a development professional in India on issues around community-based governance of land, water, and forests commons, focusing specifically at the interface of research, implementation, and public policy. Prateep is a lead author for IPBES Global Assessment of Sustainable use of Wild Species and a member of the Human Dimensions Working Group, Integrated Marine Biosphere Research (IMBeR). Prateep was a co-chair of the 2015 Biennial Conference International Association for the Study of the Commons. He is a past Trudeau Scholar, a Harvard

University Fellow in Sustainability Science, and a recipient of Canada's Governor General Academic Gold Medal. Prateep is also the Project Director of Vulnerability to Viability (V2V) Global Partnership for building strong small-scale fisheries.

Patricia E. (Ellie) Perkins is a professor in the Faculty of Environmental Studies, York University, Toronto, where she teaches ecological economics, community economic development, and critical interdisciplinary research design. Her research focuses on feminist ecological economics, climate justice, commons, and participatory governance. She directed international research projects on community-based watershed organizing in Brazil and Canada (2002–2008) and on climate justice and equity in watershed management with partners in Mozambique, South Africa, and Kenya (2010–2012). She is the editor of *Water and Climate Change in Africa: Challenges and Community Initiatives in Durban, Maputo and Nairobi* (2013). She is currently a partner in the Economics for the Anthropocene program (e4a-net.org) and directs a Queen Elizabeth Scholars program funding a global network of researchers on Climate Justice, Ecological Economics, and Commons Governance. Previously, she taught economics at Eduardo Mondlane University in Maputo, Mozambique, and served as an environmental policy advisor with the Ontario government. She holds a PhD in economics from the University of Toronto.

Jeremy Pittman is currently an assistant professor in the School of Planning at the University of Waterloo, Canada. He is also an adjunct professor with the School of Environment and Sustainability at the University of Saskatchewan. His research focuses on governance and social networks for community-based conservation and sustainability in a range of contexts.

James Robson is Assistant Professor in Human Dimensions of Sustainability, School of Environment and Sustainability, University of Saskatchewan. His substantive area of expertise lies in interdisciplinary and applied environmental research, with special emphasis on the drivers, and impacts, of demographic, social, and environmental change as they affect remote and rural communities. This includes research into community innovations, especially those targeted at or directly involving youth, to adapt customary systems of governance and resource use. He holds a PhD in Natural Resources and Environmental Management (University of Manitoba, Canada), a MA in Environment, Development and Policy (University of Sussex, UK), and a BSc in Geography (University of Liverpool, UK).

Simron Jit Singh is a professor and Associate Dean (Graduate Studies) at the Faculty of Environment, University of Waterloo, Canada. Drawing on the concept of social metabolism, his research focuses on the systemic links between material and energy flows, time use, and human wellbeing. His particular interest lies at the local and sub-national scales, as well as small islands. He has conducted social metabolism studies in the Nicobar Islands (India), Samothraki (Greece), and supervised work on biomass metabolism of Jamaica (as part of the Canadian project Hungry Cities), Region of Waterloo as well as Canada. In addition, he has played a lead role in a number of large European projects.

Vipul Singh is Associate Professor and teaches history at Department of History, University of Delhi. He is an alumnus Carson Fellow of Rachel Carson Center for Environment and Society, Ludwig Maximilian University of Munich, Germany. Over the recent few years, he has been researching on the long-term environmental history of the flood plains of the Ganga. His other research interests include inland fisheries and popular culture as depicted in folklores, migration, and vernacular literatures.

Sajida Sultana is a researcher with a PhD in Social and Ecological Sustainability. She is currently working with FAO as a Climate Smart Agriculture Specialist. Prior to that, Sajida has a diverse professional experience in operational and non-operational interventions in the areas of climate change, environment, water, and sanitation. She worked in leadership positions involving program implementation, administration, financial management, and monitoring with different UN agencies including UNDP, UNICEF, GEF-Small Grants Program, in addition to NGOs. Throughout her career, Sajida has been associated with the international donor agencies focusing on environment, agriculture, water, sanitation, and genesis of internally displacement of communities in Pakistan.

Sergio Villamayor-Tomás is a Marie Curie Research Fellow at the Institute of Environmental Science and Technology (ICTA), Autonomous University of Barcelona. Previously he held lecturing and research positions at Humboldt University and the Swiss Federal Institute of Forest, Snow and Landscape Research (WSL). His research interests include irrigation and watershed management, climate change adaptation, collective action processes for agro-environmental conservation, water-food-energy nexus, polycentrism, and the dialogue between common pool resource theory and social movements theory. He has carried out fieldwork research in Spain, Colombia, Mexico, and Germany. He serves as editor of the *International Journal of the Commons*.

Foreword

Commonisation, decommonisation, recommonise … these words are new, first used as far as I can tell in a paper the editor published in 2011 in the journal *Conservation and Society*. Useful shorthand for complex phenomena, neologisms also serve to stimulate, provoke, and disturb. Together with a related but antiquated term, commoning, the words indicate a focus on process rather than structure, on social relationships rather than institutions, on the people who use and create a commons rather than the natural resources involved.

The notion of a commons and processes related to it is old and embedded in rural history. It was revived in 1967 by an article in *Science* magazine by biologist Garett Hardin titled "The Tragedy of the Commons". This article became very well known to generations of college students to whom it was usually given to indicate that if left to their own devices, bereft of government, people would overharvest their resources and overpopulate the planet. But there was another scholarly path that explored the problem and challenges of managing certain kinds of resources, common pool resources as they came to be known, which had two key features that make them special. One is the "excludability" problem: for one reason or another it is difficult to exclude others from using it. That is a feature of public goods, as well. But common pool resources have a second problem: "subtractability". Unlike public goods, CPRs are such that one person's use can affect what is available to other people; the value of the CPR can be diminished. So not only do people have to figure out how to reasonably share in the use of a CPR, but they also have to deal with the possibility that the resource itself will decline, even disappear, with use. The "tragedy of the commons" is the scenario in which there are no limits to use of a CPR; it is "open access", and eventually it is overused and abused, and those relying on it lose out. But history and anthropology and sociology showed numerous examples of people sharing the use of a CPR but also cooperating to manage it. It became evident that CPRs could be utilized not only as "open access"; as "government property" whereby a government set up rules to prevent the "tragedy"; as "private property" where somehow the difficulties and costs of excluding others were overcome; but also as "common property".

Commonisation is a word for the process of creating common property arrangements, and decommonisation the opposite. How can a resource be converted from open-access, or private property, or state property? What relationships and events of collective action and negotiation are involved? How do people find effective and acceptable rules determining who is a rightful commoner, able to share in the resource, and what are the constraints and obligations of commoners? It is an inherently social and political process, infused with the details of culture, sense of place, and personality. Whether or not commonisation ever results in a smoothly functioning, persistent institution for commons management, the process is ongoing, and it can be transformed into a decommonisation process. The book is replete with rich cases of both as well as cases where some aspects of a resource system are treated as commons and others become privatized or state projects. There are indeed multiple faces of the commons.

The overarching focus of the book reflects the rural history of the commons. As the editor says, the focus, the agenda, is strengthening community-based commons governance. And it is true that much of the research is with small-scale fishers and farmers living in small rural communities, some in situations where they have de facto or legally recognized local community rights to use and at least partially manage CPRs. However, throughout it is clear that such people and places have long been embedded in more complex multi-scalar situations that play major roles in the options, capabilities, and motivations they have to construct, adapt, or abandon their social arrangements for managing the commons. And that some of the commons for which processes of commonisation take place, or should take place, are at a much larger scale, even global.

A very productive tension in commons scholarship, reflected in this collection, is between the "thick" and "thin" methodologies. The "thin" approach builds up from numerous cases or large n interviews, to construct general models of causation, identifying dependent and independent variables. In commons scholarship, it is also linked to assumptions about rational choice of individuals. From this perspective, we have come to learn a tremendous amount about what seems to matter to a successful community-based commons, and this volume continues the tradition very productively. The "thick" approach, also herein, is more attentive to the specifics of place, history, culture, and personality. Studies of "commoning" processes require both, the latter providing a window not only on individual agency but also the narratives and events of social life and, most of all, the actual practices through which people create, or not, more sustainable ways of living.

Bonnie J. McCay

Preface and acknowledgements

Individuals, communities, and nations in all regions of the world are experiencing the effects of climate and human induced changes in their physical and social environments. The highest and the most direct impact of these changes are seen in the case of commons (e.g., fisheries, shellfish beds, coastal spaces, lagoons, mangroves, range lands, forests, groundwater, freshwater systems, irrigation systems, urban spaces, etc.) upon which humans depend for their social, cultural, and economic needs. When impacted by a variety of drivers, commons not only go through a process of change in their biophysical characteristics, but the resulting impacts linger on to the social, cultural, political, and economic lives (e.g., loss of livelihoods, subsistence, institutions, disempowerment, loss of rights, cultural identity) of the commoners. In a similar sense, we all, as humans, are linked to some form of commons in our daily lives – we either impact the commons or get impacted by it or experience both. As a result, sustaining the commons remains an ongoing challenge that requires enhanced understanding and innovative approaches at all levels of society.

I have been fortunate to learn about the commons from several wonderful groups of people in numerous contexts. My friendship and collaboration with communities dependent on the resource commons have continued over the past three decades. My work with the self-initiated community forest management groups in the Indian Eastern Ghats (starting in the early 1990s) introduced me to the realities of the commons, which continues to act as a strong reference point for all my explorations on resource governance. The work since 2006 with the Bay of Bengal/Chilika Lagoon fishing communities, not too far from the forests mentioned above, added a crucial layer to my work by focusing on coastal commons. Here, in these commons, I experienced firsthand how the coppice forests and the community forest institutions grew in tandem, and how the development of the fishing cooperatives and the fish stock complemented one another. I have watched these relationships, interactions, and connections between the biophysical and the social (institutional) (sub)systems exposing the complexities in these commons in numerous ways. Forests stand in a place but fish continue to swim; to imagine those diverse things and the manner in which they manifest as commons has not been easy.

There is no single approach to comprehend the complex intertwining of the multiple components that make or break the commons, and none of these are bound by time and space. Through my engagement in these commons and with the commoners that occupy these collective spaces, I learned that to strive to understand and define the commons as something or the other, to put a shape and a dimension to how commons might look like, and to propose a fixed set of rules that can guide how commons might develop, are not only unrealistic but simply impossible propositions. This is when I began to think of commons as a multidimensional, complex, and continuous process. This book is one of the first to further the notion of commons as a process and, to do so, it uses commonisation and decommonisation as novel perspectives.

I have the privilege of learning from the work of a galaxy of scholars who are known for their interdisciplinary work broadly on resource/environmental governance and the society (linked to the commons): Arun Agrawal, Derek Armitage, Maarten Bavinck, Fikret Berkes, Daniel Bromley, Tony Charles, Ratana Chuenpagdee, William Clark, Ann Dale, Carl Folke, Madhav Gadgil, Ramchandra Guha, Emdad Haque, Buzz Holling, Svein Jentoft, N. S. Jodha, Leslie King, John Kurien, Bonnie J. McCay, Margaret A. McKean, Barbara Neis, Elinor Ostrom, Pauline E. Peters, Helen Ross, Himadri Sinha, Nancy Turner, Robert Wade, and many others (all in alphabetical order). I have closely worked with many of these scholars (e.g., researching, writing, presenting) but I thank each one of them for sharing their knowledge and wisdom, and help build my own perspectives on the commons.

I have been teaching a graduate course on "Governing the commons" at the University of Waterloo for over six years now, and I wish to thank all my students who have contributed to the finetuning and further development of many ideas in this book. A special thank you to Neil Craik, who inspired me to start a course on the subject of commons when I arrived in Waterloo.

I would like to thank all the chapter authors, who took up the challenge to consider commonisation and decommonisation as a lens to analyse their respective case studies and provided novel insights. Each chapter of this book has been peer reviewed by at least two referees and the editor. I sincerely thank the reviewers who took the time to provide helpful feedback (all in alphabetical order): Steve Alexander, Evan Andrews, Derek Armitage, Clare Barnes, Jessica Blythe, Maarten Bavinck, Donovan Campbell, Graham Epstein, Kate Ervine, Emdad Haque, Arthur Hoole, Svein Jentoft, Craig Johnson, Alejandro García Lozano, NC Narayanan, Patricia E. Perkins, Sisir Pradhan, Jeremy Pittman, Andrew Song, James Robson, Simron Jit Singh, Vipul Singh, Sergio Villamayor-Tomás, and Nireka Weeratunge.

I am thankful to Bernhard Glaeser and Heike Egner, Series Editors, Elena Chiu and Lakshita Joshi, Editorial Assistants, and their team from the Routledge/Taylor and Francis Group for their excellent support and guidance.

My ongoing work has been funded by the Social Sciences and Humanities Research Council of Canada (SSHRC). The initial work on the commonisation and decommonisation concepts was financially supported by the Canada Research Chairs Program (held by Dr. Fikret Berkes, University of Manitoba), Pierre Elliot Trudeau Foundation Scholars Program (2006–2010), and the Harvard University Sustainability Science Fellows Program (2010) to Prateep Kumar Nayak. The Water Institute at the University of Waterloo in Canada provided additional funding for this book project under its Seed Grants Program (2019).

Prateep Kumar Nayak

Part I

Introduction
Setting the scene

Chapter 1

Framing commons as a process

The rudiments of commonisation and decommonisation

Prateep Kumar Nayak and Fikret Berkes

Introduction

Commons are inherently dynamic and complex. Factors that appear to contribute to a stable commons regime at one time and place may be undergoing change at another. These changes can be very diverse. They respond to economic, social, environmental and political conditions and various drivers. The changes may be manifested as adaptation or fine-tuning over time, as in Japanese village common lands (McKean 1982). Or they may result in the replacement of one kind of property-rights regime by another, as in the enclosure movement in English history that resulted in the conversion of sheep grazing commons into privatized agricultural land (Dahlman 1980). It is imperative to examine these processes of change, and their implications for how commons can be governed as commons in the long run.

Both of us (Nayak and Berkes) have been working with commons and community-based resource management systems for a number of years. However, our specific interest in commons processes resulting in the development of joint use and commons institutions, or conversely, those resulting in a loss of these characteristics, started with Nayak's PhD studies in Chilika Lagoon on the Bay of Bengal. Locally called Chilika Lake (but it has a seasonal opening to the sea), this lagoon is the largest in India, and supports nearly half a million people whose livelihoods depend on small-scale fisheries. Much of the lagoon is shallow and has protected waters – ideal conditions for aquaculture. Starting in the 1970s, international markets developed for large shrimp (prawn), which previously had little value in India. Prawn now became "pink gold" (Kurien 1992). Profit motives drove outsiders and aquaculture investors into the lagoon to grow highly profitable tiger prawn (*Panaeus monodon*), and so started the displacement of small-scale fishers and the dismantling of their commons arrangements.

Chilika's small-scale fishers are caste-based. They are fishers by profession and by birth. We do not have a full historical record of how Chilika fisheries developed. But based on a number of surveys and settlement reports from pre-independence India, the development of joint use and commons institutions could be traced back to the early part of the eighteenth century. Fisher castes held rights and entitlements and conducted their fishery according to caste norms. They elaborated rules of inclusion and exclusion, rules of conduct, and social sanctions for violators. In ancient India, the caste system defined caste-based occupations. For Chilika's fishers, fishing was their primary or only livelihood source. Non-fisher castes were considered "higher" castes; they primarily undertook farming. With the advent of prawn farming, outsiders with money and political power started taking over the best sites for aquaculture, step by step. Fishers could not match the powerful outsiders and the elite (non-fisher) insiders. They were not able to defend their entitlements, even though the courts recognised their rights (Nayak and Berkes 2010, 2011).

Chilika's story is long but it is not unique. The destruction of local commons is often associated with colonial policies. In the case of India, for example, the British administration took ownership of communal forests and opened them up for colonial exploitation (Gadgil and Guha 1992). In the case of Micronesia, the demise of the traditional commons system, with elaborate spatial, temporal and species taboos, was associated with colonialism and the breakdown of traditional authority in reef and lagoon tenure. These local conservation measures were considered to be a barrier to exploitation and trade, and colonial governments made sure to suppress them so the resources could be turned into commodities (Johannes 1978).

Salmon fisheries under the control of Indigenous peoples in British Columbia, Canada, suffered a similar fate. The decline of all five species of Pacific salmon coincides with the loss of control of the resource by the local peoples and the start of commercial salmon fisheries. The area was overrun by the "canned salmon stampede". Between 1878 and 1900, commons arrangements and guardianship of Indigenous tribal fisheries were replaced by a free-for-all regime. Having dismantled tribal rules and controls, commercial fishing for canneries resulted in a dramatic decline of salmon stocks, with some 40 percent of the small stocks driven to extinction. This forced the establishment of government controls in place of open-access, but Indigenous rights were not restored. In fact, up until the 1970s, Canadian Federal fisheries policy continued to ban Indigenous fish weirs, traps and reef nets, as "wasteful and unsustainable", despite the fact that these technologies allowed for selective fishing, monitoring, and sustainable use of salmon (Turner et al. 2013). Some Indigenous practices and rights have been restored in recent decades.

Yet other cases of commons processes show different trajectories. As with Japanese village common lands, Swiss alpine commons show adaptations and fine-tuning over time, with an elaboration of rules and practices for grazing in the higher elevations (Netting 1976). Some long-standing commons cases show cycles of change, with declines followed by recovery and adjustment of institutions. An example is Sri Lanka's Negombo Lagoon shrimp fishery using *kattudel*, a type of trap net (Atapattu 1987). We also have cases in which the formation of commons institutions alternates with periods of crises brought about by market drivers and the level of government intervention. An example is southern Brazilian lagoon fisheries for shrimp in which this cycle has taken place in the last 50 years or so (Seixas and Berkes 2003).

The dynamic nature and fluctuations associated with commons development make it necessary to understand commons as a process. Fluctuations in the governance of commons respond to a diversity of influences that include social, political, economic, and ecological factors. This makes commons dynamic over time, consistent with the literature that suggests that commons institutions emerge and may go through processes of development and decline. One school of thought emphasizes a rational choice approach for the emergence of institutions, with individual people responding to perceived costs and benefits that favour (or not) cooperative action (Bromley 1992). McCay (2002) advocates a cultural, historical and ecological perspective. This approach requires looking not only at individual decision-making, but also at "who they are, what they have done, and what they will do in relation to those common-pool resources and in relation to governance issues" (McCay 2002: 393).

The issue of commons institutions is important also for policy and practice in the contemporary world. There is a great deal of interest in restoring commons systems in various parts of the world, such as Hawai'i (Gon and Winter 2019), Canadian salmon fisheries (Turner et al. 2013), and forested lands in India where ancient sacred groves can be re-tasked to provide ecological benefits (Gadgil 2018). Johannes, who had analysed the demise of local and traditional conservation systems in Oceania, wrote 24 years later about the renaissance of these systems (Johannes 2002). The issue is not about turning back the clock but about dealing with these commons systems as adaptations that we can learn from and inform sustainability. For example, it would be nearly impossible to restore the Hawaiian integrated people-environment system *ahupua'a* in its original form because the vegetation of the island has been altered so much, and because the coastal real estate is so expensive that Indigenous Hawaiians are unlikely to ever buy it back. Nevertheless, there is much to learn from these traditional systems (Winter et al. 2020).

As well, for biodiversity conservation there is also much recent attention on Indigenous and Community Conserved Areas (ICCAs), including sacred natural sites. The land under Indigenous control intersects an astounding 40 percent or so of all terrestrial protected areas and ecologically intact landscapes (Garnett et al. 2018). Sacred sites are common in Asia, Africa, North and South America, and Oceania – they are found even in Europe. Most sacred sites are not large areas, but they can form networks crucial for conservation. Some ICCAs are large as well as important from a conservation point of view. The Potato Park in Peru, locally controlled by the Quechua people as commons, is the single largest *in situ* gene bank for potato varieties in the world. Some scholars have argued that the neo-liberal concept of innovation can be decolonized by recognising the potentials of Indigenous and traditional innovations such as the Potato Park and the Andean philosophy of "buen vivir" (Jimenez and Roberts 2019). All of this leads to a search for theory that is useful to understand commons as a process.

The commonisation–decommonisation perspective

To highlight the process aspect of commons, Nayak and Berkes (2011) used two related concepts – commonisation and decommonisation – initially in an analysis of change in the governance of lagoon commons. Here commonisation is understood as a process through which a resource gets converted into a jointly used resource under commons institutions and collective action that deal with excludability and subtractability. Decommonisation refers to a process through which a jointly used resource under commons institutions loses these essential characteristics.

Excludability pertains to the question of who is and who is not a legitimate user of a resource (question of exclusion and inclusion). Subtractability deals with the rules of resource distribution and allocation among the users, without which exploitation by one user will reduce resource availability for others (Ostrom 1990). The two conditions that characterize commons are also used to define commons (common-pool resources), as "those resources in which exclusion of beneficiaries through physical and institutional means is especially costly, and exploitation by one user reduces resource availability for others" (Ostrom et al. 1999: 278).

Both of these characteristics of commons add to their complexity, generate new contestations while helping to solve existing ones. They also help explain the perspective of commons as a process. As shown in Figure 1.1, both commonisation and decommonisation are processes along a continuum. They are potentially two-way processes; they can go in either direction, as influenced by the prevalent social, cultural, economic, ecological and political history and traditions of an area, which are noted as context-specific and scale-dependent. Commonisation and decommonisation processes are either favourably or unfavourably influenced by several internal and external drivers of change that operate across the spatial, temporal and functional scales (Nayak and Berkes 2014). Figure 1.1 outlines three possible scenarios with regard to commonisation–decommonisation processes (indicated by three arrows between commonisation and decommonisation). First, the bottom arrow shows that any resource can enter into a process of commonisation. Second, the top arrow clarifies that already established commons or resources that have been commonised could also revert back towards decommonisation. Third, the middle arrow suggests that commons can go through a parallel or simultaneous process of commonisation and decommonisation. Here, some elements of the commons can undergo commonisation whereas other aspects remain subject to decommonisation processes. This two-way feedback

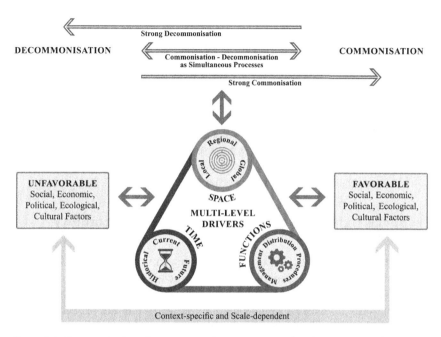

Figure 1.1 Commonisation–decommonisation perspective. A colour version of this image is downloadable as an eResource from www.routledge.com/9780367138004.

and parallel processes, with multiple possibilities around either making or breaking the commons, calls for focused scholarly attention.

In the present book, we use the perspective of commonisation–decommonisation as a novel approach to examine commons. The primary focus of the book is to explore the empirical basis of how resources are commonised or decommonised and use the outcomes to take the further step towards theorising commonisation and decommonisation as a way to understand commons as a process. We pay particular attention to the role of multi-level internal and external drivers in shaping or driving commonisation and decommonisation, and their impact on commons governance. The book aims to highlight contributing issues and dynamics associated with these processes in geographically diverse social, cultural, ecological and political contexts.

The chapters in the book aim to capture the status of commons amidst complex and uncertain social, economic, environmental and climatic changes, using the lens of commonisation and decommonisation. The chapters address one or more of the following questions:

1. What factors cause or contribute to the processes of commonisation and decommonisation?

2. What are some of the impacts and major trends emerging from these processes?
3. What is being done by the communities and the governments to sustain commonisation and respond to decommonisation?
4. What lessons for practice, policy and theory of commons governance can be learnt from our experience with commonisation and decommonisation, with particular reference to resulting threats from the privatization of commons (enclosures).
5. How can these lessons be used to maintain 'commons as commons' in the face of growing challenges from extreme social and environmental change? An overarching focus here is on lessons for strengthening community-based commons governance.

Property rights and the excludability/subtractability conundrum

This section first clarifies property-rights regimes in commons management, and then expands on excludability and subtractability. As the examples in the previous sections show, there are alternative property-rights regimes with which shared resources or commons may be held, and the property-rights regime used is crucial for commonisation and decommonisation processes. Commons scholars have defined four kinds of property-rights regimes: open-access, private-property, common-property, and state-property. These are ideal, analytic types. In practice, many resources are held in overlapping combinations of these regimes (Bromley 1992):

*   Open-access is the absence of well-defined property rights. Access to the resource is unregulated, and the resource is a free-for-all. Open-access regimes are often created by colonial governments, such as those in Oceania and British Columbia historically, as a way to decommonise resources to open them up for privatization or state-property regimes.
*   In private-property regimes, rights are held by an individual or corporation. They are often used with resources (e.g., agricultural lands) in which the costs of exclusion are relatively low. Economists argue that privatization is an appropriate way to solve the subtractability problem by internalizing the externalities (i.e., the owner can decide how to balance the costs and the benefits).
*   Common-property regimes are those in which resource rights are held by an identifiable community of interdependent users. These users exclude outsiders while regulating use by members. Rights allocation, sanctions and dispute resolution mechanisms are collectively negotiated within the community. Rights are held collectively and are unlikely to be either exclusive or transferable.

- Under state-property regimes, rights to the resource are vested exclusively in government which in turn makes decisions concerning access to the resource and the level and nature of exploitation. Examples include resources that may be held in public trust for the citizenry.

Private, state and common-property regimes are all potentially viable approaches. In practice, resources are often held in combinations of property-rights regimes, such as co-management, which is a combination of common-property and state-property. A given regime may provide a better match for a particular resource at a particular time and place. But none of the three regimes is considered intrinsically superior to any other (Bromley 1992; Dietz et al. 2003; Ostrom 2005).

Challenges to commons governance are often reflected in the discussion pertaining to rules of excludability and subtractability. Commons then becomes the mechanism through which these questions are creatively churned to find solutions each time they arise. Doing so is not an easy task and not something that can be achieved through a single or even a few attempts. It requires a process that is not bound by time limitations or the need to produce single, onetime solutions. It calls for persistence and real soul-searching engagements. Thus, the ground rules set by excludability and subtractability characteristics of commons motivate us to call it a process. Commonisation and decommonisation indicate the level of strength (clarity) or messiness (fluctuations) brought forward by excludability and subtractability.

It is no surprise that excludability and subtractability constitute key governance concerns for commons scholars and practitioners. From the perspective of commons as a process, these concerns are indisputably continuous in nature and they do not have any specific endpoints. By their very definition, questions surrounding excludability and subtractability are not meant to be resolved for once and for all. That is simply not possible given the multidimensional complexities commons historically inherit and continue to host. The core meaning of these concepts allow the commoners to engage in processes of negotiation, dialogue and informed decision-making. Such a process can continue as long as the commons, or the prospect of creating one, remains in place.

The meaning of commons fully manifests when all rigidity is removed and replaced with openness. With commons, the doors are closed to none and never, as long as claims and counter-claims on the commons are negotiated. This reflects the process dimension of the commons. Therefore, it is important to understand that excludability and subtractability are not actionable items presented by commons theory. Instead, they are to be seen as representing the core values and non-compromisable principles that keep the commons and the commoners sane. Excludability and subtractability principles ensure that there is enough flexibility, space, opportunity and reason for the commoners to deliberate and collectively fix challenges posed to the commons. In reality, the conundrum posed by excludability and subtractability warrants that commons be seen as a process and not as an end.

There is a well-developed literature related to commons that deals with issues of access and entitlements, and elaborated in the capability approach put forth by Sen (1981). Sen inspires us to argue that excludability and subtractability are linked to capability development. First, the commoners need to have the capability to act on and deliver through the mechanism of excludability and subtractability. These are sophisticated principles and to implement them in the often complex context of the commons is no easy task. Design principles, along with rules at the levels of operations, collective-choice, and constitutional-choice are developed and put to work. Here, the overall capability of the commoners defines the success of this process. Second, the claimants need a set of capabilities to engage in processes of negotiation around their inclusion in the commons and put forth their claims for a share in the collective benefit from the commons. This is no easy task either. The claimants need specific skills and capabilities to enter the claim process and successfully negotiate in the face of excludability and subtractability rule.

From myth to reality: Tragedy of the commons

We have already discussed commons theory pertaining to commonisation and decommonisation, but no discussion of commons is ever complete without dealing with the "tragedy of the commons". The tragedy is useful for us here because it illustrates how wrong or misleading a popular theory can be, and also because it gives us an opportunity to question some of its assumptions. As part of the latter, the tragedy allows us to question the "rational" behaviour and individualism, as opposed to the ability to carry out collective action, and the age-old debate on cooperation vs. competition and whether people can cooperate or not.

Hardin's (1968) paradigm was at once simple and captivating. Imagine a medieval English village commons, said Hardin, in which a number of herders graze their cattle. What is to stop the herders from adding more animals to their herds? Each herder would find it profitable to augment his or her herd, even if this meant that the carrying capacity of the grazing area would eventually be exceeded. For each herder, as an economically rational decision maker, it would be desirable to graze more animals because the herder would take all the profit from the extra animals but would bear only a fraction of the cost of range degradation. But with each herder acting by the same logic would eventually lead to overgrazing and the destruction of the commons. Thus, individual rationality would lead to a collective tragedy from which there was no escape.

The paradigm implied that all shared resources (commons) are destined to be degraded or overexploited. It strengthened recommendations for the privatization of natural resources, and/or for increasing the coercive power of the state. But was there a future for commons to remain as commons, from fisheries, grazing lands and ground water to the oceans and the atmosphere? Such questions were addressed by many case studies and comparative projects, followed by synthesis volumes published in the late 1980s, the 1990s, and the 2000s. The studies showed that, contrary to Hardin, shared resources could in fact be successfully managed by communities engaged in collective action. The conventional wisdom represented by the tragedy of the commons was overturned. The consensus was that Hardin's paradigm applied to open-access conditions, not those used as common-property. Shared resources could be managed under a common-property regime, as well as under state-property and private-property regimes, or various mixtures of the three.

In fact, Hardin's own example of the imaginary English pasture was historically incorrect. Many economic historians and others noted that commons operated successfully for several hundred years in medieval England and questioned if a tragedy of the sort described by Hardin ever occurred widely. The medieval English commons were typically used under locally devised regulations. Rules such as "stinting" limited the number of heads of animals that each owner was allowed to graze. Access was exclusive to certain members of the community, and their rights were closely regulated (McCloskey 1976; Dahlman 1980).

The new paradigm of commons, formulated by such scholars as Ostrom (1990), explicitly examined the role of collective action and local institutions in addressing the commons problem, and the conditions under which collective action may be expected to work. Hardin's assumption of individual interest unchecked by social relations, and his emphasis on competition (rather than cooperation) as the overriding relationship that shaped interactions among resource users, were rejected. In contrast to Hardin's pessimistic conclusion about the inability of users to cooperate for their mutual benefit, the new paradigm emphasized communication and trust-building, as well as perusal of self-interest. Perhaps more fundamentally, the new paradigm addressed philosophies of cooperation and non-cooperation that underlie practice.

Hardin's call for a superior force to protect the commons and the common good is similar to solutions that had been proposed a few centuries earlier. It is a philosophical debate that goes back to Thomas Hobbes (who believed that society and nature were violent and bloody places and life is "nasty brutish and short") versus his philosophical nemesis, Jean-Jacques Rousseau (who believed in a direct democracy in which everyone contributed to express the general will to make the laws of the land). The tragedy of the commons issue may be traced historically to Hobbes vs. Rousseau. In *Leviathan*, a major work in the history of Western political philosophy, Thomas Hobbes (1651) argued for the necessity of a higher authority. Society needed the absolute dominance of a sovereign ruler as the source of law (he probably had the king of England in mind). People were incapable of collective action towards the common good, Hobbes said. The rule of law, by necessity, had to be imposed exogenously from above. Hobbes's view of life as nasty and brutish colours much of the writing in both arts and science through the early industrial era.

Worster (1977) commented that Alfred Tennyson's "nature, red in tooth and claw" was a cliché even before he said it. The dominant view of nature and society, especially in the late 19th century, was one of deep pessimism. Major Western thinkers in both natural and social sciences saw nothing but strife and conflict in the world around them. Charles Darwin also believed in the centrality of conflict in nature, but sought to extract order from it (Worster 1977). Darwin observed that "the survival of the fittest" was an important means of bringing about order. Gould (1980) argued that the theory of natural selection should be viewed as an extended analogy to the *laissez-faire* economics of Adam Smith, the "father of capitalism". Order (what we would now call the market) arises naturally from the struggle among individuals even though they had not intended to produce order.

In contrast to Hobbes, Jean-Jacques Rousseau (1762) wrote *The Social Contract* about sunny, egalitarian communities in the countryside, "bands of peasants regulating the affairs of state under an oak tree". To Rousseau, the rule of law came not from external authority (exogenously), but from within (endogenously). Rousseau's optimism soon found itself at odds with the dominant pessimism of the industrial era Western Europe. His thinking inspired the French Revolution concepts of democracy and freedom, but nevertheless he was labelled a romantic. Even though the basic idea of Rousseau's *Social Contract*, that rules and laws are legitimate and binding only when they are supported by the general will of people, is now an accepted part of democracy, Rousseau had little support in his time.

One of the few thinkers to pursue Rousseau's philosophy was the Russian geographer and biologist, Petr Kropotkin. His research on animal and plant life in Siberia (e.g., lichens) convinced Kropotkin that cooperation, not competition, was the main driving force in nature. Kropotkin's major work, *Mutual Aid*, presented evidence from nature, "primitive" groups and contemporary society. The existence of informal cooperative societies in Russia, called *artels*, was one such example provided by Kropotkin: "Many of the fishing grounds on the tributaries of the Caspian Sea are held by immense *artels*, the Ural River belonging to the whole of the Ural Cossacks, who allot and re-allot the fishing grounds – perhaps the richest in the world – among the villages without any interference of the authorities" (Kropotkin 1902).

Decades of research by ecologists on mutualistic relationships in nature, such as symbiosis, and decades of research by commons scholars documenting the ability of groups to collectively govern their commons, support the notion that cooperation is an important process. We would not go so far as to say that cooperation, not competition, is the main driving force in nature. No doubt they both exist in some sort of balance and tension. Similarly, the tragedy is in essence a conflict or tension between individual interests and societal interests. Technically, the tragedy is a collective action problem, defined as any action taken by a group of people whose goal is to enhance their status and achieve a common objective. But what compels people to pursue a common objective towards collective action?

One alternative framing of the tragedy is provided by Foucault's (1991) notion of governmentality, "the conduct of conduct", everything that is relevant for governing successfully, including institutions, procedures and tactics. Foucault criticizes conventional conceptions of power, commonly wielded by authorities, punishment-driven and top-down. Foucault argues that to possess power is not the same as possessing the art of being able to govern successfully. Effective ways of governing involve working with the agency of the subjects, building trust and creating change from within the subjects themselves.

Another way to approach cooperation is provided by the Prisoner's Dilemma game. Axelrod (1984) and colleagues developed a model based on the Prisoner's Dilemma game. This is a game in which two individuals ("prisoners") can each either cooperate or defect. The payoff to a player is in terms of some benefit (e.g., resource harvest). No matter what the other does, the selfish choice of defection yields a higher payoff than cooperation. However, if both defect, both do worse than if both had cooperated. In a single round game, non-cooperation wins. But in a multi-round game (e.g., as in a face-to-face society with trust and reciprocity) cooperation wins. Deductions from the model, and the results of computer tournaments show how cooperation can evolve based on reciprocity. Cooperation can get started in an asocial world, can thrive while interacting with a wide range of other strategies, and can resist invasion once fully established (Axelrod 1984).

A third formulation is provided by Richerson and Boyd (2005) who take an evolutionary approach to collective action, looking for mechanisms that favour cooperation towards long-term survival. People in all societies hold moral beliefs about right and wrong, and these beliefs can support collective action. These beliefs and norms are culturally transmitted, guided, and favoured by natural selection. When a community member violates social norms, obtaining benefits without paying for costs, he/she will suffer social sanctions. Because norm-violators suffer costs, those who follow the norms do better than those who do not. Since simple self-interest requires adherence to norms, behaviours that undermine norms do not spread. When societies and their collective action problems are relatively small, norms that benefit the group tend to establish themselves.

The last two formulations are based on models, variations of which have been tested over the years and shown to be robust. They are in support of the rich empirical findings of commons scholars. They do have limitations: problems arise when dealing with large-scale societies and issues, such as climate change. Nevertheless, they provide clear ways of thinking on ways and strategies for commonisation, and benchmarks for the kinds of factors (e.g., loss of trust and reciprocity) that may lead to decommonisation.

Conceptualisation and theorising the commons

Commons theory has primarily focused on collective action leading to successful commons management. Ostrom (1990) suggested a number of preconditions that needs to be commonly accepted and shared among users to initiate collective action: (a) individual exploitation will seriously harm a resource which is important to all of their survival; (b) the opportunity exists for users to coordinate their resource utilization in order to prevent the degradation to the commons; (c) those participating in the management organization can trust other members to abide by the agreed-upon rules, in other words, trusting one another not to cheat the system; and (d) the costs associated with participating in the commons institution is less than the benefits which members can expect as a result of collective action.

Ostrom's (1990) seminal book *Governing the Commons*, combined with existing body of work by other scholars, laid the foundation of commons as a discipline. It established a set of eight principles for the design of durable cooperative institutions that are organized and governed by the resource users themselves:

- Clearly defined boundaries for the resource and the users (1)
- Congruence between rules and local conditions; proportionality between user benefits and costs (2)
- Collective-choice arrangements through which users can participate in the creation of rules (3)
- Monitoring rule enforcement and resource status (4)
- Sanctions appropriate to the seriousness of rule infractions (5)
- Conflict-resolution mechanisms (6)
- Recognition of rights to organize, i.e., political space for users to devise their own institutions (7)
- Nested institutions to provide a hierarchy of governance structures (8).

Cox et al. (2010) re-examined Ostrom's (1990) design principles. They analysed 91 studies to empirically evaluate the principles in light of three critiques: (1) the design principles are incomplete, and additional criteria are required; (2) there are doubts about the applicability of the principles to a wide range of cases, and (3) the lack of a more constructionist or historically, socially, and environmentally embedded perspective, and heavy reliance on rational choice. The design principles held up quite well to the 20-year accumulation of published findings, but three of them were split up, giving a total of eleven principles. Boundaries of the resource do not often match up with the boundaries of the users, giving 1A and 1B. The congruence principle (2A) had to be separated from the proportionality principle (2B). Monitoring rules enforcement was found to be distinct from resource monitoring, necessitating a split into 4A and 4B.

To examine the completeness of the design principles, Agrawal (2002) analysed three sets of principles from the work of Wade (1988, 1987), Ostrom (1990) and Baland and Platteau (1996). He examined the robustness of their conclusions by comparing them with findings from a larger set of studies. He noted that Wade, Ostrom, and Baland and Platteau together had identified 36 principal conditions. After careful elimination of duplicates, he further refined them, resulting in 24 different conditions. Agrawal (2002) categorised the critical enabling conditions for sustainability under (a) resource system characteristics, (b) group characteristics, (c) institutional arrangements, and (d) external environments. The large number of variables potentially affecting the sustainability of institutions that govern common resources has important theoretical implications for future research (Agrawal 2002).

Governing the Commons used long-standing commons institutions as key examples on which to generate the design principles, but did not look explicitly into the dynamics of commons. Several scholars have contributed to further conceptualisation and theory-building. A significant body of commons literature emerged between the late-1980s and the early 2000s, including McCay and Acheson (1987), Berkes (1989), Feeny et al. (1990), Bromley (1992), McKean (1992), Edwards and Steins (1998), Gibson et al. (2000), Ostrom et al. (2002), Agrawal (2001), Ostrom (2005), and others.

Despite these contributions, there still exist a number of scholarly concerns regarding conventional commons theory. Consistent with McCay (2002), Robbins (2004) argued that commons theory has developed along the lines of rational choice thinking which focuses on making decisions to maximize benefits and minimize costs, and does not address values and culture. Failure of collective management, some commons scholars maintain, is a misnomer because there is always an opportunity to negotiate and establish appropriate systems of rules to bring resource sustainability. Rational choice was used by some to formulate an apparently apolitical theory of commons that may prove insufficient to analyse the commons dilemma in its full complexity.

Johnson (2004) observed a normative and methodological tension within the commons theory by categorising commons scholarship into collective action and entitlement schools. It is increasingly important to recognise that commons is not an "isolated island" of resources; rather, it is situated within layers of complexities, rooted in the past, present and future discourses, and the changing social and political circumstances across geophysical boundaries influence its governance.

Interdisciplinary enrichment for thinking about the commons

Commons developed as an interdisciplinary field from the start. Commons as a process cannot be fully comprehended through a strict disciplinary approach. A process is the sum total of many interrelated components that navigate through issues, challenges, problems, opportunities and prospects. Processes are multidimensional, therefore, require contributions from a multitude of disciplines and action domains in order to produce meaningful outcomes. Commonisation and decommonisation processes are not different from such an understanding.

Recent work has directed the commons scholarship towards an even richer set of interdisciplinary approaches focusing on hybrid innovations in concepts, methods and tools to unravel new frontiers. The rules of game have changed with increases in complexity, diversity, and demands on how commons develop and persist. Scholars have continued to explore how to use existing frameworks or to develop more sophisticated ones and scholarly "angles" to understand commons governance and sustainability, especially looking at commons as a process (Armitage et al. 2017). Methodologically, such explorations have relied on either an inductive logic (i.e., do the complexities surrounding the commons offer new challenges for scholarship?) or a deductive logic (i.e., is the current commons scholarship sufficient to deal with the challenges associated with commons governance and sustainability?) or a creative combination of both.

First in the series of new interdisciplinary emphasis pertains to the idea that social and ecological processes, and linkages between the two, provide a more realistic context to examine the commons. This idea situates the commons within an integrated human-environment context. All commons are complex systems of humans and nature. They are social-ecological systems in which the social subsystem and the biophysical subsystem are coupled, interdependent and co-evolutionary (Berkes and Folke 1998; Berkes et al. 2003; Ostrom 2009).

The conceptualisation of the commons as complex social-ecological systems has tremendous influence on the understanding of commonisation and decommonisation processes. Here, social (human) and ecological (biophysical) subsystems, their interconnections and cross-influence, shape these commons-related processes. As commons are increasingly being seen as coupled social-ecological systems, the focus of inquiry has turned to the nature of relationships (MEA 2005), interactions (Kates et al. 2001) and connections (Nayak 2014) between commoners and their resources. It is understood that forms of disconnection between the commoners (people) and the physical commons (resource) are detrimental to both. Commons have many drivers, unpredictable ways in which drivers act, an array of impacts producing uncertain system dynamics, and two-way feedback interactions, all of which add to the complexity in commonisation and decommonisation processes (Nayak and Berkes 2014).

Second in line is the idea that commons are intensely contested domains and highly political spaces. While commons theory provides an entry into the areas of collective action and institutional interventions to secure access and collective rights, political ecology adds value by asking critical questions on the differentiated resource control, power dynamics, entitlements and politics of governance. In effect, this approach helps retain a critical focus on understanding how access, property rights and entitlements of the commoners may have changed, often historically over time, and with what consequences. Questions involving "who has the power, who controls, who takes decisions, and with what consequences" remain influential determinants of when and how processes of commonisation and decommonisation unfold.

The relationship of the commons with the state is an important consideration. Whether a commons is under a state-property regime or not largely depends on the context. For example, 80 percent of Mexico's forests are under a common-property regime. They are in the hands of communities through two categories of land classification, known as *ejidos* and Indigenous community lands (Bray et al. 2002). These community forests are legally recognised and managed as *de jure* commons. By contrast, fishing areas in India's Chilika lagoon are under community management through a *de facto* commons arrangement. In Chilika, commons exist through layers of rights; they do not need state enforcement, but they do need state recognition. Such questions are inherently political in nature.

Third is an area that connects commons to the questions of justice (both social and environmental), fairness and equity. Here, commonisation and decommonisation processes are tested through their ability to define how commons outcomes influence social structure and possibly impact ecosystem processes. Its focus on the elements of "how resource benefits are distributed across stakeholders, and what mechanisms and decisions on commons disproportionately influence the commoners" is critical to the understanding of commons as a dynamic process. Of course, these considerations take us to the area of distributive and procedural justice. Distributive justice is outcome-oriented and refers to the nitty gritty of sharing, allocation and entitlement in the commons. Procedural justice highlights democratic, inclusive and fair procedures as enabling conditions of commonisation, the absence of which is a key driver of decommonisation.

On the whole, justice-oriented approaches take aim at issues around who benefits and who loses. What are the dominant framings and narratives on the making and breaking of commons and who controls those? Whose views and preferences are recognised, and whose are not? And finally, who wins and who is defeated in the action arena of the commons? No doubt, these questions create multiple ripples in the way commonisation and decommonisation processes proceed. From the type of questions that they raise, it is evident that both political ecology and social-environmental justice provide cross-cutting themes to further engage in the discourse of commons as a process.

The fourth aspect pertains to commons institutions and governance arrangements (Ostrom 1990, 2005). Commons governance offers the tools to analyse the kinds of institutions (rules-in-use) that may be appropriate for maintaining connectedness between commoners and the commons. The strength of institutions lies in their ability for renewal and reorganization, learning and adaptation in dealing with change processes (Holling 2001). In the context of commons, community-based institutions (not communities in themselves) can create conditions for supporting processes of commonisation and responding to decommonisation. Provided political space is created, well designed institutions can take up the role of mediating differentiated resource access and entitlements (Leach et al. 1999; Agrawal 2002; Ostrom 2005; Nayak and Berkes 2008). Novel arrangements such as adaptive co-management of commons are often driven by key principles of partnership, collaboration, trust, power-sharing, institution-building, social learning, problem-solving and good governance, all of which can have lasting influence on commonisation and decommonisation processes and outcomes (Armitage et al. 2007; Berkes 2007).

A fifth interdisciplinary area concerns the relationship of sense of place and commons stewardship. In geography, sense of place is the meaning and attachment to a setting (place) held by an individual or group (Tuan 1977). Attachment to a place is a culturally mediated emotional bond, usually positive, between individuals or groups and their environment. Meanings are descriptive statements about a place, the images it conveys, and the felt value. Meanings can be symbolic: what does a place mean, for example, peaceful home? Traditions of stewardship are based on what people care about and what motivates them to conserve. Hence, a strong sense of place is a powerful driver for commonisation.

Sense of place theory assumes interconnection of social systems and ecological systems, and provides insights regarding the nature of the connection between the two (Masterson et al. 2017). Such connections are important for community resilience and adaptive capacity (Berkes and Ross 2013). Relationships go beyond the physical site and include social networks, heritage values and personal histories. Place-rooted identity is universal but appears to be particularly strong among Indigenous peoples. As motivators for trust-building and collective action towards commons stewardship, we can hypothesize that sense of place and rootedness are empowering, and that they develop in parallel with commonisation, with mutual feedback between the two. Conversely, it is likely that decommonisation has the opposite effect of disempowerment – but without necessarily weakening the sense of place.

Plan of the book

The chapters in this book draw from a large number of geographically diverse empirical cases – ten countries in North, South and Central Americas, and South- and South-East Asia. They involve a wide range of commons – related to forests, grazing, wetlands, coastal-marine, rivers and dams, aquaculture, wildlife, tourism, groundwater, surface freshwater, mountains, small islands, social movements, and climate. The book is transdisciplinary in nature, and contributions come from a wide range of fields of scientific research undertaken by scholars and practitioners in geography, history, sociology, anthropology, political studies, planning, human ecology, cultural and applied ecology, environmental and development studies, environmental science and technology, public policy, and environmental change and governance. Contributors include academics, community members, NGOs, practitioners and policymakers. Therefore, commonisation–decommonisation lessons drawn from these chapters are well suited for contributing to the practice, policy and theory of the commons.

The structure of the book is logically planned – an introduction followed by four distinct sections on decommonisation, commonisation, and a combination of the two, leading to a final section on governance insights on commonisation and decommonisation, and reflective comments on individual chapters. Part I, "Setting the Scene" (this chapter), provides a succinct introduction to the book by outlining its focus, objectives and key questions under investigation. It discusses key definitions, themes and issues essential to the understanding of commons as a process by focusing on decommonisation and commonisation. As the leading chapter, it offers an analytical framework that is followed through the rest of the chapters.

Having a section on decommonisation before commonisation is deliberate. The three chapters on finding the "Roots of Decommonisation" (Part II) offers a strong basis for the four chapters that focus on outlining factors of "What Enables Commonisation" (Part III). In other words, Part II generates key issues, challenges and questions around decommonisation processes which are then addressed by Part III on commonisation that aims to generate a list of enabling factors and conditions of commonisation. Furthermore, Part IV on "Commonisation and Decommonisation as a Parallel Process" uses case studies to highlight that commonisation and decommonisation are not necessarily separate and isolated, but could also be found together as parallel processes. Moreover, there are numerous ways in which commoners are able to tackle adverse effects. They may respond to decommonisation through processes of (re)(new)commonisation that is context-specific but also scale-flexible. Part V, "Closing", outlines the challenges and prospects of maintaining commons as commons through an all-inclusive governance lens, and outlines key lessons and insights on commons as a process. It also provides reflective summaries of all individual chapters.

References

Agrawal, A. (2002). Common resources and institutional sustainability. In: Ostrom, E., T. Dietz, N. Dolsak, P. C. Stern, S. Stonich and E. U. Weber (Eds.), *The Drama of the Commons*. Washington, DC: National Academy Press, 41–86. https://doi.org/10.17226/10287

Agrawal, A. (2001). Common property institutions and sustainable governance of resources. *World Development*, 29(10), 1649–1672. https://doi.org/10.1016/S0305-750X(01)00063-8

Armitage, D., F. Berkes and N. Doubleday. (2007). *Adaptive Co-Management: Collaboration, Learning and Multi-Level Governance*. Vancouver: University of British Columbia Press.

Armitage, D., A. Charles and F. Berkes (Eds.) (2017). *Governing the Coastal Commons: Communities, Resilience and Transformation*. London and New York: Earthscan/Routledge.

Atapattu, A. R. (1987). Territorial use rights in fisheries (TURFs) in Sri Lanka. *Exploitation and Management of Marine Fishery Resources in Southeast Asia*. RAPA Report 10. 379–401. Organised by Indo-Pacific Fisheries Commission. Bangkok: Food and Agriculture Organisation.

Axelrod, R. (1984). *The Evolution of Cooperation*. New York: Basic Books.

Bray, D. B., L. Merino-Perez, P. Negreros-Castillo, G. Segura-Warnholtz, J. M. Torres-Rojo and H. F. M. Vester. (2002). Mexico's community managed forests as a global model for sustainable landscapes. *Conservation Biology*, 17, 672–677.

Baland, J. M. and J. P. Platteau. (1996). *Halting Degradation of Natural Resources: Is There a Role for Rural Communities?* Oxford: Clarendon Press.

Berkes, F. (Ed.) (1989). *Common Property Resources: Ecology and Community-Based Sustainable Development*. London: Belhaven Press.

Berkes, F. (2007). Community-based conservation in a globalized world. *Proceedings of the National Academy of Sciences*, 104, 15188–15193.

Berkes, F. and C. Folke (Eds.) (1998). *Linking Social and Ecological Systems: Management Practices and Social Mechanisms for Building Resilience*. Cambridge: Cambridge University Press.

Berkes, F., J. Colding and C. Folke (Eds.) (2003). *Navigating Social-Ecological Systems: Building Resilience for Complexity and Change*. Cambridge: Cambridge University.

Berkes, F. and H. Ross. (2013). Community resilience: Toward an integrated approach, *Society & Natural Resources*, 26, 5–20.

Bromley, D. W. (Ed.) (1992). *Making the Commons Work: Theory, Practice, and Policy*. San Francisco: ICS Press.

Cox, M., G. Arnold and S. Villamayor Tomás. (2010). A review of design principles for community-based natural resource management. *Ecology and Society*, 15(4), 38.

Dahlman, C. (1980). *The Open Field System and Beyond: A Property Rights Analysis of an Economic Institution*. Cambridge: Cambridge University Press.

Dietz, T., E. Ostrom and P. Stern (2003). The struggle to govern the commons. *Science*, 302, 1907–1912.

Edwards, V. M. and N. A Steins. (1998). Developing an analytical framework for multiple-use commons. *Journal of Theoretical Politics*, 10(3), 347–383.

Feeny, D., F. Berkes, B. J. McCay and M. Acheson. (1990). The tragedy of the commons: Twenty-two years later. *Human Ecology*, 18, 1–19.

Foucault, M. (1991). *Governmentality*. London: Harvester Wheatsheaf.

Gadgil, M. (2018). Sacred groves. *Scientific American*, 32–41.

Gadgil, M. and R. Guha. (1992). *This Fissured Land: An Ecological History of India*. Berkeley: University of California Press.

Garnett, S. T., N. D. Burgess, J. E. Fa, et al. (2018). A spatial overview of the global importance of Indigenous lands for conservation. *Nature Sustainability,* 1, 369–374.

Gibson, C., M. A. McKean and E. Ostrom (Eds.) (2000). *People and Forests: Communities, Institutions, and Governance.* Cambridge, MA: MIT Press, 27–55.

Gon, S. and K. B. Winter. (2019). A Hawaiian renaissance that could save the world. *American Scientist,* 107, 232–239.

Gould, S. J. (1980). *The Panda's Thumb.* New York: Norton.

Hardin, G. (1968). The tragedy of the commons. *Science,* 162, 1243–1248.

Hobbes, T. (1651). *Leviathan, or the Matter, Form and Power of a Commonwealth, Ecclesiastical and Civil.* Republished 1958: H. W. Schneider, editor, Indianapolis: Bobbs-Merrill.

Holling, C. S. (2001). Understanding the complexity of economic, ecological, and social systems. *Ecosystems,* 4, 390–405.

Jimenez, A. and T. Roberts. (2019). Decolonising neo-liberal innovation: Using the Andean philosophy of "buen vivir" to reimagine innovation hubs. In: P. Nielsen and H. Kimaro (Eds.), *Information and Communication Technologies for Development.* Cham: Springer, 180–191. https://doi.org/10.1007/978-3-030-19115-3_15

Johannes, R. E. (1978). Traditional marine conservation methods in Oceania and their demise. *Annual Review of Ecology and Systematics* 9: 349–364.

Johannes, R. E. (2002). The renaissance of community-based marine resource management in Oceania. *Annual Review of Ecology and Systematics,* 33, 317–340.

Johnson, C. (2004). Uncommon ground: The "poverty of history" in common property discourses. *Development and Change,* 35(3), 407–433.

Kates, R., W. C. Clark, R. Corell, et al. 2001. Sustainability science. *Science,* 292, 641–642.

Kropotkin, P. (1902). *Mutual Aid.* Republished 1989: Montreal: Black Rose Books.

Kurien, J. (1992). Ruining the commons and responses of the commoners: Coastal overfishing and fishermen's actions in Kerala state, India. In: Ghai, D. and J. Vivian (Eds.), *Grassroots Environmental Action.* London: Routledge, 221–258.

Leach, M., R. Mearns and I. Scoones. (1999). Environmental entitlements: Dynamics and institutions in community-based natural resource management. *World Development,* 27(2), 225–247.

Masterson, V. A., R. C. Stedman, J. Enqvist, M. Tengö, M. Giusti, D. Wahl and U. Svedin. (2017). The contribution of sense of place to social-ecological systems research: a review and research agenda. *Ecology and Society,* 22(1), 49. https://doi.org/10.5751/ ES-08872-220149

McCay, B. J. (2002). Emergence of institutions for the commons: Contexts, situations, and events. In E. U. Weber, S. Stonich, P. C. Stern, N. Dolsak, T. Dietz, and E. Ostrom (Eds.), *The drama of the commons,* Washington, DC: National Academy Press, 361–402.

McCay, B. J. and J. M. Acheson (Eds.) (1987). *The Question of the Commons: The Culture and Ecology of Communal Resources.* Tucson: University of Arizona Press.

McCloskey, D. N. (1976). English open fields as behavior toward risk. *Research in Economic History,* 1, 124–170.

McKean, M. A. (1982). The Japanese experience with scarcity: Management of traditional common lands. *Environmental Review,* 6, 63–88.

McKean, M. (1992). Success on the commons: A comparative examination of institutions for common property resource management. *Journal of Theoretical Politics,* 4(3), 247–281.

MEA (Millennium Ecosystem Assessment). (2005). Ecosystems and human well-being: General synthesis. In: *Millennium Ecosystem Assessment.* Chicago: Island Press. Available online at: www.Millenniumassessment.org/en/Synthesis.aspx.

Nayak, P. K. (2014). The Chilika Lagoon social-ecological system: An historical analysis. *Ecology and Society,* 19(1), 1. http://dx.doi.org/10.5751/ES-05978-190101

Nayak, P. K. and F. Berkes. (2008). Politics of cooptation: Self-organized community forest management and joint forest management in Orissa, India. *Environmental Management,* 41, 707–718.

Nayak, P. K. and F. Berkes. (2010). Whose marginalisation? Politics around environmental injustices in India's Chilika Lagoon. *Local Environment,* 15(6), 553–567.

Nayak, P. K. and F. Berkes. (2011). Commonisation and decommonisation: understanding the processes of change in Chilika Lagoon, India. *Conservation and Society,* 9, 132–145. http://dx.doi.org/10.4103/0972-4923.83723

Nayak. P. K. and F. Berkes. (2014). Linking global drivers with local and regional change: A social-ecological system approach in Chilika Lagoon, Bay of Bengal. Regional *Environmental Change,* 14, 2067–2078.

Netting, R. McC. (1976). What alpine peasants have in common: Observations in communal tenure in a Swiss village. *Human Ecology,* 4, 135–146.

Ostrom, E. (1990). *Governing the Commons: The Evolution of Institutions for Collective Action.* Cambridge: Cambridge University Press.

Ostrom, E. (2005). *Understanding Institutional Diversity.* Princeton: Princeton University Press.

Ostrom, E. (2009). A general framework for analysing sustainability of social-ecological systems. *Science,* 325 (5939), 419–422.

Ostrom, E., J. Burger, C. B. Field, R. B. Norgaard and D. Policansky. (1999). Revisiting the commons: Local lessons, global challenges. *Science,* 284, 278–282.

Ostrom, E., T. Dietz, N. Dolsak, P. C. Stern, S. Stonich and E. U. Weber (Eds.). (2002). *The Drama of the Commons.* Washington, DC: National Academy Press.

Richerson, P. J. and R. Boyd (2005). *Not by Genes Alone.* Chicago: University of Chicago Press.

Robbins, P. (2004). *Political Ecology: Critical Introductions to Geography.* Oxford: Blackwell Publishing.

Rousseau, J. J. (1762). *The Social Contract.* Republished 1988: London: Penguin. First published as *Du contract social.*

Schlager, E., W. Blomquist and S. Y. Tang. (1994). Mobile flows, storage, and self-organizing institutions for governing common pool resources. *Land Economics,* 70(3), 294–317.

Seixas, C. S. and F. Berkes. (2003). Dynamics of social-ecological changes in a lagoon fishery in southern Brazil. In: Berkes, F., J. Colding and C. Folke (Eds.), *Navigating Social-Ecological Systems.* Cambridge: Cambridge University Press, 271–298.

Sen, A. (1981). *Poverty and Famines: An Essay on Entitlement and Deprivation.* Oxford: Clarendon Press.

Tuan, Y.-F. (1977). *Space and Place: The Perspective of Experience.* Minneapolis: University of Minnesota Press.

Turner, N. J., F. Berkes, J. Stephenson and J. Dick. (2013). Blundering intruders: Extraneous impacts on two Indigenous food systems. *Human Ecology,* 41, 563–574.

Wade, R. (1988). Why some Indian villages cooperate? *Economic and Political Weekly,* 23(16), 773–776.

Wade R. (1987). *Village Republics: Economic Conditions for Collective Action in South India.* Cambridge: Cambridge University Press.

Winter, K. B., N. Kekuewa Lincoln, F. Berkes, et al. (2020). Ecomimicry in Indigenous resource management: Optimizing ecosystem services to achieve resource abundance, with examples from Hawaii. *Ecology and Society,* 25(2), 26.

Worster, D. (1977). *Nature's Economy: A History of Ecological Ideas.* Cambridge: Cambridge University Press.

Part II

Roots of decommonisation

Chapter 2

The dynamics and performance of marine tourism commons (MTC) in the Karimunjawa Island Marine National Park, Indonesia

Patricia Dorn and Simron Jit Singh

Introduction

Coral reefs subject to marine tourism for snorkeling or diving are found to experience the same collective-action problems and share the same attributes as common-pool resources (CPRs) – excludability and subtractability – and are therefore perceived as marine tourism commons (MTC) (Hall 2001, Gössling and Garrod 2008). MTC are "marine resources which tourists and tourist businesses utilize, and in such destinations, residents often wholly or mainly rely on tourists for their livelihood" (Yabuta et al. 2014, p. 2). So far however, MTC have only been mentioned in terms of whale watching (Neves-Graca 2004) and therefore give ample room to explore beyond. Especially in Marine Protected Areas or Marine National Parks, marine tourism is operating within a complex web of rules and regulations, while at the same time being drawn among the two realms of environmental protection and local development (Garrod & Wilson 2003, p. 44). Once uncontrolled and uncoordinated, marine tourism has been characterized as major threat for the marine environment and challenge for marine governance (Jones et al. 2011, p. 30; Prakash et al. 2005). Yabuta et al. (2014) conclude that "a non-cooperative use of [marine] CPRs leads to an inefficient outcome including over-exploitation and environmental destruction of CPRs".

The case study of the Karimunjawa Island Marine National Park (abbreviated as KNP) in Indonesia is one such example. Within three decades only (1982–2014), the coral reef in Karimunjawa experiences a dynamic process of changing and contradicting de jure and de facto property rights leading to a complex mix of resource regimes that are divided into four phases. With the start of marine tourism development, the coral reef experiences a 'commonisation' process (Phase II) as it turns into a jointly used resource by tourist guides – the resource user – that offer snorkel- and diving trips to earn a living (Following Nayak and Berkes 2011). However, the tourist guides who were assumed to share the collective interest to gain continuing benefit of the coral reef ecosystem through snorkel or dive tourism, struggle to sustain a joint return (Phase III) of their resource units in terms of preserving the number of healthy and worth visiting coral reef sites. Phase IV identifies various drivers for a starting decommonisation that exposes the MTC to non-excludability and might lead to further overuse and damage (subtractability) of the coral reef.

The case of the KNP marine tourism commons is discussed in two parts. The first part describes the institutional development of MTC in terms of the evolution of resource regimes over a period of time. A resource regime is a (or a mixture of a) property right like Open Access, State (public) Property, Private Property and Common Property which governs the access, use and transfer of the right to a *natural* resource. The second half of this chapter applies the Social Ecological System Framework (SESF) to identify the current institutional performance of the marine tourism institutions to "track" the drivers of success or failure of sustainable management of the MTCs.

A brief overview of KNP

The Karimunjawa Marine National Park (KNP) belongs to the first marine areas in Indonesia receiving high conservation attention and is one of Indonesia's seven Marine National Parks. KNP is situated 80 km off Central Java's northern coast and is under the control of Central Java Province, Jepara District (*Kabupaten*) and Karimunjawa Sub-District (*Kecematan*). Whereas the archipelago consists out of 27 islands, only 22 are managed by the Karimunjawa National Park Authority (KNPA) under the Ministry of Environment and Forestry, leaving out the five islands within the Genting village waters (see Figure 2.1, dashed line). The KNP has a total area of 1,117 km² of which the marine area is the largest with 1,101 km², tropical lowland forest is 13 km² and mangroves 3 km². The KNPA follows an adaptive-management approach that allows to redesign the zoning of the park in a participative method. After the first zoning plan of Karimunjawa in 1989, the Marine National Park underwent another re-zoning process in 2005 and 2012 which included first 6 and then 17 marine tourism zones in the park's management.

The coral reef is the largest ecosystem in the KNP, covering around 7% of the marine area with its three types: the fringing reef, barrier reef and patch reef. With 69 coral species and 450 species of coral fish, the KNP has the highest aquatic diversity around Java. Hence, Karimunjawa is not only an important area for conservation since the last three decades, but also attracts a number of tourists to visit the "Oasis of Java" or the "Jewel of the Java Sea". The main attractions are snorkeling and island-hopping trips, as well as relaxing on uninhabited islands while enjoying the sunset views and fish cuisine.

Marine tourism in Karimunjawa substantially developed after 2003 with a peak of 25,000 tourists in 2012 (Figure 2.2), but affected by bad weather conditions leading to limited marine transportation in later years.

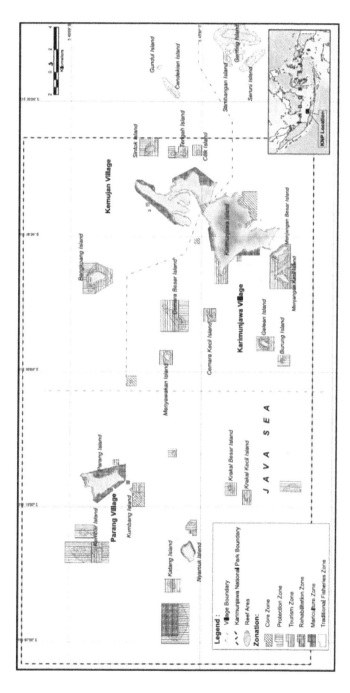

Figure 2.1 Zoning Plan 2012 (Campbell et al. 2013).

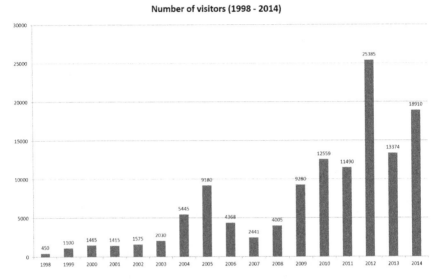

Figure 2.2 Number of visitors between 1998 and 2003 (Campbell et al. 2013); between 2013 and 2014 (TIC Karimunjawa). A colour version of this image is downloadable as an eResource from www.routledge.com/9780367138004.

Most tourists are accommodated in the main village Karimunjawa, where the tourism infrastructure is located. International tourism only counts up to 10–20% of the total tourists (Official or Civil Servant of the Kecamatan Karimunjawa).

The local population is roughly 10,000. Most of the inhabitants are immigrants from Java, Madura and Makassar and live in four villages: Karimunjawa as the southern access point with the harbor, Kemujan, Parang Island and Nyamuk Island. The locals earn their living mainly within three dominant economic sectors, that is, traditional fishery, tourism sector, and as workers in the construction sector for tourism infrastructure. The main threats to the local biodiversity are large and small-scale fishing, water pollution from infrastructure, and uncontrolled tourism (Jones et al. 2011, p. 227, Campbell et al. 2012).

Methods

The study uses a mixed-method approach using quantitative data and qualitative assessment. Primary data was collected during two field visits, first between July and September 2013, and then again between April and June 2014. Stakeholders included representatives of the tourist guide association "HPI" and tour operators, local and district civil servants, officials of the park authority, tourism and fishery department, NGOs such as the "Wildlife Conservation Society" and "Jakarta Animal Aid Network", the harbor master, investors, hotel owners, as well as researchers from the Faculty of Fisheries and Marine Science at the University of Diponegoro. A large number of official documents, reports and research papers were compiled and analysed. As a second step, a survey questionnaire was developed that was administered during the second field visit, including structured interviews with 50 Tourist Guides. Participant observation in those six months of field-work helped to gain a deeper understanding of the marine tourism situation.

The Social Ecological System Framework (SESF) was applied to the case study. The SESF originates from Ostrom's eight design principles (Ostrom 2007, Ostrom 2009) and provides a multifaceted method to analyse marine tourism in all its complexity (Garrod & Wilson 2003). In comparison to other frameworks, the SEFS is most appropriate towards a first step in perceiving an equalized interaction between the social and ecological system (Binder et al. 2013). Further, the SESF is adaptable for various research settings due to its organised variables that can be unwrapped in the multitier hierarchy. Among many other studies, the SESF has already been used for analysing and comparing coral reef managements and marine protected areas (Cinner et al. 2012, Pollnac et al. 2010). The eight highest tier variables of the SESF reflect the previous *Institutional Analysis and Development Framework* "IAD – Framework" (Ostrom et al. 1994, Ostrom 2005) and have up to 53 second-tier variables nested under them (Agrawal 2001; Agrawal 2002).

As not all variables of the SEFS were applicable to the case study due to unavailability of data, time-restrictions or irrelevance, a set of 29 variables was chosen. The SEFS of the case study differentiates between the social system which includes the resource user (U) as a group of tourist guides, nested under a governance system (GS) and depended on the ecological system, namely the coral reef resource system (RS), that produces the resource units (RU), defined as the number and quality of coral reef snorkel and diving spots. The "social, economic and political settings" (S), as well as the "related ecosystems" (ECO) variable are perceived as externalities outside of the SES. Beside the four main tiers of the social and ecological systems, the Interactions (I) between both systems offer a way of analysing the linkages within a SES. However, the variable ECO is outside the scope of this study and the predicted outcome (O) is limited to our understanding of the overall situation observed (Table 2.1).

Structured and quantitative interviews with 50 (of the 227) Tourist Guides were conducted. The questionnaire was guided by the second-tier variables under the main tiers of the social system U (U1–U9), GS (GS 1, 3, 5–8) as well as I (I 1, 2, 4, 5, 7) (see Table 2.1). Data for the ecological system RU and RS, as well as for the external tier S was obtained from management plans of the national park authority, ecological status and monitoring reports by NGOs, village statistics as well as research thesis or published articles.

Table 2.1 The Social-Ecological System Framework (SEFS) adopted from Ostrom 2009

S - Social, economic, and political setting	*No*	**ECO Related Ecosystems**	
S1 Economic Development	*weak*	ECO1 Climate patterns	
S2 Demographic Trends	*no*	ECO2 Pollution patterns	
S3 Government Resource Policies	*no*	ECO4 Flows into and out of focal SES	
S4 Market Incentives	*weak*		
S5 Media organisation			
RS Resource System	*weak*	**GS Governance System**	*weak*
RS1 Sector - Coral Reef Ecosystem		**GS1 Government Organisations**	*weak*
RS2 Clarity of System boundaries	*weak*	**GS2 Nongovernment Organisations**	*weak*
RS3 Size of Resource System	*weak*	**GS3 Network Structure**	*weak*
RS4 Human-constructed facilities		**GS4 Property Rights System**	*weak*
RS5 Productivity of System		**GS5 Operational Rules**	*weak*
RS6 Equilibrium properties		**GS6 Collective-Choice Rules**	*weak*
RS7 Predictabilities of system dynamics		**GS7 Constitutional Rules**	*weak*
RS8 Storage Characteristics		**GS8 Monitoring and Sanctioning Processes**	*no*
RS9 Location		**U Users**	*weak*
RU Resource Units	*weak*	**U1 Number of Users**	*no*
RU1 Resource Unit mobility		U2 Socioeconomic Attributes of the Users	
RU2 Growth and Recovery Rate	*weak*	**U3 History of Use**	*no*
RU3 Interaction among Resource Units		**U4 Location**	*yes*
RU4 Economic Value		**U5 Leadership**	*no*
RU5 Number of Units	*weak*	**U6 Social Capital**	*no*
RU6 Distinctive Markings		**U7 Knowledge of SES**	*no*
RU7 Spatial and temporal distribution	*weak*	**U8 Importance of Resource**	*weak*
I Interactions	*weak*	**U9 Technology Used**	*no*
I1 Harvesting Levels of Divers Users	*weak*	**Outcomes**	
I2 Information-Sharing among Users	*yes*	O1 Social performance measures	
I3 Deliberation Process		O2 Ecological performance measures	
I4 Lack of Conflicts among users	*no*	O3 Externalities to other SES	
I5 Investment Activities			
I6 Lobbying Activities			
I7 Self-Organising Activities	*no*		
I8 Networking Activities			

The 29 of the 53 variables analysed for the case study are in bold. The variables qualitative of quantitative findings are either "no" (the mean of the lower variables is not active), "yes" (the mean of the lower variables is active) or "weak" (the mean of the lower variables is weak).

To provide an assessment of each variable that allows classifying it according to its performance and to compare the variables across the framework, the study follows Ostrom's pragmatic approach in detecting robust, fragile or failing institutions: The performances are deduced from each of the variables qualitative of quantitative findings which are either "no" (the mean of the lower variables is not active), "yes" (the mean of the lower variables is active) or "weak" (the mean of the lower variables is weak) (Ostrom 1990, p. 180).

Identifying the institutional processes: The dynamics of the MTC

Within three decades only, the coral reef experiences a dynamic process of changing and contradicting *de jure* and *de facto* property rights leading to a mix of resource regimes. The period between 1982 and 2014 can be categorized into 4 phases (Figure 2.3, and discussed below). Before Karimunjawa gained any conservation status, its reefs were under a *de facto* state property combined with an open-access situation. This pre-conservation status back then might equal other coral reef areas around the world nowadays without any legal conservation framework.

Phase I – 1982 to 1989: Open-access and state property

On 26 October 1982, the proposal of the Governor of Central Java to develop Karimunjawa as a Marine National Park and marine tourism area in Jepara

Resource Regimes	>1981		Phase I 1982-1989		Phase II 1990-2004		Phase III 2005-2011		Phase IV 2012-<	
	De Facto	De Jure	De Facto	De Jure	De Facto	De Jure	De Facto	De Jure	De Facto	De Jure
State	x			x	x		x			x
Private					x	x	x	x	x	x
Open-Access	x		x		x					
Common					x		x		x	x

Starting Commonisation & Privatization

Struggling Commonisation

Decommonisation

Figure 2.3 Overview of the four phases between 1982 and 2014. A colour version of this image is downloadable as an eResource from www.routledge.com/9780367138004.

regency paved the way for Karimunjawa's future. In 1984, Karimunjawa was among 179 priority areas in Indonesia recommended as first order priority for inclusion in a national network of marine protected areas (Salm and Halim 1984). Just two years afterwards in 1986, Karimunjawa was formally declared a Strict Natural Reserve and become a formal *National Park* (KNP) in 1988. The coral reef's property regime therefore changed from a *de facto* to a *de jure* state property under a legal conservation framework.

The first zoning in 1989 further defined the coral reef's access rules by dividing the national park into a core, protection and buffer zone. Even though marine tourism did not exist back then, the core zone would have implied a no-access rule for tourism, while the buffer and protection zone allowed *"limited nature tourism activities"*. Precise rules, however, on how to limit nature tourism activities were absent. Without under any zonation, the coral reefs around the eastern islands were under an open-access resource regime. While zoning is a first precondition of coral reefs' diverse access rules, it is still an insufficient legislative framework to deal with various other issues surrounding marine tourism, such as property rights.

Phase II – 1990–2003: Starting commonisation and privatization

Based on the local's memory, the first tourists came in 1990 and shortly afterwards locals, private investors and the government saw the potential to open accommodations. Small islands or beautiful beach stretches were bought by private investors under unclear ownership rights (*de facto* mixed with *de jure*). The first coral reef intentionally opened for tourism purposes was around the Menyawakan Island with its private five-star resort lying within the buffer zone. As marine tourism began to slowly spread across the marine park in the early 90s and made coral reef subject to a joint use by locals guiding the tourists, can be called the birth hour of the MTC. However, missing rules for coral reefs usage – also those within the dedicated zones – left the coral reefs in an open-access situation.

A first attempt by the locals to manage the early tourists was the community-based group "Pokdarwis" founded in 1998 – a way forward towards commonisation of the coral reef ecosystem. The members consisted of tourism actors who played a catalytic role in supporting the tourism development and the welfare of the surrounding communities. Pokdarwis, however, never became a rule-setting or influential institution for marine tourism. The ability, power and acceptance by the whole community to proactively engage in an informal institutional set-up were underestimated. Until now the locals of Karimunjawa have the mindset that "the government has to do it". As Pokdarwis was rather a platform for exchanging experiences and ideas focusing on topics like transport, accommodation, food supply and sightseeing spots, this institutional development was also not yet prepared to create informal collective-action rules to commonly manage coral reefs for tourism.

To improve the management of the National Park, the Ministry of Forestry declared Karimunjawa as Technical Implementation Unit under the Director General of Nature Conservation to be management by the Karimunjawa National Park Authority (KNPA) in 1998. Since then, the marine area implies a property right system where the district government agency is the owner and the KNPA the manager of the marine resources including the coral reef ecosystems. Based on the decree in 1999, Karimunjawa was further officially recognized as Marine National Park and in 2001 designated as marine conservation area. While tourist transportation was limited to the slow boat departing from Jepara taking 6 hours, the fourfold increase in tourist numbers from 450 tourist per year in 1998 up to 2030 tourists in 2003 demanded an improved transportation system (Figure 2.2).

Phase III – 2004–2011: Struggling commonisation

With a slightly better transportation system in place, the third phase of Karimunjawa began. The express boat Kartini with its 156 available seats, started its weekly departures from Semarang in April 2004 taking 2½ hours journey only, and was the first catalyzer for the rise in tourism numbers from 2004 onwards. With the first peak of more than 9,000 visitors in 2005, a tourism strategy of the park's management was urgent and had to be in line with the new law on collaborative arrangements (or Co-management) for nature reserves and conservation areas (Furqan et al. 2010). The enactment of Law No. 32 in 2004 of the local government even enhanced collaborative management within the paradigm of decentralising conservation areas and supported the active participation of local communities within the local area management process. The multidisciplinary management concept *Integrated Conservation and Development Program* (ICDP) adopted by the Department of Protection and Nature Conservation under the Ministry of Forestry (which was the result of the decentralisation policy in the early 1990s), offered a politically feasible and alternative approach to include the often-confronting goals of biodiversity conservation and economic development. Hence, collaborative management and decentralisation share the same goal to strengthen community participation and to distribute power in a more equitable resource management (Yulianto et al. 2006). A first attempt of the management was therefore the revision of the previous park's boundaries via a participatory re-zoning process in 2005 with the outcome of having six dedicated marine tourism zones (MTZ) with an extent of 12.2 km² – roughly 10% of the marine park's area. In comparison to the first zoning, the marine tourism zones made the coral reef ecosystem this time to a *de jure* property right dedicated to marine tourism with clear constitutional rules prohibiting intended or unintended coral damage. However, the rules were never enforced.

Recognizing the need to provide the increasing number of visitors authorized, around 10 Tourist Guides initiated the establishment of the Tourist Guide

Association "HPI Karimunjawa" on 9 April 2005 under the regency board DPD Central Java. Similar like *Pokdarwis*, HPI is nationally recognized but a community-managed institution evolving around tourist destinations in Indonesia eager to improve the tourist guide (TG) business. Starting with 10 TGs in 2005, already 50 TGs were registered in 2009. Becoming a TG without requiring a high investment nor education offered a lucrative alternative livelihood for the locals. The HPI executive board working on a voluntary basis was eager to develop the new TG business via standard operation procedure (SOP) – collective action rules. First, HPI offered administrative support for becoming a licensed TG equipped with an official ID and t-shirts for its members and therefore enforcing excludability. Apart from this rather unofficial HPI TG license, since 2011 also the KNPA required the TGs to hold the "license for utilization of natural tourist services" allowing them to operate in the marine tourism zones. With this law, TGs gained a *de jure* common property right. However, since the license is issued in Central Java, Semarang, and doesn't bring TGs any advantages, the TGs do not consider the license as a lucrative or mandatory option worth obtaining. Only one staff of the KNPA who is also working as TG, holds such a license. So, to speak, there is only one legal authorized user for the MTC.

Then also safety standards were developed and improved. Occasionally the national park authority, HPI and the tourism department worked together to issue diving, coral transplantation and eco-tourist guide certificates/licences for interested TGs. Even if this collaboration benchmarks a peak in organising collective action for marine tourism, rules and certification schemes were limited to or applied by only several TGs. While tourism numbers quickly developed, HPI struggled to extend collective-action rules that define sustainable use of the coral reef spots (i.e. sanctioning of inappropriate tourist behaviour, closures of MTZ, tourist number controls, etc.). What Purwanti identified to be a lack of *"coordination of stakeholders to arrange resources' utilization regulation, to build a stakeholders forum and to formulate a rule of the game* (2008)" underlines that MTC never experienced a successful commonisation process. Also, the UNEP-funded project on Good Practices for Marine Environmental Governance in 2011, did not identify Karimunjawa as community-led, but as a *decentralised governance* with influences from private organisations. This already highlights the increasing role and power of private tour operators during the tourism development that might be one external factor impeding collective action among HPI. It can be argued however, that in case the park authority would have had the resources and capacity to enforce the constitutional rules – one key area of improvement identified by the UNEP report – the commonisation process by HPI could have been successful despite the strong marine tourism driven market incentives for travel agents.

Phase IV – 2012–present: Decommonisation

A turning point of the already struggling commonisation process happened in 2012 when the number of visitors exploded up to 25,000. As a response to the booming tourist industry, another re-zoning in 2012 further opened 17 marine tourism zones bringing the total area to 27.7 km² or 18.5% of the entire marine park. Most coral reefs surrounding the islands lost their previous boundaries as protection zones and become a dedicated marine tourism zone. This transformation was needed to ensure access and grant permission for tourism facilities to moor a boat and building jetties on the islands. The constitutional rules (see GS7) for the MTZ stayed the same as they were formulated in the previous zoning.

With the national law in 2014, entry fees for tourists became mandatory for all marine national parks in Indonesia (P 12 2014) – an important constitutional step for regulating access to MTC (excludability). The regional government PEMDA however, being in favour of mass tourism and concerned of declining tourism numbers in case an entrance fee would be charged, tried to hinder the KNPA to build the entrance booth at the harbor, because it is outside the KNPA responsible zones. The official entrance fees varies between local tourists (US$0.50) and foreign tourists (US$15). However, as domestic tourism is predominant in Karimunajwa, the small entry fee for domestic visitors would not hinder mass tourism. In contrast, the charges that tour operators ask tourists to pay for i.e. island entrance fees, snorkel gear, lunch etc. are far higher than the KNPA fees. At the same time, the locals mistrust the appropriate use of the charges since the fees are forwarded to the Ministry. Even though the KNPA tried to inform tourism stakeholders via social media early enough, the locals of Karimunjawa demonstrated against the new rule in fear of losing future income. The demonstration against the park fee was successful and resulted in the closure of the booth just a couple of days after its opening. Except for a few visitors during those days, only one resort is paying the official charges for the marine national park. To still meet the law, the KNPA is charging the official park fee only for those few tourists entering the mangrove trek far north of the island. In case the law would be enforced, the common property right of the coral reefs for the number of users (TGs) and authorized entrants (the tourists) would have changed from a *de facto* to a *de jure* situation.

What the SESF will in detail interpret as a decommonisation process in the next section, can be shortly described as an uncontrolled marine tourism business situation ruled by profit-seeking tour operators and unregistered TG combined with increasing tourism numbers that leads to a clear non-excludability and strong subtractability (damage and overuse) of the MTC.

Assessing institutional performance of the MTC through the SESF

This section is a detailed analysis of Phase IV starting in 2012 and applies the SEFS to identify the institutional performance during the time of this research in 2013–2014. The ecological system boundary is defined as coral reef resource system (RS) within the 17 marine tourism zones, with its resource units (RU) as the number of snorkel and diving coral reef spots in the Karimunjawa Marine National Park (KNP) in 2014. However, the analysis also includes those coral reef spots that are not within the formally declared marine tourism zones but illegally visited by marine tourism. The Social System encompasses all actors that operate or hold legal status in the 17 marine tourism zones declared in 2012. These are the group of 227 Tourist Guides (TGs) as the resource user (U) of the coral reef spots. Other actors are categorized under the Governance System (GS). The assessments of weak, yes or no were arrived at by the first author during and after field work, and was based on perception of interviewees, observations and literature.

Governance system (GS – weak)

Property Rights (GS4 – weak): As the four phases in the previous section already highlight, property rights and resource regimes for the MTC in Karimunjawa are changing over time and fail to enforce clear user and entrant boundaries leading to a non-excludability and subtractive resource use scenario for the MTC. Here we explain how the five main property rights of access and withdrawal, management, exclusion and alienation are associated with the positions of authorized entrant, authorized user, claimant, proprietor and owner: The *authorized entrant* – the tourist– only holds the right of *access* to the marine tourism zones. Because the KNPA has until now not been able to enforce the new law on entry fees, all tourists entering the marine tourism zones may be classified as unauthorized entrants. Having not the right to withdraw, leads to the false assumption that the coral reef resource system is totally unaffected by the entering tourists.

But as a matter of fact, whether it might be conscious or unconscious coral destruction, "consumption" or "withdrawal" of the coral reef ecosystem is indeed subtractive and therefore makes the problem of the marine tourism commons a collective-action problem. The *authorized user* – the TG – holds the property right of withdrawal. The term withdrawal has two meanings for the MTC: while the TGs' withdrawal as user means to gain indirect benefit of the coral reefs via offering island hoping trips, the tourists' withdrawal as entrant is the actual subtractive use of coral reefs. As the unofficial registration processes of HPI is not active anymore and the official TG license process of the KNPA not enforced, most TGs can be classified as unauthorized users. The *claimant* or manager who has the "right to *regulate* internal use patterns and *transform* the resource by making improvements to hold the position as claimant", officially is the KNPA, followed by the Department of Fishery. De facto however, the group of TGs as well tour operators have a direct impact of the internal use patterns in terms of how many boats go to which marine tourism zones and decide which coral reef sites shall be visited. Performing this right though without having operational or collective rules for sustainable marine tourism practices in place, leads to overuse of the coral reef sites. The right of *exclusion* – the right to determine who will have an access right into the marine tourism zones – and how that right may be transferred is clearly obtained by the KNPA. Both access rights i.e. park entry fee and TG licenses though have not yet been enforced. Also, the overlap between private *ownership* of small islands and the marine owned area by the Ministry of Forestry that surrounds the islands makes the position of ownership for the MTC difficult.

Constitutional Rules (GS7 – weak): For the zonings in 2005 and 2012, constitutional rules were established to define which activities are allowed and prohibited in the given zones. Tourism activities are prohibited in the core zone, rehabilitation zone, traditional use zone and the mariculture zone, but allowed in the protection zone and in the 17 MTZ. The unclear statement in the zoning plan that "nature tourism is limited" (Balai Taman Nasional Karimunjawa 2012, p. 34; 72) remained since 1989 and might be one reason for the unregulated use pattern for the MTC. The MTZs have the function to develop nature tourism and recreational activities in the concept of environmental friendliness. Taking corals or disturbing and damaging any part of the marine ecosystem – intentionally or unintentionally, are strictly prohibited within the MTZ (Balai Taman Nasional Karimunjawa 2012). As these constitutional rules are not enforced by the KNPA, they also have no further influence on the following collective-choice and operational rules.

Collective-choice rules (GS6 – weak): Collective-choice rules "affect operational activities and results through their effects in determining who is eligible and the specific rules to be used in changing operational rules" (Ostrom et al. 1994, p. 46). Further, collective-choice rules can be differentiated between formal and informal rules. A formal collective-choice rule for the MTC is the participatory and adaptive co-management process for the re-zoning in 2012. Even though the tourism sector was represented by the leader of HPI, who was back then also in the position as village chief (*Pak Lurah/Kepala Desa*), the re-zoning process did not extend its formal collective-choice rules to sustainable resource use of the coral reefs (weak). Informal collective-choice rules are identified based on (1) agreed rules (weak), the (2) participation of the TGs in decision-making processes (weak), and the (3) consensus among the TGs (weak).

Operational Rules (GS5 – weak): Operational Rules are defined as those that "directly affect day-to-day decisions made the participants in any setting" (Ostrom et al. 1994, p. 46). TGs could provide multiple answers of which rules they apply during an island-hopping trip, which were then ranked according to the number of times a rule was mentioned.[1] Rules concerning safety during the island-hopping trip, in terms of using life jacket, information of dangerous species and praying for a safe journey are the major operational rules used by the TGs. Operational rules that are being used for instructing tourists not to touch (more in terms that the coral might be hurtful to the tourist instead that the tourist might destroy the coral), stand (which tourist mostly do when putting the gear on or to take a break from snorkeling), walk (as many Indonesians cannot swim), or take the coral and encouraging them to take care of the corals, have no collective support or relevance. Other important rules to prevent coral destruction, i.e. don't dive in shallow water, clear instructions or ban of underwater camera are almost neglected. During various joined snorkeling trips, it was observed that TGs were standing on the corals to take a break after being exhausted from taking pictures underwater, sometimes diving up to 50 times within 30 minutes. Barker and Roberts (2004) found that briefings from the TGs towards the tourists are not enough to reduce coral damage. Only when the TG reprimanded a tourist for inappropriate behaviour while visiting the reefs, did the tourist reduce the level of contact with the corals. Close supervision and the TG's obligation to control tourist behaviour are highly recommended to reduce coral damage (Barker and Roberts 2004; Medio et al. 1997). Based on these findings, the operational rules mentioned for coral protection might have no impact to reduce coral damage. Missing clear defined operational rules that can restrict the subtractability of the coral reef ecosystem are one major threadhold towards the tragedy of the MTC.

Government & Non-Government organisations (GS1 & GS2 – weak): The performance of the government organisations [(GS 1) Local Government (LG), the Karimunjawa National Park Authority (KNPA), Tourism Department (TD)] as well as non-government organisations [Wildlife Conservation Society – WCS and the tourist guide association – HPI] were assessed by the TGs' perceived (1) level of trust towards the organisations, the level of success of the organisations to govern MTC and the capacity of the given organisation to improve the governance of MTC as well as TG's perceived (2) overall government effectiveness to govern the MTC. As Ostrom identified, misleading authorities can contradict the resource user's efforts in governing common-pool resources. Such misleading authorities are identified to be the local government and tourism department. Promoting Karimunjawa in favour of mass tourism, their interest to invest and make money out of that business (similar like the tour operators / travel agencies), not only contradicts the KNPA's coral reef conservation effort, but also lowers the TGs' ability to successfully governing MTC. In comparison to all other GS1 and GS2 organisations, the KNPA is seen to be the only government organisation with the highest level of trust, the most successful, and also with the most capacity to improve the MTC governance.

Because of the KNPA's 30-year existence on the island, most of the younger TGs and locals have grown up as part of the national park and acknowledge the park's constant effort to preserve the island. Several times, locals mentioned that "without the KNPA, Karimunjawa would be already broken". In contrast, the local government and the tourist department are highly distrusted for their corrupt practices. The perceived lack of trust, success and capacity by TGs towards the NGO WCS should be relativized, for the reason that WCS was working primarily together with the fisher community and supported the KNPA in management issues without any visible or recognizable effect for the TG community. That HPI lacks trust and is seen as unsuccessful by their own members, correlates with and will be further explained later. However, the higher perceived capacity of HPI might argue that TGs see themselves as an actor able to directly influence the improvement of coral reefs. The overall government effectiveness to govern the MTC is perceived as ineffective. This correlates with the earlier findings of the UNEP-funded marine protected area governance report "MPAG", where Karimunjawa reached the effectiveness of 2 (on the scale of 0–5), which refers to "some impacts partly addressed but some impacts not yet addressed" (Jones et al. 2011).

Network Structure (GS3 – weak): Network structure analyses if the cross-scale interactions produce complementary actions or actions that interfere with or undermine each other (Ostrom et al. 2002, p. 487). Promising institutions that hold cross-scale (vertical and horizontal) linkages and dynamic interactions are known as co-management and adaptive management, which are appraised in environmental governance (Evans 2012; Armitage 2008), especially in marine policy and newly recognized for tourism (Plummer 2013) and in Indonesia (Clifton 2003). A senior representative of each of the GS1 and GS2 organisations including the fishery department (PPP) rated the degree of working with other organisations using the categories none, low, medium or high. KNPA has the strongest connections with WCS and PPP, working together on sustainable coral reef fishery. In comparison, the connections between LG and the KNPA was not as strong (therefore medium): "We [the local government] have a good relationship towards KNPA, but conflicts about biodiversity conservation vs local development are evident" (Official Servant of the Kecamatan Karimunjawa). Both the tourist department (TD) and the HPI have a weak link to the KNPA (low). Despite the fact that the staff of the regional tourism department obtains monthly tourism data and forwards them to the national park, no actual working together is evident. Thus, even though the KNPA performs as the best-connected organisation in the network structure, its connection with the marine tourism sector is modest. Also, the TD is almost decoupled from the MTC governance. Even though co-management is established in Karimunjawa since 2004, so far its collaboration has been reduced unto organisations connected with fishery (Campbell et al. 2013; Purwanti et al. 2013; Yulianto et al. 2006). Despite the marine tourism zones that were developed without any significant local participation from the tourism sector, marine tourism institutions – especially the TG association HPI, but also tourist agencies – haven't been sufficiently included into the park's co-management. Especially the TGs as direct resource users has to be a respected actor of a marine tourism network structure keen to both conserve the coral reef while earning an income from it.

Monitoring and sanctioning processes (GS8 – no): There does not exist any monitoring nor sanctioning processes for wrong behaviour during the snorkeling and diving activities of tourists and TGs, either by the KNPA or by the TG community themselves in 2014. TGs were asked to rate their willingness to report wrong behaviour of a colleague to HPI and about their frequency of monitoring. While around half of the 50 TGs would report wrong behaviour and already did so very often or a few times, 44% would not. As the leadership of HPI is not reacting and seems "not to care", continuing reporting showed no effect and hence TGs lost their willingness to do so. TGs mentioned that the tension between the TGs community concerning right behaviour in the MTZ was so high, that they even started fighting in the water several times in the last years. However, since the situation did not improve, the willingness to remind each other to take care of the coral reef has vanished and is even being ridiculed. Since no sanction processes from TGs towards colleagues and tourists were active at the time of this research, the TGs were asked to at least suggest potential sanctions in case of prohibited activities. Suggested sanctions to colleagues included reminders (6 TGs); blacklisting with "yellow card" (15TGs) varying from a few days to up to 2 months; directly firing the TG of the HPI association with a "red card" (6 TGs); a fine (3 TGs); report wrong behaviour directly to the police (2 TGs); or to put to jail (1 TG). These strong suggested sanctions might reflect the frustration between the TGs of the so far failed efforts to improve the TGs behaviour.

In contrary, 62% of the TGs do not know how to give a sanction towards their own customers, in fear of losing their tip. Suggested sanctions would be either a fine (11TGs), a reminder (3 TGs), the consequence of going back to the boat (2 TGs) or even to directly stop the island-hopping trip (2 TGs) and the prohibition to further take pictures (1 TGs). In case of a fine, tourists might perceive this as another way of earning money by the TG or tour operator. As mentioned earlier, "sometimes the TG is stressed or confused, because there are too many tourists around him and he cannot control the situation. We (HPI) cannot control the tourists, we need somebody from outside to control with patrols". Even though the TG is the only person who can see, prove and report tourist misbehaviour during the snorkel trip, TGs admit their own lack of power to do so.

Monitoring by the KNPA only took place several times in 2014 and is not active anymore due to high costs of the two owned speedboats, which are a financial burden for the park. While the KNPA has precise rules concerning the tourism behavior within the MTZ, there are no active sanctioning processes for the tourists nor TGs. One possible sanction would be to take away the official TG license that allows the TG to operate in the marine national park for a certain time. However, since only one TG has such a license, this sanction cannot be enforced as the KNPA has no control over operating TGs. Another sanction of the KNPA for tourists would be a fine, but to prove the fact that the tourist has broken the coral i.e., a picture would be needed to prove the delict if it comes to a court case.

Resource user (RU – weak)

Number of Users (U1 – no): This sub-variable assumes that "the likelihood of reaching and maintaining cooperative agreements regarding the joint use of an environmental resource is greater, the smaller the size of the group, i.e. the smaller the number of resource users" (Singleton and Taylor 1992 in Huyber and Bennet 2003, p. 576). As only one TG obtained the official TG license via the KNPA, the number of users is based on HPI records until 2013. The size of the tourist guide group increased rapidly from 139 TGs in 2012 up to 187 TGs in 2013. After the mismanagement of HPI in these years, new TGs did not feel obliged to register anymore which leads to an unclear number of users. A vague number of 227 TGs of both registered and unregistered guides was counted in July 2014. This growing and unclear number of users impedes the likelihood of reaching and maintaining cooperative agreements regarding the joint use of the MTC.

History of Use (U3 – no): Usually, common-pool resources are used by a steady number of resource users over a longer period, where collective memory or experience of an event in the past can be used in times of change and uncertainty, and local traditional knowledge can be passed unto the next generations. MTC experience a different phenomenon: The history of use is limited to the timeframe of marine tourism development, hence one decade only for Karimunjawa. The average durability of the marine tourism live-lihood is around six and a half years, hence collective memory before 2008 like the founding of HPI and the re-zoning in 2005 is missing. An absent baseline of the TGs' memories contradicts their ability to find solutions for the quickly developing and changing marine tourism conditions in terms of tourist numbers and re-zoning.

Location (U4 – yes): Resource users have lower costs in self-organisation, if the geographic location is close to each other. The tour guiding business has a clear monopoly located at the main village of Karimunjawa. Short distances between the resource users should increase investment and self-organising activities as well as support information and knowledge exchange.

Leadership (U5 – no): Self-organising is more likely "when some users of any type of resource system have entrepreneurial skills and are respected as local leaders" (Ostrom 2009, p. 421). The TGs collectively agree that the current leadership is ineffective, and that HPI needs a new leader. The complaints included mistrust towards the leadership due to believed corruption and missing transparency; missing communication and collab-oration via meetings as well as no-enforcement of rules. In contrary, the leadership of HPI claimed that the marine tour guiding community has fallen apart and does not seem to care about HPI and collective arrangements anymore. Therefore, misunderstandings and mistrust between the members and leadership of HPI is making self-organisation of the TGs unlikely.

Social Capital (U6 – no): The information whether moral and ethical standards of the TGs that are likely to "lower transaction costs in reaching agreements" (Ostrom 2009, p. 421) was obtained by asking an open-ended question on the vision for and the benefit of marine tourism. As a second step, TGs were asked to rate the extent to which they felt they belonged to the HPI and the degree of trust among the TGs with none, low, medium, or high. The overall vision among the TGs for the marine tourism's future is economic development and mirrors the perceived benefit of marine tourism as income opportunity. Whereas most TGs felt either no to little relationship with HPI, the levels of trust among the TGs was equally reported with low, medium and high. Environmental or coral protection is only a minor concern for the TG community and combined with little sense of belonging to the HPI, self-organising activities geared towards sustainable use of MTC are unlikely.

Knowledge of SES (U7 – no): "When users share common knowledge of relevant SES attributes (…) they will perceive lower costs of organising" (Ostrom et al. 2002, p. 488). The two sub-variables human agency and marine environmental knowledge are examined to identify the TGs knowledge of the SES marine tourism. Human Agency indicates the degree to which TGs recognized that they and the tourists are causal agents of change in marine systems. With an open question "what could increase the wealth of the marine tourism zones", around fourteen different factors were mentioned that clearly identified human agency and show that TGs are clearly aware of their impact on the coral reef ecosystem: a professional TG who realizes his responsibility, who explains and is a good example towards tourists, coral transplantation, cleaning beaches activities, education and training, information on how to protect corals, trash bins on the islands, TGs strictness towards the tourist, a working together ethic, temporal closures of zones, right usage of fishing gear and good behaviour of tourists were all mentioned to be factors increasing the wealth of the MTZs. The statement that the wealth of the MTZs "depends on the people" directly shows the identified human agency.

The calculation of the marine environmental knowledge is based on the three variables: general marine environmental knowledge, knowledge about coral species and knowledge about fish or marine species. Answers were ranked into five categories which were differentiated between the amount and exclusivity of information. The first very general and open question on what the TG knows about the marine environment in Karimunjawa was mostly left unanswered and is interpreted as no knowledge. Knowledge about coral and fish/marine species gained similarly low levels of knowledge. All mentioned coral species are given local names reflecting the form or characteristic of the coral (table, mushroom, fire, …). Same accounts for the fish species: short fish, green fish, zebra fish, etc. Older TGs working as fishermen had much more knowledge about fish species.

The awareness of the TGs of their own impact and responsibility towards the coral reef ecosystem stands in contrast to the very low knowledge about the coral reef and marine tourism zones. Shared knowledge and experience about the SES over a longtime horizon cannot be observed in the case for the new existing MTC. Low educational levels especially on islands and missing trainings for marine tour guiding lower the learning capacity which impedes the likelihood of cooperative behaviour among the TGs.

Importance of Resource (U8 – weak): "In successful cases of self-organisation, users are either dependent on the RS for a substantial portion of their livelihoods **or** attach high value to the sustainability of the resource. Otherwise, the costs of organising and maintaining a self-governing system may not be worth the effort" (Ostrom 2009, p. 421). Two aspects are examined: The dependency on marine tourism and the occupational diversity. For the latter one, respondents were asked to list all their income activities and then rank these according to importance. The dependency of marine tourism has an equal distribution of both 24 TGs in the independency and dependency range. To crosscheck the result, TGs were asked if they were able to leave the marine tour guiding business right now: The outcome that 40% of the TGs were ready to leave, whereas 60% were not, suggests a slightly higher dependency on marine tourism. As income from marine tourism can only be gained for 6–9 month, hence most TGs have other sources of incomes such as from fishery or temporary jobs. More than half of the TGs (28 TGs) have marine tour guiding as their primary livelihood, whereas 22 TGs have their primary livelihood either in fishery (11 TGs) or in services such as bank, post office, hotel, rental (11 TGs) (Figure 2.4). Adding both livelihoods – marine

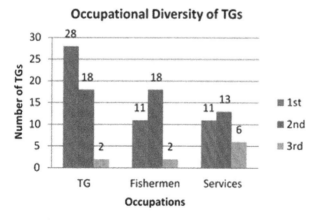

Figure 2.4 Occupational diversity of TGs. A colour version of this image is downloadable as an eResource from www.routledge.com/9780367138004.

tour guiding and fishery – the TGs are dependent on the coral reef resource system for a substantial portion of their two livelihoods. But even though self-organisation activities of TGs and fishers to achieve joint benefits through coral reef protection due to the high dependency of the coral reefs would be more probable, efforts of such kind are not the case for Karimunjawa.

Technology Used (U9 – no): The often-quoted sentence in National Parks "Take only photographs and leave only footprints" implies that taking pictures has no impact on the environment. Research found significant coral damage impact due to Underwater Camera (UWC) usage (Rouphael and Inglis 2001; Barker and Roberts 2004; Davis and Tisdell 1995). During the island-hopping trip in Karimunjawa, the picture taking process under water is a major threat to the coral damage. While most Indonesian tourist cannot swim, TGs choose shallow waters for the tourist's first snorkel experience. However, to take a picture under water with a coral and fish requires the tourist taking off the lifejacket. After the lifejacket is removed, the tourist guides push the tourist down in the water, while at the same time the other tourist guide is taking the picture of the tourist. To gain a good picture, the tourist usually tries to grab a coral or a stone to stay under water as long as possible. Hectic movements with their feet lead to severe coral damage during this picture taking procedure. Since this process is not only dangerous, but tiring for both as well, corals are used as a resting area to take a breath or even as a walking ground. While 29 TGs would disagree, and 19 TGs would agree in case the UWC would be prohibited. While on the one side the UWC is important for the tourist as memory and a lucrative sub-business to rent the cameras, many TGs acknowledged that UWC usage is damaging the reef. However, a general UWC would only be accepted by the TGs in case the rule had official status from the government, the tourist could accept the rule and the prohibition improves the marine tourism business.

Resource system (RS – weak)

Clarity of System Boundaries (RS2 – weak): Clearly defined boundaries for the MTC belong to one of the eight design principle by Ostrom which has been identified to enhance self-organisation. The designated MTZs do not match with the coral reef ecosystem boundary. The quadratic forms of the zones were designed for easier GPS coordinate markings and clear administrative units. In some cases, they overlap, are adjacent to other zones or cover half of the islands' surrounding coral reefs. To overcome that problem and to assure accurate behaviour according to the zoning, the KNPA together with the NGO WCS, HPI and community representatives including boat operators and TGs, started the *socialization*[2] of installation of floating buoys and tourist boat moorings via environmental conservation posters. The installation of floating buoys was expected to minimize the impact of tourists towards coral reef destruction, to preserve the natural resources and to assure coastal environmental cleanness. However, only 6 out of 18 floating buoys installed in 2011 endured until July 2014. Another attempt to *socialize* and promote the new MTZs boarders was the campaign by the KNPA: "Let's visit the MTZs" which included a temporal poster installation of the new 2012 zoning plan at the village center and give away t-shirts. Even though a clear system's boundary of the coral reef exists on paper, the MTC experience an extending system boundary over a short time period via the re-zonings (1989: 0 MTZ; 2005: 6 MTZ; 2012: 17 MTZ). Additionally, the coral reefs that are illegally used for marine tourism activities, hence outside the MTZs, verify the lack of clarity to define the exact boundaries of the MTC.

Size of Resource System (RS3 – weak): Highest levels of self-organisation is neither found for very large territories "given the high costs of defining boundaries, monitoring use patterns, and gaining ecological knowledge", nor for small territories that "do not generate substantial flows of valuable products", but for moderate territorial size (Ostrom 2009, p. 420). The coral reef ecosystem is the largest ecosystem, covering 79.8 km^2 of the total marine area within the KNP. 14.7 km^2 of this coral reef (or 18.5%) are open to tourists within the 17 Marine Tourism Zones (MTZ) expanding to 27.7 km^2. The 54% coral area cover within these zones therefore can be identified as a moderate territory. However, as MTC are not concentrated in one place, but dispersed, only a small portion of the coral reef ecosystem is commonly visited and intensely used (see RU5 and RU7), the coral reef might be subject to higher pressure, like congestion and overexploitation.

Resource units (RU – weak)

Number of Units (RU 5 – weak): To understand how the common-pool resources problems appear in the MTC, the number of resource units (RU5) is of major importance, since it links the problems of crowding and resource degradation. "Resource units are what individuals appropriate or use from resource systems" (Ostrom 1990, p. 30), hence are the products of the resource system for the appropriator. The number and quality of coral reef snorkel and diving spots were considered for this tier. For this research coral reef sites were identified through previous studies (Balai Taman Nasional Karimunjawa 2010), TGs statements and the identification of WCS. With 27 islands surrounded by coral reefs, the archipelago of Karimunjawa offers around 50 coral reef spots, 31 for snorkeling and 19 for diving. As the coral reefs are within mostly shallow water, diving tours only happen on special request and therefore the coral reef dive spots are excluded of the number of units. If the spots are too exposed to stronger waves or located in deeper water, with lesser quality or too far away from the harbor, TGs avoid visiting them. One spots in the north is not visited because of the mystical stories of the close by island and again two spots can only be visited by the visitors of the island resort. However, there are four more additional snorkel spots more and more visited outside the park's boundaries in the east. Due to seasonality, accessibility and the mentioned characteristics, the number of resource units is reduced to 8 up to 14 spots that are mostly and regularly visited by marine tourism.

Spatial and temporal distribution (RU 7 – weak): The spatial distribution of the snorkeling and diving spots is one essential reason why the actively used resource units are reduced to a small number. Two spatial distributions are found to have an impact on the coral reef spot usage: the distance and duration of the spots to the harbor and the spatial distribution among the spots. So far island-hopping packages only offer half-day or one day tours. Tour Operators are expected to offer at least three to four snorkel spots for a one day (8–9 hours) and two to three spots for half-day trips (4–5 hours). Whereas the 5 spots located in the east (between a 10 and 20 km radius) can only be covered in a one-day trip, the 14 spots in the west (located closer than 10 km) can be covered by both half-day and one day tours and hence are the ones most visited. To reach the nine spots located 20–30 km could only be included in a not yet offered two days tour. Also, only a few TGs know how to access those further located islands.

Karimunjawa experiences four wind seasons: During the strong west winds and monsoon season from December until February marine transportation is limited and therefore the marine park experiences a "natural" closure. The transitional seasons from March until May is usually the only time when the eastern spots can be visited together with the ones in the west. The lower east winds from June until August is high season for tourism, but usually only the spots in the west can be visited. Same counts for the again transitional season from September to November, but with lower numbers of tourists. As both spatial and temporal distributions of the resource units show, only 8 up to maximum 14 out of 31 snorkel spots are mostly visited. This enhances short-term crowding and long-term coral reef destruction and thus might lead towards the inability of the TGs to control the reefs' overuse.

Growth and recovery rate (RU 2 – weak): In 2013, coral damage by marine tourism in KNP was found to be in the range of 25.03 to 36.93 square metres per hectare (Dendy et al. 2013, p. 37). Most of this damage was found especially at a depth of one to two metres where rock fragmentation and coral damage was observed due to walking on corals or exposed fins close to the corals (Hannak et al. 2011). Those broken corals are mostly colonies of the branching and table coral (*Acropora formosa, Acropora garandis, Acropora vaughani, Acropora divaricata and Acropora hyachintus*). Campbell (2012a) recognizes that "tourism can impact coral reef ecosystems through anchor damage and trampling" and that "tourism impacts in the KNP are likely to increase in the future if (…) tourism-based activities in marine waters are not adhered to" (p. 110). If the level of damage is too severe, coral reef recovery cannot be possible. After being destroyed, coral recovery might take up to 37 years (Nababan 2010) and the resource unit reaches its limit. So far, marine tourism induced coral damage couldn't be sufficiently scientifically documented and thus has not received any political awareness and relevance.

Second, monitoring spots that have been chosen a decade ago do not overlap with the current visited snorkel and dive spots and cannot deliver proper data on coral damage induced by marine tourism. Taking the TGs' daily or weekly observations of the coral spots into account, coral damage has increased dramatically over the last decade. Still though, this does not affect their willingness to organise marine tourism institutions and maintain the MTC.

Interaction and outcomes (weak)

Harvesting Levels (I1 – weak): An appropriate calculation of the "harvesting level" in terms of a carrying capacity for the MTC cannot be sufficiently dealt with in this research. Still though, the assumption that a certain quantity of visitors leads to overuse and thus damage of the coral reef goes along with Hardin's (1968) scenario of the pasture: Every additional tourist causes a positive short-term but a negative long-term return. An approximate harvesting level of the snorkel spots is calculated with the number of tourists divided by the average coral reef area in km^2 and number of coral reef sites. Dividing the coral reef area within the marine tourism zones by the number of 31 snorkeling spots, an average area of 0.46–0.48 km^2 is calculated for each spot. Assuming that every tourist will go for one island-hopping trip, tourism numbers are divided by the number of snorkel spots. Based on the monthly tourism data, visitor numbers are categorized in three seasons: 10–50 tourists per day in case of low-season (January–March), 100–500 tourists per day in high season (April–December), and 1,000–2,000 tourists per day in peak season (appears during public holidays in case of good weather conditions only for a few days a year). Depending on the season and how many coral reef sites are visited, one snorkel site experiences up to 286 tourists per day if only the seven sites in the west can be visited, and 2,000 tourists per day in the peak season. Tourists complained: "We saw more people than fish and corals". Even if all actively visited snorkel spots, including those in the east as well, would be visited during peak season, each spot experiences a harvesting level between 71 and 143 tourists per day which clearly exceeds the suggested carrying capacity of 45 tourists per side (Hannak et al. 2011).

Information-Sharing among Users (I2 – weak): "Communication enhances cooperation" (Ostrom et al. 2002, p. 488) and "cooperation is enhanced by repeated interactions [frequency] between group members over a long time horizon [durability]' (Huybers & Bennet, 2003, p. 567). The degree of information-sharing among the TGs is identified through frequency and durability of their interactive relationships. The meeting frequency and interaction among the TGs varies considerably and is a prerequisite of self-organising. Most TGs meet quite frequently, but only in small closed groups. Only one-fifth have long relationships to each other since their childhood or school. TGs were asked to name their colleagues with which they share most of their time and information. On average, a TG has close relationships with five other colleagues which indicates that TGs have a strong relationship towards a small group, whereas levels of trust and information-sharing are decreasing beyond that. The history of their cooperation as TGs is rather recent, since tourism was only introduced in 2011, and so there is weak cooperation and self-organisation as a professional group.

Lack of conflict among users (I4 – no): According to Briassoulis (2002), "Competition becomes keener as users share a limited resource base, and the absence of governance structures for open-access resources leaves ample room for 'free riding'" (pp. 1075f). In the KNP, a high degree of conflicts was observed among the TGs, often arising from competition and perceived unfairness of the tourism sector. Competition arises between those TGs who are hired by the larger tourist agencies versus those who are freelancers with low probability of access to customers. At the same time, there are differences in work-ethics with respect to the degree of rules being followed while visiting the corals and caring for the natural environment on which they depend. The marine tourism business is perceived by most TGs as an unfair business. Despite the growing marine tourism, TGs suffer from steady low income in contrast to the profiting travel agencies. Travel agencies try to lower the prices of island-hopping trips and sell Karimunjawa as cheap as possible. The results are high competition among the over 50 local travel agencies as well as unfair working conditions for the employed TG. Misunderstandings and the overall irresponsible, careless, unmotivated and free-riding attitude of TGs that is criticized by themselves, leads to a tense and bad atmosphere among them impede the likelihood of the TGs to govern the MTC.

Self-organising activities (I5 – no): "When expected benefits of managing a resource exceed the perceived costs of investing in better rules and norms for most users and their leaders, the probability of users' self-organising is high" (Ostrom et al. 2009, p. 420). Three kinds of self-organising activities were observed during the research period. All of them were unsuccessful. Eleven TGs including one travel agent joined an English language learning project in Java. Besides learning English, the team had the vision to become an idol group to improve the marine tourism management in Karimunjawa. After returning to Karimunjawa though, mistrust and misunderstanding among the group led to the failure of the project. A second self-organising activity was undertaken by one active travel agent who organised two beach-cleaning activities in January and February 2014. Of all the 227 TGs in Karimunjawa, only 23 TG participated. The same travel agent together with another 'activist' invested his time and energy to interview 80 active TGs about the current marine tour guiding situation and organised two TG gatherings of around 10 TGs to discuss about the marine tourism problems in Karimunjawa. But due to the timing of it being in high season, the TGs the gatherings were not repeated. Also, the survey shows that the TGs have a restrained level of participation in HPI activities and a medium to low motivation to improve marine tourism. A general "wait and see" opinion and free-riding behaviour influences the TGs. Discouragement rose from the typical TGs behaviour to complain about the situation, but not taking any initiative to change. A "talk less, do more" norm would be more motivating. TGs perceived their colleagues as individualistic, since "everybody is busy with his own business" and feel demotivated to invest their time if others do not. Even though the TGs are aware that joint benefits might be created via self-organising activities, the overall non-compliance (only 4 TG reported that they were in full compliance) of operational rules deters them from investing time and effort and continue with the business as usual.

External system – Social and economic setting (S – No)

As Ostrom already identified, external factors of fast-growing economic development might lead to individual behaviour and lost relationships of trust, hence impedes commonisation. Economic development (S1) fostered by the tourism industry and the construction sector based on resource intensive and land-grabbing practices in Karimunjawa is likely to lead to negative outcomes for the related ecosystems. The demographic trend (S2) is showing a rapid population growth due to immigration driven by economic incentives. Whereas other common property regimes might "easily evolve within close-knit relation" (Ostrom et al. 2002, p. 487), Karimunjawa's society might be too fragile and diverse to quickly develop robust institutions along with some degree of social capital to deal with marine tourism management. Several interviews with the locals up to the government staff revealed that the fast tourism driven economic development immediately effected the once strong and trustworthy relations within families, kinship and friendships. Also, the increasing role of the tourism sector within Indonesia's economy and Karimunjawa's strategic location to its market – close to Java's growing middle class – show a strong and also very powerful market and economic incentives (S4) that are conflicting with marine conservation and undermine local efforts in managing the marine tourism market. Missing and/or unclear marine government resource policies (S3) are another external factor that might trigger decommonisation.

Conclusions

The Social Ecological System Framework (SESF) proved its applicability to analyse marine tourism in a holistic and structured way, but also required a vast set of methods and data sets that pushes the research's scope to a limit. Based on the decomposable systems, sub-tiers were adaptable to the case study. Twenty-nine of 53 variables of the SESF were examined to identify the institutional performance to govern marine tourism commons: with a stronger focus on the resource users and the governance system, 16 variables were analysed under the social system, 5 under the ecological system, 4 interaction, and 4 external variables. All main tiers of the SESF are classified as "weak" pointing towards a fragile between failing institutional performance interpreted as a process of decommonisation. Applying the SESF shows that decommonisation responds to a set of drivers distributed among all main tiers.

The marine tourism commons are found to possess the same characteristics as other common-pool resource problems – non-excludability and subtractability – and thus can be seen as a fruitful extension of the theory of the commons. If the MTC are interpreted like in this case study, the number of resource users is not directly linked to the size of the coral reef area (RS) or the number of coral reef spots (RU), but instead directly linked to the increase of visitor numbers (S). If supply and demand for MTC are not related with the number of resource units, but to external factors, an overcrowding effect is the direct consequence for fast developing marine tourism areas and undermines the development of social capital, shared experiences and accumulation of knowledge among the TGs. Further, the rapid transformation of coral reefs towards marine tourism commons is not consistent with the creation and enforcement of rules, institutions or marine tourism arrangements that have the power, knowledge and ability to govern coral reefs for marine tourism. Also, high variability and a limited number of coral reef snorkel spots (resource unit) due to their spatial and temporal distributions as well as other characteristics, triggers overuse and higher chances of subtractability.

Resource regimes of MTC in Karimunjawa co-evolved under a marine national park legislative framework guided by conservation priorities that imply excludability via an adaptive zoning mechanism, constitutional rules for marine tourism zones, entry fees for tourists and TG licenses. This was a private-led process by tour operators and investors seeking non-excludability for maximum profit of marine tourism and supported by the tourist guide association that creates collective-action and operational rules. Confronted with the stress to create new working rules and at the same time being confronted with ongoing changes like the rapid development of tourism and altering quality of snorkeling spots, the TG community as resource user fails to successfully manage MTC as commons (i.e., the so-called "uncontrolled" marine tourism).

Acknowledgements

The first author acknowledges financial support received from Alpen-Adria University, Austria, for conducting fieldwork. In Indonesia, she is thankful to a number of individuals and organisations for their valuable support that made this research possible, in particular: Dr. Dicky Muslim (University of Padjajaran, Bandung) for his local mentorship; Ms. Puji and her colleagues at the Karimunjawa National Park Authority and the NGO Wildlife Conservation Society for providing relevant data and contacts; Mr. Eddy Permana for guiding through the administrative processes, translations for the interviews and building social connections with the locals.. The first author also thanks all the Tourist Guides and the local community for participating in the survey.

Notes

1 Rules and the number of times they were mentioned by TGs: Life Jacket was stated 23 times; Prayer prior to departure, 20; don't throw trash, 15; Information about dangerous animals, 15; don't touch the coral, 14; Information about the destination, 12: don't stand on the coral, 9; Explain the equipment, 8; don't walk on the corals, 5; don't take the coral, 5; safety procedures, 5; follow the TG, 3; don't take sand, 2; number of tourist per guide, 1; don't snorkel in shallow water, 1; how to use the underwater camera, 1; 6 TGs – no rules mentioned
2 This refers to the typical Indonesian local or regional event to proclaim an official regulation.

References

Agrawal, A. (2001). Common property institutions and sustainable governance of resources. *World Development 2 (10)*, pp. 1649–1672.
Agrawal, A. (2002). Common resources and institutional sustainability. In Ostrom, E., Dietz, T., Dolšak, N., Stern, P. C., Stonich, S., & Weber, E. U. (Eds.). *The drama of the commons*. Washington, DC: The National Academies Press. https://doi.org/10.17226/10287.
Armitage, D. (2008, January). Governance and the commons in a multi-level world. *International Journal of the Commons 2 (1)*, pp. 7–32.
Balai Taman Nasional Karimunjawa. (2010). *Zonasi Taman Nasional Karimunjawa Tahun 2012*. Departemen Kehutanan Direktorat Jenderal Perlindungan Hutan Dan Konservasi Alam, Semarang, Indonesia.
Balai Taman Nasional Karimunjawa. (2012). *Zonasi Taman Nasional Karimunjawa Tahun 2012*. Departemen KehuTanan Direktorat Jenderal Perlindungan Hutan Dan Konservasi Alam, Semarang, Indonesia.
Barker, N., & Roberts, C. (2004). Scuba diver behaviour and the management of diving impacts on coral reefs. *Biological Conservation 120 (4)*, pp. 481–489.
Berkes, F., George, P., & Preston, R. (1991). The evolution of theory and practice of the joint administration of living resources. *Alternatives 18 (2)*, pp. 12–18.
Binder, C., Hinkel, J., Bots, P., & Pahl-Wostl, C. (2013). Comparison of frameworks for analyzing social-ecological systems. *Ecology and Society 18 (4)*, p. 26.
Briassoulis, H. (2002). Sustainable tourism and the question of the commons. *Annals of Tourism Research 29 (4)*, pp. 1065–1085.
Campbell, S.J., Cinner, J.E., Ardiwijaya, R.L., Pardede, S., Kartawijaya, T., Mukmunin, A., Herdiana, Y., Hoey, A.S., Pratchett, M.S., & Baird, A.H. (2012a). Avoiding conflicts and protecting coral reefs: customary management benefits marine habitats and fish biomass. *Oryx 46*, pp. 486–494.
Campbell, S., Hoey, A., Maynard, J., Kartawijaya, T., Cinner, J., Graham, N. A., & Baird, A. H. (2012b). Weak compliance undermines the success of no-take zones in a large government-controlled marine protected area. *PloS ONE 7 (11)*, pp. 1–12.
Campbell, S., Kartawijaya, T., Yulianto, I., Prasetia, R., & Clifton, J. (2013). Co-management approaches and incentives improve management effectiveness in Karimunjawa National Park, Indonesia. *Marine Policy 41*, pp. 72–79.

Cinner, J., McClanahan, T., MacNeil, M., Graham, N., Daw, T., Mukminin, A., Kuange, J. (2012). Comanagement of coral reef social-ecological systems. *PNAS* *109 (14)*, pp. 5219–5222.

Clifton, J. (2003). Prospects for co-management in Indonesia's marine protected areas. *Marine Policy 27*, S. 389–395.

Davis, D., & Tisdell, C. (1995). Recreational SCUBA diving and carrying capacity in marine protected areas. *Ocean & Coastal Management 26*, pp. 19–40.

Dendy, W., Saefudin, Y., Rohman, E., Gunawan, Roestiana, E., Sutisna, E., ... Prihatiningsih, P. (2013). *Laporan Kajian Dampak Wisata Terhadap Ekosistem Terumbu Karang di Taman Nasional Karimunjawa*. Laporan Non Penelitian, University of Diponegoro (UNDIP), Semarang, Indonesia.

Evans, J. (2012). *Environmental Governance*. London: Routledge. https://doi.org/10.4324/9780203155677

Furqan, A., & Som, A. (2010). Effects of decentralization policy on island destination in Indonesia, Penang. *World Applied Sciences 10 (Special Issue of Tourism & Hospitality)*, S. 63–70.

Garrod, B., & Wilson, J. (2003). *Marine Ecotourism: Issues and Experiences*. New York: Channel View.

Gössling, S., & Garrod, B. (2008). *New Frontiers in Marine Tourism. Diving Experiences, Sustainability, Management*. Amsterdam: Elsevier Science.

Hall, C. (2001). Trends in ocean and coastal tourism: The end of the last frontier? *Ocean and Coastal Management 44 (9)*, pp. 601–618.

Hannak, J., Kompatscher, S., Stachowitsch, M., & Herler, J. (2011). 1 Snorkelling and trampling in shallow-water fringing reefs: Risk assessment and proposed management strategy. *Environmental Management 92 (10)*, pp. 2723–2733.

Hardin, G. (1968). The tragedy of the commons. *Science 162* (December), pp. 1243–1248.

Huybers, T., & Bennet, J. (2003). Inter-firm cooperation at nature-based tourism destinations. *Journal of Socio-Economics 32*, pp. 571–587.

Jones, P., Qiu, W., & De Santo, E. (2011). Governing Marine Protected Areas – Getting the Balance Right – Volume 2. Technical Report to Marine & Coastal Ecosystems Branch. UNEP. Nairobi.

Kartiwijaya, T., Prasetia, R., & Ripanto. (2011). *Rencana Aksi Ekowisata di Taman Nasional Karimunjawa*. Bogor: Wildlife Conservation Society.

Medio, D., Ormond, R., & Pearson, M. (1997). Effect of briefings on rates of damage to corals by SCUBA divers. *Biological Conservation 79*, pp. 91–95.

Nababan, M., Munasik, Yulianto, I., Prasetia, R., Ardiwijaya, R., Pardede, S., Syaifudin, Y. (2010). *Status Ekosistem di Taman Nasional Karimunjawa: 2010. Wildlife Conservation Society – Indonesian Program*. Bogor.

Nayak, P., Berkes, F. (2011). Commonisation and Decommonisation: Understanding the Processes of Change in the Chilika Lagoon, India. *Conservation and Society 9(2)*: 132–145.

Neves-Graca, K. (2004). Revisiting the tragedy of the commons: Ecological dilemmas of whale watching in the Azores. *Human Organisation 63(3)*, S. 289–300.

Ostrom, E. (1990). *Governing the Commons: The Evolution of Institutions for Collective Action*. Cambridge: Cambridge University Press.

Ostrom, E. (2005). *Understanding Institutional Diversity*. Princeton: Princeton University Press.

Ostrom, E. (2007). A diagnostic approach for going beyond panaceas. *PNAS 104 (39)*, S. 15181–15187.

Ostrom, E. (2009). A general framework to analyzing sustainability of SES. *Science* *325:* 419–422.

Ostrom, E., & Schlager, E. (1992). Property-rights regimes and natural resources: A conceptual analysis. *Land Economics 68 (3)*, pp. 249–262.

Ostrom, E., & Schlager, E. (1996). The formation of property rights. In S. Hanna, C. Folke, & K.-M. Mäler, *Rights to Nature* (pp. 127–156). Washington, DC: Island Press.

Ostrom, E., Dietz, T., Dolsak, N., Stern, P. C., Stonich, S., & Weber, E. U. (2002). *The Drama of the Commons.* Washington, DC: National Academies Press.

Ostrom, E., Gardner, R., & Walker, J. (1994). *Rules, Games and Common-Pool Resources.* Ann Arbor: The University of Michigan Press.

Plummer, R., Armitage, D., & Loë, R. (2013). Adaptive co-management and its relationships to environmental governance. *Ecology and Society 20 (3)*, S. 21.

Pollnac, R., Christie, P., Cinner, J., Dalton, T., Daw, T., Forrester, G., ... McClanahan, T. (2010). Marine reserves as linked social-ecological systems. *PNAS 107 (43)*, pp. 18262–18265.

Prakash, S., Wieringa, P., Ros, B., Poels, E., Boateng, F., Gyampoh, B., & Asiseh, F. (2005). *Potential of ecotourism development in the Lake Bosumtwi Basin. A caste study of Ankaase in the Amansie East District, Ghana.* Socio-Economics of Forest Use in the Tropics and Subtropics Working Paper No. 15. University of Freiburg, Germany. ISSN 1616-8062.

Purwanti, F. (2008). *Concept of Co-Management for Karimunjawa National.* Ph.D. thesis, Bogor Agricultural University.

Purwanti, F., Alikodra, H., Basuni, S., & Soedharma, D. (2008, September). Pengembangan Co-Management Taman Nasional Karimunjawa. *Ilmu Kelautan 13 (3)*, pp. 159–166.

Rouphael, A., & Inglis, G. (2001). "Take only photographs and leave only footprints?": An experimental study of the impacts of underwater photographers on coral dive sites. *Biological Conservation 100*, S. 281–287.

Salm, R.V., & Halim, M. (1984). A protected area system plan for the conservation of Indonesia's marine environment. V.1. Bogor, Indonesia. A IUCN/WWF report prepared for the Directorate General of Forest Protection and Nature Conservation, Bogor: 19 (21) (PDF) Recent Development of Marine Protected Areas (MPAs) in Indonesia: Policies and Governance. Retrieved from https://www.researchgate. net/publication/266354376_Recent_Development_of_Marine_Protected_Areas_ MPAs_in_Indonesia_Policies_and_Governance. Accessed 13 December 2020.

Singleton, S., & Taylor, M. (1992). Common property, collective action and community. *Journal of Theoretical Politics 4 (3)*, pp. 309–324.

Yabuta, M., Scott, N., & Ozawa, T. (2014). *The management of common-pool resources in tourism destinations: A simple model analysis of marine resource management.* Tokyo: Institute of Economic Research Chuo University.

Yulianto, I., Herdiana, Y., Halim, M., Ningtias, P., Hermansyah, A., & Campbell, S. (2013). Spatial analysis to achieve 20 Million Hectares of Marine Protected Areas for Indonesia by 2020. *Wildlife Conservation Society and Marine Protected Areas Governance.* Wildlife Conservation Society – Indonesia Program, Bogor, Indonesia.

Yulianto, I., Purwanti, F., Sujarot, H., & Widyatuti, E. (2006). *Pengelolaan Kolaboratif Taman Nasional Karimunjawa.* WCS Program Kelautan Indonesia, Semarang, Indonesia.

Chapter 3

The cascading effects of coastal commonisation and decommonisation

Jeremy Pittman

Introduction

Coastal areas throughout the globe are facing a "quadruple squeeze" from multiple pressures: population increase (and associated resource needs), climate change, environmental change, and the possibility of crossing tipping points or initiating regime shifts (Glavovic et al., 2015). These pressures ultimately require changes to governance or institutional regimes in order to manage their potentially deleterious effects, while simultaneously grasping any opportunities that arise (Bennett, 2018; Glavovic et al., 2015; J. Pittman and Armitage, 2016). Ideally, these changes would support the sustainability and wellbeing of coastal ecosystems and communities. However, the paths towards such sustainable social-ecological systems in the coastal zone are not always clear, and they are full of uncertainties, many of which are irreducible at the time of taking crucial decisions to manage our future coasts (Ramesh et al., 2016).

Some of these decisions ultimately involve defining – from an institutional standpoint – the desired relationships between people and the coast. Common pool resource theory provides a valuable lens for examining these relationships and their potential implications (Nayak and Berkes, 2011; Ostrom, 2005; Ostrom, 1990). Within common pool resource theory, and other fields of economics, there are two key features used to categorise resource types: excludability and subtractability. Excludability is the degree to which users of a resource can keep other users from using the resource (Ostrom et al., 1999); while subtractability is the degree to which a resource is depleted through use (Ostrom et al., 1999).

Considering both excludability and subtractability results in a typology of resources (Table 3.1). Private resources are those which are highly subtractable, but also highly excludable (Ostrom, 2005). When an individual owns a resource, they can keep others from using that resources (i.e., it is excludable) and they deplete the resource through their use (i.e., subtractable). Club resources are those that are easy to exclude, but non-subtractable (Ostrom, 2005). For club resources, a certain group or club can access the

Table 3.1 A typology of resources (Ostrom, 2005; Ostrom and Ostrom, 1977)

	Easy to Exclude	Difficult to Exclude
Subtractable	Private resources	Common pool resources
Non-Subtractable	Club or toll resources	Public resources

resource, but their use does not deplete it. Public resources are not excludable nor subtractable (Ostrom, 2005). These are accessible by the entire public in different places, and the public's use or enjoyment of the resource does not deplete it. Finally, common pool resources are those which are difficult to exclude but also highly subtractable (Ostrom, 2005). These are resources that are depleted through use, and it is also difficult to keep others from using the resource. For example, a beach used for public recreation is neither excludable nor subtractable (i.e., it is a public resource). However, a beach mined for sand is a common pool resource, since it is subtractable, but often not excludable.

The purpose of this chapter is to trace how the categorisation of resources changes considering various drivers, and then how these changes cascade through systems to affect the use and institutional characteristics of resources in other places – hereafter referred to as processes of (de)commonisation (Nayak and Berkes, 2011). The chapter aims to accomplish this purpose by exploring the (de)commonisation processes in Small Island States of the Lesser Antilles Island of the Caribbean. It uses sand from beaches and river banks – a resource facing a potential "looming tragedy" at the global scale (Torres et al., 2017) – as an example to illuminate these processes in the local and regional contexts.

Case study and methods

The Lesser Antilles are a group of islands in the Eastern Caribbean (Figure 3.1). These islands support a range of livelihood activities and economic sectors, including fisheries, tourism, and agriculture. Tourism is a major economic activity in the region (CTO, 2018), and different forms of tourism can be found there, including mass tourism, elite tourism, and eco-tourism (Dehoorne et al., 2010). To a lesser extent, the region also hosts expatriates from the Global North, who migrate to the region for various reasons (OIM, 2014).

This chapter treats the Lesser Antilles as a case study and draws mostly on semi-structured interview data gathered in six Small Island States in the Lesser Antilles (Table 3.2): St. Lucia, Dominica, Antigua and Barbuda, St. Kitts and Nevis, St. Vincent and the Grenadines, and Grenada. The data were gathered between July and December 2014 as part of a research project focused on governance across the land-sea interface. Interviews were

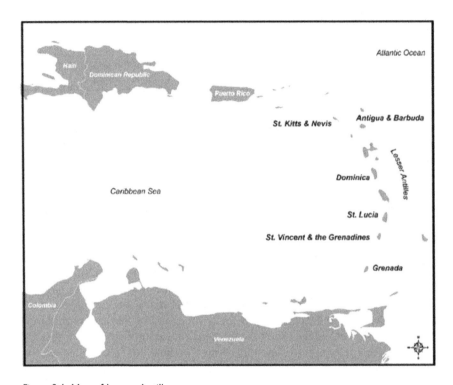

Figure 3.1 Map of Lesser Antilles.

Table 3.2 Interviews for each island

	St. Lucia	Dominica	Antigua	St. Kitts	St. Vincent	Grenada	Total
Interviews (n)	55	56	13	27	24	22	197
Participants (n)	65	60	16	28	24	27	220

conducted with individuals within national governments (e.g. beach management organizations), local communities (e.g., fisheries cooperatives), the private sectors (e.g., hotel owners and operators), and non-governmental organizations (e.g., conservation organizations) with relevance to coastal-marine sustainability. Interviews took place in the respondents' offices or in places of mutual convenience (e.g., by the beach). They were digitally recorded and later transcribed. In most cases, respondents were interviewed individually; however, some group interviews were conducted, often at the respondents' request, to enhance scheduling convenience for the respondents. The data were analyzed using qualitative content analysis, and the issues discussed in this chapter were emergent themes in the data. The respondents' voice was maintained by using direct quotes in the interpretation of findings. The interpretation of interview data was triangulated with media sources and policy documents from the region.

Beaches as public resources

In many islands of the Lesser Antilles, beaches are by law intended to be low subtractable, low excludable public resources. For example, the Queen's Chain in Saint Lucia – a relic from colonial times – establishes the area from the high-water mark to 165.5 feet landward as public property, which can be enjoyed by anyone. The Queen's Chain was established in 1704 and was originally intended to protect the interests of the French Monarchy in maintaining ship landing sites and the right to develop towns in the face of expanding plantations. It has since become a means of ensuring – or at least attempting to ensure – public rights to access Saint Lucia's many beaches for the purposes of recreation in the face of an expanding tourism sector. Other islands have similar institutional arrangements guiding beach access, but they are all slightly different. Antigua and Barbuda, for example, in their Physical Planning Act of 2003 even go so far as to ensuring that the public can access beaches for recreational use through private property by establishing a public right of way across private property for beach access. Nonetheless, many of these institutions are contested and their enforcement can sometimes raise issues, which are discussed in greater detail in subsequent sections.

Drivers of (de)commonisation of sandy beaches

The expansion of the tourism sector is a major driver of beach (de) commonisation in the Lesser Antilles. The many beaches in the region are prime locations for tourism activity, and the tourism sector has expanded considerably in recent years (CTO, 2018; Dehoorne et al., 2010). Tourism brings people from all over the world (CTO, 2018), who also wish to enjoy the region's beaches, which greatly expands the pressure on these beaches for recreational purposes. However, these added pressures also challenge the existing institutional arrangements that maintain beaches as public resources. Tourists have different preferences for privacy while enjoying beaches, and similarly, their perceptions of how beaches ought to be accessed by the public are likely grounded in the institutional frameworks of their home countries, which may or may not be consistent with the prevailing rules in the Lesser Antillean islands.

Considering these factors, the onslaught of tourist use initiates a process of (de)commonisation of sandy beaches, which changes their resource use characteristics and potentially the rules in use governing these interactions. Tourism operators, to align with their clients' demands, sometimes attempt to exclude the public from beaches by various means. Although not always successful, these attempts are important to consider as a driver of (de)commonisation.

A secondary driver associated with the expanding tourism sector is the increased need for construction materials to build the resorts, restaurants, accommodations, and other infrastructure necessary to support the sector. Depending on the type of infrastructure being developed, sand is often a major input to construction projects (Krausmann et al., 2017; UNEP, 2016). Expansion in the construction sector associated with tourism means increased consumptive use of sand in building projects. While sand is imported in some islands (UN Comtrade, 2018), often developers and residents look to the islands' many beaches and river banks as a cheap local source of sand for construction purposes. This secondary driver places pressure on existing public uses of beaches for recreation and similarly initiates (de)commonisation.

How does (de)commonisation progress?

Beaches: From public resources to club resources?

Tourism resorts can sometimes convert select beaches from public resources to club resources. These beaches become more excludable than prior, but remain non-subtractable, as much of the new use is still for recreational purposes. Their excludability changes due to the way some resorts operate, which is often counter to existing formal institutions. Resorts respond to their clients' demands, or perceived desires, and sometimes aim to manage resort beaches as exclusive to the resorts' guests, and in doing so the beaches become club resources for the guests during their stay. Resorts employ different means for attempting this excludability. For example, the Mill Reef Club on the island of Antigua does not provide public access through its private lands in order to access approximately five miles of beach located off the seaward side of the property. Although Antigua's Planning Act does have provisions for ensuring situations like this do not arise, it is difficult to ensure these provisions are followed, even when the government recognises the problem:

> All beaches are public. But before you get to the beach … people own land … so what is happening is that in order to access the beach you have to walk through their private land and they are seeking to literally ensure their own privacy and, in the process, cutting off access to the beach.
> (P. M. Brown, August 27, 2018, the Jamaica Gleaner)

Sand: A common pool resources under changing exploitation

As mentioned earlier, the tourism sector often relies on the construction of hotels, resorts, expat housing, etc., and this construction enables the type of (de)commonisation discussed above. Beaches cannot be transformed from public resources to club resources without the development of infrastructure to support the tourism sector. However, construction also produces a cascading effect to beaches and riverbanks that are not the focus of recreation for tourists. Construction often requires a reliable and cheap supply of sand for concrete, which developers and builders often find in beaches and riverbanks (i.e., gut sand). These beaches and riverbanks may be in very different parts of the islands in relation to the homes, resorts or other developments, but nonetheless construction can impact the types of resource use on distant beaches and riverbanks and initiate changes in usage levels, which in this case are predicated on the (de)commonisation process affecting tourist beaches. During this process, sand extraction from beaches and riverbanks is increased. Sand mining for construction is a subtractable use, but the sand remains largely not excludable.

> Construction, a lot of [sand] is used for construction. And as the island is developing more, you have not only locals who are building and improving their homes, but an increasing number of expats – wealthy expats. The problem of sand mining has always been there, but it's exacerbated more. So, you have the increasing problem of sand mining.
>
> (SK0026)

However, it is important to note that the treatment of beaches as common pool resources and their exploitation is also not necessarily new on these islands. Illegal sand mining occurred before the expansion of tourism and the expat population:

> Sand mining, if you [are] building in the rural areas you not buying sand you just go on the beach [and] you take up the sand.
>
> (SV0013)

Although, the effect of tourism is synergistic with these other factors that contribute to illegal sand mining, as it potentially increases demand – and therefore the price – of sand gained through non-illegal or less detrimental means. The combined effects of factors leading to illegal sand mining – including the expansion of the tourism sector – lead to potentially unsustainable use of beaches and riverbanks, which have several compounding impacts with other activities and issues threatening coasts and coastal communities.

The impacts of (de)commonisation

Sand mining significantly impacts coastal-marine ecosystems by increasing erosion and sedimentation, which affects food webs and degrades species' habitat (Torres et al., 2017). Furthermore, the impacts of sand mining are compounded with other activities, some of which are related to development in the tourism sector:

> There are other issues, too. There are issues of sand mining, you know, we have situations where people go to the beach and take buckets and buckets of sand, so you have erosion issues being compounded by the fact that people are building drains in a way that might not be taking into account sediment transport systems. You have sea walls going down in the same vein, so there have been a number of direct impacts on the coast from these tourism plans.
>
> (ANU0003)

The combined environmental impacts of sand mining, resort development, and other drivers have implications for other livelihoods, such as small-scale fisheries – an issues found in other parts of the globe as well (Marschke, 2012; Marschke et al., 2014). Either through displacement, or by impacting fish habitat, these drivers can be problematic:

> development poses a lot of challenges and when you take the beaches and develop the beaches then it hampers the fishers, like the hotels that build near to the sea shore bring more pollution to the sea shore [and they] become like the container port in Campden Park which was a beach where I live. The container port [took] up almost the whole beach, so then that part of my livelihood – I have to say – [it has] been bothered there. So, we see some changes; we see some changes in erosion, because sand mining has taken a lot of the sand from the beach and you find the water come into the land and when the water mix with the dirt, because the sand is already removed, it brings more erosion around there and have the water dirty for some time, so some changes do happen.
>
> (SV0008)

Is governance changing?

Governing and managing the issues discussed above often requires multilevel and multisectoral approaches to account for the diverse and interconnected resources, uses, and users involved (Epstein et al., 2015; Pittman and Armitage, 2017). While much of the current governance system in the Lesser Antilles region can be characterised as top-down or command-and-control (Scobie, 2016), there is some evidence to suggest that more collaborative and networked forms of governance are emerging (Pittman and Armitage, 2019). These developing modes of governance likely do not replace top-down approaches, but can co-exist to produce, or attempt to produce, more sustainable patterns of resource use. For example, the following system in Antigua and Barbuda demonstrates how a top-down regulatory approach can be used simultaneously with a more networked approach that involves multiple government agencies:

> We developed an application process for anyone choosing or wishing to mine gut sand, which is coming down from the hills along the stream way. It's a cooperative work between APUA, Forestry, the Environment Division, and Extension. … The application process requires a signature from the Forestry officer, a signature from the Environment officer and a signature from the APUA Water manager. So, it's a system that we had tried to develop to cut down on illegal mining of gut sand. And not just that but put a more structured approach to extraction, because an individual would just go down with their bulldozer and trucks and dig ad hoc and just destroy the banks and such. What we have done is that we made it a requirement that they get an engineer to make the assessment to determine how it's going to be extracted, and we will tell them how much we are going to allow them to extract. The engineer would say how much can be safely extracted, and then we would look at it and determine whether this engineer's report stands any weight. And then we will determine okay, we will move ahead based on this. But all of this would be covered by the applicant; they will make the application, they will pay for all of this thing, and then we will, "Okay, no problem". They will go ahead with the extraction and we will have an officer on site watching to ensure that they're doing what they say they're going to do.
>
> (ANU0010)

There are also emerging opportunities to manage and govern these issues at the community-level. Communities in the region often have many latent capacities to address sustainability challenges, and finding ways to connect and mobilize these latent capacities can be especially important to advance governance (Epstein et al., 2015; Pittman and Armitage, 2019). The following example from Grenada demonstrates local leadership and the need to connect with community-level institutions (i.e., religion) to address a suite of sustainability challenges:

> There's one thing that you would realize in the Caribbean, people do love their religion, and if it's one thing that's able to get people to actually do positive things in the community, it's the church … this is one great story of one of the beaches here in St. Patrick's called Mount Rodney. It's just plagued with a lot of problems- illegal dumping; legal and illegal sand mining. … We tend to see with a lot of beaches in the area that it's connected to a river, the river sort of flushes everything out to the beach. And so, you have a lot of dumping in the river, that gets pushed out into the beach. And so, there's this one guy who basically has claimed the

beach as his own, and just for himself, without getting any sort of compensation for himself, is just cleaning the beach, getting people organized to raise awareness; when the turtles come up, he's patrolling in the night.

(GRE0001)

Summary

This chapter shows how (de)commonisation processes cascade through resource systems, and how these processes can shift the same resource in different ways across different places. Sand – a resource of emerging global concern (Torres et al., 2017) – is used to exemplify how these processes move through and affect Small Island States in the Lesser Antilles region of the Caribbean. In the Lesser Antilles, the beaches are intended to be public resources. However, tourism is inherently linked to sandy beaches, and tourists' desire for exclusivity can sometimes lead to beaches changing from public resources to club resources, as tourism operators attempt to enclose public beaches and prevent locals from accessing them. The construction necessary to support the tourism sector leads to a secondary impact of (de) commonisation, as beaches and riverbanks in other parts of the islands find themselves under increasing pressure from sand mining activities to satisfy the demand for building materials and concrete. In the process, these sources of sand are common pool resources, and increased exploitation of these resources creates problems for existing governance regimes. Nonetheless, governance regimes are responding by (1) creating collaborative mechanisms at the national-level to deal with the interconnected and intersectoral nature of the issues and (2) engaging local leadership and community-level institutions to address sustainability challenges. Despite progress, beach (de)commonisation still poses significant challenges for existing governance and more work is needed to fully contend with the problem.

References

Bennett, N. J. (2018). Navigating a just and inclusive path towards sustainable oceans. *Marine Policy*, June, 0–1. https://doi.org/10.1016/j.marpol.2018.06.001

CTO. (2018). *Key Stats 2017*. Caribbean Tourism Organization. Available online at: https://create.piktochart.com/embed/27958259-key-stats-from-the-caribbean-tourism-organization

Dehoorne, O., Murat, C., and Petit-Charles, N. (2010). International tourism in the Caribbean area: Current status and future prospects. *Etudes Caribeennes*, 16.

Epstein, G., Pittman, J., Alexander, S. M., Berdej, S., Dyck, T., Kreitmair, U., Raithwell, K. J., Villamayor-Tomas, S., Vogt, J., and Armitage, D. (2015). Institutional fit and the sustainability of social-ecological systems. *Current Opinion in Environmental Sustainability*, *14*, 34–40. https://doi.org/10.1016/j.cosust.2015.03.005

Glavovic, B., Limburg, K., Liu, K.-K., Emeis, K.-C., Thomas, H., Kremer, H., Avril, B., Zhang, J., Mulholland, M., Glaser, M., and Swaney, D. (2015). Living on the margin in the Anthropocene: Engagement arenas for sustainability research and action at the ocean–land interface. *Current Opinion in Environmental Sustainability*, 1–7. https://doi.org/10.1016/j.cosust.2015.06.003

Krausmann, F., Wiedenhofer, D., Lauk, C., Haas, W., Tanikawa, H., Fishman, T., Miatto, A., Schandl, H., and Haberl, H. (2017). Global socioeconomic material stocks rise 23-fold over the 20th century and require half of annual resource use. *Proceedings of the National Academy of Sciences*, *114*(8), 1880–1885. https://doi.org/10.1073/pnas.1613773114

Marschke, M. (2012). *Life, Fish and Mangroves*. Ottawa, Canada: University of Ottawa Press.

Marschke, M., Lykhim, O., and Kim, N. (2014). Can local institutions help sustain livelihoods in an era of fish declines and persistent environmental change? A Cambodian case study. *Sustainability (Switzerland)*, *6*(5), 2490–2505. https://doi.org/10.3390/su6052490

Nayak, P., and Berkes, F. (2011). Commonisation and decommonisation: Understanding the processes of change in the Chilika Lagoon, India. *Conservation and Society*, *9*(2), 132. https://doi.org/10.4103/0972-4923.83723

OIM. (2014). Migration in the Caribbean: Current trends, opportunities and challenges. In *Working Papers on Migration*. https://doi.org/10.1093/toxsci/kft290

Ostrom, E. (2005). *Understanding Institutional Diversity*. Princeton: Princeton University Press.

Ostrom, E. (1990). *Governing the Commons: The Evolution of Institutions for Collective Action*. Cambridge: Cambridge University Press.

Ostrom, E, Burger, J., Field, C. B., Norgaard, R. B., and Policansky, D. (1999). Revisiting the commons: Local lessons, global challenges. *Science*, *284*(5412), 278–282. https://doi.org/10.1126/science.284.5412.278

Ostrom, V., and Ostrom, E. (1977). Public goods and public choices. In E. Savas (Ed.), *Alternatives for Delivering Public Services: Toward Improved Performance*. Boulder, CO: Westview Press.

Pittman, J., and Armitage, D. (2016). Governance across the land-sea interface: A systematic review. *Environmental Science and Policy*, *64*. https://doi.org/10.1016/j.envsci.2016.05.022

Pittman, J., and Armitage, D. (2017). How does network governance affect social-ecological fit across the land–sea interface? An empirical assessment from the Lesser Antilles. Ecology and Society, *22*(4), 5.

Pittman, J., and Armitage, D. (2019). Network governance of land-sea social-ecological systems in the Lesser Antilles. *Ecological Economics*, *157*(February 2018), 61–70. https://doi.org/10.1016/j.ecolecon.2018.10.013

Ramesh, R., Chen, Z., Cummins, V., Day, J., D'Elia, C., Dennison, B., Forbes, D. L., Glaeser, B., Glaser, M., Glavovic, B., Kremer, H., Lange, M., Larsen, J. N., Tissier, M. L., Newton, A., Pelling, M., Purvaja, R., and Wolanski, E. (2016). Land-ocean interactions in the coastal zone: Past, present and future. *Anthropocene*, *2015*. https://doi.org/10.1016/j.ancene.2016.01.005

Scobie, M. (2016). Policy coherence in climate governance in Caribbean Small Island Developing States. *Environmental Science & Policy*, *58*, 16–28. https://doi.org/10.1016/j.envsci.2015.12.008

Torres, A., Brandt, J., Lear, K., and Liu, J. (2017). A looming tragedy of the sand commons. *Science, 357*(6355), 970–971. https://doi.org/10.1126/science.aao0503

UN Comtrade. (2018). *International Trade Database.* Available online at: https://comtrade.un.org/

UNEP. (2016). *Global Material Flows and Resource Productivity. An Assessment Study of the UNEP International Resource Panel.* https://doi.org/10.1111/jiec.12626

Chapter 4

Governing fluvial commons in Colonial Bihar

Alluvion and diluvion regulation and decommonisation

Vipul Singh

Introduction

The floodplains have always been at the centre of conflict in historical past because of its huge agricultural potential. Like any other early modern state in India, the colonial state's prime concern was permanence of land revenue, and that could be possible only when exactness of property is ascertained. In the case of non-riparian upland such collection based on assessment or lease out is feasible, but on riparian and fluvial land it is particularly challenging due to ephemeral nature of the property. This case study discusses the different bodies of acts that were introduced to address the problem of revenue collection in *diara* land of colonial eastern India. While doing so it examines the process of decommonisation of the common land. The analysis is further extrapolated to its impact on boatmen and fisher communities.

Background and context

The Ganga has historically been one of the most revered rivers of India. Many rivers traverse the Ganga basin, and of them the Ganga itself is the largest that flows eastwards from the northwest. During its long route of about 2,500 km from the Himalayas to the Bay of Bengal, the river creates a huge catchment area of 980,000 km². All along its flow, the Ganga is not only treated as a sacred, but also a conjointly used river for the communities living along it. The very nature of its flow has led the social scientists to divide it into three stretches – upper, middle and lower (Chakrabarti, 2001). Six head-streams, originating in the Himalaya glaciers, confluence at Rishikesh and form the mainstream of the Ganga. The "imaginary" axis at Allahabad separates the upper course of the Ganga from the middle section because now the gradient decreases and the riverbed has a more spread-out path. The depth of the river is quite generous here as compared to the lower stretch, which is flatter and shallow. In the lower segment, the Ganga tends to be braided and gets divided into several channels and forms a delta nearer to the Bay of Bengal. All these physiognomies of its flow also coincide with the path and direction it takes. From its origin in the Himalayas the Ganga flows in the south-easterly direction, but when it reaches the mid-Ganga section, it flows from west to east, and in its lower part the river again turns towards south-east. The Himalayan range runs almost parallel to the Ganga in this section. As a result, many other rivers descending from the Himalayas meet the Ganga. The major portion of the middle section of the Ganga lies in the modern state of Bihar. Here many rivers flowing down from the Himalayas such as the Gomati, Ghaghara, Gandak and Kosi meet the Ganga from the north. The Betwa, Chambal, Ken and Sone rivers that originate in the Deccan Plateau join the Ganga from the south. These confluences allow the Ganga to maintain a decent amount of flow throughout the year. That is why, unlike its upper part the Ganga remains navigable for the entire year. However, the proximity to the Himalayan ranges also pose physiographical challenges for the communities living in Bihar. Due to the sharp descent from the Himalayan Mountains, the rivers draining the Ganga basin have enormous sediment transfer in active floodplain (Figure 4.1). The monsoon rains further add to the flow engendered by the melting of the glaciers in the higher reaches of the Himalaya during June, July and August. The loose soil wash down into the rivers and the deposited sediments in the rivers often cut a new path in the hugely spread-out riverbed of mid-Ganga section. This in turn leads to frequent avulsion and formation of new land called *diara*.[1]

Figure 4.1 Geomorphic map of Ganga river valley. A colour version of this image is downloadable as an eResource from www.routledge.com/9780367138004.

Diara as fluvial common

Diara is essentially a landmass in the river like islands. Its formation is a long drawn process, and is the result of sand and silt deposition over a long period of time. In the initial years, a new land is created with sand, which is not useful for cultivation at all. In subsequent years, it is then leveled by fertile silt. After eight to ten years the river tide starts chiseling out deposited sand and silt from the earlier avulsed land. Thus, *diara* was a cyclical phenomenon. Because of its non-permanent nature, the community of boatmen and fishers live on these lands in temporary settlements (Singh 2018). They are severely dependent on the river for their irrigation needs, fishing and communication.

The rulers in the region also understood the local ecology, and therefore, never imposed any taxes on these lands. The *Zamindars* were although the traditional holders of much of the upland of the floodplains, the *diara* commons was left for the boatmen and fishers and the *Zamindars* stayed away from it. The land here was available for cultivation only six months from November to April as during rest of the months the Ganga inundated the entire low land. During these months the local community sowed wheat and few pulses that were just enough for their survival for the entire year. Since the land was newly avulsed, therefore, the family of boatmen and fishers would identify a suitable land and begin cultivation.

In the entire stretch of the Ganga basin, the Mughals emerged as a powerful state during early modern times. To enhance the income of their state they not only brought more and more wasteland under cultivation but also converted some of the forest area into agricultural land. The mid-Ganga Bihar was not an exception to this development. However, the complex web of rivers in the region did not leave much scope for such conversions. The riverine geography of the region had already made its control difficult for the Mughal governors as the local chieftains often defied the revenue collection deed (Singh 2018). Some of the *Zamindars* were, however, integrated into the Mughal system by being given lands for revenue collection for the state outside their traditional holding.

Riverine ecology influencing history

For the cavalry centred early modern regimes rivers always posed a challenge, but for the British East India Company the rivers were a blessing (Singh 2018).[2] The Ganga and its tributaries limited Turkic and Mughal control, and although they did manage to have a firmer hold in the upper Ganga basin, they were not so stable in Bihar. For the control of Bihar province (*suba*), the Mughals in particular, had to negotiate with local actors. Taking the advantage of the riverine ecology the local chieftains in Bihar saw even a slight absence of the imperial official as an opportunity to take control.

The destabilisation of Bihar was essentially due to its topography. To control Bihar from Agra-Delhi axis was challenging. The axis denotes the geographical zone of the two cities of Agra and Delhi. Both the cities have broadly similar ecological setting as they are located on the banks of the Yamuna. Delhi was the capital of the Turkic rulers for a long time. When the Mughals established their rule, they built their capital at Agra, some 200 km away from Delhi. The capital was later shifted to Delhi under the Mughal emperor Shah Jahan in the early 17th century.

In riverine Bihar, the Mughals had to face many rebellions. Even though the Mughal emperors were able to counter the rebellion with their huge cavalry, the triumphs were only temporary. Once the Mughal army withdrew, the local chiefs often re-surfaced crossing the rivers from different directions to defy the orders of the Mughal officers and refusing land revenue. The early modern history of conflict in the region indicates that its river ecology was unique and needed a one-off military system that was in sync with the local setting. Only those who handled navigability of the rivers of Bihar well could have been successful. To some extent this could be one of the reasons for preference of the Dutch and English East India Companies to ask for the land revenue rights and trading rights from the later Mughal rulers in Bihar (and also Bengal). In fact, Bihar was one of the first provinces of the Mughal territory where the revenue collection rights were handed over to the British.

Prudent tradition

From the perspective of monsoon pattern, Bihar is situated in between the wet eastern coastal regions and the relatively dry continental region of the western plains (Figure 4.1). The variability of monsoon rains is quite common and sometimes it leads to drought in certain parts of the province. During the same year, the melting of glacier in the Himalaya hills results in massive amount of water flow in the rivers, and by the time the inundated water enters the cultivable fields the ideal hot weather for wet rice variety is already over. Quite often than not, the overflow of water in the rivers take monstrous form leading to flood. Inundation in that sense is an annual phenomenon in the region, but flood as a disaster also occurs once in every few years. Sometimes the two disasters – drought and flood – come in the same year, drought followed by flood. Traditionally, the cultivators believed in flood utilization and dependence on it for agricultural production instead of perceiving inundation as flood. They evolved a cropping pattern that was in tune with the annual occurrence of inundating rivers. Traditional irrigation methods were evolved to face such challenges. Flush irrigation was one of the most common methods. When water level in the rivers was higher than in the fields, cultivators only had to make a cut in the water channel and allow the water to flow into their fields as required. Many a times, however, the water level in the rivers was at a lower level, and therefore, it was lifted through various traditional methods. Wells were the most popular modes of irrigation and a lever called *dhenkula* or *lattha* was used to raise water in pots. Water from deeper wells was drawn through cattle power. *Ahar* and *Pyne* were quite common among the cultivators. *Ahar* were natural reservoirs with embankments across the line of drainage with one side left open for drainage water to enter the catchment during annual flooding. It is also used to conserve rainwater. *Pyne* were of two types. Smaller ones originated from *ahar* and carried the water to cultivable fields. Larger ones originate in rivers from where water is diverted to *ahar* through the temporarily erected embankments. The same methods of irrigation were also followed in the fluvial *diara* land.

The pre-colonial states never tried to extract any revenue from these lands, as they understood its ephemeral nature. The medieval and early modern accounts are silent on any kind of revenue generation from the *diara*. That is why the administrators of the British East India Company, who relied on local agents, did not get any input on including such temporarily avulsed territories. So initially they did not include such land into revenue settlement. *Diara* was not mentioned in the proclamation of the Bengal Permanent Settlement of 1793. Even the maps drawn just before the settlement by James Rennell in 1780 did not mention such land (Singh 2018). It was only after the government was able to put the Permanent Settlement in place that it began to include the *diara* in the maps. Maps drawn after 1801 started referring to the avulsed land and starting in the 1860s the maps categorically mentioned the newly formed lands each year.

Beginning of decommonisation

The Dutch, French and British East India Companies used the Ganga for their commercial activities in Bihar ever since the seventeenth century (Madan 2005). The East India Company proved to be more successful in the region and it used the downstream flow of the river to export the bulk of grains and saltpetre to the port of Calcutta on the east coast, from where they were shipped to Europe.[3] The river navigability in the area also helped the British East India Company to get a firmer hold over the region. In 1765 it had got the land revenue collection rights (*diwani*) from the Mughal rulers. After few years, in 1793 it introduced the Permanent Settlement for the collection of revenue from the remote villages and signed an agreement with the *Zamindars* or the landlords. The landlords were asked to pay fixed revenue to the government, and in return they were recognised as hereditary proprietors of the land.

When the British East India Company acquired the rights of revenue collection from the Mughal ruler, the ideas of local governance and ecological regime of the earlier period were upturned by the European notion of a strictly regimented Bengal after 1765. By the end of the eighteenth century, the Company was able to get a firmer hold over the territory, and then it decided to increase the land revenue base. The British preferred to get into a contract with the *Zamindars* or the traditional big landholders, who had enormous influence on the local population. Their role was that of a middlemen who collected revenue from the title-holders of land. The *Zamindars* had the right to collect any amount of revenue as they wished from the title-holders but only the fixed portion of the revenue was deposited in government treasury. In that sense, the Permanent Settlement was a system of direct settlement of revenue with the local *Zamindars*. They were responsible for paying a fixed amount of land revenue to the British East India Company while enjoying the power to collect unlimited amounts of land revenue. The method of revenue assessment was broadly similar in nature to the Mughal revenue system of earlier period. However, the Mughal administration at the local level was strong with appointed officials like the *qanungo, chaudhuri, taluqdar*, etc., and the revenue system "incorporated a degree of flexibility".[4] Many concessions were granted. For example, crop failures due to flood or drought was always taken into consideration by the Mughal administration in assessing land revenue. The Mughal state also shared the loss of revenue when gross produce was lower. One of the main differences between the Mughal and the British system of revenue settlements was, however, the way in which the land revenue was calculated. The land revenue under the Mughals was fixed as a share of the crop, and therefore, varied according to the crop cultivated. In contrast, the land revenue under the British was a tax on land. So, the very basis of assessment was different. The Company's assessment was not based on what crop was grown on the land but on the quality of the land itself irrespective of the crop type.

Despite its long presence in Bihar and reliance on river communication, the British East India Company could not fully comprehend the river ecology and the traditional knowledge of irrigation and the fluvial commons when it came to actually administering the territory. In contrast, the early modern governors and local chieftains in Bihar were able to sustain themselves by extracting land revenue from cultivators from the uplands, and not interfering with the traditional common lands.

The 1770 famine pushed the colonial government to think in terms of widening the land revenue base. During the early 19th century, the East India Company looked for inclusion of more and more potential crop land under the revenue calculation. The fluidity and temporariness of the *diara* land, however, posed a challenge for the administration to achieve permanence of revenue collection.

Under the Permanent Settlement system, the landlord was obliged to pay the entire revenue fixed by the Company even if a particular area had not been able to produce anything, or the production was lower than expected due to drought or flood. It had an immediate implication on the avulsed lands. Since the British government was to be paid a fixed revenue the landlords passed on the burden to the cultivators, and started making "excessive demands from the cultivators" (Buchanan 1928). Very soon, they started taking control of the *diara* cultivable fields so that the burden of revenue is shared. The earmarking of *diara* land for revenue collection went unrecorded in the British accounts because they often mentioned the avulsed land as wasteland. Thus, there was no liability of revenue payment from such land. Very soon the British government began taking control of these lands and auctioned them off. This led to another, much larger problem. The *Zamindars* started buying up these huge tracts of land for a nominal amount (Hill 1997). They were kept as revenue-free for years, on the grounds of being wasteland, but in reality, these lands were leased out to cultivators (Hunter 1877). Gradually, the East India Company began to consider *diara* land in terms of lost revenue. It assumed that these lands were "underutilized" and thus needed to be included under the regular revenue assessment.

The British government started working on a regulation to bring the fluvial *diara* land under permanent land revenue settlement and tried to compensate itself for the loss of revenue. In 1825, the Regulation XI called the Bengal Alluvion and Diluvion Regulation (ADR) was approved. Its preamble mentioned that since the lands gained from the rivers by way of shifting of the sands are a "frequent source of contention", and the rules being generally not known, the Courts of Justice find it difficult to determine the rights of litigant parties claiming the avulsed land, the regulation has been enacted. The Bengal Alluvion and Diluvion Regulation XI thus contained the guidelines for determining the ownership of the land gained by alluvion or diluvion in order to resolve disputes arising between individuals, and were passed to guide the courts in deciding the ownership of *diara* lands. One of the most startling provisions related to the changing course of the river and the newly emerging land is that "when land is gained by gradual accession, from the river's recess, it should be considered an increment to the tenure of the person to whose land or estate it is thus annexed". But at the same time, it also mentioned that this accession should not be understood to exempt the holder of it from the payment to the East India Company. The main objective of the government was to bring even the fluid landscape under some kind of proprietorship. An important provision of the regulation was that the right over a piece of land would not to be affected merely because it went under water. The owner of the submerged land is deemed to be in "constructive possession" of the same during the period of its submergence and is thus allowed to claim back the same land when it re-emerged from the river. The revenue accounts officers started writing to the Deputy Collectors of various districts instructing them to bring the newly avulsed track on to the rent roll.[5]

The Bengal Alluvion and Diluvion Regulation of 1825 is still referred to by the Courts of Justice in India in property matters relating to disputes in the *diara* land. The major problems with this regulation during those years and even today is, however, establishing the actual gain over the occupied land. The regulation guidelines suggest that the courts shall be "guided by the best evidence they may be able to obtain of established local usage", and this left much scope for varied interpretations and disputes. After the enforcement of the Act, there were numerous litigations. The government could not assert its title to the possession of "island which was thrown up in a river" as it was surveyed a few years back and could not be surveyed "till the expiration of at least ten years from the time of the previous survey". The court in that situation also believed that "the status of the island at the time the Government came into Court must be the guide by which the right of Government ought to be determined".[6]

The *Zamindars* often refused to pay rent on the pretext of the frequent changes in the *diara* land due to inundation.[7] Consequently, the government decided to bring in special provisions in the Bengal Rent Act of 1859. Through this Act, the government tried to ensure that the tenant was liable to enhancement of rent in case of increase of the area of his land by alluvion. All these provisions, however, were in the form of guidelines and did not give the government machinery the authority in real sense to collect rent from the *diara* land. To do that, the Alluvial Lands Possession Bill was passed in the Council in 1868.[8] The bill was moved "to amend the provisions of Act IX of 1847". The Act, implemented in 1847, was regarding the assessment of lands gained from rivers by alluvion. The existing practice was that the revenue authorities would recognise the claim of the nearest proprietor to a prior right to the purchase of the same or to a settlement of the lands. But now the proposed change to the Act of 1847 was that all lands gained shall be considered an increment and would be at the disposal of the Government (Phillips 1884). The new portion of a *diara* was taken possession of by the local revenue officers when the channel between such island and the shore was "not fordable" [which could be crossed on foot]. Even when such channel became fordable an individual could not take possession of the land (Phillips 1884).

The various regulations and acts of the government did serve the purpose with which they were brought into effect. But the local communities of boatmen and fishers lost out massively in terms of livelihoods. These communities often moved from one avulsed land to the other and lived in temporary settlements and used the land for winter crop cultivation. In the 19th century, even such temporary lands were taken away from them either by the *Zamindars* or by the state declaring it as rent roll property. There were written protests against the government regulations, but no one advocated for the landless communities. The Indian members of the Council such as Baboo Ramnath Tagore, were promoting the rights of the *Zamindars* only. In his letter Tagore wrote that he was not agreeable to Section 4 of the proposed Bill and believed that the proposed change was against the principle of Clause 3, Section 4 of Regulation XI of 1825. According to that clause, when a *diara* land might be thrown up in a large navigable river (the bed of which was not the property of an individual) and the channel of the river and the shore might not be fordable, it should, according to established usage, be placed at the disposal of the government. But if the channel between such an island and the shore was fordable at any season of the year, it should be considered an accession to the land or tenure of the person whose estate might be contiguous to it. People opposing the proposed bill believed that by Section 4 of the present bill, the effect of that provision would be completely destroyed, and that with it the government intended to deprive the *Zamindars* of a right that they had enjoyed since the Permanent Settlement.

The Bengal Tenancy Act of 1885 had grave implications on the *diara* community. After the passing of this Act, a survey and assessment of landholdings of the *Zamindars,* their tenants and other holdings were done to facilitate rent realisation. This assessment led to an increased and more regular rent demand. Resultantly, measures had to be taken by the tenants to increase agricultural production, and that was done in two ways. One, double cropping was started, and two, there was an attempt to increase the cropping area itself. So there were attempts to assert ownership of the *diara* land and then cultivate crops such as potatoes, linseeds, pulses, etc., on this land (Bindeshwar 1997). Under the provision of the Act, any person holding a particular piece of land for 12 years continuously, whether under lease or otherwise, became a "settled *raiyat*" (Rampini and Finucane 1889). The status of a "settled *raiyat*" could not be acquired by purchase or sale and was, therefore, different from "occupancy *raiyat*". The "occupancy *raiyat*" could be purchased as rights of occupancy and was transferable. The acquisition right was allowed even if a person held as *raiyat any land* in the same village for twelve years, either before or after the passing of the Act, and that too either by himself or through inheritance. This rule, however, did not apply to the *raiyats* of *diara* land. For the acquisition of rights of "settled *raiyat*" in *diara*, the prerequisite was that the person held the *same land* for 12 years. Till such time the person was eligible for the right of occupancy in the given land, he had to pay the rent agreed upon between him and the landlord (Rampini and Finucane 1889). Although Clause 180 (3) of the Act gave the collector the power to declare any *diara* land as regular land after receiving the application either from the landlord or tenant, or on a reference from the civil court adjudicating a dispute, this was rarely done. The special provision in the case of *diara* land practically debarred the *raiyats* from acquiring the right of occupancy as the landlord kept shifting them around so as to prevent them from occupying the *same land* for twelve years *continuously*. Thus, until the completion of these twelve years, the tenant was neither a "settled" nor a "non-occupancy" *raiyat*, and thereby was a tenant-at-will. A new Section, 86A, was inserted into the Bengal Tenancy Act by an amendment which provided that the tenant's right to the "diluvion land" would be considered as being relinquished if he had obtained a reduction of rent.

In the river ecology of the mid-Ganga plain, despite these regulations there were administrative hurdles, especially for deciding on disputes over possession of land. The very fluid nature of the *diara* land did not allow the British government to control it properly for all practical purposes. The uncertainty of the *diara* also made it a property of "speculative nature" (Sinha 2014). It was difficult for the government administrators to fix criteria by which the "estimated produce of the lands" for the next ten years might be correctly calculated. Therefore, auction-based settlements were preferred. The communities of boatmen and fishers could not compete with the *Zamindars* as they were always the highest bidders. The *diara* community could no longer claim the newly avulsed land as common property in such a scenario of revenue farming.

Migration

The Bengal Alluvion and Diluvion Regulation of 1825 appeared to be rational, but it had much wider implications in environmental terms. It brought a major transformation of the social and economic life of the *diara* community of boatmen and fishers. The revenue-intensive agriculture, post the Permanent Settlement, ruined the elasticity of their production, and, in a way, they were now supposed to compete with the peasants of the plains by taking the land on lease. The very meaning of land as common property, which the communities had possessed for centuries, changed into the absolute right of proprietorship. The ADR Regulation also proved to be the defining moment for the ecology of the mid-Ganga flood country. It initiated a cycle of transformation in which the crops with highest revenue potential were sowed, because the lands were now being leased out by the *Zamindars* to highest bidders amongst the *diara* cultivators.

Traditionally, the poor peasants had always been migrating as the temporary nature of the *diara* landscape did not allow any permanence in cultivation. After the promulgation of the Permanent Settlement in 1793 and the ADR in 1825, with not much land left as *diara* wasteland, however, their "adaptive strategy" changed to a "livelihood strategy". With no land to cultivate the traditional boatmen and fisher community had to look for alternative options. In the various reports sent by officers to Hunter in 1885, I find references to the "peasants forced to look elsewhere for work and sustenance" (Rothermund 1997).

Fishing community of the *diara*

For the communities living in *diara*, fisheries were another main livelihood. The loss of livelihood through cultivation forced the fisher community to fully depend on fisheries. But that too gradually came under government regulation and decommonisation of inland fisheries also began. By the last quarter of the nineteenth century, many British reports recommended that fisheries might prove as a valuable source of revenue for the state. It was after this that the British government passed inland fisheries acts, which clearly distinguished the *zamindar* entitled fisheries and state entitled fisheries. Within two decades the situation emerged that there were no free fisheries that the public could access without license, except the sea. It may be reiterated that although the fisheries rights got divided into *Zamindars* and states, in all the cases the fishing rights were leased out.

It meant that river water for fishing was decommonised, and public fishing in the rivers was normally not allowed. The pre-colonial tradition of free fishing in rivers and ponds changed. The *Zamindars* began the practice of leasing out *jalkar* to *ijaradars* (i.e. water tax/revenue to the highest bidder). In most cases the right of fishing was transferred with the land. They gave out the fishing rights to the renters (*mustajirs*), who sometimes employed men to catch the fish for wage, or for a share. It was sometimes re-let to the traditional fishermen. The fishermen who caught fish from *zamindar* controlled areas gave one-third of the fish to the agents of the landlords. In Patna and Shahabad, in the parts of the channel of the Ganga, which in the dry season contained not much flow, the fisheries were leased out to the fishers. In this way, the colonial rule re-defined all rights and tried to take control over access to the water and its resources, including fish. The various acts, contrary to their stated intents led to more privatisation of water bodies and consequently of the fishes, thus adversely affecting the income of the fisher community living in *diara* landscape. This may not be proved with a statistical account because of the paucity of data on the actual income of the communities living in *diara,* but the "increased migration pattern" (Singh 2018) over the last decade of the 19th century suggests that the community surviving on inland fishery might have been affected economically.

Conclusion

The very natural process through which *diara* land is created – cutting and deposition of soil – leads to instability and uncertainty in the life of the community dependent on it. It is because of this frequent process of creation and dissolution of the *diara* land that no permanent land tenure system could develop here historically in pre-colonial times. *Diara* as fluvial common resource had existed for centuries and was outside any governmental and institutional control. It was a jointly used territory, but with the introduction of a series of new acts during the nineteenth century it lost its basic characteristic of commons and a process of decommonisation started. After the dreaded 1770 famine in Bengal, the colonial government of the British East India Company claimed that there had been a huge amount of revenue loss both in terms of collection and area of land assessed. Therefore, by the early nineteenth century the state began to plan for widening the base of land revenue. The colonial government went on to pass the ADR in order to bring even newly avulsed land under Permanent Settlement and thus tried to maximise its revenue. But the temporary nature of the newly formed *diara* land and frequent changes in river-courses posed an ecological challenge, and problem of assessment similar to the floodplain uplands. The easy way out for the government was to lease out the fluvial *diara* lands to highest bidders, who were often the *Zamindars*, and the *diara* community of boatmen and fishers lost their livelihoods. The government was successful in taking economic control of the avulsed territories through various acts and rules, but these led to massive *diara* community migration to the surrounding areas. The alternative livelihood strategy of the communities living here was inland fisheries which was also brought under governmental control. The driving forces of decommonisation were not ecological, rather political and socioeconomic despite the fact that fluvial commons were ecologically ephemeral territories. The *diara* community needed to be reconnected to their environment to restrict their migration. However, such reconnection was only possible when their livelihood remains intact.

For common property resources such as *diara,* homogenous regulations may not do justice to the local communities. The enactments of laws and new lease policies often ignore the long-established traditional rights. Even today the *diara* landscapes property ownerships and its disputes are governed by almost two centuries old ADR, and the traditional community of boatmen and fishers have been written off. It is essential that fluvial and ephemeral lands be commonised once again and the customary livelihood rights of the communities living here are respected.

Notes

1 It has been estimated that some 40 million hectares of land in India lies in the flood plain, and out of it 2.64 million hectares is *diara* land. Gopal Kumar et al., "Land Use Land Cover Change in Active Flood Plain using Satellite Remote Sensing", *Journal of Agricultural Physics,* vol. 8, 2008, p. 22. Tracking of *diara* land in eastern India through the technique of remote sensing has also been done by B. C. Panda, R. N. Sahu and Manju Sharma, "Land Use Mapping of Brahmani–Birupa *Diara* in Cuttack, Orissa", in *Remote Sensing for Natural Resources*, Dehradun: Indian Society of Remote Sensing (ISRO), 1996, pp. 167–70.
2 In contrast, Victor Liberman argues that because of the exposed position of the Indo-Gangetic zone the Turkic or Mongol nomads, moving on horses, found it easier to invade these plains. He uses the term "exposed zones" to distinguish it from the "protected zones" of Eurasia. Eurasia was located far away from central Asia that kept the nomads at arm's length. See Victor Lieberman, *Strange Parallels: Southeast Asia in Global Context, c. 800–1830—Volume 2: Mainland Mirrors: Europe, Japan, China, South Asia, and the Islands*, New York: Cambridge University Press, 2009.
3 James Rennell published his survey of the course of the Ganga and the Brahmaputra rivers. Rennell, *An Account of the Ganges.*
4 For the two contrasting views, see Mann, "A Permanent Settlement"; Habib, *Agrarian System of Mughal India*; Siddiqi, *Agrarian Change*. Rohan D'Souza has

also done a survey of literatures on the Mughal and colonial system of revenue administration. See D'Souza, *Drowned and Dammed*, pp. 51–96.

5 Miscellaneous Letters Monghyr, V.4, 1831–37; Shahabad Correspondence Volumes, 1835–57, Bihar State Archive, Patna.

6 Proceedings of the Council of the Lieutenant Governor of Bengal for the Purpose of Making Laws and Regulations, Nehru Memorial Library and Museum, New Delhi (Microfilm) V. no. 1–47, 1868, p. 136.

7 Shahabad Correspondence Volumes, 1835–57, Bihar State Archive, Patna.

8 Alluvial Land Possession Bill, Proceedings of the Council of the Lieutenant Governor of Bengal for the Purpose of Making Laws and Regulations, Nehru Memorial Library and Museum, New Delhi (Microfilm) V. no. 1–47, 1868, pp. 131–34.

References

Alluvial Land Possession Bill, Proceedings of the Council of the Lieutenant Governor of Bengal for the Purpose of Making Laws and Regulations, 1868. Nehru Memorial Library and Museum, New Delhi (Microfilm) 1–47.

Buchanan, F. (1928). *An Account of the District of Purnea in 1809–1810*, Patna: Bihar and Orissa Research Society.

Chakrabarti, D. K. (2001). *Archaeological Geography of the Ganga Plain: The Lower and the Middle Ganga*, Delhi: Permanent Black.

D'Souza, R. (2016). *Drowned and Dammed: Colonial Capitalism and Flood Control in Eastern India*, Delhi: Oxford University Press.

Habib, I. (2013). *Agrarian System of Mughal India: 1556–1707*, Delhi: Oxford University Press.

Hill, C. V. (1997). *River of Sorrow: Environment and Social Control in Riparian North India, 1770–1994*, Ann Arbor: Michigan University Press.

Hunter, W. W. (1877). *A Statistical Account of Bengal: Districts of Monghyr and Purneah*, vol. 15, London: Trubner and Co.

Kumar, G. et al. (2008). Land Use Land Cover Change in Active Flood Plain using Satellite Remote Sensing, *Journal of Agricultural Physics*, 8, 2008, 22–28.

Lieberman, V. (2009). *Strange Parallels: Southeast Asia in Global Context, c. 800–1830—Vol 2: Mainland Mirrors: Europe, Japan, China, South Asia, and the Islands*, New York: Cambridge University Press.

Madan, P. L. (2005). *Ganga: A Cartographic Mystery*, Delhi: Manohar.

Mann, M. (1995). A Permanent Settlement for the Ceded and Conquered Provinces: Revenue Administration in North India, 1801–1833, *Economic and Social History Review*, 32, 2, 245–69.

Miscellaneous Letters Monghyr, 4, 1831–37. Bihar State Archive, Patna.

Panda, B. C., Sahu, R. N. and Sharma, M. (1996). Land Use Mapping of Brahmani–Birupa *Diara* in Cuttack, Orissa, *Remote Sensing for Natural Resources*, Published jointly by Indian Society of Remote Sensing and NNRMS, (ISRO), 1996, 167–70.

Phillips, H. A. D. (1884). *Manual of Revenue and Collectorate Law with Annotations*, Calcutta: Thacker, Spink and Co., 1884.

Proceedings of the Council of the Lieutenant Governor of Bengal for the Purpose of Making Laws and Regulations (1868). Nehru Memorial Library and Museum, New Delhi (Microfilm) 1–47.

Ram, B. (1997). *Land and Society in India: Agrarian Relations in Colonial North Bihar*, Delhi: Orient Blackswan.

Rennell, J. (1781). *An Account of the Ganges and Burrampooter Rivers*, London: J. Nicholas.

Rothermund, D. (1997). "A Survey of Rural Migration and Land Reclamation in India, 1885", *Journal of Peasant Studies*, 4, pp. 230–42.

Shahabad Correspondence Volumes (1835–57). Bihar State Archive, Patna.

Siddiqi, A. (1973). *Agrarian Change in a Northern Indian State: Uttar Pradesh, 1819–1833*, Oxford: The Clarendon Press.

Singh, V. (2018). *Speaking Rivers: Environmental History of a Mid-Ganga Flood Country, 1540–1885*, Delhi: Primus Books.

Sinha, N. (2014). Fluvial Landscape and the State: Property and the Gangetic Diaras in Colonial India, 1790s–1890s, *Environment and History*, 20, pp. 209–37.

Rampini, R. F. and Finucane, M. (1889). *The Bengal Tenancy Act: Being Act VIII of 1885*. Calcutta: Thacker, Spink & Co.

Part III

What enables commonisation?

Chapter 5

Five key characteristics that drive commonisation

Empirical evidence from Sri Lankan shrimp aquaculture

Eranga Kokila Galappaththi and
Iroshani Madu Galappaththi

Introduction

The chapter examines five key characteristics that can drive commonisation in the face of social-ecological system change based on the case of Sri Lankan shrimp aquaculture. We argue that commonisation in shrimp aquaculture is possible when the five identified characteristics, or combinations thereof, create the atmosphere for establishing commons. We studied five small-scale shrimp farming communities in northwestern Sri Lanka. All coastal aquaculture in the northwestern region produces "black tiger shrimp" (*Penaeus monodon*). Sri Lanka is a small-scale shrimp producer in terms of quantity, but this case study provides unique insights into commonisation and its key characteristics. In Sri Lanka, from 1992 to 1996, the shrimp industry witnessed rapid and uncontrolled growth which resulted in a harvest of up to 8,000–9,000 kg/ha per year in large-scale classical earthen ponds (Galappaththi & Berkes, 2014). Yet, this growth couldn't be sustained due to resource mismanagement that led the industry into multiple disease outbreaks and environmental problems, including impacts from climate change. After 2005, shrimp aquaculture started moving in a positive direction under the ownership of small-scale producers and laid the foundation of Sri Lankan shrimp aquaculture commonisation – after a series of painful lessons learned from the past.

"Commonisation is understood as a process through which a resource gets converted into a jointly used resource under commons institutions that deal with excludability and subtractability, and "decommonisation" refers to a process through which a jointly used resource under commons institutions loses these essential characteristics" (Nayak & Berkes, 2011: 132). Obtaining a better understanding of the processes of both commonisation and decommonisation requires further examination of their characteristics. Such inquiries allow us to answer some critical questions, such as: How can shrimp aquaculture be managed as commons? What are the key characteristics of commonisation in the context of lagoon-based shrimp aquaculture? How do such characteristics support commonisation in the context of SES? Why is it important to understand such characteristics? Yet, most shrimp aquaculture literature concentrates on the wide range of adverse social and environmental implications resulting from unsustainable large-scale aquaculture (Benessaiah & Sengupta, 2014; Bhari & Visvanathan, 2018; Bush et al., 2010). The impacts of large-scale shrimp aquaculture are unpredictable and inequitable, as they depend on the level of vulnerability in a SES (Handisyde, Telfer, & Ross, 2017; Paprocki & Huq, 2018).

A limited number of scientific studies illustrates how to engage in sustainable shrimp aquaculture (Bush et al., 2010; De Silva & Davy, 2010; E. Galappaththi, 2013; Harkes, Drengstig, Kumara, Jayasinghe, & Huxham, 2015). For instance, Galappaththi and Berkes (2015) examined northwestern Sri Lanka shrimp aquaculture using an SES approach, focusing on the surviving small-scale shrimp farmers and how they creatively deal with uncertainties and complexities. Small-scale shrimp aquaculture operations have maintained close relationships with the environment, on which, along with natural resources, they depend for their livelihoods and well-being. With Sri Lanka's history of practicing community-based management and co-management of small-scale fisheries (for example, culture-based fishery) (Amarasinghe & Bavinck, 2017; De Silva, Amarasinghe, & Nguyen, 2006), an original research project was aimed at proposed community-based shrimp aquaculture as an alternative to large-scale aquaculture operations (Galappaththi, 2013). Galappaththi and Nayak (2017) used the story of Sri Lankan shrimp aquaculture to illustrate the two faces of shrimp aquaculture: commonisation and decommonisation. Collective action in the Sri Lankan shrimp aquaculture was used to illustrate the process of commonisation. Interestingly, even after the primary data collection in 2012, government statistics showed incremental improvement in aquaculture shrimp production since 2005. Almost all national shrimp aquaculture production comes from tiger shrimp farming in northwestern Sri Lanka (Figure 5.1).

Study area: Lagoon system

This study was conducted primarily in the five coastal communities of *Ambakandawila*, *Koththanthive*, *Muthupanthiya*, *Pinkattiya*, and *Karamba*, located in northwestern Sri Lanka. These shrimp farming operations rely on three different lagoon water bodies that provide a consistent water supply for shrimp farming – the *Chilaw* (700 ha), *Mundal* (3,600 ha), and *Puttalam* (32,000 ha) lagoon systems (Galappaththi & Berkes, 2015). Dutch Canal is a man-made canal that mainly connects the aforementioned three lagoons (Chandrasekara, Weerasinghe, Pathirana, & Piyadasa, 2018). Furthermore, this canal connects to several rivers and streams in the northwestern area, creating an interconnected system of common lagoon water body (Figure 5.2).

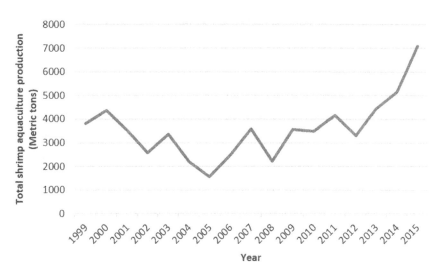

Figure 5.1 Total shrimp aquaculture production over the years (metric tons). A colour version of this image is downloadable as an eResource from www.routledge. com/9780367138004.

Data source: NAqDA (2017)

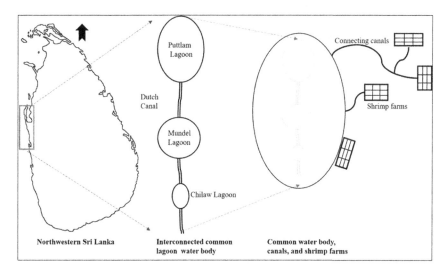

Figure 5.2 Sketch of the ponds and the canal/common water body where water is discharged/drawn. A colour version of this image is downloadable as an eResource from www.routledge.com/9780367138004.

Source: Adapted from Galappaththi et al. (2019a)

Almost all the shrimp farms in the northwestern coastal area are directly or indirectly connected to this water system. Hundreds of natural or man-made channels (inlet canals) and branches bring water to the shrimp ponds as well as drain excess/used water from them (outlet canal). Inevitably, all the shrimp farming operations in the northwestern area depend on this interconnected common water body (Galappaththi & Berkes, 2015).

The interconnected nature of the lagoon water system allows shrimp viral diseases to spread unpredictably. In addition, climate change impacts such as unexpected and extreme weather increase the uncertainty and complexities surrounding shrimp disease control. In the past, Sri Lankan shrimp aquaculture had experienced three major shrimp disease outbreaks (Galappaththi & Berkes, 2014; Munasinghe, Stephen, Abeynayake, & Abeygunawardena, 2010). The first major outbreak took place in 1988/9 and was due to the Monodon Baculo Virus (MBV). A second major disease outbreak occurred in 1996, causing White Spot Syndrome (WSS) in shrimp infected by the WSS Virus (WSSV). This was followed by a third outbreak in 1998, which was due to both WSSV and the Yellow Head Virus (YHV). WSS continues to remain as the largest threat to shrimp aquaculture in Sri Lanka. WSS infects mainly the penaeid shrimp species; it can act quickly and kill shrimp within a day. It can also spread quickly through other aquatic animals – crustaceans and birds – as carriers. Thus, shrimp diseases can quickly spread throughout the water system and to the shrimp farms that this water system connects, thereby directly affecting the livelihoods and well-being of small-scale shrimp farmers.

In this case study, we explain how shrimp farmers collectively respond to this shrimp disease challenge by managing the interconnected lagoon water body through a process of commonisation, which eventually led to establishment of aquaculture commons in Sri Lanka. The chapter's aim is to examine the characteristics of the commonisation process in Sri Lankan shrimp aquaculture. Proposed characteristics are major thematic areas that emerged during the qualitative data analysis ("manifest" and "latent" content analysis supplemented with "discourse" analysis). Data were collected using participant observations, interviews, and focus groups during 2012–2013. The authors considered some insights from the first author's experience as a shrimp farmer in the same region during the transition of shrimp aquaculture management in Sri Lanka (2003–2006). The following section discusses this commonisation by first exploring the sample profiles, then by covering the history and development of Sri Lankan shrimp aquaculture. Third, the chapter explains the Zonal Crop Calendar system through which shrimp farmers manage aquaculture resources as commons following their multi-layered institutional structure. Next, under discussions and conclusion, the chapter covers five characteristics that drive commonisation in facing SES change, including climate change.

Sample profile

Almost all existing shrimp aquaculture operations in northwestern Sri Lanka were small-scale (Galappaththi & Berkes, 2015). Recorded pond size varied from 0.2 to 0.8 hectares and total farmland area varied from one to seven hectares. Farmland ownership varied among farmers. Fifty-three percent of farms were on state-owned lands while 37 percent were farmer-owned. There were some unresolved legal issues, related mostly to the use of state-owned lands for shrimp farming. The remaining 11 percent of farmers rented land from previous shrimp farmers. Forty-two percent of farmers carried out farming activities on their own. While 39 percent of farms were family-owned businesses, 11 percent were organised through partnerships. Eight percent of farmers operated their businesses as private limited companies.

Farmers' general practice was to employ the minimal number of employees to reduce input costs. Forty-seven percent of farms employed two to five people; 24 percent had fewer than two employees; and 29 percent employed five to eight people. The involvement of family members in farming operations was a common phenomenon due mainly to the high input cost of farming, which was the main factor limiting the ability to hire more people. Seventy-four percent of farmers said that they received family support. Sixty-four percent of farmers received family support from women – wives, daughters, mothers, and/or other close relatives. These women were involved in diverse ways: labour (shrimp harvesting), bookkeeping, day-to-day farm administrative activities, financial contributions towards farming (investment), and participation in the community association activities.

Famers also had multiple revenue streams, arguably a way to manage livelihood risk (Galappaththi, Galappaththi, & Kodithuwakku, 2017). Fifty-eight percent of the farmers engaged in a secondary income-generating activity. Some of these activities were related to shrimp aquaculture: shrimp post larvae production, shrimp feed sales, and shrimp and fish integrated farming. Lagoon-based capture fishery, salt production, and the cultivation of coconut, paddy (rice), and vegetables were additional livelihood activities undertaken other than shrimp aquaculture.

History and development of Sri Lankan shrimp aquaculture

At present, the major activity in these lagoon water bodies is shrimp aquaculture. Lagoon capture fishery still exists in the area, but at a negligible scale. Sri Lankan shrimp aquaculture operations began in the late 1970s with four multi-national companies (Andrew's, Carson, Enris, and Liver Brothers) operating as commercial scale ventures. Initially, these farms were geographically limited to the eastern part of the country (the Batticaloa District). These companies reportedly earned high profits partly due to their technical know-how with respect to aquaculture systems, input supply, and marketing, which was not accessible by anyone from the outside.

Before the 1980s, lagoon capture fishery dominated lagoon water bodies in the northwestern coastal belt. Villages used to fish for shrimp and fin fish mainly for subsistence purposes. These fishers used wooden fishing canoes and various fishing gears, such as cast nets, gill nets, and other traditional fishing equipment. In the early 1980s, some of the employees of pioneer shrimp farming companies started their own farms to practice what they had learnt while working for large-scale operations by companies. The profit-making potential of shrimp farming attracted new investors, such as politicians, bank managers, and wealthy business owners.

In the early 1990s, the Sri Lankan government started promoting shrimp aquaculture as a profitable self-employment opportunity among locals in the northwestern coastal area. Many community-level small-scale farmers started shrimp farming, leading to an expansion of shrimp aquaculture throughout the northwestern coastal area. Small-scale farmers continued farming within the same community area while large- and medium-scale farmers shifted from place to place by converting mangrove and coconut cultivation lands into shrimp farms. The civil unrest that prevailed in the eastern part of the country limited the industry's expansion to that area.

In the late 1990s, as small-scale shrimp farming operations rapidly grew, farmers across the northwestern area began organising into associations. This led to the emergence of community-based institutions. In terms of shrimp production volumes and quality standards, the government or any other regulatory body had no control over the industry. For instance, no specific timeframe existed for stocking shrimp post larvae (baby shrimp or seed). Shrimp farmers and hatcheries continued their production throughout the year, and no rules were in place to govern the starting or closing of farming operations. Post larvae producing shrimp hatchery owners self-organised into a shrimp breeders' association as a means of sharing technical knowledge and obtaining better selling prices for post larvae.

In the early 2000s, the shrimp breeders' association took the initiative of calling a meeting of all the stakeholders in the shrimp aquaculture sector to develop a strategy for overcoming the industry's difficult position. In 2005, these discussions resulted in the formation of a national-level sector association called SLADA (Sri Lanka Aquaculture Development Association), in collaboration with all the industry stakeholders. SLADA asked the Ministry of Fisheries to form a government institution responsible for supporting and monitoring the northwestern shrimp aquaculture sector. In 2003/4, the Sri Lankan central government was directly involved in the supervision of the shrimp aquaculture sector through a line institution called the National Aquaculture Development Authority of Sri Lanka (NAqDA). NAqDA's approach was to work in collaboration with SLADA, community-level shrimp farmers' associations, and shrimp breeders' associations. One of the initial tasks of the SLADA and NAqDA collaborative management arrangement was to respond to the shrimp disease problem.

In 2005/06, SLADA designed and introduced a Zonal Crop Calendar (ZCC) to control access to the natural lagoon water body for purposes of managing shrimp diseases. NAqDA's role in the implementation of ZCC was to coordinate, monitor, and facilitate the implementation process. The crop calendar significantly changed the way in which farming operations were conducted in the area. Initially, the historically independently operated people of the sector (especially farmers and breeders) had trouble adjusting to the new management system. They resisted mainly due to the limited number of production cycles allowed per year. During the first few crop cycles under the new ZCC system, some relatively large- and medium-scale shrimp farmers and hatchery owners left the industry after realizing that it would not be profitable to keep their farms and hatcheries in an idle state during some parts of the year.

Farmers and hatchery owners who adapted to the Zonal Crop Calendar experienced a successful year mainly in terms of controlled disease spread. This success story caused some of the previous farmers (those who had left shrimp farming) to resume farming during the following season. However, the next season was less successful in terms of shrimp production and selling prices. Most of the medium-scale farmers stopped farming because of the uncertain nature of production as well as the significant increase in labour costs and inputs such as fuel and chlorine. White Spot Syndrome, which had been assumed to be under control, returned from time to time, resulting in fluctuations in shrimp production and prices.

By 2009/10, most farmers and hatchery owners who remained in the industry were abiding by the ZCC system. NAqDA worked towards strengthening the existing community-level associations. NAqDA became more flexible in its approach towards learning from previous experiences, and the shrimp farmers started cooperating. All the changes that had taken place during the previous stages resulted in the establishment of a multi-layered management structure. After years of battling shrimp diseases, about 600 shrimp farms remained in northwestern Sri Lanka by 2012.

Zonal Crop Calendar (ZCC)

ZCC is a self-protective approach towards managing shrimp diseases, implemented in northwestern Sri Lanka (Galappaththi & Berkes, 2015). The uncontrollable nature of shrimp disease conditions and the resulting impacts on the industry led to the development of a crop calendar. SLADA introduced it in 2004 and its implementation was legalised by the Ministry of Fisheries and Aquatic Resources Development in Sri Lanka. The crop calendar's main objective was to minimize the damage caused by shrimp diseases (mainly WSS disease) to increase national-level shrimp production. Zonal and sub-zonal geographical boundaries were developed that considered the connected nature of the area's natural water system and the shrimp disease spreading patterns through the lagoon water body. One (or two) shrimp farming communit(ies) was (were) recognised as a sub-zone and a collective of sub-zones became a zone. Thus, the northwestern shrimp farming area was divided into 5 zones and 32 sub-zones (Figure 5.3).

ZCC provides an annual plan for water allocation for shrimp farming in the northwestern area. SLADA/shrimp farmers and the government collectively decide which zone(s) and/or sub-zone(s) can access the interconnected common water body for shrimp farming during each crop season. A commonly agreed-upon annual crop calendar is designed and implemented. In other words, consensus is achieved regarding who can engage in shrimp farming during a season and who cannot. A calendar year is divided into three seasons of shrimp production: pre-*yala* (February to April); *yala* (April to September); and *maha* (October to February). Production seasons are

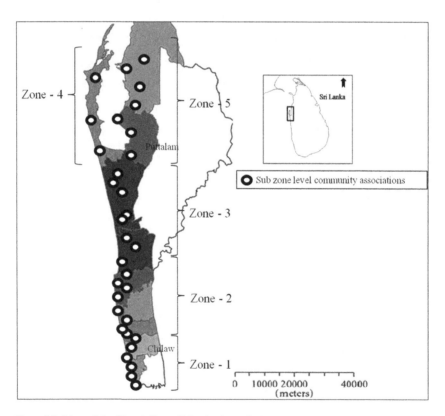

Figure 5.3 Map of the Zonal Crop Calendar boundaries.
Source: Adapted from Galappaththi and Berkes (2015)

assigned to sub-zones/communities based on the disease spread patterns along the water system. Each community receives at least one or two production season(s) per year. This way, the seasonal crop calendar creates buffer zones through geographical (zones/sub-zones) and temporal (seasons) boundaries. Furthermore, the ZCC is subjected to changes on an annual basis – an adaptive learning process. Changes are made based on feedback from farmers escalated through the multi-layered structure and from lessons learned during previous crop seasons responding to the changing climate. ZCC is the most significant component of the existing governance system, as it determines all the other activities related to shrimp farming, such as post larvae production and quantities.

As part of the ZCC system, community institutions practise Better Management Practices (BMPs) for shrimp aquaculture operations. BMP is a set of guidelines that NAqDA developed for adaptation at the community level. For example, BMPs specify a stocking density reliant on the use of aerators, i.e., four to six post larvae/m^2 for a pond with no aerators and a maximum of 10 post larvae/m^2 for a pond with aerators. Community associations are expected to adapt and fine tune these BMPs to suit their own environments and social conditions, such as salinity levels (which affect the use of aerators), the availability of mangrove vegetation closer to farms, and the success of previous crops. The multi-layered institutional structure reinforces the shrimp aquaculture governance system.

Multi-layered institutional structure

The Sri Lankan shrimp aquaculture production system is managed by a multi-layered institutional structure that, since the 1990s, has evolved from less complex community associations (Figure 5.4). This is a private-communal-state mixed management regime. At the heart of this mixed regime is the community-based institution (called *samithiya* in the local language), i.e., the shrimp farmers' association. These community-based institutions together serve as the bottom (community) level, self-organised community entities within the hierarchy of existing shrimp farmers' associations (community to national level). Community-level shrimp farming associations formulate and implement their own rules to manage community-level resources. Every shrimp farmer in the community (100 percent) must be a member of the community association. Most of the community associations are small collective groups (20 to 60 members). The elected officers of a community association include the president, vice president, secretary, treasurer, and assistant treasurer. Most of the community associations have government aquaculture extension officers that work closely to ensure that practices comply with national regulations. However, these officers do not have the power to influence any of the decisions that the associations make. The community-level rules for managing shrimp aquaculture practices/resources are created through collective

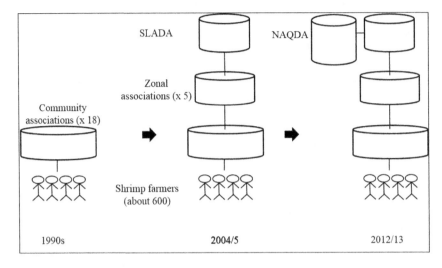

Figure 5.4 Adapting commons institutions.
Source: Adapted from Galappaththi et al. (2019a)

decisions. The collective decision-making process is one of the important characteristics of a community association. The community association also acts as an information hub by sharing information about shrimp aquaculture operations among member farmers. Such information includes post larvae prices; feed brands/prices; farm gate shrimp (harvest) prices; production quotas and stocking dates based on the national crop calendar; disease prevalence/spread; and shrimp farming techniques and management practices.

Community-level institutions are well-organised and interconnected through overriding zonal-level associations. Some zonal associations represent just one sub-zone, whereas the others may represent up to eight sub-zones. While the community associations are represented by community-level shrimp farmers, leaders of these sub-zonal associations represent the zonal association. All the zonal associations and sub-zonal associations are collectively represented in SLADA – there is at least one representative from each zone and sub-zone.

SLADA, the national-level association representing all the direct stakeholders in the shrimp farming sector – farmers; hatchery owners; feed suppliers; and shrimp processors – was established in 2005 with an initial membership of 16 people. Later, zonal and sub-zonal associations were granted permission to become members of SLADA. Consequently, the membership increased to about 50. To improve the shrimp farming sector, SLADA appointed six committees that targeted different subject areas, such as environmental protection, hatchery development, and shrimp farm development. Furthermore,

Table 5.1 Roles and responsibilities of each management level

Level	Specific Roles and Responsibilities
Community-level associations (samithi)	To regulate community-level farming practices with the support of NAqDA field extension officers. For this purpose, there is a shrimp farm monitoring and extension unit in Battulu Oya (established in 2008).
Zonal associations	To develop the infrastructure of shrimp farming areas in collaboration with divisional secretariat offices and provincial councils. Zonal associations also maintain a link (mainly communication) between the sub-zonal and national levels.
SLADA and NAqDA collaboratively	To improve the performance of the overall national-level shrimp aquaculture system. In this role, the management body has the authority to take legal action in response to any illegal activities, such as shrimp post larvae stocking beyond the crop calendar and the release of disease-infected water into the natural water body.

SLADA and NAqDA jointly developed a Technical Advisory Committee representing expertise from local universities and research institutions.

SLADA and NAqDA collaboratively form the top layer of the management structure. It is a joint management body and the decision-making pattern is a participatory process. The most interesting feature of this top management body is its composition; SLADA includes representation from all the stakeholders while NAqDA brings the government authority to the table. This body is powerful and effective at formulating as well as implementing guidelines to better regulate and ensure the industry's sustainability. Its ability to influence community-level actions and compliance is due mainly to the participatory nature of making decisions and creating guidelines. Furthermore, each layer of the management structure is tasked with specific roles and responsibilities (Table 5.1).

Major changes in the shrimp aquaculture management system over time (i.e., the time before and after implementation of the ZCC system) influence the lagoon SES. The lagoon has many other resource users besides shrimp farmers (e.g., fishers, gleaners, salt farmers, and hotels and tourism). Lagoon resource stakeholders express dynamic viewpoints about how major changes in shrimp aquaculture management have affected their lagoon-related livelihood activities (Table 5.2).

Discussion

The connected nature of the three lagoon water bodies and Dutch Canal has a large impact on Sri Lankan shrimp aquaculture management. Shrimp disease spreading along this common water body represents the key challenge

Table 5.2 Dynamics and critical perspectives resulting from commonisation of shrimp aquaculture

Lagoon Resource Users	Quotes
Salt farmer from Puttalam Lagoon	… I used to be a shrimp farmer … now I'm using my abundant shrimp ponds for salt farming …
Cast-net fisher from Mundel Lagoon	… we have a different samithi [cooperative] to discuss our [lagoon fishers] matters … It's hard to live now … it's a matter of survival … as long as I and my family survive, that is what I think about. My friends [fishers] already moved to other jobs in off-show trawling and seasonal labour in shrimp farm[s] …
Tourist guide working in lagoon-based eco-tourism	… this [hotel in the lagoon area] is fine, but there are some other places [lagoon area] [that need] dredging and cleaning … water is not flowing well … it's going to be worse in [the] coming rainy season. We don't get many people [tourists] that time [monsoon season].
Broker/middleman for selling land/ shrimp/fish	… land prices [around Chilaw Lagoon] are increasing every day … sometimes foreigners are also looking [to buy] land … shrimp price margins are not attractive anymore … we can't make good money like in the early days [before 2000] … actually, they don't produce much shrimp now …

facing shrimp farmers. Shrimp farmers have self-organised with government support and have implemented a calendar system to manage shrimp disease impacts. Arguably, this interconnected common water body acts as a common-pool resource. The ZCC is essentially a way of responding to shrimp disease challenge and creating aquaculture commons (Galappaththi & Berkes, 2015). The ZCC system addresses the excludability problem in commons theory (Ostrom, 1990), as it controls access to the common water body.

The second method of addressing the problem of excludability is through community-based institutions (*samithi*) (Galappaththi & Berkes, 2014). Individually owned farms are managed under community-level rules. Community-level shrimp farmers' associations collectively establish their own rules to avoid movable shrimp farming. These rules deny access to outsiders. The subtractability problem in shrimp aquaculture is associated mostly with the discharge of used pond effluents (Galappaththi & Berkes, 2015). A farmer may release disease-infected water from a shrimp farming pond into the surrounding environment (to an interconnected lagoon water body). This action affects the ability of other shrimp farmers to continue farming without being infected by shrimp diseases which can affect their livelihoods.

This chapter shows how shrimp farmers have experienced SES change, how they have responded to such changes, and how they are undergoing the process of commonisation. Commonisation is a complex process (Nayak & Berkes, 2011), but in this chapter we recognise its five vital characteristics, including essentials based on the case of Sri Lankan shrimp aquaculture: (1) bottom-up multi-level institutions with a mixed commons governance regime; (2) collaboration and collective action among resource users to share uncertainty and common challenges; (3) partnerships and government support for the commons governance system; (4) an adaptive nature throughout the commons governance process; and (5) effective networking and information sharing through commons institutions. Table 5.3 shows how such characteristics drive commonisation in the context of community-based shrimp aquaculture.

Table 5.3 Five key characteristics of community-based shrimp aquaculture that can drive commonisation

Key Characteristic	Description/How It Enables Commonisation	References
Bottom-up multi-level institutions with a mixed commons governance regime	Multi-level institutional structures will integrate all the organised commons institutions at all levels (community, zonal, and national) to enable better decision making related to shrimp aquaculture management (for example, the annual crop calendar). The bottom-up approach allows feedback (for example, updates about past crop and disease conditions) to be obtained from community-level to national-level decision making for ZCC development. A mixed commons governance regime (private, communal, and government) brings diversity and a broad range of knowledge to the overall institutional structure while improving the effectiveness of decision making. A multi-level institutional structure plays a key role in the process of commonisation by adjusting to changing SES.	(E. K. Galappaththi & Berkes, 2014)
Collaboration and collective action among resource users to share uncertainty and challenges	Shrimp farmers co-operate with each other by working collaboratively/collectively to overcome shared challenges (mainly shrimp diseases). Collaboration happens at multi-levels involving diverse interest groups. For instance, the shrimp farmers' association facilitates community-level collaboration and collective action among shrimp farmers (e.g., shrimp harvests, disease situations, charity work). At the national level, the joint body of the government (NAqDA) and the sector association (SLADA) collaborate on annual ZCC planning, with the representation of all zonal and community levels. Competition over scarce resources is typical and broadly occurs all over the world, leading to the process of decommonisation. Collaboration and collective action can facilitate the process of commonisation.	(E. Galappaththi & F. Berkes, 2015; E. K. Galappaththi & F. Berkes, 2015)

(Continued)

Table 5.3 Cont.

Key Characteristic	Description/How It Enables Commonisation	References
Partnerships and government support of the commons governance system	Decision making at all levels follows a participatory approach. This involves the participation of regional, provincial, and central government institutions and academic institutions for ZCC planning. The ZCC is developed by the shrimp farmers with the support of the government. The government facilitates the mainstreaming of the commons management system (for example, registering community associations, providing technical know-how, monitoring the ZCC system, providing capacity-building programs). Farming operations are owner-managed under community-level rules, with government oversight and coordination. Though no formal co-management arrangement exists with the government, the small-scale aquaculture practiced in Sri Lanka since 2012 is de facto co-management. Overall, government support and partnerships can be used throughout commonisation.	(E. K. Galappaththi & F. Berkes, 2015)
Adaptive nature throughout the commons governance process	First, adapting institutions (Boyd & Folke, 2012), from community associations to multi-level institutional structures, allows for adaptation to the changing SES conditions over the years (Figure 5.4). Second, ZCC is an adaptive process, as the annual ZCC continually changes according to the prevailing SES conditions, such as disease dominant (sub)zones, the changing climate, and extreme weather events. Third, BMPs are used based on the prevailing conditions in the communities (e.g., lagoon salinity levels, availability of mangrove forests). This adaptive nature allows for improved updates in response to changing conditions as a means of supporting the process of making commons.	(E. Galappaththi, Berkes, & Ford, 2019b; E. K. Galappaththi & F. Berkes, 2015)
Effective networking and information sharing through commons institutions	Effective networking takes place with relevant stakeholders in a shrimp aquaculture supply chain and specific information (e.g., related to disease and price) is shared among such stakeholders through community associations. According to Galappaththi et al. (2019b) when shared broadly and available readily, information can behave as commons – information commons. Information commons can enable commonisation, as a positive correlation exists among effective information sharing, the functionality of community associations, and the overall performance of the small-scale producers' supply chains.	(E. Galappaththi et al., 2019b)

The aforementioned five characteristics of resource governance in small-scale coastal aquaculture can be recognised as different but interrelated means of driving commonisation in shrimp aquaculture. These characteristics, in different combinations, allow for commonisation under specific SES conditions. However, we are not arguing that the shrimp aquaculture governance in Sri Lanka is perfect in terms of equitable distribution of benefits among farmers; power imbalances inherent in the process can affect SES resilience (Bournazel et al., 2015; NAqDA, 2017). Still, the overall effectiveness of the ZCC system and the methods of building commons in this aquaculture system are reflected in the sustainability of – and gradual increase in – aquaculture shrimp production (Figure 5.1). Furthermore, based on the application of collective action design principles (Cox, Arnold, & Tomás, 2010; Ostrom, 1990), the shrimp aquaculture management system in northwestern Sri Lanka is a success story, as most of the design principles (eight out of eleven) indicate a high degree of fit (Galappaththi & Berkes, 2015).

Commonisation and decommonisation are two faces of shrimp aquaculture (Galappaththi & Nayak, 2017). To better understand the process, it is important to understand the characteristics and aspects that drive each face. Ultimately, the two faces of shrimp aquaculture can be identified in the same SES. For instance, before commonisation, Sri Lankan shrimp aquaculture underwent the process of decommonisation. This decommonisation process had its origin along with the beginning of large-scale aquaculture (late 1970s), when shrimp aquaculture expanded across the northwestern coastal areas through the conversion of coconut lands and mangrove forests into shrimp farms. This aggressive expansion of aquaculture disturbed and encroached into lagoon space for capture fisheries. Shrimp disease outbreaks were the result of a decommonisation process that led shrimp farmers to create the ZCC system. The introduction of this system, coupled with the collective action of individual owners through cooperatives and a collaborative multi-level management structure, caused the shrimp aquaculture system to undergo the process of commonisation. Because of this persistent process, shrimp aquaculture SES has become much more resilient. Examination of the characteristics of the two faces of aquaculture advances the knowledge necessary to address issues of theoretical significance for aquaculture governance and policy development (Krause et al., 2015), as well as of practical significance for sustainable aquaculture (DeBey, Foco, & Alder, 2017).

While shrimp aquaculture goes through a process of commonisation, the lagoon SES indicates dynamic critical perspectives (Table 5.2). For example, a number of sub-systems (or resource users) – such as lagoon fishers, salt farmers, mangrove eco-systems, and lagoon-based tourism – that rely on the interconnected lagoon waterbody report how the lagoon system has changed with shrimp aquaculture. Arguably, the "commonisation" process of small-scale shrimp farmers might have led to the "decommonisation" of the resource base of small-scale capture fishers and/or gleaners. As such, the use of the term "commonisation" for lagoon SES could be challenged. In this case, "decommonisation" may be inherent to the process of "commonisation". However, in reality, use of the ZCC system evidently minimizes adverse impacts on the lagoon system as compared to the pre-ZCC era (a time of the "decommonisation" of shrimp aquaculture). This highlights the importance of studying and understanding the "big picture" of lagoon SES as a process using commons and SES perspectives.

In an aquaculture commons, the impacts of climate change affect the process of commonisation. Climate change impacts, such as unexpected weather and extreme events (for example, floods and droughts), increase the uncertainties and complexities of shrimp disease control and the ZCC system. The ZCC system is the prime mechanism for building resilience in the face of the challenges that shrimp disease poses. Crop calendar planning is based on the prevailing shrimp disease in the lagoon, while weather predictions rely on past weather experiences. Furthermore, unexpected climate change limits the effectiveness of BMPs as shrimp farmers modify and adapt best management practices, as appropriate, to community conditions. However, shrimp farmers seeking to manage the complexities and uncertainties created by climate change use a learning-by-doing approach (adaptive management) to practice ZCC. From a social-ecological resilience perspective (Berkes, Colding, & Folke, 2003), unexpected and extreme weather increases the uncertainties and complexities of northwestern shrimp aquaculture SES. Galappaththi et al. (2019b) illustrate how the ZCC system's implementation is supported by the system resilience, which are: living with change and uncertainty (shrimp disease and weather changes); nurturing diversity (non-aquaculture livelihood options); using different kinds of knowledge (shrimp production techniques, marketing knowledge, local environmental knowledge); and fostering learning (collective learning via *samithi*). Thus, such sources of resilience (Folke, 2016) are positively corelated with the performance of commonisation.

Conclusions

The geographical context of an aquaculture system (for example, the interconnected nature of a lagoon system) can be an important aspect to consider in the process of making commons, i.e., commonisation. ZCC is an innovative way to create aquaculture commons in the context of lagoon-based aquaculture. Environmental and climate change can increase the uncertainties and complexities related to commons governance. Based on Sri Lankan shrimp aquaculture, the five key characteristics that drive commonisation in the face of SES change are: bottom-up multi-level institutions with a mixed commons governance regime; collaboration and collective action among resource users to share uncertainties and challenges; partnerships and government support for the commons governance system; an adaptive nature throughout the commons governance process; and effective networking and information sharing among commons institutions. These key characteristics, combined with the sources of resilience, can help shrimp aquaculture persevere (i.e., remain sustainable) because commonisation can make such SES adaptive and resilient to change.

Acknowledgements

We sincerely appreciate the support of the shrimp farmers and community members of northwestern Sri Lanka. Furthermore, we appreciate the support of NAqDA field extension officers and ex-officers of SLADA. This study was supported by the Canada Research Chairs program (www.chairs-chaires.gc.ca) grant to Prof. Fikret Berkes. Finally, the author owes a debt of gratitude to Dr. Fikret Berkes, Canada Research Chair in Community-Based Resource Management, for his financial and intellectual support and advice throughout the project.

References

Amarasinghe, O., & Bavinck, M. (2017). Furthering the implementation of the small-scale fisheries guidelines: Strengthening fisheries cooperatives in Sri Lanka. In Jentoft, S., Chuenpagdee, R., Barragán-Paladines, M.J., Franz, N. (Eds.), *The Small-Scale Fisheries Guidelines: Global Implementation.* The Netherlands: Springer, pp. 379–399.

Benessaiah, K., & Sengupta, R. (2014). How is shrimp aquaculture transforming coastal livelihoods and lagoons in Estero Real, Nicaragua? The need to integrate social–ecological research and ecosystem-based approaches. *Environmental Management, 54*(2), 162–179.

Berkes, F., Colding, J., & Folke, C. (Eds.). (2003). *Navigating Social-Ecological Systems: Building Resilience for Complexity and Change.* New York: Cambridge University Press.

Bhari, B., & Visvanathan, C. (2018). Sustainable aquaculture: Socio-economic and environmental assessment. In Hai, Faisal I., Visvanathan, Chettiyappan, Boopathy, and Ramaraj (Eds.), *Sustainable Aquaculture.* The Netherlands: Springer, pp. 63–93.

Bournazel, J., Kumara, M. P., Jayatissa, L. P., Viergever, K., Morel, V., & Huxham, M. (2015). The impacts of shrimp farming on land-use and carbon storage around Puttalam lagoon, Sri Lanka. *Ocean & Coastal Management, 113,* 18–28.

Boyd, E., & Folke, C. (Eds.). (2012). *Adapting Institutions: Governance, Complexity and Social-Ecological Resilience.* New York: Cambridge University Press.

Bush, S. R., Van Zwieten, P. A., Visser, L., Van Dijk, H., Bosma, R., De Boer, W. F., & Verdegem, M. (2010). Scenarios for resilient shrimp aquaculture in tropical coastal areas. *Ecology and Society, 15*(2), 15.

Chandrasekara, C. M. K. N. K., Weerasinghe, K., Pathirana, S., & Piyadasa, R. U. (2018). Stresses over surface water sources in a human dominated environment: A case study in Hamilton canal, Sri Lanka. *International Journal of Disaster Resilience in the Built Environment, 9*(2), 184–197.

Cox, M., Arnold, G., & Tomás, S. V. (2010). A review of design principles for community-based natural resource management. *Ecology and Society, 15*(4), 38.

De Silva, S. S., Amarasinghe, U. S., & Nguyen, T. T. (2006). Better-practice approaches for culture-based fisheries development in Asia. *ACIAR Monograph, 120,* 50–72.

De Silva, S. S., & Davy, F. B. (Eds.). (2010). *Success Stories in Asian Aquaculture.* Ottawa: Springer.

DeBey, H., Foco, Z., & Alder, J. (2017). Advancing sustainable aquaculture through blue growth. *FAO Aquaculture Newsletter* (57), 39–42.

Folke, C. (2016). Resilience (republished). *Ecology and Society, 21*(4), 44. doi:10.5751/ ES-09088-210444

Galappaththi, E. (2013). *Community-Based Shrimp Aquaculture in Northwestern Sri Lanka* (Master of Natural Resources Management, Winnipeg), University of Manitoba, Winnipeg, Manitoba. Retrieved from https://umanitoba.ca/ institutes/natural_resources/Left-Hand%20Column/theses/Masters%20Thesis%20 Galappaththi%202013.pdf

Galappaththi, E., & Berkes, F. (2015). Drama of the commons in small-scale shrimp aquaculture in northwestern Sri Lanka. *International Journal of the Commons, 9*(1), 347–368.

Galappaththi, E., Berkes, F., & Ford, J. (2019a). Climate change adaptation efforts in coastal shrimp aquaculture: A case from northwestern Sri Lanka. In Johnson, J., De Young, C., Bahri, T., Soto, D. & Virapat, C. (Eds.) *Proceedings of FishAdapt: the Global Conference on Climate Change Adaptation for Fisheries and Aquaculture.* Bangkok, 8–10 August 2016. FAO Fisheries and Aquaculture Proceedings No. 61. Rome, FAO. 240 pp. Licence: CC BY-NC-SA 3.0 IGO. Retrieved from http://www. fao.org/documents/card/en/c/CA3055EN/

Galappaththi, E., Berkes, F., & Ford, J. (2019b). Climate change adaptation efforts in coastal shrimp aquaculture : A case from northwestern Sri Lanka. In : Johnson, J., De Young, C., Bahri, T., Soto, D. & Virapat, C. (Eds.), *Proceedings of FishAdapt: The Global Conference on Climate Change Adaptation for Fisheries and Aquaculture, Bangkok, 8–10 August 2016.* FAO Fisheries and Aquaculture Proceedings No. 61. Rome, FAO.

Galappaththi, E. K., & Berkes, F. (2014). Institutions for managing common-pool resources: the case of community-based shrimp aquaculture in northwestern Sri Lanka. *Maritime Studies, 13*(1), 1–16.

Galappaththi, E. K., & Berkes, F. (2015). Can co-management emerge spontaneously? Collaborative management in Sri Lankan shrimp aquaculture. *Marine Policy, 60,* 1–8.

Galappaththi, E. K., & Nayak, P. K. (2017). Two faces of shrimp aquaculture: Commonising vs. decommonising effects of a wicked driver. *Maritime Studies, 16*(1), 12.

Galappaththi, I. M., Galappaththi, E. K., & Kodithuwakku, S. S. (2017). Can start-up motives influence social-ecological resilience in community-based entrepreneurship setting? Case of coastal shrimp farmers in Sri Lanka. *Marine Policy, 86,* 156–163.

Handisyde, N., Telfer, T. C., & Ross, L. G. (2017). Vulnerability of aquaculture-related livelihoods to changing climate at the global scale. *Fish and Fisheries, 18*(3), 466–488.

Harkes, I., Drengstig, A., Kumara, M., Jayasinghe, J., & Huxham, M. (2015). Shrimp aquaculture as a vehicle for climate compatible development in Sri Lanka: The case of Puttalam Lagoon. *Marine Policy, 61,* 273–283.

Krause, G., Brugere, C., Diedrich, A., Ebeling, M. W., Ferse, S. C., Mikkelsen, E., ... Troell, M. (2015). A revolution without people? Closing the people–policy gap in aquaculture development. *Aquaculture, 447*, 44–55.

Munasinghe, M. N., Stephen, C., Abeynayake, P., & Abeygunawardena, I. S. (2010). Shrimp farming practices in the Puttallam district of Sri Lanka: implications for disease control, industry sustainability, and rural development. *Veterinary Medicine International, 2010.* doi:10.4061/2010/679130

NAqDA. (2017). National aquaculture development authority of Sri Lanka. Retrieved from www.naqda.gov.lk/statistics/Production-of-Shrimp/

Nayak, P. K., & Berkes, F. (2011). Commonisation and decommonisation: Understanding the processes of change in the Chilika Lagoon, India. *Conservation and Society, 9*(2), 132.

Ostrom, E. (1990). *Governing the commons: The evolution of institutions for collective action*. New York: Cambridge University Press.

Paprocki, K., & Huq, S. (2018). Shrimp and coastal adaptation: On the politics of climate justice. *Climate and Development, 10*(1), 1–3.

Chapter 6

Vicuña conservation and the reinvigoration of Indigenous communities in the Andes

Gabriela Lichtenstein and Carlos Cowan Ros

Introduction

Local people´s perceptions, beliefs and views on wildlife have changed over time. However, in the case of vicuñas, *Vicugna vicugna,* they were highly regarded by local herders since the early development of pastoralism (Yacobaccio 2009) and are still considered "the herds of the Gods" by most local Andean communities.

The populations of vicuña – a small member of the camelid family that roams in the Puna and Altiplano high Andean ecoregions in Argentina, Bolivia, Chile, Ecuador and Peru, reaching altitudes between 3,500 and 5,000 metres – have followed a volatile trajectory over the past several hundred years. While most of the literature on traditional commons deals with fisheries, forests, water management, irrigation and animal husbandry (Laerhoven and Ostrom 2007), wildlife use has not been as widely explored (see Bjørklund 1990; Smith et al. 2019). Although vicuñas can be considered an "uncommon" common-pool resource (CPR), they do exhibit the two principal characteristics of CPRs: (a) exclusion or the control of access of potential users is difficult; and, (b) each user is capable of subtracting from the welfare of all others. These are known as the *excludability problem* and the *subtractability problem*, respectively (Ostrom 1990; Berkes 1996; Ostrom et al. 1999). Both characteristics shape the history of vicuña use and conservation. According to Nayak and Berkes (2011), '*commonisation*' refers to a process through which a resource gets converted into a jointly used resource under commons institutions that deal with excludability and subtractability, and "*decommonisation*" refers to a process through which a jointly used resource under commons institutions loses these essential characteristics. In this chapter, we provide a historical background on the *decommonisation* processes of vicuñas and their near extinction that occurred following the Spanish Conquest in the Andean Region. We then analyse their recent *commonisation* led by Indigenous communities and state agents at different levels of government in the province of Jujuy, Argentina to identify the enabling conditions, and the socio-political, cultural, economic, and ecological benefits generated for those involved.

Study sites and methods

Data was collected in the Yavi district, in the NW of Argentina, during the period 2016–2018, through participant observation in seven vicuña captures (*chakus*), and participation in community workshops organised by the Secretary of Family Agriculture (SAF). Participant observation at the "Introductory course on vicuña monitoring and management", subsequent field visits offered by community representatives and technicians from Bolivia (2014), and two International Meetings of Vicuña Management Communities (2012 and 2017). We performed informal and semi-structured interviews with community members from El Condor, Suripugio, Larcas, and Escobar Tres Cerritos, technicians, legislators, local authorities and reviewed available secondary data.

A brief history of vicuña use and local institutions

The vicuña has a long history of association with humans. Remains of bones, fibres and skins were found in the archaeological record from the beginning of human settlement in the *Altiplano* (Yacobaccio 2009). By Incan times (1470–1535 ce), management of the wild vicuña was ritualized and followed strict rules, which ensured not only the fibre was available for the exclusive use of the Incan royal family, but also maintained a pattern of sustainable utilization of the wildlife resource (Flores de Ochoa 1994). Vicuñas were captured, sheared and released again into the wild every three to five years using a technique known as *chaku*, which required the organisation and participation of thousands of people. The rules and regulations under the *chaku*, including the death penalty for poachers, prevented overexploitation by controlling access to and use of the species (Custred 1979). A certain proportion of the animals were killed while the remainder were sheared and released. The fibre obtained was used for making special garments meant for exclusive use by the Inca, which warranted a limited use of the resource.

The pre-Hispanic Andean society was organised in *ayllus*. The *ayllu* was the basic kin unit of the Andean social structure; it functioned prior to Inca conquest, during the Inca and Spanish colonial periods. The dispersed fields, waters and animals that could be used by local Andean families belonged not only to them as alienated property but rather to the collective domain of the *ayllus*, communities and ethnic groups (Stern 1993). Households and *ayllus* activated and reinforced community or ethnic bonds by engaging in reciprocal exchanges of labour among relatives. The extension of cooperation allowed groups to reach out to access further resources and to engage in collective activities such as irrigation, bridge building or terracing. In short, these activities were meant to increase the productive forces at their disposal. The *ayllu* involved collective land stewardship and social relations within communities. Equal exchange was the core principle governing mutual reciprocity. The term *ayni* refers to specific forms of morally grounded cultural or economic reciprocity in both Quechua and Aymara languages. The *ayllu* and *ayni* were key cultural values that enabled Andean communities to cope and adapt to the hard environment where they lived (Walshe and Argumedo 2016).

The Spanish brought a completely new (foreign) worldview to the Andes. They had little respect for *ayllu* institutions, "safety nets" and principles, such as reciprocity, duality, common property, rule by consent, kinship ties and membership rights. A market driven extractivist economy was imposed over the years, and local communities were gradually alienated from the resources.

During the colonial period, in the province of Jujuy, the Spanish Crown gave part of the Indigenous land to the *Conquistadores* in the form of a gift (*merced real*). Many Indigenous communities were forced into the *encomienda* system, another colonial institution that regulated and ensured the rights of some *Conquistadores* to profit from Indigenous labour. In addition to these violent processes, mass population displacements and resettlements favoured the miscegenation of different ethnic groups, and the breakdown or total disintegration of customary institutions, such as the *ayllu*. This process of *decommonisation* intensified during the Republican stage, after 1810, through the exclusion of community land tenure in the Civil Code in favour of private property. The imposition of the rule on the Indigenous people to rent land, now under fiscal or private propriety, and their forced inclusion in the temporary labour market through a dedicated focus on capitalist relations of production (Madrazo 1982, Rutledge 1987). In the first half of the 19th century, what used to be a collective mode of production and organisation, gave rise to a "free peasantry" (Madrazo 1982) or a "semi-proletarian peasant" (Isla 1992) that still lived in rural villages, locally named as "communities". Unlike the Bolivian communities of the Central Andes where the existence of *ayllus* was still recorded in the 1990s, in Yavi only disjointed remnants of the *ayllus* institutions were found (Isla 1992).

The inclusion of vicuña fibre in the world trading system and its export to Europe beginning in the 16th century onwards produced a drastic decrease in its populations (Yacobaccio 2009). Vicuñas became, within little over a century, an open-access resource that was persecuted and hunted to the brink of extinction in order to obtain "the silk of the new world". By 1960, it was estimated that the vicuña population had dropped from its pre-colonial population of 2 million to an estimated 10,000 individuals. In summary, the destruction of local institutions and inclusion in the world trading market led to the near extinction of the species.

From near extinction to recovery

The decline in the status of vicuña had become so acute by the mid-1960s that concerted action among Andean countries to stop trading its fibre, and banning exports into manufacturing countries, appeared necessary to save the species from extinction (Custred 1979). A trade ban under CITES[1] on the export of vicuña pelts and the establishment of the Vicuña Convention paved the way to create a shared vision and collective conservation effort which led the recovery of the species. Today, the vicuña population is around 500,000 individuals (Acebes et al. 2019). Once population recovery was underway, the opening up of international trade – albeit regulated – and the subsequent incentives for sustainable use by local communities have further improved the status and long-term outlook for the species.

In 1979, Argentina, Bolivia, Chile, Peru and Ecuador signed the Convention on the Conservation and Management of the Vicuña. In Article I of the Vicuña Convention, and in the signatory states' subsequent submissions to CITES meetings, Andean people that had borne the burden of vicuña conservation were named as the main beneficiaries of future vicuña use. However, translating this article into national legislation and ensuring exclusive benefits to local people has proven difficult. In Bolivia, exclusive rights were granted to Andean communities to benefit from vicuñas. In the case of Chile, the rights of usufruct are not specified. In Argentina, only recently have usufruct rights been given to Andean communities in the province of Jujuy. In the province of Catamarca, however, international textile companies are allowed to manage vicuñas found on their land, and compete with local communities for access.[2] In Peru, the exclusive usufruct rights given to the communities were later extended to persons and businesses distinct from *campesino* communities, thus preparing the ground for large companies to take part in vicuña management (Lichtenstein 2010).

The establishment of vicuña management programmes

Vicuña management programmes developed in the Andes follow the logic of community-based wildlife management (CWM) (Western and Wright 1994; North, 1990, Hulme and Murphree 2001). These CWM programmes are a variation of what are collectively referred to as community-based natural resource management (CBNRM) initiatives, a form of natural resource management that emerged as a strategy to link conservation and community development through local participation and sustainable use. The rationale behind vicuña use projects is similar to the "linked incentives" model proposed by Salafsky and Wollenberg (2000), whereby allowing for the commercial utilization of fibre obtained from live-shorn vicuñas would encourage local participation and the development of positive local attitudes towards vicuña conservation. In turn, it was anticipated that such a model would result in a decrease in poaching (or a decrease in local support for poachers), the replacement of domestic livestock with vicuñas, an increase in tolerance for vicuñas on community lands, and greater support for their conservation measures. This rationale was based on the assumption that commercial use of vicuña fibre was a viable economic option that could contribute sufficient benefits to lower the cost of conservation for local communities. Vicuña conservation has been perceived as a cost by local people, who must allow vicuña to graze on their properties ("eating the best pastures") and mix with their livestock ("catching and transmitting diseases to domestic animals and bathing at drinking points") (Stollen et al. 2009). The hope is that instead of being antagonistic towards vicuñas, rural residents would assist in the government efforts to monitor and protect the species.

The five vicuña countries have adopted different models for vicuña management. The first management systems, developed in Peru and Bolivia, comprises vicuña management under common property regimes by *Aymara* and *Quechua* speaking communities. They use a capture and release system evolved through the traditional Inca *chaku* tradition, whereby large numbers of community members holding colourful flags chase vicuñas into a funnel from where vicuñas are taken to be shorn. Modern *chakus* incorporate animal welfare considerations and the use of modern technology (such as motorcycles in Chile) to support the vicuña roundup (Lichtenstein 2010).

Subsequently, in the 1990s, there was a trend in Peru, Argentina and Chile towards managing vicuñas in captivity and a management entity that ranged from single producers to families and communities. At present, both captive and wild vicuña management co-exist in Argentina, Chile and Peru. Bolivia is the only country that remains committed to managing vicuñas in the wild under common property regimes. Whereas wild management has the potential to create economic incentives for the conservation of vicuña and its habitat, the link between captive management and conservation is less obvious (Lichtenstein 2006). Vicuña is one of the most valuable and highly priced sources of animal fibre on the international market. The luxury garments made from vicuña fibre are sold in the most exclusive fashion houses in Europe, USA, Asia and Australia to the world's wealthiest elites (Lichtenstein 2010). Although vicuña poaching decreased significantly with the implementation of trade regulations and management systems, it still has an impact in all Andean countries, which is a prime concern for policymakers.

Vicuña management in Jujuy, legal framework and early experiences

In Argentina, vicuñas are distributed over five provinces, but only vicuña populations from Jujuy, Catamarca, and just recently Salta provinces have been transferred to CITES Appendix II.[3] In the case of Jujuy province, until 2005, the predominant management method was captive management by individual ranch owners (Lichtenstein 2010). The justification for developing a scheme based on individual production given by the Argentinean Government to CITES in 1997 grossly disregarded existing local communities and the possibility of *commonisation,* and stated that contrary to what we see in Peru or Bolivia, lands in Argentina had no community (but individual) titles in the Puna, and local people had an "individualistic" form of production.

During 2003–2005, the Cooperative *Los Pioneros*, in Cieneguillas, Jujuy, managed vicuñas in the wild with the technical support of a group of scientists and the MACS project. This was later followed by a cooperative in Santa Catalina (Arzamendia et al. 2008). These early experiences contributed to a different outlook on vicuña management in the province.

A brief portrait of Andean communities from Yavi

The rural population of the Puna Jujeña is traditionally grouped in sparse localities called "parajes" or "villages" and more recently "communities" most of which are inhabited by elders (Cowan Ros 2013a). The Yavi district is located in the Puna region of the province of Jujuy, extreme North of Argentina (Figure 6.1). The Puna is a uniform plateau located more than 3,300 metres above sea level and characterised by very harsh conditions such as low annual rainfall, a high daily temperature range, and low primary productivity. Climatic and management factors such as altitude, harsh weather conditions, destructive frosts, soil erosion, pasture reduction caused by overgrazing, scarcity of water, and periodic droughts reduce the options for agriculture and limit economic activities. This is compounded by the lack of special techniques for enhancing production in desert environments, distance from markets, and low demand for regional products (Lichtenstein and Vila 2003). The lack of opportunities can encourage locals to leave their homes to find paid work in rural areas and cities at lower altitudes.

At present, rural social reproduction strategies are defined in families or domestic groups and are subject to community rules and institutions. Households have difficulties in meeting their social reproduction needs and implement multi-purpose strategies in which they combine income from agricultural production that results from temporary or permanent labour, services (from transport, warehouses, etc.), social assistance or pension schemes. Regarding agricultural production, capital and labour are the two resources that are most scarce. The lack of labour is usually compensated by mutual help between neighbours, in a balanced reciprocity modality that is locally called "*tornavuelta*", whereas the lack of financing is compensated through contributions that sporadically arrive through development programmes (Cowan Ros 2013a).

Community life implies fulfilling rights and obligations. The roads, the community hall, the chapel, the soccer field and patronal parties are managed through collective action. The community land is common property. The community territory is usually divided into three areas: residence, cultivation and grazing. Agricultural production and sale of agricultural produce are mostly

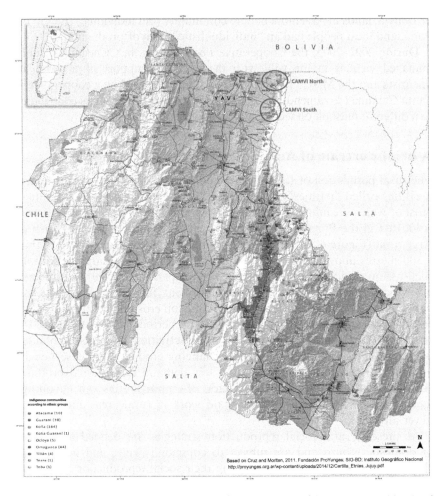

Figure 6.1 Yavi district in the Puna region of the province of Jujuy, extreme North of Argentina. A colour version of this image is downloadable as an eResource from www.routledge.com/9780367138004.

at the household level. Some resources, as water, are managed as commons (Cowan Ros 2013a). The community assembly is the institution within which the distribution of roles and jobs is planned and organised, and the performance of each family regarding community work is controlled and evaluated according to their rights and obligations. In terms of their relationships the outside world, especially relating to claims and negotiations with the government authorities, family representatives are expected to accompany and assist the President of the community.

The beginning of the (re) commonisation

In Argentina, according to the 1994 Constitutional reform, the management of natural resources is given provincial jurisdiction. In Jujuy, a Provincial Law (No. 5634) was passed in 2009 with regards to vicuña management. In agreement with the Convention for the Conservation and Management of the Vicuña, this law specified that vicuña shearing could be carried out only on live animals in the wild and it granted the right of sustainable use of vicuña to the Andean inhabitants with effective residence in the Puna.[4] A provincial management plan (PCMSV) was established in 2014 with the participation of an advisory board composed of experts from scientific and technological institutions as well as consultations with referents of Indigenous communities and agricultural producers (Arzamendia et al. 2012). In 2016, a Registry of Andean Aboriginal Communities and Local Producers Managers of Vicuñas was created.[5] In order to get permission to manage vicuñas, local communities had to be registered and present to the Provincial Authority of Biodiversity (DPRGB), a local management plan (the contents of which are defined in the PCMSV), as well as the endorsement of the community. Thus, in Jujuy occurred a paradigm shift in vicuña management, moving from captive management to wild management. Additionally, through legislation at the national and, fundamentally, the provincial level, and the alignment of such legislation with international treaties, a multi-level governance system was created for the conservation and sustainable management of vicunas for the benefit of local communities.

Beginning in the second half of the 1990s, communities in the Puna from Jujuy were re-invigorated, with vicuña management leading the way in promoting collective action and commonisation. The reinvigoration of communities resulted from a process of re-articulation and reaffirmation of Indigenous identity associated with recognition in the national and provincial legislation of Indigenous peoples as subjects of collective law, in particular through the categorization of the Indigenous community as a legal figure of public law, and their right to obtain titles to the communal lands that they traditionally inhabited (Cowan Ros and Nussbaumer 2013).

In the following years, communities received legal recognition with support from the Church and rural development NGOs. They had to formalise a representative organisational structure for their memberships – a "community assembly" – demarcate their territories, censor their members and channel their legal claim to recover ownership of the lands they had traditionally inhabited but mostly owned by the provincial state (Cowan Ros 2013a). Until 2010, 124 communities of the Puna, belonging to the Kollas, Atacamas and Toara ethnic groups, had been registered in the Provincial Registry of Aboriginal Communities of Jujuy (García Moritán and Cruz 2011).

Community institutions in the Puna were reinforced by the work of rural extension workers, NGOs and state agencies that since 1990 have implemented collaborative projects, frequently inspired by a certain idealisation of Andean *ayllu*. Projects have mostly involved improving community infrastructure, agricultural production and marketing. From their interventions, they have sought to mobilise the families of each community group, and promote intra and inter-community organisational structures around the resolution of common problems and the production and commercialisation of Andean products (Cowan Ros 2013b).

From conflicts with vicuñas to the formation of the CAMVI

In 2010, leaders of the Yavi community expressed their interest in managing vicuñas to the rural extension agents from the SAF with whom they were already working on several rural development projects. The Yavi communities complained that vicuñas were competing with their livestock for grass and water and they wanted either to be able to benefit from them or be allowed to reduce their numbers. However, not all communities in the area were interested in managing vicuñas. Some communities considered vicuñas as sacred animals and preferred not to manage them, while others were not interested in incorporating another productive strategy. Finally, members of eight Indigenous communities from the Yavi district accompanied by an interdisciplinary group with technicians from the SAF, the National Institute of Agricultural Technology (INTA), and the Provincial Authority of Biodiversity (DPRGB) undertook the project, which resulted in mutual learning amongst all the parties. The costly materials for building the infrastructure for capturing vicuñas (funnel and corral) were provided by the Ministry of Environment of Jujuy, and the shearing equipment and training by the INTA.

Between 2012 and 2014, technical support (through 12 workshops) was given to the communities by the SAF with regards to different aspects of vicuña management (e.g., national and international legislation; animal welfare, population monitoring, etc.). A very important keystone was a visit by technicians and community members from across the border in Bolivia in 2014 and 2015, who shared their approach and experiences of collective vicuña management. At the end of the process, local communities developed their own local vicuña management plans with the technical support from SAF and DPRGB and following the guidelines of the Provincial Management Plan.

The process had a positive impact on vicuña conservation. Over the time, community members assumed responsibility of contributing towards the conservation of the vicuñas that inhabited in the communal territory. This involved mutual surveillance, avoiding attacks by domestic dogs, and alerting the police in case of poaching. Some community groups chose not to fence or remove fences when they existed in "vegas" (highland wetlands) to facilitate access to vicuñas. In other cases, it was decided to reserve part of the community grassland area for exclusive grazing of vicuñas, with a view to increasing forage availability and attracting more animals.

Over the years the vicuña management communities created an organisational structure called the Andean Managing Communities of Vicuña or CAMVI (for the acronym in Spanish). The CAMVI is divided in CAMVI Norte (North) and CAMVI Sur (South), each of them is composed by Vicuña Management Committees of nearby communities (Figure 6.2). In the case of CAMVI Norte, the communities of Larcas, Inticancha, Suripugio and Quirquinchos manage the vicuñas on their individual territories. Each community has its own Vicuña Management Committee which develops a local management plan and carries out the procedures before the DPRGB to be registered. Given that *chakus* require around 100 people, which is not that easy to get in the rural area, communities "lend" community members to participate in *chakus* in other communities with the logic of "tornavuelta", a traditional practice of mutual aid widely practiced among relatives and neighbours in the area based on the principle of "balance reciprocity" (as

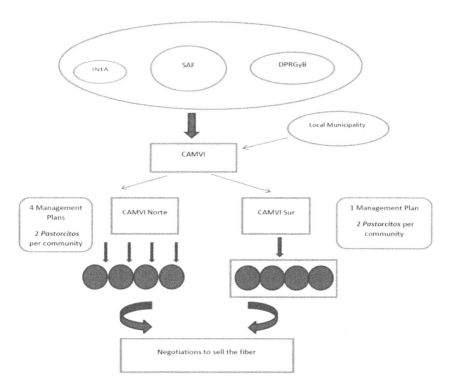

Figure 6.2 Key institutional linkages facilitating the activities of the vicuña management project. A colour version of this image is downloadable as an eResource from www.routledge.com/9780367138004.

mentioned earlier). As a result, if 18 members of Larcas attended the *chaku* in Suripugio, Suripugio will send 18 of its members to Larca's *chaku*. The fibre obtained is commercialised by each community of CAMVI Norte individually.

In the case of CAMVI Sur, some communities that have been already associated since the end of the 1990s for the production and marketing of handicrafts, llama meat and agricultural products, created a single management committee and formulated a single management plan comprising all activities. In this case, the communal area for vicuña management encompasses the four communities of Corral Blanco Cieneguillas Azul K'asa, Cholacor, Escobar Tres Cerritos, and El Condor. The families of each community interested in the production of vicuña fibre elect a representative who meets with those of the other communities to coordinate actions to implement the management plan. Members of the four communities participate in all of the *chakus*. The fibre that results from the *chakus* from CAMVI Sur is sold as block sale. Around 60 percent of families from the communities in CAMVI Sur, and 80 percent of the families from the communities in CAMVI Norte are involved in vicuña management.

Community members involved in vicuña management in CAMVI meet regularly from March to August with the SAF rural extensionists, to discuss options for fibre commercialisation, and negotiate a capture calendar, which goes from September to early December every year, plan activities, divide roles and responsibilities among the attendees, and evaluate the performance of the previous year. Agreeing on a *chaku* calendar enables communities to share the infrastructure and shearing equipment which rotates from one community to the other, and for the technical staff to be present at all events.

CAMVI meetings result in an opportunity for discussion and agreement. In this context communities agree on local norms and practices as well as sanction measures for communities that do not follow the norms or have high vicuña mortality in their *chakus*. High vicuña mortality in one community can result in the members missing a whole year of not being allowed to perform vicuña management by the other communities. In such cases, customary institutions have devised effective governance rules that are stricter than common law.

The chaku

The *chakus* are led by the *pastorcitos* (little shepherds). These are young community members (two per community) who have received training in vicuña monitoring and are trained to follow vicuña groups throughout the year. It is the *pastorcitos*, after their intensive observation of vicuña movements, the topography and the availability of labour, who decide where to install the funnel for the *chaku* with the supervision of technicians. The *pastorcitos* work *ad honorem*. In each *chaku*, *pastorcitos* from other community groups participate to help, observe and learn from the experiences of other communities. The new communities that join the vicuña management are invited to participate in the *chakus* of neighbouring communities, to receive training and gain experience. These exchanges contribute to the strengthening of social capital, enabling collective action and improving the *chaku* technology.

The day before the *chaku* takes place, a request for permission from *Pachamama* (Mother Earth) and *Coquena* (mythological protector of camelids) is undertaken. Part of the community group is mobilised to the area where the *chaku* will take place and they make an offering to the *Pachamama* following ancestral rituals, in order to thank and ask for good results (which imply no vicuña casualties and many animals being captured). This ancestral practice provides evidence to the persistence of Andean cultural references, in particular the link between people and nature. *Chakus* articulate ancient traditions such as coloured flags and modern technology in the shape of walkie-talkies). The human display parallels those used to capture donkeys, foxes or pumas. Around 100 people participate in each *chaku*. In the early hours of the morning they are divided into ten groups (8–10 participants each) of *arreo* and are arranged along a distant perimeter of approximately 2 km from the enclosure pen. The starting voice is provided by the group that commands the herding, led by a *pastorcito*. The groups advance in silence stretching out ropes with coloured stripes to make a human barrier (Figures 6.3 and 6.4), which is used to herd vicuñas into a funnel trap where the animals are sheared. Each member assumes a specific function. Young men are most involved in catching vicuñas from the pen, weighing, holding, shearing, and moving them, along with the removal of the infrastructure. Collecting the fleece, bagging, and separating the sow, are among the roles that women usually play. Once the shearing is finished and the sleeve and capture pen are removed, the vicuñas are released and all the participants share lunch (prepared by the women from the community) where the *chaku* took place.

The *chakus* are inspected by DPRGB technicians. They classify and register the captured animals, determine which are suitable for shearing based on age, sanitary and gestational status, and fleece length. Animal welfare criteria are also agreed upon to complement those of the PCMSV. At present, the rule is to use a threshold of three dead vicuñas and five hours of *chaku* beyond which activities are to be suspended, and captured vicuñas (whether sheared or not) released. This is to avoid further deaths of vicuñas.

Socio-economic impacts of vicuña management

Between 2014 and 2018, 64 *chakus* were carried out by nine communities (eight from the department of Yavi and one from the department of Rinconada) harvesting 1003.03 kilograms of fibre (Table 6.1). Vicuña mortality fell over time, even though the number of captured vicuñas increased.

Figure 6.3 Community members from El Condor, Jujuy, making a human barrier to herd vicuñas. A colour version of this image is downloadable as an eResource from www.routledge.com/9780367138004.
Source: Lichtenstein.

Figure 6.4 Last stage of vicuña herding, with vicuñas already inside the corral in El Condor, Yavi. A colour version of this image is downloadable as an eResource from www.routledge.com/9780367138004.
Source: Cowan Ross.

Table 6.1 Chakus in Yavi and Rinconada Departments, Jujuy

Year	N° chakus	N° of communities	N° vicuñas captured	Kilograms of fibre	% de vicuñas dead/ captured vicuñas
2014	3	3	556	40,825	0.36
2015	6	N/A	N/A	116,310	N/A
2016	11	5	810	136,590	1.36
2017	25	9	1.813	316,140	0.83
2018	19	9	2.530	393,165	0.27
Total	64			1003,030	

New communities were trained to conduct *chakus*. Given that personnel from the DPRGB and SAF have to be present to oversee the *chakus*, the lack of public resources to control and support the *chaku* operations created a bottleneck to increase the number of vicuñas captured and communities involved in these activities.

In 2018, the CAMVI member communities made their first sale of 600 kilograms of raw fibre harvested between 2014 and 2017. To improve their negotiation power, the communities that make up the CAMVI as its members jointly negotiated the sale to a single company. The proceeds were distributed among the community groups according to what each one had produced. Some community groups chose to allocate the money raised for the purchase of community goods and / or for the maintenance of existing ones. In other cases, the money was distributed among the families, according to the labour contributed by them. Given the ban on the use of vicuñas over previous decades, spinning and handicraft weaving infrastructure and technology was lost in the region. In the case of the CAMVI Sur, 10% of the fibre harvested was used for spinning and making garments with an objective of recovering the lost textile tradition of the region and provide added value to the fibre.

Vicuña management by Yavi communities resulted in the creation of a shared vision and collective conservation effort for the species and its fragile environment, resulting from the convergence of Andean culture and scientific knowledge. The *commonisation* of vicuña management strengthened and enhanced community identity, and social cohesion, revitalised old traditions of collective action (such as *ayni* and *tornavuelta*), strengthened and created relationships among communities and new institutional arrangements, recuperated local knowledge, developed a framework for local participation, solidified land claims, provided incentives to avoid migration to cities (specially for young people), and created alternative sources of income for Indigenous people that are usually forgotten by the state. CAMVI representatives have participated yearly in the Vicuña Convention since 2015; and they hosted an international meeting of vicuña producers in 2017 which aimed to enhance collaboration across borders, discuss common concerns, and facilitate

tangible participatory mechanisms for full and effective Indigenous participation at the Vicuña Convention. Participating in vicuña use helped remote
(and usually neglected) communities to become visible to local and central
governments, and to strengthen their voice and power in policy processes in
order to be better placed to ask for land titles, credit, schools, health service,
better roads, infrastructure and support for economic activities. The social
capital generated enabled and encouraged cooperation and strengthened
collective action for the management of other commons such as grasslands,
water for human consumption and irrigation, bushes for cooking and heating,
roads, etc.

Key factors of the commonisation process

According to Nayak and Berkes (2011), the processes of *commonisation* and
decommonisation are continuous, and potentially two-way. Vicuña management was *decommonised* following the Spanish Conquest, due to the expro-
priation of land and resources from Indigenous peoples, in addition to mass
population displacement and resettlement. The case study in Yavi district,
however, illustrates a reversal process of *commonisation* driven by cooperation
among members of Indigenous communities and state agents at different
levels of government in Jujuy. This process is not unique to Jujuy, collective
action for vicuña management in Peru and Bolivia could also be analysed in
the light of a *commonisation* process that resulted in social cohesion and a
revival of local traditions (Renaudeau d'Arc 2005).

In this study we identified a series of factors that promoted *commonisation*
in the Yavi district, many of which overlap with the factors that account for
sustainable institutional arrangements to manage the commons (Ostrom
1990, Agrawal 2002) (Table 6.2).

Resource system characteristics: The population recovery of the vicuña, after
indiscriminate hunting, has created a good resource base that has enabled the
performance of the *chakus*. Two models were developed: the one, practiced in
the CAMVI Norte (each community performing a *chaku* in its own territory);
and the one, practiced in the CAMVI Sur (communities performing *chakus*
collectively in different communities). Given the mobility of vicuñas and the
unpredictability associated with the captures, a model followed by CAMVI
Sur could be predicted to increase the chances of success.

Relatively low population densities: Low human population density,
resulting from the continuous rural-urban migration, creates a strong need
for collaboration among community members and work together with other
communities when it comes to vicuña herding.

Rules about inclusion and exclusion: Only community members participate in the *chakus* and are entitled to the benefits derived. The CAMVI has
formulated rules for allowing communities to enter CAMVI and graduated
sanctions for those communities whose *chakus* result in large vicuña casualties.

Socio-cultural factors: *commonisation* in vicuña management occurs within the framework of a wider process of ethnic re-articulation led by Indigenous groups whose life in the community emerges as a diacritical feature. The existence of traditional community institutions with a customary governance regime enabled the adaptation of already existent rules as well as the development of new ones for conflict resolution, sanctions, and monitoring as a part of vicuña management. The customary systems of reciprocity or *tornavuelta* facilitated collective action. Vicuña management in the wild follows the local agricultural production mode (i.e. open pastures without fencing). In addition, the Andean worldview of nature and the norms about the use of natural resources for *Pachamama* contribute to the sustainable use of vicuñas. As in the case of Chillika lagoon (Nayak and Berkes 2011), a traditionally established strong connection between the people and the resource – material and spiritual – facilitated resource *commonisation* in the case of vicuña management.

Enabling legislation: The configuration of a multi-level governance system (transnational, national and provincial) for the conservation and regulation of the production and commercialisation of vicuña fibre favours *commonisation*. Through multiple benefits to the local inhabitants the governance system creates conditions that discourage poaching and promote wild vicuña management in a collaborative manner. By recognising local communities, providing land titles and allocating exclusive use rights to communities, the government of Jujuy created legal pre-conditions for the effective functioning of local level institutions. This is extremely important because such legislation does not exist in some other provinces of Argentina, such as Catamarca, where private companies are allowed to compete with local communities for vicuña management.

Land tenure: The territorial structure in the *Puna* is mostly occupied by Indigenous communities who hold or can claim titles to land. Under this condition, availability of private land and market for it is minimal. The National Constitution recognises community tenure of land by Indigenous people which is non-transferable or inalienable.

Supportive government policies: The existence of public policies (and funding) targeted at Indigenous communities aims to enhance collective action in the area. These resources have also enabled public institutions and increased the involvement of local communities. The *chakus* were visited by the governor of Jujuy on several occasions, which was considered symbolic in terms of political support to the communities.

Strong cross scale linkages with rural development institutions: According to Berkes (2007), for effective community-based conservation the project needs to find strategies to strengthen existing commons institutions, build new linkages horizontally and vertically, engage in capacity-building, build trust, encourage mutual learning, and invest enough time and resources to achieve these objectives. All of these features contributed towards *commonisation* in this study. Horizontal and vertical linkages between the CAMVI and different state agencies at the national, provincial and municipal levels significantly contributed to the vicuña management process. Further, strong accountability and trust between these institutions along with a past history of working together added to the process.

Economic factors: There is a need for rural people to increase their household income and incorporate new economic activities that take place beyond the individual (household) level. Vicuña management can easily fit in with already existing activities and does not overlap in terms of labor, land, water or capital. Due to the nature of the product, i.e., as opposed to meat or wool that can be sold at the individual level, collective action is the best way to capture vicuñas and commercialise vicuña fibre. This is a group activity and requires collective action for success.

Technological innovation: When it comes to common-pool resources that are mobile, such as vicuña, wild management is the most appropriate technique (Renaudeau d´Arc, 2005). The amount of labour required for vicuña management is best facilitated by cooperation among community members. The involvement of the government departments brings training and innovation in technology that is crucial for vicuña management.

(Re)commonisations of vicuñas, benefits and some threats

The *commonisation* of vicuña management produces benefits for the inhabitants of the Yavi area, and society in general. It provides a new source of income for rural families that live in poverty, while contributing towards local and regional development. It also generates ecosystem services by species conservation and the maintenance of biodiversity. So, the benefits of vicuña management and commonisation around it has benefits that are social-ecological in nature. It has helped to reinforce the ongoing ethnic re-articulation processes, contributing to the revaluation and updating of Andean cultural references and the recognition of rights of the Indigenous communities.

Nevertheless, those benefits are threatened by *decommonisation* processes: Firstly, persistent rural-urban migration creates a deficiency in the labour force that could compromise the possibility of conducting *chakus*. Secondly, in economic terms, since the start of the operations, CAMVI has sold fibre on only one occasion. The continuity of vicuña fibre production and the *commonisation* process relies not just on socio-cultural benefits but also on satisfactory sustainable financial gains from the sale of the fibre and crafts over the long term. Thirdly, in political-institutional terms, the redefinition of the legislative and institutional framework and the discontinuity in the political support of the successive provincial governments of Jujuy could threaten the continuity of the processes of commonisation. Encroachment

Table 6.2 Key factors of the *commonisation* process of vicuñas

Key factors	Description
Resource conditions	• Good resource base • Vicuña mobility • Unpredictability of resource flows
Relatively low population densities	• Small population size meant less competitor and the need to collaborate • Easier to form more cohesive and manageable groups
Rules about inclusion and exclusion	• Only community members can participate • Graduated sanctions
Socio-cultural factors	• Pre-existence of community institutions with a customary governance • Traditionally strong link with the resource • Already in place mechanisms of reciprocity • Vicuña management in the wild follows the local agricultural production mode
Enabling legislation	• Multi-level governance system (transnational, national and provincial) for the conservation and regulation of the production and commercialisation of vicuña fibre to the benefit of the local inhabitants • Allocation of exclusive use rights to communities in Jujuy
Land tenure	• Non-transferable or inalienable condition of community land tenure by Indigenous people
Supportive government policies	• Public policies (and funding) targeted at Indigenous communities in place
Strong cross scale linkages and development institutions	• Strong horizontal and vertical linkages between the CAMVI and state agents of different dependencies
Economic factors	• Previous experience in collective commercialisation • It pays selling large volumes of fibre, which can only be gathered collectively
Technological innovation	• Wild management is the most appropriate technique and given the amount of labour required, it is facilitated by cooperation

by the private sectors through offering "partnerships" in which they "finance the captures and provide wages" is fast becoming a major concern. Lastly, the sustainability of the state support with regards to technical and financial assistance to the vicuña communities is a key factor to guarantee the continuity of the *commonisation* process.

However, despite the threats, the number of communities involved in the process and the number of *chakus are* increasing in Jujuy every year, as well as the links between communities. The recent change of appendix of vicuñas from Salta Province at the CITES Cop 2019 provides the opportunity of *commonisation* to extend to communities in the neighbouring provinces.

Community members from Salta were already involved in training and *chakus* in Jujuy, which created new collaborations and network among these communities.

As in the case of other commons, the global market has commodified vicuña fibre while integrating it to the capital accumulation logic. In contrast, some areas of the Puna such as Yavi host significant processes of commonisation that are reshaping ancient knowledge, traditions and local forms of production while re-connecting local communities with one another and the vicuñas.

Acknowledgements

We thank CONICET for funding. Tojo Sardinas, and colleagues from SAF, Sandra Romero and technicians from INTA for their logistic support that enabled us to participate in chakus and meetings. We are grateful to the CAMVI for sharing chakus, community meetings, and their knowledge with us, and to Fikret Berkes and James Robson for revising the manuscript.

Notes

1 The Convention on International Trade in Endangered Species of Wild Fauna and Flora (CITES) is an agreement between governments that regulates the international trade of wildlife and wildlife products. The Convention has three Appendices (I, II, and III) that denote different level of protection from trade.
2 www.diputados.gov.ar/proyectos/proyecto.jsp?exp=2117-D-2014.
3 The vicuña population from Salta province was transferred to CITES Appendix II at the CITES CoP18 (Geneva 2019).
4 For further details please refer to www.ecolex.org/details/legislation/ley-no-5634-plan-de-conservacion-y-manejo-sustentable-de-la-vicuna-en-silvestria-lex-faoc122954/.
5 For further details, please refer to the Official Gazette 2017 on creation of a registry for Indigenous communities and local producers and managers of vicuñas at http://boletinoficial.jujuy.gob.ar/?p=17647.

References

Acebes, P., Wheeler, J., Baldo, J., Tuppia, P., Lichtenstein, G., Hoces, D. and Franklin, W. L. (2018). Vicugna vicugna: The IUCN red list of threatened species, e.T22956A18540534. Accessed on 14 October 2019 at: www.researchgate.net/publication/329276857_Vicugna_vicugna_The_IUCN_Red_List_of_Threatened_Species_2018.

Arzamendia Y., Maidana R., Vilá B. and Bonacic C. (2008). Wild vicuñas management in Cieneguillas, Jujuy (Argentina). In: *South American Camelids Research*. Editor: Frank E., Antonini M. & Toro O. Wageningen Academic Publishers. The Netherlands: Wageningen, 139–146.

Arzamendia, Y., Baldo, J. and B. Vila. (2012). *Lineamientos para un Plan de Conservación y Uso Sustentable de vicuñas en Jujuy, Argentina*. Jujuy: EDIUNJU.

Berkes, F (2007). Community-based conservation in a globalized world. *Proceedings of the National Academy of Sciences,* 104(39), 15188–15193.

Berkes, F. (1996). Social systems, ecological systems, and property rights. In: Hanna, S., Folke, C. and Maler, K. G. eds. *Rights to Nature,* Washington, DC: Island Press, 87–107.

Bjørklund, I. (1990). Sami reindeer pastoralism as an Indigenous resource management system in northern Norway: A contribution to the common property debate. *Development and Change,* 21, 75–86.

Cowan Ros, C. (2013a). *La trama de lo social: Familia, vecindad y facciones en la producción de prácticas políticas en comunidades aborígenes de la Puna argentina.* Madrid: Editorial Académica Española.

Cowan Ros, C. (2013b). Laberintos de emancipación: Reciprocidad y conflicto en las relaciones de mediación entre agentes de promoción social y dirigentes campesinos. *Revista de Antropología Social.* Universidad Complutense de Madrid. n° 22, 287–312.

Cowan Ros, C. and Nussbaumer, B. (2013). "Comunidad indígena": (Des)encuentros de sentidos. *Cuadernos de Antropología Social,* 37, 109–137. Buenos Aires: Universidad de Buenos Aires.

Custred, G. (1979). Hunting technologies in Andean culture. *Journal de la Societe des Americanistes, Musee de l'Homme, Paris,* 7–12.

Flores-Ochoa, J. (1994). Man's relationship with the camelids. In: Martinez, J; Patthey, F y O. Sons (eds.) *Gold of the Andes: the llamas, alpacas, vicuñas and guanacos of South America.* Barcelona: Francis O. Patthey and Sons.

García Moritán, M. and Cruz, B. (2011). *Comunidades originarias y grupos étnicos de la provincia de Jujuy.* Tucumán: Ed. Del Subtrópico.

Hulme, D. and Murphree, M. (2001). (eds.) *African Wildlife and Livelihoods: The Promise and Performance of Community Conservation.* Oxford: James Currey Ltd.

Isla, A. (1992). "Dos regiones, un origen: Entre el 'silencio' y la furia". In: Isla (org.) *Sociedad y articulación en las Tierras Altas jujeñas. Crisis terminal de un modelo de desarrollo.* Buenos Aires: Proyecto ECIRA, ASAL, MLAL, 167–215.

Jujuy. (2009). Ley 5.634 Plan de Conservación y Manejo Sustentable de la Vicuña en Silvestría. Legislatura de la Provincia de Jujuy. Boletín Oficial e Imprenta del Estado, Provincia de Jujuy, San Salvador, Argentina. Sancionada 26/11/2009.

Jujuy. (2014). Decreto N° 5175-G-2014. Plan de Conservación y Manejo Sustentable de la Vicuña. Poder Ejecutivo de Jujuy. http://boletinoficial.jujuy.gob.ar/?p=39886

Kellert, S. R., Mehta, I., Ebbin, S. A and Lichtenfeld, L. L. (2000). Community natural resource management: Promise, rhetoric and reality. *Society and Natural Resources,* 13, 705–715.

Laerhoven, F. and Ostrom, E. (2007). Traditions and trends in the study of the commons. *International Journal of the Commons,* 1, 3–28.

Lichtenstein, G. (2006). Manejo de vicuñas en cautiverio: El modelo del CEA INTA Abrapampa. In: Vilá, B. (eds.), *Investigación, conservación y manejo de vicuñas.* Lujan: Proyecto MACS, Universidad Nacional de Lujan, 133–146.

Lichtenstein, G. (2010). Vicuña conservation and poverty alleviation? Andean communities and international fibre markets. *International Journal of the Commons,* 4 (1), 100–121.

Lichtenstein, G. and Vila, B. M. (2003). Vicuna use by Andean communities: An overview. *Mountain Research and Development,* 23(2), 198–202.

Madrazo, G. (1982). Hacienda y encomienda en los Andes. *La Puna argentina bajo el marquesado de Tojo. Siglos VIII a XIX*. Buenos Aires: Fondo Editorial.

Nayak, P. and Berkes, F. (2011). Commonisation and decommonisation: Understanding the processes of change in the Chilika Lagoon, India. *Conservation and Society*, 9(2), 132–145.

North, D. C. (1990). *Institutions, Institutional Change and Economic Performance*. Cambridge: Cambridge University Press.

Ostrom, E. (1990). *Governing the Commons: The Evolution of Institutions for Collective Action*. Cambridge: Cambridge University Press.

Ostrom, E., Burger, J., Field, C. B, Norgaard, R. B. and Policansky, D. (1999). Revisiting the commons: Local lessons, global challenges. *Science*, 284, 278–282.

Renaudeau d'Arc, N. (2005). Community-Based Conservation and Vicuña Management in the Bolivian Highlands. PhD thesis, School of Development Studies, University of East Anglia.

República Argentina. (1987). Examen de enmienda a los Apéndices I y II. www.cites.org/esp/cop/10/prop/index.shtml.

Rutledge, I. (1987). *Cambio agrario e integración: El desarrollo del capitalism en Jujuy. 1550–1960*. Buenos Aires: Proyecto ECIRA, FFyL-CICSO, UBA-MLAL.

Salafsky, N. and Wollenberg, E. (2000). Linking livelihoods and conservation: A conceptual framework and scale for assessing the integration of human needs and biodiversity. *World Development*, 28(8), 1421–1438.

Smith, H., Marrocoli, S., Garcia Lozano, A. and Basurto, X. (2019). Hunting for common ground between wildlife governance and commons scholarship. *Conservation Biology*, 33, 9–21. doi:10.1111/cobi.13200.

Stollen, K. A, Lichtenstein, G. and Renaudeau d' Arc, N. (2009). Local participation in vicuña management. In: Gordon, I. (eds.) *The vicuña: The theory and practice of community-based wildlife management*. New York: Springer, 81–96.

Sonogorwa, A. N. (1999). Community based wildlife management (CWM) in Tanzania: Are the communities interested? *World Development*, 27(12), 2061–2079.

Stern, S. J. (1993). *Peru's Indian people and the challenge of the Spanish Conquest: Huamanga to 1640*. Madison: University of Wisconsin Press.

Walshe, R. and Argumedo, A. (2016). Ayni, Ayllu, Yanantin and Chanincha: The cultural values enabling adaptation to climate change in communities of the potato park, in the Peruvian Andes. *GAIA – Ecological Perspectives for Science and Society*, 25(3), 166–173.

Western, D. and Wright, R. M. (1994). *Natural Connections: Perspectives in Community-Based Conservation*, Washington, DC: Island Press.

Yacobaccio, H. (2009). The historical relationship between people and the vicuña. 7–20. In: Gordon I. J. (eds.) *The vicuña: The theory and practice of community-based wildlife management*. New York: Springer, 124.

Chapter 7

Commoning and climate justice

Patricia E. (Ellie) Perkins

Introduction

As a settler and an immigrant in Canada, I acknowledge and thank the First Nations and Indigenous peoples of the territories where I live and work: the Anishinaabe, Haudenosaunee, Huron-Wendat, and many other First Peoples. Their gifts, traditions and ongoing climate justice leadership inspire reciprocity.

A recent, sobering book by James Daschuk tells the story of the six years from 1885 to 1891 in which at least a third of the Indigenous population of the Canadian plains died of disease and starvation (Daschuk 2013). During this period, many communities held *matahitowin*, or the Give-Away Dance, a sacred dance for Pahkahkos, the spirit of famine, in which people gave away everything they had in order to change their fortune. We may all be entering into a new period of crisis and insecurity due to climate chaos. Will our first reaction be to give away and share what we have?

For some cultures, such a response to calamity is natural. Culture and governance traditions play a key role in material and psychic wellbeing. The greed and selfishness that we often assume are "human nature" may not be as deeply-engrained as we think. I believe this has important implications for commoning, which depends on sharing well-governed common pool resources and works best when giving is respected and socially rewarded so that there can be "reciprocity between what is given and what is taken" (Federici and Caffentzis 2014: i102).

Indigenous economist Ronald Trosper states:

> (T)he world is in the midst of a change in thinking. ... Climate change is showing that the world depends on a common pool resource, the atmos-phere. Other common pool resources, such as fresh water and forests, are also important. Simply put, the world is discovering that people depend upon these common pool resources more than they believed. How should people organize themselves when they depend upon a common pool

resource? We need to study examples of people who have developed complex and productive systems using a common pool resource as the fundamental source of wealth.

(Trosper 2009: 4)

Indigenous peoples on the Pacific Coast developed complex socio-political-cultural systems centred around the potlatch, a ceremony where leaders demonstrated and confirmed their status by respectfully distributing wealth to all community members (Trosper 2009; Umeek 2011). "The chief shows his worthiness by generating the surplus required for the feast, and the guests acknowledge his position when they accept the gifts" (Trosper 2009: 20). Or as Nuu-chah-nulth hereditary chief Umeek says, "(G)iving is associated with abundance, whereas not giving is associated with stagnation (since the circulation, or giving, of goods and assistance is essential to life)" (Umeek 2011: 152).

The embeddedness of commons in appropriately rich social systems is essential to their successfully creating resilient livelihood conditions. Elinor Ostrom's exploration of the requirements for commons governance – high levels of general *civic consciousness, co-operation,* the ability to listen and *mediate differing goals, conflict resolution, flexibility* and good will throughout society, especially in the context of *social dynamism* and diversity – approaches this from an empirical settler stance (Ostrom 2012). Federici and Caffentzis, in seeking to build anti-capitalist commons that prefigure a new mode of production grounded in collective solidarity, focus on a different set of indicators: the collective *co-production of commons* by those whose livelihoods depend on them; *shared natural or social resources* for non-commercial use that are held in common, not as public goods; also, the *gradual re-appropriation of public wealth* created by communities and public workers; the *existence of a community* which does care-work to reproduce and regenerate the commons; *regulations* that stipulate how shared wealth must be used and cared for; and *equal access and egalitarian decision-making* for all commons members (Federici and Caffentzis 2014: i101–i103).

In this chapter, my goal is to explore these sorts of indicators, preconditions, and opportunities for commoning processes, specifically in relation to climate justice – which is simultaneously a visionary hope that human beings can find a way to reduce climate change fairly, an activist movement aiming to bring this about, and a field of research focusing on how this might happen. Commoning in the face of climate chaos involves building the institutions that, as Ostrom said, can "bring out the best in people", since all humans are in this crisis together even though just a few are mainly responsible for causing it. For many, reforming capitalism and its supporting structures would not be desirable, as this would leave the door open for future climate crises in coming years; only a significantly new system offers hope of a more sustainable and egalitarian livelihood provisioning system.

Cooperatives and commons – used here as linked concepts[1] – are more prevalent and more important in assuring people's livelihoods globally than many may realise. The United Nations has estimated that the livelihood of half the world's population is made secure by co-operative enterprises (COPAC 1999: 1). At some level, thus, it is arguable that commons are widely understood as backstop livelihoods protection when times get difficult.

While it is not inevitable, those dependent on commons are often the most marginalised; this may be because resources valuable enough for private capital and entrepreneurs to take an interest in might not remain commons for long. Countering pressure to privatise anything seen as valuable under capitalism, collective economic structures such as mutual aid, utopian communities, grassroots collaborative economic initiatives and coops have allowed Black Americans to persevere in "finding alternative economic strategies to promote economic stability and economic independence in the face of fierce competition, racial discrimination, and White supremacist violence and sabotage" while building leadership and community stability (Gordon Nembhard 2014: 28). This underscores the insurgent potential of commons to safeguard community livelihoods against threats from outside / dominant economic interests (Quarter et al. 2009); the Brazilian quilombos discussed below provide another example.

Understanding commons in their complex historical and anticolonial context is key to equitable economic transformation. Colonial and capitalist economic structures developed together, forcing Indigenous peoples and racialised peoples to bear the brunt of enclosures, slavery, land theft and other forms of exploitation which ultimately led to the climate crisis. Untangling these destructive intertwined systems, in processes of commoning, requires solidarity and strategy. Dene activist Glen Coulthard, in his book Red Skin White Masks, discusses the hope and the promise of commons.

What must be recognised by those inclined to advocate a blanket "return to the commons" as a redistributive counterstrategy to the neoliberal state's new round of enclosures, is that, in liberal settler states such as Canada, the "commons" not only belong to somebody – the First Peoples of this land – they also deeply inform and sustain Indigenous modes of thought and behaviour that harbour profound insights into the maintenance of relationships within and between human beings and the natural world built on principles of reciprocity, nonexploitation and respectful coexistence. By ignoring or downplaying the injustice of colonial dispossession, critical theory and left political strategy not only risks becoming complicit in the very structures and processes of domination that it ought to oppose, but it also risks overlooking what could prove to be invaluable glimpses into the ethical practices and preconditions required for the construction of a more just and sustainable world order.

(Coulthard 2014: 12)

Justice-oriented economic transformation requires significant and ongoing education about the damage and legacies of colonialism in order to begin to envision alternative economic institutions that respect the contributions and rights of women and Indigenous peoples, both individually and collectively (Davis 2010; Tuck 2012).

One definition of commons is: "territorial entities and those resources that are collectively owned or shared between and among populations as well as socio-nature – the air, water, plants, etc. of socio-nature as well as the results of social (re)production and interaction such as knowledge, languages, codes, information" (Chatterton et al. 2012: 610). Another definition is "the organised provision of the essentials of life to all" (Turner and Brownhill 2001: 806). But *whose* collectivity and *whose* life essentials? Equity and decolonisation may be obscured by commons ideas, as Fortier points out: "Projects to reclaim the commons remain ensnared within settler colonial logics in three important ways: through the evasion of complicity in producing and maintaining the structures of colonization, through the attempt to naturalize settler spaces and systems of governance, and through the appropriation of Indigenous territories and ways of being" (Fortier 2017: 35). He says the only way to address this is by building co-conspiratorial relationships for decolonisation (Fortier 2017: 50, 64).

The starting point for this chapter is thus that social justice and equity, far from being assured by commons approaches to livelihoods and governance, must be critically examined as indicators of the legitimacy of emergent collective institutions and processes. Climate change, by heightening the urgency and gravity of livelihood threats for growing numbers of marginalised people, is raising the stakes. Decolonisation is enmeshed in both the causes of climate change and in approaches to solutions. The commoning examples in the following section are discussed in relation to climate resilience and the potential they seem to offer for creating co-conspiratorial relationships for decolonisation.

How can commoning advance climate justice and decolonisation?

Commons scholars and activists are optimistic about the potential of commons and commoning – building new commons of diverse kinds – to transform and replace capitalism, protect vulnerable groups from climate threats, and incorporate ecological sustainability in new livelihood initiatives (De Angelis 2017: 12–13, 267–270; Bollier and Helfrich 2012; Alldridge 2018; Ostrom 2009b; Murota and Takeshita 2013; Rowe 2008; Turner 2011; Ricoveri 2013). For example, De Angelis says:

> The process of social revolution is ultimately a process of finding solutions to the problems that capital systems cannot solve: …. social justice, a dignified life for all, climate change, environmental disaster…. What

has become increasingly clear from the various movements in the recent decades, from the Zapatistas in the mid-1990s to the Occupy movement in 2011, is that whatever the alternative put forward by an idiosyncratic section of the movement – whether micro or macro, whether participatory budgets, reconfiguration of social spending by the central state, transition towns, renewable energy cooperatives, self-managed factories, non-criminalised cyber-activism, defence of traditional communities along a riverbed threatened by enclosures, general assemblies, self-managed public squares and so on – they all depended on some form of commons, that is social systems at different scales of action within which resources are shared, and in which a community defines the terms of the sharing, often through forms of horizontal social relations founded on participatory and inclusive democracy.

(De Angelis 2017: 270)

Esteva similarly emphasises the diversity, grassroots practicality, and social relationship aspects of new commons, in contrast to "resources" or ownership, thus equating commoning with decolonisation. "Modern colonisation 'economises' the commons, that is, transmogrifies then into economic goods, commodities, imposing on them a regime of public or private property and the corresponding norms … Resources and commons are opposed and in fact conflicting conditions" (Esteva 2014: i155).

The following examples of commonisation in the face of changing weather, extreme weather events, food shortages, and other climate-induced threats illustrate how this can take place. While they are very diverse, examining them yields clues to how they developed, what grounds their success, and how they relate to decolonisation.

- In eThekwini/Durban, South Africa, a number of ecosystem reforestation projects covering nearly 80,000 hectares rely on women's work (in collecting and planting Indigenous seeds, planting forests, eradicating invasive plants, etc.) and benefit women-headed households through job creation, entrepreneurship training, and education. Community-based waste management initiatives also generate job creation, improved recycling and waste reduction, poverty alleviation, and reuse of materials – central climate adaptation goals for the city (Gumede 2018: 29–30; D'MOSS 2018; C40 Cities 2018). These initiatives involve coalitions among postcolonial local government bodies, community conservation groups, and environmental civil society organisations.
- The World March of Women, an international feminist action movement connecting grassroots groups and organisations working to eliminate the causes of poverty and violence against women, has a long history of organising collectively and even globally for "bread and roses", with an understanding that capitalism, patriarchy, and war sustain and reinforce

each other (Asselin 2010). Their movement links women's groups internationally for commoning ("the common good – food sovereignty – access to resources. … A long chain of solidarity") (Asselin 2010: 14–16) in response to climate change and economic induced threats to water, food sovereignty, commodification of the environment, extraction and cuts in public services. This includes "reparation of the ecological debt owed by industrialised countries, most of which are in the North, to peoples in the South. This debt is the result of the gradual appropriation and looting of natural resources and abusive appropriation of communal spaces such as the atmosphere or the oceans, which has created numerous socio-environmental problems at local levels; (and) support for countries where the consequences of climate change and intensive, chemical-based agriculture have increased the effects of natural disasters" (WMW 2009).

- In Brazil, more than 2,600 communities of Afro-descendant Brazilians known as *quilombos* maintain communal property, farms, work systems, and social organisation. Many of these communities have maintained their communal livelihood systems since the 16th century when they were established by self-liberated former slaves. Along with Indigenous communities which make up about 14 percent of Brazil's territory, the rights and commons governance of these "traditional communities" are protected by the 1988 Brazilian constitution and by Presidential Decree 6040 of 2007 (FUNAI 2017; Programa Brasil Quilombola 2013), although they remain under threat from extraction, development, ecological and population pressure.
- Lakes in Bangalore, India provide shared drainage, irrigation, microclimate moderation, waste treatment, water supply, and other benefits for local populations. Rajapalayam Lake, following large-scale privatisation and the exclusion of many community members who formerly had access to the common lake, more recently has been the focus of a "recommoning" effort by local activists who have worked with "a wide range of actors from inside and outside government and the local geography … through claiming the public sphere of urban governance" to reassert common rights to the lake (Sundaresan 2011: 78).
- Land and housing movements in many countries organise landless and homeless people to claim urban and rural space for houses, farms and communal access. They resist forced removal of poor people's settlements, carry out demonstrations and marches, occupy unused land, push for public housing, set up mutual aid services, and organise schools and universities. These movements include Abahlali base Mjondolo (South Africa), the Landless Workers' Movement (Brazil), Narmada Bachao Andolan (India), EZLN (Mexico), Fanmi Lavalas (Haiti), Bhumi Uchhed Pratirodh Committee (India), and many others.
- Inspired in part by the people's movement in Cochabamba to oust Bechtel as designated private water provider after it drastically raised water prices

(Oliveira 2004), a coalition of citizens' groups and local cooperatives called Initiative 136 in Thessaloniki, Greece has fought the privatisation of the city's water system by the French water corporation Suez, in order to keep the water in public hands (Swift 2014; Moss 2013; see also Municipal Services Project 2018).

The following are a few additional examples of organisations and projects in Toronto which are building local commons and also addressing social resilience, food insecurity, local redistribution, and political change to meet common needs. These groups and initiatives are thus advancing climate justice in the face of climate change and livelihood threats.

- The Parkdale Neighbourhood Land Trust works to protect the social, cultural and economic diversity of Toronto's Parkdale neighbourhood which is facing pressures from development, gentrification and infrastructure erosion. The Trust leases land to nonprofit partners who provide affordable housing and spaces for social enterprises, recreation, and urban agriculture. It promotes food security, poverty alleviation, and community participation in local land-use decisions to keep the area affordable and diverse (PNLT 2018).
- Not Far from the Tree puts Toronto-grown fruit to good use by picking and sharing it locally. Fruit trees planted long ago in the city are still producing apples, pears, cherries, berries, and other fruit. According to the organisation's website, "When a homeowner can't keep up with the abundant harvest produced by their tree, they let us know and we mobilise our volunteers to pick the bounty. The harvest is split three ways: 1/3 is offered to the tree owner, 1/3 is shared among the volunteers, and 1/3 is delivered by bicycle to be donated to food banks, shelters, and community kitchens in the neighbourhood so that it is possible to put this existing source of fresh fruit to good use. This simple act has profound impact. With an incredible crew of volunteers, this initiative is making good use of healthy food, addressing climate change with hands-on community action, and building community by sharing the urban abundance" (Not Far from the Tree website, 2013).
- The Yes in My Backyard (YIMBY) program links volunteers and landowners in Toronto. "YIMBY is a garden-matching program that connects gardeners and yard-owners in the neighbourhood. Eligible gardeners and garden hosts within the catchment area … are able to specify what they are looking for in a garden match: Would they like to work together, or have the gardener take care of the space? How would they like to share the produce? …. In addition to finding the perfect garden match, YIMBY offers bulk-buying opportunities, a seedling giveaway, gardening workshops, potlucks, a tool-share, and a seed library. … Why wait in line for a community garden plot or watch your yard go to weeds when there's a YIMBY match just around the corner?" (YIMBY 2018).

- Community supported agriculture farms exist across Canada and in many other countries around the world. Food consumers purchase a share of each year's mixed vegetable crop at the beginning of the growing season, providing cash up-front for farmers and spreading the risks and rewards of agriculture. In some CSAs, consumers also help out in the fields. An Ontario website provides a directory of CSA farms across the province so that potential customers can find one in their area (Community Supported Agriculture website 2018).

The same skills of collaboration and negotiation across diversity to build flexible and sustainable governance structures in times of climate chaos are also being mobilised at regional and global scales.

- The nonprofit Marine Conservation Institute brings together scientists, local conservation groups and activists, and governments to advocate for transboundary protection of oceans, and is working with government officials, activists and conservation organisations to publicize and begin organising a "Baja to Bering" ocean conservation corridor, including important offshore biological diversity conservation sites in the Pacific (Marine Conservation Institute 2018).
- Great Lakes Commons is an "activist bioregional initiative working to transform water governance in the Great Lakes along the lines of governance principles rooted in Indigenous traditions, through education, community building, visioning and storytelling, developing respect and understanding of water commons, and networking in the watershed. Questions of justice related to water access, affordability, rules, agency, authority and culture are central to the Great Lakes Commons Charter, an agreement calling for renewed attention to the waters and their governance, which can be used to focus decolonisation and climate justice activism" (Baines 2019).

These diverse, brief examples indicate, at different scales, how commons can be assembled, managed, enjoyed and governed by groups of people using a combination of NGO, government, and private structures, rules, and incentives. Each is different, each has its own constituency and provides distinct services or generates value for its members or "commoners". When considered broadly, these benefits extend beyond the commoners to others in society, which is partly what motivates the commons' development and existence, and also shows why commons fill important gaps in state or private/market forms of governance (see also Shimada 2010). Themes that emerge from these wide-ranging cases include:

1) Job creation for the underemployed, particularly women and youth, allows skills to be used and developed through social enterprises that meet community needs.

2) People everywhere will mobilise to protect their common access to necessities of life: water, housing, land, food, space.

3) Marginalised people (ex-slaves, the racialised, ethnic minorities, Indigenous people, women) often have deep historic traditions of commons, skills, and experience with reliance on commons.

4) Multi-scale networking including global partnerships can strengthen commoning movements and initiatives.

5) The many synergies among ecological protection, basic needs provision, food and water sovereignty, education, political engagement, and cultural flourishing are enhanced by and through commoning.

6) Decolonisation and post-colonial development can advance in parallel with commoning where Indigenous leadership and cultural traditions are respected and at the forefront.

A commons perspective on climate justice, which Chatterton et al. term "co-constitutive logics" (2012: 607), allows us to use insights from commons theory – such as the concepts of socio-ecological systems (SES) and polycentricity – to identify crucial challenges to climate justice, and find ways to address these challenges. For example, skills of communication, collaboration and respect may need fostering in order to build the potential for commons governance and also climate justice. Where borders and limits are problematic in access to resources by local groups in the context of climate change-induced migration, a focus on access and borders – perhaps ecosystem borders such as watersheds – may help to encourage a sense of common purpose and internal purpose. At the global scale, where redistribution and dissemination of promising climate justice solutions are desperately needed, respect and solidarity through diaspora communities, ethical commonalities, and polycentricity may be very helpful.

As Chatterton et al. note:

> The commons, then, creates new vocabularies, social and spatial practices and repertoires of resistance which activists are creatively using to challenge a problem as complex as climate change. Commoning evokes a political imaginary which can be anti (against), despite (in) and post (beyond) capitalist." … What is crucial is that (commons) are prefigurative (i.e. they practice the future that they wish to see), open, experimental and have the potential to generate solidarities.
>
> (Chatterton et al. 2012: 611)

Concepts of property rights (which as Arturo Escobar notes are problematic in reference to commons) are in constant flux in response to changing social, economic and political circumstances (Escobar 2014; Demsetz 1967; Carlson 2009: 64). As legal scholar Jonathan Carlson points out:

until scientists discovered the impact of climate change, the international community did not need to consider whether there was a "right" to emit greenhouse gases or whether there was a right to be free of changes in the chemical composition of the atmosphere caused by greenhouse gas emissions. These issues simply did not arise. Consequently, the treatment of the atmosphere and the climate system as unowned commons is a treatment not founded on social judgements about rights but on the previous lack of need for such a judgement.

(Carlson 2009: 64)

Climate change underscores that it is time to acknowledge the importance of commons as an emergent way of structuring and governing Earth affairs.

Climate justice is itself polycentric, in the sense that there are many ways to move towards it, and local people know best how. Even at the global scale, polycentricity is a useful frame:

1) The same skills and methods (trust, reciprocity, respect, transparency, clear monitoring for compliance) that work locally are helpful globally.
2) Short-term and episodic responses to crises (disease outbreaks, earth-quake or storm relief) can be built into long-term, more institutionalised support for local justice initiatives, if this is done concertedly with new frames (beyond State and Market) and led by local people.
3) Diasporic communities have tremendous potential to motivate and facilitate global links and transfers.
4) Opposing fossil fuel use, investment, exploration, extraction and technologies is a global priority (as is developing, fostering and spreading decentralised renewable energy and energy-storage initiatives). Decentralisation is potentially more just because it interferes with exploitative global market systems. This is an emergent aspect of the post-fossil fuel era, and it opens the way for local commoning.
5) Indigenous peoples' leadership is powerful; First Nations have deep experience with the damage and destruction of colonialism, are more open to commons, often less enmeshed in the Market, more critical of the State, more culturally and politically creative. They also have moral, historical and legal claims to their traditional territories, and experience with the socio-political requirements for sustainable life there.

Commons are both an end and a means toward climate justice. To quote Chatterton et al.: "Exploring, understanding and promoting novel spatial forms constituted through communing practices, then, is central to mobilising the alternatives that are developing through place-based movements, networks, and translocal alliances for climate justice" (2012: 612).

Indigenous activism and scholarship offers guidelines for reconciliation which start with settlers' doing the work required to rectify their ignorance about the colonial repression of Indigenous histories and the damages of colonialism; redressing these wrongs through return of control and decision-making power over Indigenous territories and their wealth; respecting Indigenous knowledge, knowledge-keepers, and diversity in their richness; building ongoing relationships of respect; and prioritising the land and all its inhabitants (Simpson 2017; Manuel 2017; Coulthard 2014; Tuck and Yang 2012).

No economic or theoretical concepts – including commons, feminism, and climate justice – can be separated from the effects of colonialism. Colonialism, due to its global nature and interdependence with the history of capitalism, has changed human thought patterns as well as all the relationships among humans and other life on Earth (Nixon 2015). Using Western theoretical and even activist frames to attempt to describe co-conspiratorial relationships of decolonisation is a bit like trying to use the Master's tools to dismantle the Master's house (Lorde 1979). As we build new commons for livelihood provision in times of climate change, we can find inspiration and hope in the creative collective solidarity that arises from the grassroots, grounded in skills and desires that predate capitalism, colonialism and patriarchy.

Conclusion

The goal of this chapter was to advance a series of indicators of commons-readiness or commoning opportunities, and to point to how climate justice challenges may create both the need and the desire for commons. Based on the examples briefly cited above, let me venture the following thoughts. A community's ability to sustainably govern its livelihood-protecting commons (its "commons-readiness"), and to build co-conspiratorial relationships of decolonisation in times of climate change, is positively correlated with:

- Respected Indigenous leaders, elders, languages, and cultural programs
- Ongoing efforts to combat colonialism and redress its legacies through education, and shared traditions
- Community members' recognition of each other, respect for each other, and history together
- Depth of social, cultural, sustenance, and political networks among community members
- Shared socio-cultural values that prioritise sustainable relationships with the land and more-than-human nature
- Social institutions that ensure material redistribution and equity, limit the impunity of leaders, and emphasise relationships of reciprocity
- Dynamic possibilities for social learning by recognising diverse contributions and perspectives
- Community flexibility in adapting to new situations within a stable social framework

- Mechanisms for transmitting and developing skills
- Shared recognition of the boundaries for the community's responsibilities
- Interactions, networks, and relationships with other communities
- Transparent information-sharing
- Equitable political/cultural roles for all
- Strategies for meeting outside threats to the community's commons and their governance

Noticing, acknowledging, and assessing these factors in appropriate ways will vary according to each specific situation, and will need to be discussed and derived collectively by community members themselves as they develop their own processes of commoning.

Note

1   Greig De Peuter and Nick Dyer-Witheford, in linking cooperatives and commons, explain that cooperatives help workers and community members learn the art of collective association, build decentralized control of common resources, and become integrated in broader currents of social change.

> Cooperatives can be seen as a response, at once antagonistic and accommodative, to capitalism … (but) the extension and actualization of the radical potential of worker cooperatives requires interconnection with other commons struggles – a process we term the *circulation of the common*.
>
> (De Peuter and Dyer-Witheford 2010: 32)

References

Alldridge, Celia (2018). "How the defense of the commons and territories has become a core part of feminist, anti-capitalist struggles," in *Friends of the Earth and C40 Cities, Why Women Will Save the Planet* (2nd ed.), pp. 141–153. London: Zed Books.

Asselin, Michèle (2010). "2010 Women on the March until We Are All Free! A Brief History of the World March of Women." www.dssu.qc.ca/wp-content/uploads/a_brief_history_of_world_march_of_women.pdf. Accessed 5 August 2019.

Baines, Paul (2019). "The Great Lakes Commons: Working with water and adapting our movement to the Great Lakes." In P. E. Perkins (ed.), *Local Activism for Global Climate Justice: The Great Lakes Watershed*. London/New York: Routledge, chapter 17.

Bollier, David and Silke Helfrich, eds. (2012). *The Wealth of the Commons: A World beyond Market and State*. Amherst, MA: The Commons Strategies Group/ Levellers Press.

C40 Cities (2018). "100 resilient cities pilot project: Community based interventions to improve river health (Aller River)." www.c40.org/case_studies/community-based-interventions-to-improve-river-health

Canadian Co-operative Association (2013). "Co-op facts and figures," CCA website, http://coopscanada.coop/en/about_co-operative/Co-op-Facts-and-Figures. Accessed 29 October 2013. See also: www.planetfriendly.net/coop.html http://www.coopscanada.coop/assets/firefly/files/files/Ethnocultural_co-ops_report_final.pdf.

Carlson, Jonathan C. (2009). "Climate change and the rights of states," *Transnational Law and Contemporary Problems* 18: 45–67.

Chatterton, Paul, David Featherstone, and Paul Routledge (2012). "Articulating climate justice in Copenhagen: Antagonism, the commons, and solidarity. *Antipode* 35(3): 602–620.

Community Supported Agriculture (2018). http://csafarms.ca/wp/.

Co-operative Housing Federation of Toronto (2013). www.coophousing.com/.

COPAC – Committee for the Promotion and Advancement of Cooperatives (1999). *The Contribution of Cooperatives to the Implementation of the World Summit for Social Development Declaration and Programme of Action.* Geneva: COPAC. Available online: www.copac.coop/publications/1999-coops-wssd5.pdf. Accessed 5 November 2016.

Coulthard, Glen Sean (2014). *Red Skin White Masks: Rejecting the Colonial Politics of Recognition.* Minneapolis/London: University of Minnesota Press.

Daschuk, James (2013). *Clearing the Plains: Disease, Politics of Starvation, and the Loss of Aboriginal Life.* Regina, SK: University of Regina Press.

Davis, Lynne, ed. (2010). *Alliances: Re/Envisioning Indigenous–non-Indigenous Relationships.* Toronto: University of Toronto Press.

De Angelis, Massimo (2017). *Omnia Sunt Communia: On the Commons and the Transformationto Postcapitalism.* London: Zed.

Demsetz, Harold (1967). "Toward a theory of property rights," *American Economic Review*, 57(2): 347–359.

De Peuter, Greig and Nick Dyer-Witheford (2010). "Commons and cooperatives," *Affinities: A Journal of Radical Theory, Culture, and Action*, 4(1): 30–56.

D'MOSS (2018). Durban Metropolitan Open Space System. www.durban.gov.za/City_Services/development_planning_management/environmental_planning_climate_protection/Durban_Open_Space/Pages/What-can-you-do-to-protect-biodiversity.aspx.

The Ecologist (1992). Special issue: Whose Common Future? 22(4), July/August.

Escobar, Arturo (2015). "Commons in the pluriverse," in D. Bollier and S. Helfrich (eds.), *Patterns of Commoning.* Available at: http://patternsofcommoning.org/commons-in-the-pluriverse/

Esteva, Gustavo (2014). "Commoning in the new society," *Community Development Journal* 49(1-1): i114–i159.

Federici, Sylvia (2004). *Caliban and the Witch.* Brooklyn, NY: Autonomedia.

Federici, Sylvia (2011). "Feminism and the politics of the commons," *The Commoner*, No. 15. www.commoner.org.uk/?p=113

Federici, Sylvia (2018). *Re-Enchanting the World: Feminism and the Politics of the Commons.* Oakland, CA: PM Press.

Federici, Sylvia and George Caffentzis (2014). "Commons against and beyond capitalism," *Community Development Journal* 49(S1): i92–i105.

Fortier, Craig 2017). *Unsettling the Commons: Social Movements Within, Against, and Beyond Settler Colonialism*. Winnipeg: ARP Books.

FUNAI (2017). "Terras indígenas no Brasil." www.funai.gov.br/index.php/indios-no-brasil/terras-indigenas.

Gordon Nembhard, Jessica (2014). *Collective Courage: A History of African American Cooperative Economic Thought and Practice*. University Park: Pennsylvania State University Press.

Great Lakes Commons (2013). www.greatlakescommons.org/. Accessed 6 January 2014.

Great Lakes Commons Map (2013). http://greatlakescommonsmap.org/main. Accessed 6 January 2014.

Gumede, Zandile (2018). "What's happening in Durban: From "tree-preneurs' to trendsetters," in *Friends of the Earth and C40 Cities, Why Women Will Save the Planet*. London: Zed, pp. 27–31.

Harvey, David (2011) "The future of the commons," *Radical History Review* 109: 101–107.

Hess, Charlotte and Elinor Ostrom (2007). *Understanding Knowledge as Commons: From Theory to Practice*. Cambridge, MA: MIT Press.

Hyde, Lewis (2010). *Common as Air: Revolution, Art and Ownership*. New York: Farrar, Straus & Girous.

IPCC (2007). "Climate change 2007: Appendix to synthesis report." In *Climate Change 2007: Synthesis Report. Contribution of Working Groups I, II and III to the Fourth Assessment Report of the Intergovernmental Panel on Climate Change*. Geneva: IPCC.

Jones, Van and Conrad, Ariane (2008). *The Green Collar Economy*. New York: HarperOne.

Kretzmann, John P. and John L. McKnight (1993) *Building Communities from the Inside Out*. Chicago: ACTA Publications.

Lorde, Audre (1979). "History is a weapon: The master's tools will never dismantle the master's house." www.historyisaweapon.com/defcon1/lordedismantle.html.

Marine Conservation Institute (2018). www.marine-conservation.org/what-we-do/program-areas/mpas/baja2bering/#sthash.0erSPrqb.dpuf. Accessed October 30, 2013.

Manuel, Arthur (2017). *The Reconciliation Manifesto: Recovering the Land, Rebuilding the Economy*. Toronto: Lorimer.

Mellor, Mary (1997). *Feminism and Ecology*. New York: NYU Press.

Moss, Daniel (2013). "Greeks stand up to protect their water from privatization." *On the Commons*, January 8. www.onthecommons.org/magazine/greeks-stand-protect-their-water-privatization#sthash.RvgrzZqx.dpbs.

Municipal Services Project (2018). www.municipalservicesproject.org/.

Murota, Takeshi and Ken Takeshita (2013). *Local Commons and Democratic Environmental Governance*. Tokyo/New York/ Paris: United Nations University Press.

Nixon, Lindsay (2015). "Ecofeminist appropriations of Indigenous feminisms and environmental violence," *thefeministwire.com*, April 30.

Not Far from the Tree (2013). www.notfarfromthetree.org/about/what-we-do. Accessed October 31, 2013.

Oliveira, Oscar (2004). ¡*Cochabamba!: Water War in Bolivia*. New York: South End Press. On the Commons (published monthly). http://onthecommons.org/. Accessed 28 October 2013.

Ostrom, Elinor (1990). *Governing the Commons: The Evolution of Institutions for Collective Action*. New York: Cambridge University Press.

Ostrom, Elinor (2009a). "Beyond markets and states: polycentric governance of complex economic systems." *Nobel Economics Prize lecture*, December 8, 9009. Available online: www.nobelprize.org/nobel_prizes/economic-sciences/laureates/ 2009/ostrom_lecture.pdf. Accessed October 28, 2013.

Ostrom, Elinor (2009b). "A Polycentric Approach for Coping with Climate Change." www10.iadb.org/intal/intalcdi/PE/2009/04268.pdf.

Ostrom, Elinor (2012). *The Future of the Commons: Beyond Market Failure and Government Regulation*. London: Institute of Economic Affairs.

Parkdale Neighbourhood Land Trust (2018). www.pnlt.ca/about/.

Programa Brasil Quilombola (2013). *Guia de políticas públicas para comunidades quilombolas*. Brasília. www.seppir.gov.br/portal-antigo/arquivos-pdf/guia-pbq.

Quarter, Jack, Ann Armstrong and Laurie Mook, eds. (2009). *Understanding the Social Economy: A Canadian Perspective*. Toronto: University of Toronto Press.

Ricoveri, Giovanna (2013). *Nature for Sale: The Commons Versus Commodities*. London: Pluto Press.

Rowe, Jonathan (2008). "The parallel economy of the commons." *State of the World Report* 2008. Available online: http://jonathanrowe.org/the-parallel-economy-of-the-commons. Accessed October 29, 2013.

Shimada, Daisaku (2010). "How can societies create common access to nature? The roots and development process of the Bruce Trail, a Canadian case study." Post-doctoral research paper, York University Faculty of Environmental Studies.

Simpson, Leanne Betasamosake (2017). *As We Have Always Done: Indigenous Freedom Through Radical Resistance*. Milwaukee: University of Minnesota Press.

Swift, Richard (2014). "The commons as a fount of hope," *The Bullet*, E-bulletin No. 1006, July 9, 2014, n.p.

Sundaresan, Jayaraj (2011). "Planning as commoning: Transformation of a Bangalore lake," *Economic and Political Weekly*, XLVI(50): 71–79.

Trosper, Ronald L. (2009). *Resilience, Reciprocity, and Ecological Economics: Northwest Coast Sustainability*. London / New York: Routledge.

Tuck, Eve and K. Wayne Yang (2012), "Decolonization is not a metaphor," *Decolonization: Indigeneity, Education and Society*, 1: 1–40.

Turner, Matthew (2011). "Political ecology III: The commons and commoning," *Progress in Human Geography*, 41(6): 795–802.

Turner, Terisa E. and Leigh S. Brownhill (2001). "Gender, feminism and the civil commons: Women and the anti-corporate, anti-war movement for globalization from below," *Canadian Journal of Development Studies* 22(4): 805–818.

Umeek, E. Richard Atleo (2011. *Principles of Tsawalk: An Indigenous Approach to Global Crisis*. Vancouver: UBC Press.

World March of Women (2009). "The common good and public services," www. marchemondiale.org/actions/2010action/text/biencomun/en/base_view.

YIMBY (2018). http://thestop.org/find-your-garden-match/.

Chapter 8

Understanding groundwater common-pool resources

Commonisation and decommonisation of cenotes in Yucatan, Mexico

Yolanda Lopez-Maldonado

Introduction

Groundwater systems, or all water found beneath the ground, are crucial environments for the planet and humanity (MEA, 2005; UN-Water, 2016). An important aspect of its conservation is to find the right balance between its use and management to avoid future problems (Giordano, 2009; Montanari et al., 2013). All societies around the world rely, directly or indirectly, on groundwater resources and several among those manage it as a common-pool resource. Common-pool resources are held in common by identifiable groups of people for which exclusion is difficult and joint use involves subtractability (Berkes et al., 1989; Ostrom et al., 1999; Ostrom, 2009). For example, in a groundwater system wastewater discharge from one user affect the use by others who share the same resource, and if one user extracts water from an aquifer, it impacts the ability of others to use the resource.

Historically, many societies have witnessed a sharp decline in their common-pool resources (e.g. forest, fisheries, groundwater basins). Groundwater is no exception, especially in places where they are open access, governed by top-down approaches, and where the establishment of boundaries and property rights is a challenge. This can generate severe free-riding problems (Levin et al., 2013). While an open access resource is competitively used, property rights arrangements may develop and experience several adjustments attempted through time. These possible shifts in property rights arrangements suggest that what appears to be stable in one spatiotemporal scale may undergo changes into another (Cash et al., 2006).

One key issue with groundwater conservation is that it is temporally and spatially cross-scale (Gleeson et al., 2012). Groundwater sustainability is difficult due to the long timescales involved (Figure 8.1). For example, at global scale, groundwater residence times can be important for geological processes, but groundwater ages are often inconsistent with social timescales. At local scale, human activities commonly affect distribution, quantity, and quality of groundwater basins making them susceptible to contamination and

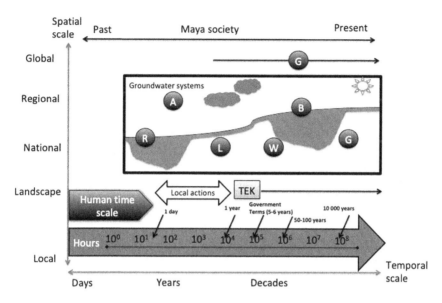

Figure 8.1 Schematic representation of the interaction of human and hydrologic time scales. A colour version of this image is downloadable as an eResource from www.routledge.com/9780367138004.

Black circles are for: freshwater in biota (B), atmosphere (A), rivers (R), wetlands (W), lakes (L), and groundwater (G). TEK is for Traditional Ecological Knowledge. This diagram is based on an original figure by Gleeson et al. (2012) with own additions.

producing global long-term impacts, having consequences in the short and long run (Montanari et al., 2013).

Much of the research on freshwater follow hydrological sciences traditions. But, considering that groundwater systems interact with social systems and are dynamic over time (Berkes and Folke, 1998), a proper analysis will require a perspective that focuses on groundwater as a social-ecological system. A recent step in regards to such an integration is the incorporation of insights from social sciences and humanities into hydrological research (Hoekstra and Mekonnen, 2012; Sivapalan, Savenije and Blöschl, 2012). However, information about how societies develop strategies and actions to access groundwater resources and how some of these initiatives may undergo shifts through time have not been well documented (Ostrom, 2009; Nayak and Berkes, 2011).

Groundwater systems, for example, are known to be particularly important in places without surface rivers, like in Yucatan, Mexico, where the common groundwater reservoir remains as the primary and only source of freshwater for the population. Yucatan is in the southeast region of Mexico, and the landscape is defined by a high permeable karstic soil with a notable absence of permanent freshwater resources on its surface. In Yucatan, it is easy to find *cenotes* from which societies extract usable water. Cenotes, coming from the Mayan word *d'zonot* (sinkhole), are formed because a significant amount of rainwater infiltrates the soils creating streams and channels that disappear under the ground. Currently there are more than two thousands *cenotes* and more than two million people withdrawing water from these sources that are undergoing challenges of pollution (INEGI, 2015). Consequently, the system has been experiencing a social-ecological crisis since increasing demands on groundwater resources, combined with changing land use practices, and human impacts have created significant threats (Pérez Ceballos and Pacheco Ávila, 2004). The environmental consequences of a "groundwater free for all" situation, combined with the fact that groundwater has been poorly managed, the population is confronting a greater groundwater risk than is currently recognised (Lopez-Maldonado, 2019).

However, it is not just the present what matters in the case of Yucatan since water management has evolved from long surviving traditional commons institutions (Lopez-Maldonado and Berkes, 2017). In this place the system has remained the same, but resource uses and users have largely changed over hundreds of years, along with the cultural, ecological and socio-political contexts. The Maya, for example, emerged in this place more than 4,000 years ago, prospered for thousands of years until its collapse (Turner and Sabloff, 2012). The reasons for the collapse have been attributed to several factors. Some scholars propose that a possible drought caused the lack of water as the principal cause of the fall (Curtis, Hodell and Brenner, 1996). Even though there is no consensus on the main reason, archaeological evidence suggests there was close correspondence between water and the Mayan society as a whole. Mayas knew, for example, how to take care of their water resources, that water was sacred, and rituals and ceremonies were performed to protect this precious resource as commons.

This chapter is based on a case study of the Mayas of Yucatan since it can provide groundwater management insights at different time scales. It considers the different aspects of past and present groundwater management with the aim to develop better understanding of how best to govern a groundwater common resource used by many individuals (in this case a local groundwater basin) to prevent its destruction, and how to contribute to its proper management. To do this, I follow a three-step approach in this chapter: First, I analyse the interactions of the social and the ecological subsystems in the study area. Social-ecological systems are composed of an ecological subsystem (represented by the biophysical conditions) of the resource (a groundwater basin); and the social subsystem (represented by the society) of resource users (the Maya of Yucatan) (Ostrom, 2009; Berkes 2011; Levin et al., 2013). Second, I examine the knowledge system of users, defined as the body of knowledge, practice, and belief, evolving by adaptive processes and handed down through generations by cultural transmission, about the relationship of living beings with another and with their environment (Gadgil, Berkes and Folke, 1993; Berkes, 2012). Third, because the Yucatan groundwater basin is a common-pool resource, I apply the concepts of commonisation and decommonisation (Nayak and Berkes, 2011) to the Mayan groundwater context. Here 'commonisation' of groundwater resources is defined as a process through which the resource gets converted into a jointly used resource under commons institutions and collective action that deal with excludability and subtractability. Likewise, the term "decommonisation" refers to a process through which groundwater is a jointly used resource under commons institutions loses these essential characteristics.

Considering my own Indigenous background, and the large database of information and research results obtained during my doctoral work, this chapter aims to understand how a resource that is used for an entire society – a common groundwater resource – lost its main characteristics, broke down and got decommonised. To demonstrate these changes and analyse the processes of earlier commonisation of the system, I use the Social-Ecological System (SES) framework (Ostrom, 2009) (Figure 8.2). I develop a series of conjectures about how a particular society (the ancient Maya) organised itself to govern and manage common-pool groundwater resources and the same society (the Maya, at present) is currently facing serious decommonisation. This chapter examines several questions: What are the main variables that helped promote successful protection of groundwater in the past? Why present water management in Yucatan has failed, while past management succeeded? What can we learn from the Maya groundwater management system? Can *cenotes* get reconverted into a jointly used resource under commons institutions and collective action?

First challenge: Analysis of past and present management of cenotes

This chapter is based on the analysis of two cases: the past and present management of *cenotes* in Yucatan. *Cenotes* are the common-pool resource used for this study.

For the first case on the past management of cenotes, I draw from books, articles, scientific publications, and archaeological evidence on the important role the ancient Mayas played in water management. Archaeological evidence ranges from precisely dated monuments and ceremonies to human bones, fauna, and cultural artifacts found in the *cenotes*. Documenting this, therefore, I relied mostly on scientific literature, archives, and reconstructing past from such data.

Considering that contemporary water management practices in Yucatan are strongly associated with past Mayan traditions and that groundwater management have deep roots in the history, a second step was to investigate present management of the *cenotes*. I organise the analysis into five phases and applied a set of tools and methods: (1) To understand biophysical conditions of the resource I quantified groundwater flows associated with present-day economic sectors (e.g., determined water fluxes, extraction rates, trends, system boundaries, etc.). (2) To elicit mental models of users, I determined user's knowledge of the system and its characteristics. (3) I obtained insights about current status of *cenotes* and to assess the level of pollution and cultural material, I performed underwater exploration. (4) To integrate local values, beliefs and perceptions, I obtained information from the user's through interviews and informal conversations. (5) To explore levels of collaboration among users and trustworthiness, I performed communitarian activities. I conducted interviews in Mayan villages between 2014 and 2018, used participant observation, developed workshops, and performed field visits to communities (Lopez-Maldonado and Berkes, 2017; Lopez-Maldonado et al., 2017). In the context of the past and present data, I used Ostrom's SES framework (2009) as an analytical tool.

Second challenge: Using the SES framework and identifying variables

There is no doubt that the Maya had an impact on the environment, which is evident for their current water management techniques and the earlier traditions. In this section, I analyse whether the groundwater basin in Yucatan fulfilled the characteristics of a common-pool resource and compare this with present situation. I first consider the Ostrom's SES framework (Figure 8.2) which helps to identify variables for studying the groundwater basin and the relationships among the first-level core subsystems of the natural system, the resource unit (the amount and flow of water), the governance system (those who manage the system), etc. The framework also allows for a systematic study of the past and present governance systems (Basurto, Gelcich and Ostrom, 2013). Given the similarities in the level of complexities between the two segments (past and present), findings are presented separately.

Were cenotes managed as commons in the past?

This section addresses the question: were *cenotes* managed as commons in the past? Overall, results indicate that some social and governance factors might successfully influence the way in which cenotes were managed as commons for the ancient Maya. To survive, for example, the Mayas had to collectively organise themselves for the management of water resources collectively that included water bodies and natural and human-made reservoirs (Akpinar-Ferrand et al., 2012). Users organised themselves and took part in making use rules and acted as stewards of the resource. The Mayan hydraulic system was adaptively engineered to the evolving needs of a growing population (Diamond, 2011; Medina-Elizalde and Rohling, 2012; Turner and Sabloff,

Social, Economic, and Political Settings (S)

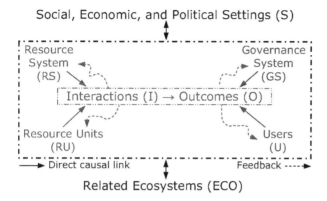

Figure 8.2 Schematic representation of the core subsystems on the framework for the study of Social-Ecological Systems (Ostrom, 2009). A colour version of this image is downloadable as an eResource from www.routledge.com/9780367138004.

Second-level variables are described in Tables 8.1, 8.2, 8.3, 8.4, 8.5 and 8.6.

2012; Lucero, 2018). Overall, water was a significant resource across the region. Thus, I speculate here that *cenotes* were used as a commons along with other resources in the area that were shared and protected for the whole society under joint use (Toledo et al., 2003). Evidence supporting this explanation, including the second-level variables under first-level core subsystems found in past groundwater management and the sources of data, is presented in Table 8.1, 8.2 and 8.3.

Natural system

The natural system comprises the *cenotes* and the groundwater system in Yucatan (**RS1**). Having firm boundaries and uniform territorial control (**RS2**), Maya cities were well established so they could extract water for use and the aquifer size (**RS3**) was not an ecological obstacle for its protection. Despite system boundaries being unclear, communities were able to locate and identify the bounded water territories.

In the absence of surface rivers, the Maya also learned how to manage water resources by building human-made reservoirs, constructing dams on the top of hills (**RS4**). They were able to deal with the variations resulting from environmental conditions (**RS6**) by transforming their local environment. Maya people managed the *cenotes* including their maintenance. In addition to pyramids and ball courts, they significantly modified the landscapes to centralise their water needs, capture rainfall, and create channels to provide water to several communities. The Maya built their water structures on

Table 8.1 Second-level variables describing resource systems identified in past groundwater management

Variable		Description	Past Management	References
RS1	Sector	Groundwater	All water found beneath the ground surface	(Lucero, Gunn and Scarborough, 2011)
RS2	Clarity of system boundaries		High RS2. Well defined boundaries, individuals and rights	
RS3	Size of resource	Spatial extent of resource system	RS3 very large; unlikely to be self-organised given the high cost of monitoring and gaining knowledge	(Lucero, 1999)
RS4	Human-constructed facilities	Human-made constructions	High RS4 attributed to their successful landscape engineering. The Mayas engineered features to prove access to water resources from small-scale household systems to massive centres. They captured rainfall; created channels, constructed reservoirs, dams on the top of hills, to provide water for human needs	(Killion, 1990; Lucero, 2006; Dunning, Beach and Luzzadder-Beach, 2012; Lentz et al., 2014)
RS5	Productivity of the system	The curvilinear effect on self-organisation across all sectors	High RS5 due to the seven-month dry season, followed by seasonal droughts	(Lucero, 2019)
RS6	Equilibrium properties	Lower intensities of stress, balancing loops tend to lead the system to an equilibrium state	High RS6 found in paleo-climatic data. At some point the system was pushed away this equilibrium and it is thought that a consequence collapse happened	(Curtis, Hodell and Brenner, 1996; Scarborough et al., 2012)
RS7	Predictability of system dynamics	Degree to which users are able to identify patterns in environmentally driven variability	Low RS7. Droughts may have undermined system dynamics (including institutions of Maya rulership) when existing ceremonies and technologies failed to provide sufficient water	(Scarborough and Gallopin, 1991; Scarborough, 2003)
RS8	Storage characteristics	Space for water that can be storage for later use in natural water sources (e.g. soil water, wetlands, tanks, reservoirs, etc.)	High RS8. The Maya would have needed to store water in rainy seasons to have sufficient supplies throughout the dry season.(by building cisterns called chultuns in their houses to store rainwater for use)	(Weiss-Krejci and Sabbas, 2002; Yaeger and Hodell, 2008; Scarborough et al., 2012)
RS9	Location	Accessibility to the resource	High RS9 because water was accessible through cenotes, wells, and a few deep caves allowing settlements. Lower elevations meant a higher and more accessible water table, this would have been favoured by interior locations	(Brady et al., 1997; Masson, 2012; Dunning et al., 2014)

Table 8.2 Second-level variables under first-level core subsystems describing users attributes that were identified in past groundwater management

Variable	Description	Past Management	References
U1 Number of users	Those who have rights to withdraw resource units from resource affecting decision-making	Large U1 consuming water (estimates at the peak of the Classic period range from 3 million to 13 million inhabitants), which impacted supply and quality	(Kepecs and Mason, 2003)
U2 Socio-economic attributes	Includes age, marital status, heterogeneity, etc.	High U2. Hierarchical order associated with water's limited availability. Growing geopolitical influence of policies and ruling Maya lineages have been found (e.g. Tikal, Calakmul). Evidence of political fragmentation	(Davis-Salazar, 2003; Kepecs and Mason, 2003)
U3 History of use	Successors, traditional ecological knowledge passed by generations, changes in water management strategies	High U3 due to management based on ancient traditions handed down through generations	(Lucero, 2006)
U4 Location	Spatial location of the resource	High U4. Most of the Maya cities were built near the cenotes and water bodies	(Scarborough, 2007)
U5 Leadership, entrepreneurship	Refers to users who have skills to organise collective action or communitarian members which are seen as influential in the decision-making process	Good U5. Leadership, mainly political leaders, impact political cohesion as well as community involvement in resource management and some connected to local traditional elite	
U6 Norms/social capital	Involves the extent to which members feel confident with other members decisions/agreements and monitoring	High U6. Cooperation and development of rules and norms took place during different times	
U7 Knowledge of SES's/ Mental models	User's knowledge of the resource, dynamics, and attributes	High U7: well-known resource that allows ancient Mayan cities to determine chemically distinct water sources for agricultural, sacred and domestic uses. The challenge of keeping water clean was met by maintaining a balance of plants that purified the water (e.g. water lilies)	(Beach et al., 2009)
U8 Importance/ dependence of the resource	Value of the resource reflected in the dependence on the resource for a substantial portion of their livelihoods (e.g. economic dependence, etc.)	High U8: water used for all activities (including building of pyramid complexes), which might require prodigious quantities of water. Limited dry season water supplies meant that people had to rely on reservoirs at centres and cenotes	(Lucero, 2016, 2019)
U9 Technology used	Technological means available to exploit the resource can transform the cost-benefit ratios of harvesting products	High U9 because the small-scale extensive and intensive subsistence technologies including terraces, dams and canals	(Lucero, 2019)

Table 8.3 Second-level variables describing governance attributes identified in past groundwater management

Variable	Description	Past Management	Reference
GS1 Government organisations	Government systems that control the rules of use of the resource in question	High GS1 due to centralised water management, implying control by an elite. Kings served as water managers, organising the expansion and maintenance of water systems and supplicating gods and ancestors on behalf of their subjects	(Scarborough and Gallopin, 1991; Scarborough, 1998; Lucero, 2002; Scarborough et al., 2012)
GS2 Non-government organisations	Further institutions that control, develop rules of use of the resource in question	High GS1 because the different alliances among organisations in the area and on ranging contacts in the Mesoamerican world setting the stage for the amplification of mercantile institutions	(Chase and Chase, 1982)
GS3 Network structure	Networking with government agencies or external aid	High GS3 with external communities and sophisticated market system that emphasised adaptation conducive to cooperative strategies around water management and complex networks of exchange	(Kepecs and Mason, 2003; Kepecs, 2007)
GS4 Property rights system	Common property institutions specify the rights of a community to a resource	High GS3. The CPR was centralised allowing access to the resource suggesting levels of community association, cooperation, and interactions	(Gunderson and Holling, 2002)
GS5 Operational rules	Practical decisions, norms and the activities permitted for managing the resource by individuals authorised to take these actions	High GS5. Population had access rights for water uses and extraction. Centralised political organisation based on divine kingship in those polities, a system that had been pervasive in the Classic Period Maya lowlands	(Sharer and Golden, 2004)
GS6 Collective-choice rules	It refers to collective actions performed by users	High GS6. Archaeological evidence suggests that water bodies may have been maintained as communal property. Water was an immediately shared collective resource in proximity to a set of neighbours	(Davis-Salazar, 2003)
GS7 Constitutional rules	Institutional regimes and arrangements concerning monitoring, sanctions, adjudication and accountability	Medium GS7, rights were monitored, imposed and controlled by the Mayan elite and supernatural beings and population might have received sanctions	(Kepecs, 2007)
GS8 Monitoring and sanctioning processes	Formal/informal norms for monitoring within the community, by local users or outsiders legitimised by them, observe that other users comply behaviour in the use of the resource (includes sanctions given to the users who violate rules)	High GS8. Communal acts of venerations to water spirits have been reported in the Mayan area. Failure to this could cause disappearance for the water body; those venerations ensured the water supply	(Scarborough, 1998)

topographic heights to use the hydraulic gradient for distribution water from canals into complex irrigation systems. As access routes for the exchange of goods between communities and commercial centres, these roads (called *sacbes*) (**RS4**) were created to provide access to sacred centres (e.g., temples) and also to get access to water reservoirs and cenotes, and to connect cities and towns. Productivity of the system (**RS5**) was stable due to good maintenance of the resource. Occasional droughts did create erosion and land problems including human overuse and misuse. However, during the past, the system was mostly resilient and sustainable based on a Stone Age technology, which prevented an overexploitation of the resources undergirding water access.

To deal with seasonal variations in rainfall, the Mayas also developed strategies to store water. They developed a complex system of water management dependent on water collection and storage devices (**RS8**) and this supported a better control of the resource. Cities were designed to catch water from rainfall and quarries and excavations were converted into water reservoirs (**RS9**). Communities had neither rivers nor springs due to which most of the Maya cities were strategically located around permanent water sources. Location and access to the resource was likely an important factor in determining which large population centres could survive. In addition, slow incremental modifications were possible without significantly altering existing pathways and disrupting the natural flow of nutrients and energy (**RS5, RS6**). Overall, it is thought that the system was resilient and sustainable, which prevented its pollution and overexploitation (Scarborough and Lucero, 2010).

Groundwater was the major source of water for the communities in the Yucatan. But surprise is inevitable in systems of people and nature (Holling, 2001). For the Mayas, the system was unpredictable (**RS7**) and their management system required confronting multiple uncertainties. For example, at some point the Mayas were not able to deal with the droughts that may have undermined institutions of Maya rulership when existing ceremonies and technologies failed to provide sufficient water. Instead, they learnt how to deal with such uncertainties by managing complexity and technical challenges. Unpredictability in the system dynamics was probably the reason why they learned how to take care of it. Replacement rate of the resource (**RS2**), was affected due to widespread conditions and episodes of drought, which were consistent with a reduction of annual precipitation (Medina-Elizalde and Rohling, 2012). For example, variations in annual precipitation might have significantly alter the groundwater table in the area and the replenishment rate.

Social system

The social system includes the governance and management of the resource. The large and homogeneous number of users (the peak of the Classic period ranging from 3 million to 13 million inhabitants) (**U1**) was not an issue in the way in which the resource was managed. With an homogeneous but hierarchical society (**U2**), management of groundwater was based on ancient traditions handed down through generations (**U3**). Higher levels of authority may, or may not, be able to control water indirectly by exerting pressure on those individuals responsible for water management through the other social roles that they hold. Rules and norms are likely to have been in place during earlier times and local communities might have had greater control over the resource (**U3**). Communities were organised near the cenotes and other sources of water making it possible to use and manage the resource (**U4**). Strong social capital (**U6**) along with good leadership, mainly political leaders (**U5**), had impact on political cohesion as well as community involvement in resource management. Knowledge about the resource allowed ancient Mayas cities to determine chemically distinct water sources for agricultural, sacred and domestic uses, including also the use of sand and water lilies to clean water (**U7**). The Mayas believed in the concept of a holy world beneath the ground, and the cenotes were known as portals to enter that world. Some authors have emphasised that such events involved societal decisions about the use and maintenance of the environment (Turner and Sabloff, 2012). The importance of groundwater in a hostile environment creates high dependence of local communities on the resource (**U8**) for its survival and cultural traditions. Overall, water was used for drinking, food processing, cooking, bathing, but also construction, lime cement production and for the erection of pyramid complexes that required significant quantities of water. Productively, earlier civilisations like the Mayas tended to have growing population and rapidly expanding cities that needed to be supplied with enough natural resources, including freshwater, for their basic human needs. However, satisfying this demand in a place were no rivers on the surface existed was an extremely difficult task (**U9**).

Governance

Governance of the resource is also important, which might require a well-structured landscape planning, substantial political and social organisation as well as reinforcement of values of institutions and traditional local practices. The need to manage water resources in a water-dependent society might lead to the establishment of institutions for its management (**GS1, GS2**). *Cenotes*, as important sacred places, were also maintained based on a body of traditional ecological knowledge and were often associated with guardians, spirits and supernatural forces as a way of monitoring and protection. Community members had access rights for extraction, and most of those rights were monitored and controlled by the Mayan elite and supernatural beings. Networking with external communities and governments (**GS3**) were evident in all the Mesoamerica and solidarity among communities to use and protect their natural resources has been described in the literature. In the past the system was managed as commons (**GS4**) and protected for the whole society for joint use. Archaeological evidence indicates that *cenotes, aguadas* and lagoons may have been conceptualised, utilised and maintained as communal property (**GS5**). Operational rules as well as formal or informal norms for monitoring (including supernatural sanctions) (**GS7, GS8**) were probably critical variables that positively influenced groundwater management and its conservation. For example, some communal acts of veneration to water spirits have been reported in the Mayan area as a way of supernatural monitoring and sanctions. Collective actions in Yucatan were successful and led to protect and improve environmental conditions of *cenotes* (**GS6**) and sanctions imposed by governmental authorities (**GS7**) also influenced its conservation.

Are cenotes currently used as commons?

Once all possible variables from the past management of the *cenotes* were listed, it was possible to broaden the analysis to include current variables pertaining to the causes and conditions affecting levels of collective action among the users of the present Mayan society. This section addresses the question: are *cenotes* currently used as commons? Overall, current use, protection, and management of *cenotes* in Yucatan is anything but not successful. Rather, the system has lost several of its characteristics and has been decommonised. Table 8.4, 8.5 and 8.6 shows the second-level variables, causes and conditions currently affecting collective action around groundwater.

Natural system

The system at present is shared by three different states: Yucatan, Campeche and Quintana Roo. In Yucatan, all socio-economic sectors rely directly or indirectly on this resource (**RS1**). The main uses are agriculture and industry, which causes pollution and overexploitation at high rates. Clarity of boundaries and size (**RS2, RS3**) limit conservation since the groundwater basin is located in one of the biggest aquifers in the country. Large number of *cenotes* (ca. 2,000 cenotes), and the lack of reliable hydrological data, make monitoring and management a difficult task for users. For example, locals having a *cenote* (or *pozo*) on their lands have self-defined the outer boundaries of their water and territory over time. Physical resource boundaries do not overlap with social-user boundaries causing lack of control of water extraction, tax declaration and high levels of pollution in open access places (Lopez-Maldonado and Berkes, 2017). Physical and virtual boundaries (administrative, protected areas, etc.) are not well defined and the people do not recognise them clearly. Communities can withdraw water from almost any place including the neighbouring water bodies. Total volumes available for extraction are not well determined due to the lack of monitoring of extraction patterns and boundaries of use. Overall, absence of well-defined property rights has been reported. For this study, boundaries concerning who owns the resource were

Table 8.4 Second-level variables describing resource attributes in present groundwater management

	Resource Attributes	Description	Current Management	References
RS1	Sector	Groundwater	The groundwater basin of Yucatan state	(CONAGUA, 2016)
RS2	Clarity of the system boundaries	Represents which entities are inside the system and which are outside	High RS2: shared by three different states: Yucatan, Campeche and Quintana Roo; in Yucatan 106 municipalities share the groundwater system	(Lopez-Maldonado et al., 2017)
RS3	Size of resource system	This is the total aquifer groundwater volume available for extraction	High RS3. Total volumes available for extraction are not well determining due to the lack of tax declaration and private wells in which communities extract their own water. Locals having a cenote on their lands they have self-defined the RS1 and RS2 of their water/territory over time	(Lopez-Maldonado and Berkes, 2017; Lopez-Maldonado et al., 2017)
RS4	Human-constructed facilities	Communication and facilities to integrate distant resources and their users with other users	Low RS4, including pumping wells, local infrastructure for extraction such as windmills, roads and private wells to obtain water directly from the aquifer	(Lopez-Maldonado, 2018b)
RS5	Productivity of the system	It refers as a curvilinear effect on self-organisation across all sectors	Low RS5. No investments made to improve RS5. The system is not overexploited (elevated rainy season) and groundwater is apparently very abundant. Society do not see scarcity, they do not need, or see the need, to manage for future	(Lopez-Maldonado and Berkes, 2017; Lopez-Maldonado, 2018a)
RS6	Equilibrium properties	In CPR some resources perform near the Nash equilibrium over time	Low RS6. In Yucatan a change in water storage might represent trend in the basin over time. In this case, the change in storage is negligible over our particular period, thus the basin is in an apparent equilibrium under current use	(CONAGUA, 2009)
RS7	Predictability of system dynamics	System dynamics need to be predictable that users can estimate what would happen if they were to establish particular harvesting rules or no-entry territories	Low RS7. High soil porosity and permeability cause rapid rainwater evaporation and infiltration of water and pollutants. Combining this with high warmer temperatures during the year makes storage poor contributing to a low RS7	(Lopez-Maldonado et al., 2017; Lopez-Maldonado, 2018b)
RS8	Storage characteristics	In systems without storage, water is strictly tied to the land but not rotation is used	Lack of RS8: Population does not tend to preserve ancient practices for water storage like the ancient Mayas did in the past	(Lopez-Maldonado et al., 2017)
RS9	Location	Geographical setting	Low RS8. Impact on the resource due to location (e.g. cenotes located near the capital city, cenotes currently used for tourism activities in Natural Protected Areas)	(Steinich et al., 1996)

Table 8.5 Second-level variables describing the users attributes in present groundwater management

Variable		Description	Current Management	References
U1	Number of users	Large, medium or small number of users	Large U1 adversely affecting its long-term productivity	(INEGI, 2015)
U2	Socio-economic attributes	Include age, marital status, levels of wealth or income, heterogeneity, etc.	Large U2, users from rural and urban areas and they are not only locals. Users have little autonomy to make their own rules	(Lopez-Maldonado, 2018a)
U3	History of use	Successors, traditional ecological knowledge passed by generations, changes in management strategies	Low U3 that has been eroded during the decades. Local communities might have had greater control in the past over resource management that today	(Lopez-Maldonado and Berkes, 2017)
U4	Location	Spatial location	High U3 since cenotes are rooted in Indigenous communities. However, resources are difficult to control since cenotes suffer pollution problems and vandalism despite of being located on protected areas	(Lopez-Maldonado and Berkes, 2017)
U5	Leadership, entrepreneurship	Communitarian members which are seen as influential in the decision-making process (young, familiar with changing external environments, connected to local traditional elite)	Low U5. Lack of influential elders and students tend to migrate. Local members do not perceive themselves as leaders and leader positions are subject to government terms	(Lopez-Maldonado and Berkes, 2017; Lopez-Maldonado, 2018a, 2019)
U6	Norms/social capital	Trust among users in reaching agreements and monitoring	Lack of U6. Absent trustworthiness and reciprocity, locals and non-locals do not develop their own norms. Local owners of cenotes or wells make decisions independently without established norms. Non-locals did not share norms related to harvest practices	(Peba, 2018)
U7	Knowledge of SES's/ Mental models	User's knowledge of the resource and their attributes	Lack of U7 and not consensus among stakeholders about the system. Mental models of users (experts, locals, etc.) are diffuse and do not overlap. Lack of literacy	(Lopez-Maldonado and Berkes, 2017; Lopez-Maldonado et al., 2017)
U8	Importance/ dependence of the resource	Value of the resource reflected in the dependence on the resource for a substantial portion of their livelihoods	High U8: resource used in all socio-economic sectors. No other sources of water for the entire population. Low spiritual and cultural value	(Lopez-Maldonado and Berkes, 2017; Lopez-Maldonado et al., 2017)
U9	Technology used	Technological means available to exploit the resource can transform the cost-benefit ratios of harvesting products and this may undermine the sustainability of institutions	Medium U9. Change in power relations since locals dependent on common-pool resources loss certain levels of access. Enough time is needed before users are able to adapt to the new technologies	

Table 8.6 Second-level variables describing the governance of the system in present groundwater management

Variable		Description	Current Management	Reference
GS1	Government organisations	The government systems that control the rules of use of the resource in question	Low GS1. Ownerships and management of cenotes are vested in the government and not in the communities	(Lopez-Maldonado and Berkes, 2017)
GS2	Non-government organisations	Further institutions that control, develop rules of use of the resource in question	Low GS2. NGO's and local cooperatives are using the resource to evolve a more valuable activity by offering tourism services	(Lopez-Maldonado and Berkes, 2017)
GS3	Network structure	Networking with government agencies or external aid	Low GS2. No solidarity among users, cooperation and involvement of locals is limited	(Lopez-Maldonado, 2019)
GS4	Property rights system	Common property institutions specify the rights of a community to a resource	Low GS4. Cenotes are under a mix of property regimes and user rights (private property, open access, etc.)	(Lopez-Maldonado and Berkes, 2017)
GS5	Operational rules	Operational community norms for managing the resource and the different activities permitted	Low GS5. Government is likely to develop rules of use but population does not follow them up. There is no regulation nor punishment to those who over extract and pollute the system	(Lopez-Maldonado, 2019)
GS6	Collective-choice rules	It refers to collective actions performed by users	Lack of GS6. Efforts have been made by groups to protect and restore the resource (e.g. clean-ups). Locals do not protest (or have been unable to do this effectively) against pollution (they protect the wells located on their own houses)	(Lopez-Maldonado and Berkes, 2017)
GS7	Constitutional rules	Institutional regimes and arrangements concerning monitoring, sanctions, adjudication and accountability	Lack of GS7. Rules are used for assessing water fees to pay for water and maintenance activities. However, lack of control and declaration of taxes makes developing rules and assessing water fees problematic	(CONAGUA, 2014; Lopez-Maldonado, 2019)
GS8	Monitoring and sanctioning processes	Formal or informal norms for monitoring within the community	Low of GS8. As an aquatic resource, monitoring and control it is difficult. Supernatural sanctions on some cenotes mentioned but population does not follow them up	(Lopez-Maldonado and Berkes, 2017)

defined and estimations were performed in order to obtain groundwater flows associated with present-day socio-economic sectors by considering substance flow analysis (Lopez-Maldonado et al., 2017).

Currently, a company (JAPAY) supplies water to 90 percent of the urban households. Rural households are self-sufficient with their water but do receive technical support from JAPAY. In addition, municipalities also receive water from a main pumped source that consists of legal concessions available to those wanting to extract water for multiple uses from the aquifer. Roads, human-constructed facilities, and other modifications to the natural system including pumping wells, technology for groundwater extraction and modification to build infrastructure for tourism have impacts on the resource (**RS4**). According to National parameters, the aquifer is not overexploited since rainy season is remarkable elevated (**RS5**). Thus, groundwater is apparently abundant for a majority of the population. Locals do not perceive scarcity and they do not see the need to manage the resource for the future.

Despite water related practices, knowledge and actions of the ancient Maya, and that the current community members possess considerable traditional knowledge of the flora and fauna in the *cenotes* in the region, evidence suggests a lack of equilibrium properties, predictability and storage characteristics (**RS5, RS6, RS7**). In Yucatan, a change in water storage might represent trends in the basin over time. In this case, the change in storage is negligible over particular periods, which suggests that the basin is in equilibrium under current use. High unpredictability of resource flows affects the ability of users to allocate available resources or undertake activities that would augment supply. For example, Yucatan possesses soil characteristics of high porosity and permeability causing rapid rainwater evaporation and infiltration of water and pollutants. A combination of this two, with high warmer temperatures during the year, makes storage poor. High unpredictability of resource flows affects the ability of users to manage it. Thus, equilibrium of the system is currently jeopardised in many parts of Yucatan (**RS5**), which in turn makes it difficult to predict future behaviours. People also have not cared to preserve ancient practices for water collection and storage (e.g. rainwater harvesting) like the Mayas did in the past (**RS8**). Evidence suggests that only one percent of the water is recycled and there is a lack of traditional rainwater harvesting practices and mechanisms for efficient use (Lopez-Maldonado et al., 2017). *Cenotes* and similar water bodies are located in all of Yucatan. Many of them are still used for agriculture and cattle ranching. Location of the resource does influence its use and protection: those located in private lands are better protected than those that are managed as common property (**RS9**).

Social system

Social barriers include many resource users (**U1**), but also exclusion of almost all of them from resource management and planning. With 106 municipalities in the Yucatan state, the only water source is the local basin. It means that water can also be extracted from local wells and stored in tanks without a concession. Groundwater is pumped directly to the households but most rural households also extract water from their own wells (Lopez-Maldonado et al., 2017). Different socio-economic attributes can be found in the area (**U2**), but traditional ecological knowledge has weakened (**U3**). Lack of leadership (**U5**) was also evident during the community survey and trust among users in reaching agreements and monitoring was not found when eliciting mental models (**U7**). Users do not share norms related to extraction levels and cultural practices (**U6**). Despite significant increase in the role of communitarian leaders, the younger generation seems less interested in preserving ancient traditions. Over the years, several activities have been implemented in an effort to involve Indigenous leaders in groundwater management and conservation. Some groups have carried out numerous activities to highlight the need for *cenotes* conservation but still little has been done for the recognition of ancient traditions (Lopez-Maldonado, 2019). Similarly, there is a profound lack of system knowledge and, overall, there is an absence of groundwater literacy and poor monitoring. The local population is not interested in protecting all the *cenotes*, they want to protect just one of them, or to protect individual wells. This might be seen as a way of lack of understating of the interconnectedness of the system (Lopez-Maldonado, 2019). Mental models allowed seeing discrepancies among those organisations regarding problem definition and knowledge of the system. Scientists and experts do not include the social system in their analyses and mental models of users do not overlap (**U7**). Social and physical boundaries, and characteristics of system functions, were not clearly defined for the users, which suggest lack of system knowledge (**U7**).

With regard to autonomy in rule-making rules there have been some activities in order to protect the *cenotes* but the participants in most of those instances were not locals (**U2**). Dependence on the resource (**U8**) is high but this is not reflected in the value systems of the locals towards their resource. During fieldwork, I found that *cenotes* in general displayed significant human alterations (**U9**), although some of these places are under environmental protection from government. Monitoring is not vested in community members who were accountable to the community, and sanctions were not used (**U6, U8**). Monitoring is entirely in the hands of the water distributor and the local authority. Conflict resolution and sanctions are violated due to the lack of community associations and there is ignorance about legal actions related bad management practices (**U8**).

Governance system

In modern times, *cenotes* are usually held in a combination of different property regimes as described by Lopez-Maldonado and Berkes (2017). The current governance system is polycentric but does not work properly (**GS1**). Some cenotes are located in private lands, others on ejidos lands, some of them are managed by the government and others are open access (Lopez-Maldonado, 2018a). Ownership and management are vested in the government and not in the communities; the system is operated by the local water supply company (JAPAY) (**GS5**). Access to information and networks (from local to international levels) were almost absent outside agencies that manage and provide potable water for both rural and urban areas. For the villages, for example, the local water provided had little influence on water uses since it is in charge only for distribution. This has left local people free to extract, manage, dispose, and observe their own water withdrawals but not to set their own rules. Indeed, villages do not pay for water since it has been established that any political party in charge of the government will cover the fees for the entire municipality. Thus, everyone in the village knows that they can use as much water as they want without worrying about its payment in the future. Knowledge of the rules is not distributed through the communities, rather they are concentrated in the hands of the municipal authorities and the supply company. There are NGOs but they work in an isolated way and are not able to develop rules to promote better management practices or to solve problems regarding groundwater (**GS2**). NGOs do not influence groundwater management and society does not organise to manage the resource. In general, people are not confident about their ability to deal with water problems or to protect the system.

Even more importantly, water rights are disproportional since some members have more land for agriculture, cattle ranching, etc. and they use more water than others. More water also means increased amounts of wastewater discharges, which makes it even more disproportional. Group size for collective action is mediated by other variables and there is a lack of networking with government and external agencies (**GS3**). *Cenotes* that are in open access spaces or that do not have well-established common property regimes (**GS4**) are more vulnerable to overexploitation. Collective-choice arrangements are also notably absent (**GS5**). Government and policy makers do not influence decision-making processes made by associations and communitarian cooperatives. Rule-making is not developed collectively since it involves a very small group of experts and just few representatives of the population elected by the former (**GS6**).

Rules of use and local conditions do not overlap. Users can take water from any part of the aquifer and the related water bodies for use in industry, agriculture or for their human needs. Mismatches among institutions and jurisdictions, changes in values and perceptions, and lack of rules created a transition from local common groundwater management to an open access use of the resource (Lopez, 2015). Apparently *cenotes* are less valued for their cultural and spiritual role by the population than they used to be (Lopez-Maldonado, 2019). Efforts have been made by local groups to protect and restore the resource by clean-ups, but locals do not tend to be involved (or have been unable to do this effectively). Local people have little incentive to conserve *cenotes*; since they do not own the *cenotes*, they cannot regulate their own joint use (**GS5, GS6, GS7**). There are no horizontally and vertically integrated institutions for decision-making and government do not recognise traditional ecological knowledge as an important part of monitoring (**GS8**) to promote better groundwater management (Lopez-Maldonado and Berkes, 2017). Information about internal or external sanctions and authority structure at different levels for their application is diffused. Supernatural sanctions in some *cenotes*, for example, were identified but local people do not follow them strictly (**GS9**).

Third challenge: Reversing the process of decommonisation and calls for the future

This chapter uses Ostrom's SES framework to analyse groundwater as a social-ecological system (Ostrom, 1990) with the aim to understand how it was used for an entire society – a common groundwater reservoir, lost some of its characteristics after a period of time, broke down and got decommonised. The analysis uses past and present examples from the Mayan and provides evidence in relation to the use of *cenotes* as a commons (commonisation) and as a non-commons (decommonisation). But can the cenotes get converted into a jointly used resource under commons institutions and collective action? What can we learn from the Maya?

The first point to consider is that groundwater systems are open systems, their boundaries are difficult to delineate and the system components and their relationships are highly dynamic. Thus, any resource can enter a process of commonisation; already established commons or resources that are being commonised could also revert to decommonisation (Nayak and Berkes, 2011). In the case of governing the groundwater commons in Yucatan, there has been a failure to understand large-scale management processes with the interplay between institutions at multiple levels and scales. For example, the Mayas were a water-oriented society (Lucero, 1999; Lucero, Gunn and Scarborough, 2011; Turner and Sabloff, 2012). They were aware that to maintain their water resources a number of regulatory mechanisms had to be followed and respected by the society (Scarborough et al., 2012). Apparently, it was clear to the Maya that to ensure clean water for the survival of all, rules of management and use had to be established. All of this suggests that the water and *cenotes* were important resources (protected and respected) in the past.

Currently, *cenotes* are still important since they provide clean water for thousands of people in a place where water is scarce. However, the system has remained in a decommonised state and groundwater problems are growing. Thus, it is important that water problems in Yucatan are seen as a result of different forces and complex concerns dictated by current and past hydrological conditions, political and economic dynamics, and technical considerations (Lopez-Maldonado, 2018a).

A second fact to consider is that the process of decommonisation may have had different starting points due to several factors:

1. *Decline of Mayan civilisation (before Spanish colonisation):* if the decline occurred due to lower precipitation then the groundwater would have become more valuable, not less. Therefore, the rules for protection (kings, priest, chiefs, or supernatural powers) would have become stricter and, as a consequence, making collective action also stricter.
2. *Colonisation process:* Colonisation for example, resulted in the destruction of many Mayan institutions including (I assume) commons institutions. This process, however, cannot be the only and single explanation for the environmental problems since Spanish people were also interested in clean water. However, their focus was on the concept of management through individual ownership of water instead of communal use of the aquifer under commons institutions that is based on collective action. This may have contributed to the process of decommonisation.
3. *Commodification and commodity production:* This was especially related to sisal (*Agave sisalana* – a species of Agave native to southern Mexico, which was used in making various products). Water intensive processes for sisal production and transport might have occurred here with the industrial process to obtain and commercialise the fibre. This stage was crucial to convert the economy from local-scale production to haciendas-production, commercialisation and export of commodities.
4. *Change in political power:* This might have influenced the decommonisation process since most of the Mayas were treated as workers (and semi-slaves) by the Spanish-descendant owners of haciendas. I consider this as the starting point of the overall process of decommonisation that continues to the present times.
5. *Control of the land:* This might have been a crucial factor because of the change from communal land ownership to large private holdings by the Spanish hacienda owners.
6. *Change from community to individual values:* In the past the local population protected their *cenotes* collectively as commons.
7. *Mayan uprising and suppression:* Probable destruction of any remnants of ancient Mayan institutions at this stage happened. Here formal and informal rules were replaced at the time of the Spanish invasion, which dominated the traditional ancient institutions.

How is it possible that the ancient Maya organised themselves to govern a common-pool resource and the contemporary Maya do not? Some factors currently influencing the way in which *cenotes* are being decommonised include a lack of institutional diversity to manage groundwater, low interest in establishment and definition of common property rights, absence of community involvement, lack of enforcement of rules by government, management strategies of *cenotes* do not include Indigenous peoples in the decision-making processes.

From all those factors mentioned above, point 6 is of special interest for the case of the Maya. It appears that today's disconnection of people from the resource is a driver of the difficulties the society is currently facing. *Cenotes* underwent decommonisation after a period in response to a shift or loss in how people value the system. This is because societal values towards water might vary with time, changing under the influence of education and due to the dynamics of the resource system in question. In general, communities thought that their relationship with the resource had deteriorated over the years and the common-pool resource is not considered commons anymore. To explore the mechanisms that contributed to this shift, we should explore social-ecological systems based on the hypothesis that values reflect human preferences at different time periods. As suggested by Nayak and Berkes (2011), disconnection of people from the resource is a driver of decommonisation, which is evident in the case of *cenotes* of Yucatan.

But can the *cenotes* get converted into a jointly used resource under commons institutions and collective action? To reverse the process of decommonisation, and to secure water for the future, a major issue is to understand the thousand years of history of communities actively involved in the use of groundwater resources and this has undoubtedly influenced the ways in which the resource is currently used (Lopez-Maldonado, 2019). The case of Yucatan provides key lessons for commonisation and decommonisation. For example, the longstanding traditional ecological knowledge of the Mayan is not linked with the current management policies or the faster development of the current Mayan society. Thus, emphasis on collective-choice rules and revitalisation of ancient traditional institutions are necessary.

The past Mayan society may have organised to extract their resources and established multifaceted institutional arrangements to manage them and to avoid failures. However, the society has evolved, the natural system and institutions to manage have also changed, some cultural practices have been lost and other characteristics have changed. So, we now have a completely changed situation within which the *cenotes* exist. As a result, there are new users, a more contaminated resource, and new kinds of governance systems. To match this, we need a new commonisation process, not simply reversing the decommonisation but creating opportunities for further innovations in how the cenotes can be back under commons regime. How such a new process would look like needs to be further examined.

References

Akpinar-Ferrand, E. et al. (2012) "Use of aguadas as water management sources in two Southern Maya Lowland sites", *Ancient Mesoamerica*, 23(1), pp. 85–101. doi: 10.1017/S0956536112000065.

Basurto, X., Gelcich, S. and Ostrom, E. (2013) "The social–ecological system framework as a knowledge classificatory system for benthic small-scale fisheries", *Global Environmental Change*, 23(6), pp. 1366–1380. doi: 10.1016/ J.GLOENVCHA.2013.08.001.

Beach, T. et al. (2009) "A review of human and natural changes in Maya Lowland wetlands over the Holocene", *Quaternary Science Reviews*, 28(17–18), pp. 1710– 1724. doi: 10.1016/J.QUASCIREV.2009.02.004.

Berkes, F. et al. (1989) "The benefits of the commons", *Nature*, 340(6229), pp. 91–93. doi: 10.1038/340091a0.

Berkes, F. (2011) Restoring unity: The concept of marine social-ecological systems. Pages 9–28 in R. E. Ommer, R. I. Perry, K. Cochrane, and P. Cury (eds) *World fisheries: A social-ecological analysis*. Blackwell, Brighton, UK. http ://dx.doi.org/ 10.1002/9781444392241.ch2.

Berkes, F. (2012) *Sacred Ecology*. 3rd edn. New York: Routledge.

Berkes, F. and Folke, C. (eds) (1998) *Linking Social and Ecological Systems: Management Practices and Social Mechanisms for Building Resilience*. New York: Cambridge University Press.

Brady, J. E. et al. (1997) "Glimpses of the dark side of the Petexbatun Project: The Petexbatun Regional Cave Survey", *Ancient Mesoamerica*, 8(2), pp. 353–364. doi: 10.1017/S0956536100001784.

Cash, D. W. et al. (2006) "Scale and cross-scale dynamics: Governance and information in a multilevel world", *Ecology and Society*, 11(2), p. 8.

Chase, D. Z. and Chase, A. F. (1982) "Yucatec influence in terminal classic northern Belize", *American Antiquity*, 47(03), pp. 596–614. doi: 10.2307/280237.

CONAGUA (2009) *Actualización de la disponibilidad media anual de água subterránea. Acuífero (3105) Península de Yucatán: Estado de Yucatán*. México, D.F. Available at: http://dof.gob.mx/nota_detalle.php?codigo=5327360&fecha=20/12/2013

CONAGUA (2014) *Estadísticas del agua en México*. Available at: www.conagua. gob.mx/CONAGUA07/Publicaciones/Publicaciones/EAM2014.pdf (Accessed: 13 February 2016).

CONAGUA (2016) *Estado de Yucatán: Títulos y volúmenes de aguas nacionales y bienes inherentes por uso de agua*. Available at: www.gob.mx/cms/uploads/attachment/file/ 131038/yuc.pdf (Accessed: 10 August 2016).

Curtis, J. H., Hodell, D. A. and Brenner, M. (1996) "Climate variability on the Yucatan peninsula (Mexico) during the past 3500 years, and implications for Maya cultural evolution", *Quaternary Research*, 46(1), pp. 37–47. doi: 10.1006/ QRES.1996.0042.

Davis-Salazar, K. L. (2003) "Late classic Maya water management and community organization at Copan, Honduras", *Latin American Antiquity*, 14(03), pp. 275–299. doi: 10.2307/3557561.

Diamond, J. (2011) *Collapse: How Societies Choose to Fail or Succeed*. 2nd edn. New York: Penguin Books.

Dunning, N. P. et al. (2014) "Xcoch: Home of ancient Maya rain gods and water managers", in Stanton, T. W. (ed.) *The Archeaology of Yucatan: New Directions and Data*. Oxford: Archaeopress Pre-Columbian Archaeology 1, pp. 65–80.

Dunning, N. P., Beach, T. P. and Luzzadder-Beach, S. (2012) "Kax and kol: Collapse and resilience in lowland Maya civilization", *Proceedings of the National Academy of Sciences of the United States of America*, 109(10), pp. 3652–3657. doi: 10.1073/pnas.1114838109.

Gadgil, M., Berkes, F. and Folke, C. (1993) "Indigenous knowledge for biodiversity conservation", *Ambio*, 22(2–3), pp. 151–156.

Giordano, M. (2009) "Global groundwater? Issues and solutions", *Annual Review of Environment and Resources*, 34(1), pp. 153–178. doi: 10.1146/annurev.environ.030308.100251.

Gleeson, T. et al. (2012) "Towards sustainable groundwater use: Setting long-term goals, backcasting, and managing adaptively", *Ground Water*, 50(1), pp. 19–26. doi: 10.1111/j.1745-6584.2011.00825.x.

Gunderson, L. H. and Holling, C. S. (eds) (2002) *Panarchy: Understanding Transformations in Human and Natural Systems*. Washington, DC: Island Press.

Hoekstra, A. Y. and Mekonnen, M. M. (2012) "The water footprint of humanity", *Proceedings of the National Academy of Sciences of the United States of America*, 109(9), pp. 3232–3237. doi: 10.1073/pnas.1109936109.

Holling, C. S. (2001) "Understanding the complexity of economic, ecological, and social systems", *Ecosystems*, 4(5), pp. 390–405. doi: 10.1007/s10021-001-0101-5.

INEGI (2015) *Instituto Nacional de Estadística y Geografía, Censo General de Poblacion y Vivienda*. Available at: www.inegi.org.mx/ (Accessed: 9 November 2016).

Kepecs, S. (2007) "Chichén Itzá, Tula and the Epiclassic/Early Postclassic Mesoamerican world system", in Kowalski, J. K. and Kristan-Graham, C. (eds) *Twin Tollans: Chichén Itzá, Tula and the Epiclassic to Early Postclassic Mesoamerican World*. Washington, DC Dumbarton Oaks.

Kepecs, S. and Mason, M. A. (2003) "Political organization in Yucatán and Belize", in Smith, M. E. and Berdan, F. F. (eds) *The Postclassic Mesoamerican World*. Salt Lake City: University of Utah Press, pp. 40–44.

Killion, T. W. (1990) "Cultivation intensity and residential site structure: An ethno-archaeological examination of peasant agriculture in the Sierra de los Tuxtlas, Veracruz, Mexico", *Latin American Antiquity*, 1(03), pp. 191–215. doi: 10.2307/972161.

Lentz, D. L. et al. (2014) "Forests, fields, and the edge of sustainability at the ancient Maya city of Tikal", *Proceedings of the National Academy of Sciences*, 111(52), pp. 18513–18518. doi: 10.1073/PNAS.1408631111.

Levin, S. et al. (2013) "Social-ecological systems as complex adaptive systems: Modeling and policy implications", *Environment and Development Economics*, 18(02), pp. 111–132. doi: 10.1017/S1355770X12000460.

Lopez-Maldonado, Y. et al. (2017) "Local groundwater balance model: Stakeholders' efforts to address groundwater monitoring and literacy", *Hydrological Sciences Journal*, 62(14), pp. 2297–2312. doi: 10.1080/02626667.2017.1372857.

Lopez-Maldonado, Y. (2018a) "Can the cenotes be saved? Biocultural conservation in Yucatan, Mexico", *Langscape Magazine*, 7(1), pp. 42–47. Available at: https://medium.com/langscape-magazine/can-the-cenotes-be-saved-biocultural-conservation-in-yucatán-mexico-586bee1b81fb.

Lopez-Maldonado, Y. (2018b) *Understanding Socio-Groundwater Systems: Framework, Toolbox, and Stakeholders' Efforts for Analysis and Monitoring Groundwater Resources.* Ludwig-Maximilians-Universität München. Available at: https://edoc. ub.uni-muenchen.de/21697/.

Lopez-Maldonado, Y. (2019) "Protecting our sacred water: Cenote conservation in the Maya area of Yucatan, Mexico", in Liljeblad, J. and Verschuuren, B. (eds) *Indigenous Perspectives on Sacred Natural Sites: Culture, Governance, and Conservation.* Abingdon, UK, and New York: Routledge, pp. 193–206.

Lopez-Maldonado, Y. and Berkes, F. (2017) "Restoring the environment, revitalizing the culture: Cenote conservation in Yucatan, Mexico", *Ecology and Society*, 22(4), p. 7. doi: 10.5751/ES-09648-220407.

Lopez, Y. (2015) "Groundwater common pool resources in Yucatan, Mexico: Understanding commonisation processes – and anticipating decommonisation – in the cenotes of the Mayan area", in *15th Biennial Global Conference: International Association for the Study of the Commons.* Edmonton, Alberta, pp. 1–48.

Lucero, L. (1999) "Water control and Maya politics in the southern Maya lowlands", *Archeological Papers of the American Anthropological Association*, 9, pp. 35–49. doi: 10.1525/ap3a.1999.9.1.35.

Lucero, L., Gunn, J. and Scarborough, V. (2011) "Climate change and classic Maya water management", *Water*, 3(2), pp. 479–494. doi: 10.3390/w3020479.

Lucero, L. J. (2002) "The collapse of the classic Maya: A case for the role of water control", *American Anthropologist*, 104(3), pp. 814–826. doi: 10.2307/3567259.

Lucero, L. J. (2006) *Water and Ritual: The Rise and Fall of Classic Maya Rulers.* Austin: University of Texas Press.

Lucero, L. J. (2016) "Ancient Maya water management, droughts, and urban diaspora: Implications for the present", in *Tropical Forest Conservation: Long-Term Processes of Human Evolution, Cultural Adaptations and Consumption Patterns.* Mexico, DF: UNESCO, pp. 162–188.

Lucero, L. J. (2018) "A cosmology of conservation in the ancient Maya world", *Journal of Anthropological Research*, 74(3), pp. 327–359. doi: 10.1086/698698.

Lucero, L. J. (2019) "Water management in lowland Mesoamerica", in Scarborough, V. L. (ed.) *Water and Humanity: Historical Overview.* Paris: UNESCO.

Masson, M. A. (2012) "Maya collapse cycles", *Proceedings of the National Academy of Sciences of the United States of America*, 109(45), pp. 18237–18238. doi: 10.1073/pnas.1213638109.

Medina-Elizalde, M. and Rohling, E. (2012) "Collapse of classic Maya civilization related to modest reduction in precipitation", *Science*, 335(6071), pp. 956–959. doi: 10.1126/science.1216629.

Millenium Ecosystem Assessment (2005) *Ecosystems and Human Well-Being: Synthesis.* Washington, DC: Island Press.

Montanari, A. et al. (2013) "'Panta Rhei – Everything Flows': Change in hydrology and society – The IAHS Scientific Decade 2013–2022", *Hydrological Sciences Journal*, 58(6), pp. 1256–1275. doi: 10.1080/02626667.2013.809088.

Nayak, P. and Berkes, F. (2011) "Commonisation and decommonisation: Understanding the processes of change in the Chilika Lagoon, India", *Conservation and Society*, 9(2), pp. 132–145. doi: 10.4103/0972-4923.83723.

Ostrom, E. (1990) *Governing the Commons: The Evolution of Institutions for Collective Action.* Cambridge: Cambridge University Press.

Ostrom, E. et al. (1999) "Revisiting the commons: Local lessons, global challenges", *Science*, 284(5412), pp. 278–282. doi: 10.1126/science.284.5412.278.

Ostrom, E. (2009) "A general framework for analyzing sustainability of social-ecological systems", *Science*, 325, pp. 419–422. doi: 10.1126/science.1172133.

Peba, R. (2018) "Múuch' xíinbal: El "ya basta" al "negocio verde" a costa de los pueblos Mayas", *MayaPolitikon*, 22 July. Available at: http://mayapolitikon.com/negocio-verde/.

Pérez Ceballos, R. and Pacheco Ávila, J. (2004) "Vulnerabilidad del agua subterránea a la contaminación de nitratos en el estado de Yucatán", *Ingeniería*, 8(1), pp. 33–42.

Scarborough, V. L. (1998) "Ecology and ritual: Water management and the Maya", *Latin American Antiquity*, 9(02), pp. 135–159. doi: 10.2307/971991.

Scarborough, V. L. (2003) "How to interpret an ancient landscape", *Proceedings of the National Academy of Sciences of the United States of America*, 100(8), pp. 4366–8. doi: 10.1073/pnas.0831134100.

Scarborough, V. L. (2007) "Colonizing a landscape: Water and wetlands in ancient Mesoamerica", in Scarborough, V. L. and Clark, J. E. (eds) *The Political Economy of Ancient Mesoamerica: Transformations During the Formative and Classic Periods*. Albuquerque: University of New Mexico Press, pp. 163–174.

Scarborough, V. L. et al. (2012) "Water and sustainable land use at the ancient tropical city of Tikal, Guatemala", *Proceedings of the National Academy of Sciences of the United States of America*, 109(31), pp. 12408–12413. doi: 10.1073/pnas.1202881109.

Scarborough, V. L. and Gallopin, G. G. (1991) "A water storage adaptation in the Maya lowlands", *Science*, 251(4994), pp. 658–662. doi: 10.1126/science.251.4994.658.

Scarborough, V. L. and Lucero, L. J. (2010) "The non-hierarchical development of complexity in the semitropics: Water and cooperation", *Water History*, 2(2), pp. 185–205. doi: 10.1007/s12685-010-0026-z.

Sharer, R. J. and Golden, C. W. (2004) "Kinship and polity: Conceptualizing the Maya body politic", in Golden, C. W. and Borgstede, G. (eds) *Continuities and Changes in Maya Archaeology: Perspectives at the Millennium*. New York: Routledge, pp. 23–50.

Sivapalan, M., Savenije, H. H. G. and Blöschl, G. (2012) "Socio-hydrology: A new science of people and water", *Hydrological Processes*, 26(8), pp. 1270–1276. doi: 10.1002/hyp.8426.

Steinich, B. et al. (1996) "Determination of the ground water divide in the karst aquifer of Yucatan, Mexico, combining geochemical and hydrogeological data", *Geofísica Internacional*, 35(2), pp. 153–159.

Toledo, V. M. et al. (2003) "The multiple use of tropical forests by indigenous peoples in Mexico: A case of adaptive management", *Conservation Ecology*, 7(3), p. 9. Available at: www.consecol.org/vol7/iss3/art9/.

Turner, B. L. and Sabloff, J. A. (2012) "Classic Period collapse of the Central Maya Lowlands: Insights about human-environment relationships for sustainability.", *Proceedings of the National Academy of Sciences of the United States of America*, 109(35), pp. 13908–13914. doi: 10.1073/pnas.1210106109.

UN-Water (2016) *Towards a Worldwide Assessment of Freshwater Quality. A UN-Water Analytical Brief*. Geneva: United Nations.

Weiss-Krejci, E. and Sabbas, T. (2002) "The potential role of small depressions as water storage features in the central Maya lowlands", *Latin American Antiquity*, 13(03), pp. 343–357. doi: 10.2307/972115.

Yaeger, J. and Hodell, D. A. (2008) "The collapse of Maya civilization: Assessing the interaction of culture, climate, and environment", in Sandweiss, D. H. and Quilter, J. (eds) *El Nino, Catastrophism, and Culture Change in Ancient America*. Washington, DC: Dumbarton Oaks, pp. 197–251.

Part IV

Commonisation and decommonisation as parallel processes

Chapter 9

Commoning and the commons as more-than-resources

A historical perspective on Comcáac or Seri fishing

Xavier Basurto and Alejandro García Lozano

Introduction

How commons emerge and what processes contribute to their formation or dissolution are questions scholars have been interested in for decades, given the implications they pose for the self-governance of civil societies and healthy environments (Axelrod, 1984; Baland & Platteau, 1996; Berkes, 1989; McCay & Acheson, 1987; Olson, 1965; E. Ostrom, 1990; V. Ostrom, Tiebout, & Warren, 1961; Pagdee, Kim, & Daugherty, 2006; Persha, Agrawal, & Chhatre, 2011). The concepts of commonisation and decommonisation proposed by Nayak and Berkes (2011) illustrate the enduring interest in better understanding these issues. In particular, notions of commonisation and decommonisation signify the dynamic and processual rather than fixed nature of commons. However, as these concepts are anchored in common-pool resource theories, they also emphasize the institutional and resource-based aspects of commons (i.e. when resources are jointly governed by a collectivity) over other dimensions.

The purpose of this chapter is to bring commonisation/decommonisation into conversation with *commoning*, an explicitly relational concept that has emerged in more critical engagements with the commons to emphasize process and embodied forms of praxis as central for the maintenance and formation of commons. Reading the concepts of commoning and commonisation/decommonisation through one another, we argue, contributes to a more balanced understanding of the intricate, nuanced processes of emergence and dissolution of commons. Commoning describes the constant coming together of humans with(in) their broader milieu, and can be understood as a constantly changing and evolving relationality between humans, nonhumans, their territories and histories, and the forging of subjectivities that ultimately give meaning to issues such as tenure, substractability and excludability emphasized in common-pool resource theories. Working together, these concepts can help to prevent us from thinking about the governance of commons as static moments of institutional alignment. Instead, they facilitate thinking of these moments as constituted by diverse, ongoing, and interrelated processes of governance, which inherently escape binary categor-isation, and thus, at times contribute to processes of commonisation and in other times to decommonisation (or both at the same time), depending on the optic from which these processes are observed or analyzed.

In this chapter, we engage this perspective of commons as intertwined relational processes, specifically in the context of a society where struggles for the self-governance of fishing commons have been prominent. The Seri or Comcáac have inhabited the Sonoran Desert of Northwest Mexico for thousands of years and were the last hunters and gatherers in North America to become sedentary – but they did not become an agricultural or cattle-ranching society, like other groups in similar biomes elsewhere in Mexico (Cariño, 1996). Instead, fishing politics and fish trade were the main motiv-ations to sedentarise. Tracing historically the processes of collective action that emerged to govern property rights over fish and fishing territories by the Comcáac provides fertile ground on which to better understand the dynamic processes of emergence of commons as moments of commoning. These processes inevitably entangle other material and symbolic aspects of daily life, such as the idea and expression of what a community is, among other issues of consequence related to societal development. Our own engagement with the history of the Comcáac and thus, the data presented here, is grounded in long-term research and ties to the region that go back for two decades for the first author, and includes encounters with the Comcáac annually during a field course, entanglements of friendship and care with some of the people in Punta Chueca, and lots of interviews over time and with students most recently. As a starting point, we provide a brief explanation of how we engage ideas of commoning and commonisation/decommonisation in the context of the Comcáac's history of fish governance and politics.

Theoretical framing: Complementarities between commonisation and commoning

Nayak and Berkes' (2011) ideas of commonisation and decommonisation are anchored in the larger literature on common-pool resources (CPRs), most prominently developed by Lin Ostrom and colleagues associated to the Workshop in Political Theory and Policy Analysis at Indiana University (now known as the Ostrom Workshop). Nayak and Berkes (2011) define commonisation as the "process through which a resource gets converted into a jointly used resource under commons institutions that deal with excludability and subtractability". Conversely, they use decommonisation to describe any "process through which a jointly used resource under commons institutions loses these essential characteristics [dealing with excludability and subtractability]". There are two key elements to their definition of these concepts. On the one hand they attend to the emergence of collective action, which according to Ostrom (1990, 2007) takes place through processes in which individuals engage in rule-building or changing existing rules pertaining to joint use of a common-pool resource, as in the well-documented case of the Chilika Lagoon, the largest in India (Nayak, Armitage, & Andrachuk, 2016). On the other hand, Nayak and Berkes' definition states "joint use" to be exercised through "commons institutions". This is an important condition because it suggests that all right-holders can participate in decision-making processes about a shared common-pool resource, in order to produce new rules or rule modifications. This view of commons as resource base, governed by certain kinds of property relations, reveals much about the institutional dimensions shaping both the maintenance and potential breakdown or enclosure of commons, as Nayak and Berkes (2011) demonstrate (see also Bromley, 1992; National Research Council, 2002; McCay & Acheson, 1987).

However, we identify fruitful avenues for engagement between this perspective and emerging literature on *commoning*, which conceptualises commons as performative and embodied 'doing' rather than as 'things' or resources pre-existing the relations that constitute them (Bresnihan, 2016; Dawney, Kirwan, & Brigstocke, 2015; Linebaugh, 2008). Such a relational vision of the commons emphasizes the importance of ongoing and situated praxis, discourses and subjectivities, and entanglements between humans and more-than-human natures. Through this lens, commoning emerges as multiple processes of struggle and negotiation, and also as productive or generative of different natures, environments, and communities (Dawney et al., 2015; Gibson-Graham, Cameron, & Healy, 2016). This more relational perspective on the commons emerges as distinct from the intellectual tradition in which CPR theories have emerged. Namely, relational perspectives resist anthropocentric and individualist epistemologies, emphasizing instead the ways in which commons are always already embedded in webs of constitutive relations – an understanding that "our world is already shared" between humans and nonhumans (Bresnihan, 2016, p. 147).

It would be naïve to suggest common-pool resource scholarship does not attend to relationships, such as those shaping distinct articulations of community (Agrawal & Gibson, 1999). Scholarship on self-governance and institutional diversity seeks to explain how individuals form institutional arrangements with one another and the wide variation of forms and structures we experience in the world (Ostrom, 2005). What we want to emphasize in this piece is that commons are co-produced dynamically by different actors, the material and symbolic relations in which they are enmeshed, and the non-human entities with which they interact at particular moments in time. In this sense commons are much more than resources (Bresnihan, 2016; Linebaugh, 2008; De Angelis 2017). Take for instance small-scale fisheries, where individuals employ many 'resources' simultaneously, including vessels, technologies and diverse social relations, not just harvested species (Bresnihan, 2016; Johnsen, 2005). Sometimes their catch will be sold for profit and other times used for subsistence or cultural practice. Boats become both means of production and vessels for leisure with the family (Berkes, Mahon, McConney, Pollnac, & Pomeroy, 2001), as well as necessary mediators of the relations between humans and their dynamic environment. In many instances it is challenging to distinguish the nature of the good, the property-right and the governance system under which the property-right is governed (McCay, 1996). In such cases, using one common-pool resource as a starting point for analysis makes it harder to envision how diverse practices and particular subjectivities and interdependencies come into play in the formation of commons, beyond the actual decisions about harvesting fish.

In essence, we argue for entry points to the understanding of the commons that allow praxis to come to the forefront of the analysis, based on the view that a 'commons' needs to be practiced in order to become one. That is, those holding the rights to access, withdrawal or manage the common-pool resource need to engage in performative moments where the collective is more salient than the self (MacKenzie, Muniesa, & Siu, 2007; Roelvink, 2009). It is through moments of practice that a number of material and symbolic elements and subjectivities are entangled in commoning, simultaneously contributing to the emergence of what we understand as commons. In some instances, elements that contributed to the appearance of commons could not have been easily identified a priori, a sort of emergent property dynamic as described by Lansing (2003) and suggested as well by Nayak and Berkes (2011). We find the term "commoning" useful to capture continuous action, moments of encounter between different actors, instances of performativity in collective action.

Dynamic processes of commonisation and decommonisation in the history of Comcáac fishing commons

The history of fish governance among the Comcáac or Seri offers an excellent canvas on which to better understand dynamic processes of commonisation and decommonisation, as a function of both institutional changes and the kinds of interdependencies and struggles that constitute commoning or commons-as-practice. Before proceeding, it is worth noting that "Seri" is the name given to this indigenous group by European colonisers (which they also adopt to varying degrees), and "Comcáac" is how they refer to themselves in their native tongue (*Cmiique Iitom*). We use the term Comcáac throughout but use Seri to refer to certain understandings of the group from the perspective of outsiders (e.g., the "Seri community"). We present three key moments in the history of Comcáac collective action to govern fishing commons in order to illustrate our argument. Each one constitutes an opportunity to reflect more broadly about processes and practices of emergence and dissolution of collective action and common-property institutions, and who benefited from these processes. We argue that considerations of who benefited from collective action are crucial for understanding its emergence, since this is a fundamental question for individuals deciding whether or not to join group efforts (McCay, 2002). In this sense, our work builds on notions of bounded rationality (Schlager, 2002) to work through a broader concept of the commons as ongoing practice.

The first historical moment we consider involves collective action resulting in the formation of the Seri fishing Cooperative, a quintessential 'commons institution' in the sense that property rights that govern joint access and use of fishing commons are held collectively. Formally, the Seri Cooperative bylaws stipulated that only their members could legally harvest and commercialise fish. Classifying the formation of the Cooperative as a form of commonisation produces some tensions, however, since by some accounts the Comcáac did not actively participate in decision-making through this institution. Rather, a fish buyer used the formation of this commons institution to control Seri labor and the production of fish in Seri territory. Nonetheless, the formation of the Seri Cooperative produced new material and symbolic relations both among the Comcáac, and between them and their broader political milieu in Mexico. For instance, the Cooperative contributed to outsiders' perception of the Seri as engaged in joint collective action, which has benefited the Comcáac when they have articulated their collective interests in other contexts. In addition, the Cooperative led to the establishment of a collective physical space: "the town of el Desemboque" (Figure 9.1). This collisional physical space – a place of encounter for different formerly nomadic social groups, outsiders, and new configurations of humans with(in) nature (Moore, 2015) – also acted as a foundation for new forms of commoning among the Comcáac that had never been possible when they lived as hunters and gatherers.

The second historical moment follows from the first and takes place when a confluence of material and symbolic events allows the Comcáac to build a collective vision of self-determination and take control of decision-making related to the access and use of fishing resources inside their territory. The Comcáac came together and enacted this collective sense of self-determination to control access by outsider fishers and fish buyers, whom they saw as encroaching on their resources and their collective future. During this period the Comcáac achieved more control of their fisheries, and more sustainable catch rates, than in any other moment in time (Basurto et al., 2012).

Finally, the third moment illustrates the tension between commonisation and decommonisation and their fluidity as continued processes of change. This moment is represented by the decommonisation of the Seri Cooperative and the simultaneous move towards commonisation of fish harvesting through the creation of several smaller family cooperatives among the Comcáac. Organising fishing institutional arrangements at the scale of the family or extended family networks (parents, children and close cousins and uncles) is better fitted to the existing traditions of decision-making in place among the Comcáac. Yet, as Comcáac fishers recognize themselves, this reorganisation

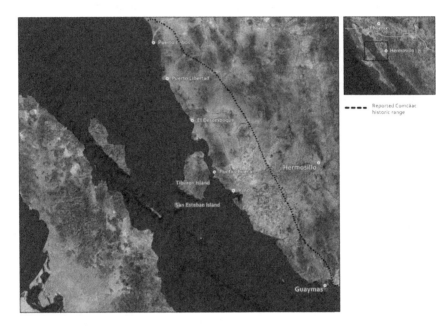

Figure 9.1 Map of the Gulf of California region indicating important coastal sites, with the historic range of the Comcáac shown in dashed lines. A colour version of this image is downloadable as an eResource from www.routledge.com/9780367138004.

presented insurmountable coordination challenges for controlling access and use, and likely contributed to the perceived sharp decline of fishing resources in Comcáac territory.

Altogether, these moments help us illustrate productive tensions between thinking of the commons as webs of relations and moments of becoming on one hand, and commons as resources and their associated institutional regimes on the other. In the next sections we describe in greater detail these three moments in the history of the Comcáac. This historical analysis demonstrates the fluid processes of governance of fishing commons in Seri territory, where commonisation/decommonisation and ongoing practices of commoning are inevitably entangled with place, fish, social traditions of decision making, and strong symbolic representations of the community, among other material-discursive elements.

The creation of the Seri fishing cooperative: Assembling community and Comcáac collective action

It is well established that for thousands of years the ethno-linguistic group known as the Comcáac likely were organised around small nuclear groups of related kin, which were in turn grouped into six bands loosely affiliated through intermarriage and sharing similar core linguistic patterns, but inhabiting different regions (Moser, 1963). This social organisation was similar to other nomadic groups living in the desert and allowed them to best take advantage of the patchy distribution of food, water and other material resources needed for daily life. Felger and Moser (1985) beautifully described the diversity of plants and animals used by the Comcáac in the Sonoran Desert. Different bands could be distinguished by their different specializations on the hunting and gathering of some animals and plants over others, based on their availability in their locality. For instance, the hunting of sea lions (*Zalophus californianus*) is said to have been unique to the band inhabiting the remote island of San Esteban (Bowen, 2000) (Figure 9.1).

In the 1920s, the Comcáac started shifting from nomadic to semi-sedentary strategies to appropriate fish. This change was facilitated by the emerging fish trade and the ensuing cash economy in the region. It was then that fish buyers increasingly took a leading role in organising collective action among the Comcáac by controlling the appropriation of fish. Sometime between 1926 and 1928, the Mexican brothers Roberto and Luis Thompson became the first fish buyers of the region finding in the Comcáac 'willing' and 'resilient labor' amenable to receiving clothing, sugar, coffee, food, and other goods in return (Smith, 1954). Soon the area of Kino Bay (Figure 9.1) became the most populated winter camp for the Comcáac, who settled around the landing of fish, a focal point of employment and easier access to material goods in demand by Comcáac families.

The following decade (1930s) saw a rapid expansion of Kino Bay as a permanent settlement. Comcáac and Mexican fishers regularly landed fish for an increasing number of fish buyers. Thompson was able to secure support from the State to the Comcáac in the form of vessels and fishing gear, and educational resources through the establishment of the first school in Kino for the primary benefit of Comcáac children (Smith, 1954). Yet, the increasing Mexican mestizo population in the locality resulted in Comcáac displacement, disease, and increased conflicts between them and with the immigrant fishers. According to Smith's (1954) diary notes, however, fish buyers still preferred Comcáac fishing labor since they were "efficient and dependable", they accepted material goods as payment, and were easy to trick when weighing their catch. As a result, fish buyers increasingly competed for Seri fishing labor as the demand for seafood and vitamin A obtained from shark liver increased in the advent of World War II.

In parallel, at the end of the Mexican Revolution of 1910 the emerging Mexican centralized State started defining its main policies to govern fisheries and ocean resources. The Fisheries Law of 1925 defined permits as the main policy tool to manage a number of species including sharks, sea-turtles, finfish, bivalves, lobster, shrimp, among others (Soberanes Fernández, 1994). Access to fishing permits became exclusive to fishers organised into fishing cooperatives. Cooperatives constituted the main mechanism by which the

Mexican State channelled benefits to dispersed, isolated harvesters of seafood in an effort towards building a political constituency similar to that built with agricultural societies through the *ejido* land tenure system (Taylor, 2003). These constituencies were to become the rural base of the emerging official party (now known as the Partido Revolucionario Institucional, PRI), which governed practically unopposed for 70 years until the year 2000.

In this new national political context, in 1939 a fish buyer named Jesus Solorzano saw the opportunity to outcompete other fish buyers by organising Seri production within the structure of a fishing cooperative in what is now the town of El Desemboque, more than 50 km north of Kino. According to Smith (1954) the move was mutually enabled: On the one hand, Solorzano was interested in capturing all Seri labor for himself and monopolising their catch, and on the other hand, the Comcáac desired to avoid assimilation and conflict with Mexican fishers in Kino. In this context, the agreement between Solorzano and Comcáac fishers to move to El Desemboque (Figure 9.1) and create the Seri Cooperative constituted an important moment of collective action. Although Smith's (1954) diary provides evidence that Solorzano controlled decision-making of the Cooperative, by organising fishing around a common-property institution, Solorzano created the idea of Seri fisheries governance as a collective endeavour. No recorded evidence exists that the Comcáac worked collectively beyond the small family unit in other areas of life (except when waging war), or that they had developed other traditions of collective decision making. However, this moment of commonisation through the establishment of the Seri Cooperative, and the associated sedentarism that has continued until the present, helped build the powerful idea of the "Seri community", an enduring external image of the Comcáac as a monolithic cultural group. While members of different bands were now living in the same spatial unit, how can we assume a priori they shared the same collective interests? Yet living together created the possibility or the basis for commoning, by more closely knitting their lived and collective histories with an already shared cosmology and sense of place.

Another tension to note is that the creation of the Seri Cooperative ("commonisation") likely at the same time accelerated the decommonisation of fish in Seri territory by essentially transforming fish into a cash crop, particularly because decision-making of access and use of the fish were under the control of outsider groups. Between the years 1940 and 1948, Solorzano controlled the Cooperative and the territory of Desemboque (Smith, 1954). During this time, he built the Cooperative's office and ice-house, obtained its first fishing permits, provided credit loans to its members, and established a school. Smith (1954) describes Desemboque during this time as a "model community in which the Seri tribe outnumbered the Mexicans approximately 2 to 1, and where the sale of Marijuana and liquor was prohibited". Malkin (1962, p. 33) described the production arrangements surrounding the Seri Cooperative differently:

[t]he Seris' commercial fishing is pretty much controlled and exploited by the two or three Mexican fish traders from Nogales and Hermosillo. These have their tiendas [stores] in El Desemboque, which at set prices sell things to the villagers. They also provide the Indians with the five horse-power motors for fishing trips and pleasure cruises and with the oil and gasoline essential to run these – also at set price. They finally purchase the fish – at a set price – and from the proceeds the Seris purchase goods at the tiendas, completing the cycle.

While increasingly living together (i.e., in Desemboque) and working within the same institutional arrangement (the Seri Cooperative), it is intriguing how the institutional arrangement of a fishing cooperative could have accommodated the Comcáac's deeply engrained nomadic tendencies to work and benefit only their own clan or familial lines. As found by Nenadovic et al. (2018), for a cooperative to function as a basis for the generation of public and collective goods for their members, those members need to make contributions to it (e.g., develop a rule structure, land their fish at the cooperative, sanction rule breakers). The indication that this common-property institution was not well fitted for the Comcáac might have been evident from the conflicts that eventually emerged between Solorzano and the Comcáac. Solorzano eventually left Desemboque in 1948 and according to Smith (1954) the Cooperative declined under Comcáac leadership, unable to maintain basic administrative procedures and collective benefits (e.g., the school or credit to fishers) achieved during Solorzano's tight grip. While the Comcáac were now in control of decision-making of the Cooperative, they still depended on outside fish buyers for the commercialisation of their catch. The Comcáac also lacked the appropriate political connections and capital to foster necessary economic development for the Cooperative and their town of Desemboque.

In summary, the establishment of the Seri fishing Cooperative fostered the idea or image in the public imaginary of community collective action among the Comcáac. Yet, the same institutional arrangement can be viewed as having provided a formal mechanism for decommonisation of Seri fisheries by outsiders. The dynamic could well be understood as one of exploitation by outsiders, aiming to control the fishing commons of the Comcáac. Although it is unclear whether the Comcáac would have been better off without the emergence of the Seri Cooperative, its formation also made Seri labor more legible (Scott, 1998) or governable, allowing outsiders to more easily organise production of Comcáac fishing commons.

Commonisation in the Infiernillo Channel: A space for commoning through self-determination and collective action

Not much has been written about Comcáac fisheries governance between the 1950s and 1970s, and it is unclear how active the Cooperative was during this time. Yet, two events in the 1970s and 1980s possibly reinvigorated it. First, in 1975 the Comcáac, through the Seri Cooperative, were granted permanent and exclusive property rights (i.e., the right to withdraw) over the marine resources in "the waters surrounding Tiburon Island", in the form of a marine concession (Diario Oficial de la Federación, 1975). These rights were part of a larger allocation of property rights over territory on land to the Comcáac (Basurto, 2005), which included Tiburon Island (the largest island in Mexico, Diario Oficial de la Federación, 1978) and a strip of coastal land using the ejido system of communal land tenure (Diario Oficial de la Federación, 1970). Indigenous territorial rights were advocated by the National Indigenous Institute through a presidential executive decree to prevent further acculturation and eventual disappearance of the smallest indigenous groups in Mexico through interaction with mestizo populations. The marine tenure granted to the Seri was territorial in nature, that is, not species-specific like the fishing concessions that the Mexican fisheries policy agency (CONAPESCA, its acronym in Spanish) can issue to cooperatives or individuals elsewhere in Mexico. The concession was also limited to those individuals belonging to "the Seri tribe and the Seri fishing cooperative" (Diario Oficial de la Federación, 1975).

Second, in 1971 the President Luis Echeverria created a parastatal company, Productos Pesqueros Mexicanos (PROPEMEX), to provide technical and infrastructure support to fishing cooperatives in Mexico, which reached the Comcáac in the early 1980s (Lobato González, 1996). PROPEMEX provided fishing means of production and built ice houses mainly in El Desemboque and Punta Chueca (or *Socaaix*, the second permanent Comcáac settlement established after Desemboque, 25 km north of Kino Bay, see Figure 9.1). By increasing fishing infrastructure and providing conditions for steady employment to Seri and non-Seri fishers alike, PROPEMEX propelled once again the economic development of El Desemboque (and Punta Chueca). It also renewed interactions and conflict between the Comcáac and newcomers, as during this time several non-Seri fishers intermarried with Comcáac, gaining permanent access to the Comcáac fishing concession (Basurto, 2006). This seems to have been a particularly sensitive issue for the Comcáac inhabiting Punta Chueca, who had moved there looking to distance themselves from outside influences present in El Desemboque (Figure 9.1). This latter point has some implications for our understanding of commoning. The formation of Punta Chueca emerges from an oppositional expression of Comcáac identity as collective, a means to produce a community without outsiders or invaders who historically harmed the Comcáac. By 1984, PROPEMEX left Seri territory due to overfishing of finfish for export and internal administrative issues, transferring fishing boats and gear to the control of the Seri Cooperative. At the same time commercial diving for the sessile bivalve pen shells (*Atrina tuberculosa* and *Pinna rugosa*) boomed, fostering incentives among divers from Kino to seek access to the best banks found inside the Infiernillo Channel (Basurto, 2006; Basurto & Coleman, 2010) (Figure 9.2).

According to local informants, in lieu of the renewed sense of encroachment of outsiders to Comcáac territory, Genaro Herrera, a particularly strong and vociferous leader of the Comcáac at the time, proposed to "tax" outsiders in exchange for gaining entry to harvest pen shells inside the Channel. Effectively establishing the idea of "la cota" (the fee) which was paid to the Comcáac leaders in the form of a certain number of kilos of pen shells or their monetary equivalent. It is unclear whether the fee was to be paid to the overall leader of the Comcáac or to the president of the Seri Cooperative. This initial idea of a fee catalysed the design of a variety of rules by a number of different fishing families, which effectively allowed the Comcáac to regain control on access and withdrawal of pen shells in the Infiernillo Channel, a portion of their fishing concession. These rules have been documented previously in detail by Basurto (2005) and included equity-enhancing provisions

Figure 9.2 (A) Comcáac or Seri fishers harvesting pen shells by free-diving in the Gulf of California (photo by Ian Markham); (B) Fishing gear assembled in Puerto Libertad, Sonora, characteristic of working waterfronts in Mexican fishing towns (photo by Juliana Mayhew); (C) Pen shell harvest by fishers from Kino Bay, whose access to the mollusk banks is influenced by informal rules put in place by the Seri – here they have harvested pen shells using a breathing apparatus made from plastic hoses attached to a gasoline-fueled compressor (photo by Shannon Switzer Swanson). A colour version of this image is downloadable as an eResource from www.routledge.com/9780367138004

so that different segments of the Comcáac population could benefit or retain access to pen shells and other bivalves by the presence of outsiders. For instance, a rule stipulated that a Comcáac must be part of the fishing crew. This "aboard monitor" rule effectively provided employment and cash to those among the Comcáac without their own fishing means of production (i.e., boat) because it is customary to split in equal parts the catch among all crew members. Another rule stipulated that areas of low tide harvesting (and thus no need for diving gear) be reserved to women, children and elders in what is known as the "callo de bajamar" practice. In any case, outsiders were regularly asked to leave the Infiernillo Channel waters when the perception of excess fishing effort or too many outsiders prompted the Comcáac leader to give a vacating order. Enforcement, during this time was done by the informal Traditional Guard. Those not obeying it risked the confiscation of their fishing boat and gear, which was known to happen occasionally (Basurto, 2005).

These diverse informal rulemaking processes emerged as an important form of commonisation by the Comcáac, preventing what they perceived as encroachment and enclosure on their territory and its resources. The emergence of collective action beyond the family group and through the design of local rules to control access and withdrawal of pen shells worked because the different rules benefited different segments of the population, and therefore different family groups, who saw these rules as means for their own economic well-being. For instance, while the *cota* benefited mostly those families in leadership positions, the "aboard monitor" rule benefited those without ownership of fishing means of production, and the "callo de bajamar" rule guaranteed access to pen shells for subsistence or cash income to those without access to diving technology.

The Seri Cooperative did not influence the emergence of these informal rules, since it did not effectively foster joint decision making, nor did it operate as an institution to organise production or commercialisation of catch during this time. The Cooperative only generated income by selling of formal invoices to fish buyers, who controlled the commercialisation of pen shells and other fishery products. Given that the catch was obtained from the Seri fishing concession, which legally could only be exploited by the Seri Cooperative, all catch needed to be invoiced through the Cooperative. In turn, income from the sale of invoices benefited the president of the cooperative and his family. An in-depth explanation of the functioning of fishing permits is provided in Cinti et al. (2010) and Basurto et al. (2012) but here it suffices to state that only permit holders can provide legal invoices (or *facturas*), which constitute proof of legal ownership of the harvest. Invoices are necessary to sell or buy and transport the catch to markets. Without an invoice from the Seri Cooperative it was not possible to show proof that the catch was obtained legally so fish buyers were willing to pay a fee for every invoice in order to truck the catch away.

In summary, during this time, different Comcáac family units were able to design a variety of rules that benefited them economically and imposed an additional cost for outsiders considering fishing in the Infiernillo Channel. The collective action needed for the enforcement of these rules was motivated by a strong narrative, led by a strong elder leader, of a new form of invasion to their territory. This narrative effectively elicited a collective sense of self-determination, facilitating engagement in decision-making beyond individual or strict familial self-interest. As such, these narratives fostering collective action worked by articulating a shared past of the Comcáac, in which previous invaders had encroached on their ancestral territories, as well as a precarious future worth fighting for. However, continued motivations for collective action and sustained control of access to Comcáac rich fishing grounds would end with the creation of family cooperatives by 2010. Family-based cooperatives likely constituted a better fitted institutional arrangement to Comcáac kin structure but were not well suited for controlling access and use (and therefore sustainable use) of common-pool resources inside their fishing concession.

Commonisation or decommonisation? The proliferation of family fishing cooperatives

The original Seri Cooperative never really worked as a collective institution partly because the Comcáac could not organise and sustain decision-making across Comcáac familiar alliances, and by the 1990s some Comcáac fishers started forming their own family-size cooperatives. The Law of Cooperatives of 1992 made this institutional change possible, since it reduced the minimum number of members required to form cooperatives, while the Law of Fisheries of 1992 had also eliminated the exclusive access benefits enjoyed by cooperatives over certain commercial species, opening them up to private firms and individuals. The formation of family cooperatives has been controversial, since these are perceived as less legitimate by the broader cooperativist sector – a kind of enclosure by quasi-private entities. However, this new form of collective action among closely related Comcáac kin could be characterised as a new moment of commonisation: joint use became organised under common-property institutions that were better fitted to their traditions of decision-making along kinship lines. At the same time, it was a moment of decommonisation from the perspective of the Seri Cooperative, as any collective benefits produced by the Seri Cooperative ended in this period. These tensions reveal the ways in which national policies come into assemblage with local realities and shape the space of possibility for local collective action, in ways that are not straightforward and can become subject to conflicts and contestation.

More generally, a national-level study in Mexico has found that the four main reasons fishers start new cooperatives are: (1) to be able to access fishing permits and other benefits offered by the State, (2) to have their organisation be legally recognized, (3) dissatisfaction with their previous organisation, and (4) to improve their own working conditions (Nenadovic et al., 2018). Of these four, obtaining benefits from the State and being legally recognized are the most important across the country. Legal recognition is the first step towards accessing fishing permits and State benefits that are still reserved only for cooperatives such as the subsidy program for the upgrade of boats and motors, the most coveted among fishers. Fishing permits are not only valuable because they allow fishers to move away from working outside the purview of the State and avoid penalties, particularly since enforcement of fishing regulations is limited. A fishing permit is particularly valuable because it functions as a tracking number to which the catch is referenced throughout the commercialisation chain.

Given that many fishers work independently and without fishing permits, fishers need to associate their catch to a permit number, and therefore, there is demand to buy *facturas* or invoices from cooperatives with valid fishing permits. Selling invoices is common practice enabling fishers or cooperatives without valid permits to land their catch and sell it further up the commercialisation chain. In some cases, cooperatives that are not actively fishing maintain a legal status so that they can continue to sell *facturas*. Like many other cooperatives in Mexico, the Seri Cooperative has also participated in this practice. According to our informants, as the activities of outside fishers and fish buyers increased inside of Comcáac territory, the sale of *facturas* increasingly became one of the few reliable sources of income to the Seri Cooperative. A *factura* from the Seri Cooperative was valuable to have when harvesting from the Infiernillo Channel even when the Cooperative itself did not carry fishing permits anymore. That is because the Executive Decree of 1975 that established the Seri fishing concession stipulated the Cooperative as exclusive holder of harvesting rights inside Seri waters (Diario Oficial de la Federación, 1975). A *factura* from the Seri Cooperative constituted a tangible materialisation of the symbolic power held by the Seri Cooperative as representative of 'Seri Collectivity' or of "the Seri Community". Outside fish buyers have described to us that buying a *factura* from the Seri Cooperative was akin to gaining the "okay" of the Seri community and safe passage inside Comcáac territory.

The above described symbolic power held by the Seri Cooperative withered away with the advent of Seri family cooperatives. In the early 2000s, a number of family cooperatives were created as the State provided the Seri new boats and motors, likely in association with upcoming federal elections. These cooperatives, unintentionally perhaps, started competing with the monopolistic control the Seri Cooperative had in the sale of *facturas*, and its symbolic power as a representation of the Seri Community. Perhaps indicative of these processes of destabilization, outside fishers and fish buyers during this time expressed frustration saying that nowadays there is no clear person from whom to buy a *factura* or pay the *cota*:

"Ahora cualquier persona puede pedirte la cota. Terminas pagando ¡dos o tres veces!"
"Now anyone can come and ask you for the *cota*. You end up paying two or three times!".

(Fish buyer Informant A)

In 2012, we had the opportunity to survey the twelve leaders of these new cooperatives (Basurto, unpublished data). We asked them a variety of questions aimed to understand why they organised into family cooperatives and what were their institutional characteristics. The Comcáac expressed their motivations to create these new institutions in a variety of ways that suggested entanglements with their collective economic well-being and their aspirations of self-determination, as illustrated by these statements:

"[Formamos nuestra cooperative para] [p]oder vender marisco a mayor precio e iniciar un negocio familiar. Poder transportar fuera del territorio y tener apoyos de equipos y artes de pesca. La cooperativa Seri no podia dar apoyos a todos los socios, eran muchos y no funcionaba bien ..."
"[We established our cooperative] [t]o be able to sell our seafood at a better price, start a family business, be able to transport [our seafood] outside of our territory and obtain [State] support and fishing means of production. The Seri [cooperative] could not give support to all its members. They were too many and it did not work well". (Fisher Informant B)

"Queríamos obtener mejores precios, saltarnos al intermediario, bajar apoyos y proyectos".
"We wanted to get better prices, skip the middle-man, and access State resources and support".

(Fisher Informant C)

These responses signal a duality between organising new cooperatives to fulfil narrow economic incentives and also to enable the continuing struggle for self-determination. This dual purpose also illustrates the usefulness of thinking of the commons simultaneously as a verb and a noun (i.e., as ongoing processes and as institutional arrangements over a resource). Commonisation in the form of establishing a common-property institution (i.e., a cooperative) serves as a basis for commoning in broader collective desires and efforts towards self-determination – a more long-term vision, yet a grand motivator shared across families. In other words, the interest in capturing benefits offered by the State to acquire boats and motors was not only for increasing economic well-being through enhanced harvesting activities, but also about exercising greater control over who benefited from this activity. An underlying sentiment is that the control of their territory is incomplete as long as they are dependent on fish buyers for the commercialisation of their catch.

In this sense, commoning through self-determination is able to transcend self-interest within close kinship ties, at least in certain moments. It also suggests that commoning cannot necessarily be viewed as rational processes of decision-making. Indeed, we see mixed evidence of Comcáac investments in building their common-property institutions to realize some of the above aspirations based on an initial review of their characteristics (Table 9.1). While most of them owned boats and motors collectively, because in many instances that was the State requirement to grant them, only half of the cooperatives used them to land their catch collectively. Less than a fourth mentioned being

Table 9.1 Characteristics of Comcáac family cooperatives

Name	Year established	Owns boats and motors	Lands catch collectively	Transport catch	Valid fishing permit
Soc. Coop. Prod. Pesq. y Acuicola Axol Ihoom	1998	YES	NO	YES	NO
Soc. Coop. Estrella Seri SC de RL de CV	1990	YES	NO	YES	YES
Punta Sargento	2008	NO	NO	YES	NO
Sociedad Cooperativa Canal del Infiernillo SCL	1996	YES	YES	YES	YES
Sociedad Cooperativa de Produccion Pesquera Coofteocl SC de RL de SC	2009	YES	NO	NO	NO
Haoxl Hihom SC de RL de CV	2010	YES	YES	NO	YES
Sociedad Cooperativa de Produccion Pesquera y Acuicola Kamanti Xana SC de RL de CV	2000	YES	NO	NO	NO
S.C.P.P. Marlin XV SC de RL de CV	2007	NO	NO	NA	NO
Sociedad Cooperativa Romero Punta Chueca SC de RL	1998	YES	YES	YES	NO
Segovia Esquivel SC de RL de CV	2007	YES	YES	YES	YES
Sociedad Cooperativa Socaix	2007	YES	YES	NO	NO
Cooperativa de Produccion Pesquera y Acuicola Tacsen SC de RL de CV	2005	YES	NO	NA	NO
Sociedad Cooperativa de Produccion Pesquera Acuicola Punta Perla SC de RL	2000	YES	YES	NO	YES

able to transport their catch to the first point of commercialisation and skip a middleman, only three cooperatives had current fishing permits, and all claimed to fish five species on average.

Nonetheless, the creation of new cooperatives has resulted in more economic experimentation among the Comcáac than in the past. Never before could the Comcáac transport their catch outside of their territory or act as middlemen between Comcáac fishers and outside fish buyers. Moreover, access to boats and motors is another form in which the Comcáac enact their self-determination. For the Comcáac, boats have many other uses besides fishing. They are a means to go gathering plants and fruits and hunting in the islands, and otherwise conduct culturally meaningful activities in their territory which are more easily accessed by water. Seafaring vessels also offer other potential sources of income, including the occasional tourism outing or bighorn sheep hunting trips (Figure 9.3 illustrates the kinds of seascapes along which these activities take place).

However, it is also the case that coordination among the Comcáac has become more challenging and controlling access by outsiders is at an all-time low. According to our Comcáac informants, their once abundant pen shell banks are now in a constant state of overexploitation and there is no agreement among Comcáac fishers on how to let them recover. In addition,

Figure 9.3 View of the Gulf of California from Kino Bay, Sonora; a typical view of the kinds of seascapes navigated by fishers in the region, Comcáac and Mexican alike (Photo by Juliana Mayhew). A colour version of this image is downloadable as an eResource from www.routledge.com/9780367138004.

our research suggests the Comcáac are not actively working to enact their self-determination through building collective institutions, such as cooperatives, which would allow them to gain greater control over the commercialisation and marketing of fishery harvest. Lack of capital and political power are often mentioned as some of the major impediments to doing so. There are increasingly more actors and centers of power shaping the Comcáac's relations of production, distribution and conservation of fishing resources. Meanwhile, the hegemony of the Seri Cooperative as a unifying symbol of the 'Community' is fading away, perhaps to be replaced by social media and other new symbols of togetherness like the highly successful music festival organised by Comcáac youth every year in the village of Punta Chueca.

The more recent history of the Comcáac, and their evolving relations to both their territories and the surrounding marine life, is difficult to separate from long histories of colonisation and subsequent forms of subjection by the Mexican State. Recent processes through which one Seri cooperative became a proliferation of smaller, family cooperatives complicate any simplified understanding of commonisation or decommonisation, since as Nayak and Berkes (2011) suggest, these are dynamic and ongoing. Furthermore, the history of the Comcáac suggests the distinction might be one of optics (i.e., commonisation from one perspective might signify exclusion and enclosure from another). By revealing the tensions surrounding the formation and fragmentation of cooperatives, what emerges is an ongoing and disjointed picture of commoning as relational assemblage – a processual coming together and pulling apart of humans with(in) their broader milieu. This commoning may be understood as an evolving relationality between the Comcáac and their territories or towns, one that is always embedded in the historical relations with Mexico as well as with the "natural" environment or more-than-human natures around them. This latter part has been less the focus of our work here, but one that remains important to examine, as the Comcáac's particular cosmovision and understandings of nature distinctly give shape to their practices of commoning.

Conclusions

As we have argued in this chapter, the history of the Comcáac (parts of which we must inevitably simplify in order to examine their relations to fishing commons) reveals a diversity of ongoing and interrelated processes that might be understood through the lens of commonisation and decommonisation. These insights benefit from the incorporation of concepts such as commoning that emphasize relational understandings of commons (i.e., commons as process and praxis). Particularly, see Bresnihan's (2016) work on commoning and more-than-human commons in fisheries, which has inspired us. By way of concluding, we emphasize some key theoretical insights that emerge through the incorporation of "commoning" to common-pool resources theory and their implications for understanding commons as processual using the evolving governance of fishing commons in Comcáac territory as our illustrative canvas.

First, our case illustrates tensions and complex socio-historical processes that complicate discrete conceptual categorisations for which common-pool resources theory is mostly known, here illustrated by the framings of commonisation and decommonisation. Our argument is not that such categorisations are not useful. They can be most useful, for instance, as analytical building blocks and entry points for understanding complex phenomena. However, focusing primarily on the institutional arrangements or the resource dimensions of commons obscures their processual and relational nature. Placing the concept of commoning in conversation with commonisation/ decommonisation, we have focused on specific practices, encounters, meanings, and socio-historical processes that constitute commons, elucidating productive tensions between structural understandings of institutional arrangements and the more fluid nature of governance processes.

Consider the question of whether or not the original Seri Cooperative (defined as a new institutional structure with a particular combination of rules and norms) might be considered a form of commonisation. The Cooperative's institutional aspects (i.e., decision-making practices) and historical emergence suggest this is contradictory and a sole explanation based on structure masks these contradictions: The Comcáac did not actually control the Cooperative, and although they did agree to form it with an outsider like Solorzano (suggesting an element of consent or agency), the exchange was vastly unequal. Indeed, through some analytical framings, it might be considered a form of exploitation or primitive accumulation (in a Marxist sense), taking place through the appropriation of the "unpaid labor" of human and non-human natures (Moore, 2010, 2015). Such a Marxist understanding of these dynamics might also illustrate the ways in which the body itself becomes a site of enclosure and exploitation vis-à-vis the appropriation of labor (De Angelis, 2007). However it is important to point out, as our case illustrates, capitalism works and takes shape through the agency of diverse subjects and natures – which are not merely passive recipients of some unified capitalist logic or state-capitalist control (for such a framing in Mexican fisheries, see Breton & Estrada, 1989; Quezada Domínguez, 1995).

As De Angelis's (2007, 2017) work suggests, practices of commoning have emancipatory potential for pushing back on exploitative modes of capitalist production. The Comcáac's initial move towards cooperativism (albeit an exploitative one, rooted in colonial histories) facilitated other forms of commoning, including the formation of towns as sites where the "Seri community" continues to evolve. Over time, the Comcáac have enacted considerable agency in shaping the conditions of production in Desemboque and Punta Chueca including the formation of new, less-exploitative forms of cooperative organisation of labor (e.g., family cooperatives). Note that these forms of commoning around the formation of cooperatives, for instance, are not just about resources but also historical struggles, the forging of collective subjectivities and communities-as-commons (Gibson-Graham et al., 2016). In this sense, our work here also resonates with Bonnie McCay's work on the historical emergence of commons and enclosures (McCay, 1987), as well as her work more generally, which inspires us to understand the situated or embedded historical context in which collective action and commoning take shape.

A second, related point worth emphasizing from our work, which Nayak and Berkes' (2011) case study also illustrates, is the importance of understanding how processes of commonisation/decommonisation and commoning are embedded in broader assemblages of national policies, discourses, and understandings of the world. For instance, in our case the role of PROPEMEX or legal changes at the national level (e.g., to the Law of Fisheries), the latter of which can be seen as an instance of decommonisation through the State's elimination of exclusive benefits to fishing cooperatives, can also be understood as generative, co-producing the space of possibilities for practices of commoning at the local level. Indeed, the issue of scale has been examined extensively in the common-pool resources literature, yet our case draws attention to the inherent contradictions that emerge for assessing benefits and outcomes when processes of collective action at different scales are incorporated into the analysis.

Third, our case study demonstrates the ways in which narratives and stories shape efforts of collective action, much as they influence property relations and understandings of the commons (Rose, 1990, 1994). Powerful narratives for the Comcáac weave together shared pasts and instances of unity in the face of invasions. These insights suggest a deeper understanding of commoning (or commons as ongoing process) will require recognition that discursive and symbolic dimensions are important for understanding collective action and the articulation of collective subjectivities.

Lastly, we want to emphasize the importance of examining the more-than-human entanglements that constitute diverse forms of commoning and which underlie our understandings of commonisation/decommonisation. Certainly, the forms of commonisation and commoning that have taken place in Comcáac territories have been possible because of the rich biodiversity and bioabundance of the Gulf of California. We acknowledge this has not been the central focus of our work here. Nonetheless, we have pointed to the relationships between the Comcáac and technological objects such as fishing vessels, and it is worth noting both the importance of these objects for enacting diverse forms of commoning (e.g., through uses beyond fishing, such as traveling to ancestral territories), and the ways in which these objects serve to articulate forms of citizenship or subjection to the Mexican State. Understanding the future of Comcáac fishing commons, as well as fishing commons more generally, will require us to understand the ways in which commons institutions are embedded in and constituted through such evolving relations with diverse non-human entities.

Acknowledgements

We are indebted to Comcáac friends, informants, and colleagues for sharing with us over the years their knowledge about Comcáac history and their relations with their territory. We also thank Samantha Huff for her assistance with figures. Finally, we would also like to thank the editor and two anonymous reviewers for their feedback on this chapter.

References

Agrawal, A., & Gibson, C. C. (1999). Enchantment and disenchantment: the role of community in natural resource conservation. *World Development, 27*(4), 629–649.

Axelrod, R. (1984). *The Evolution of Cooperation*. New York: Basic Books.

Baland, J.-M., & Platteau, J.-P. (1996). *Halting Degradation of Natural Resources: Is There a Role for Rural Communities?* Rome: Food & Agriculture Org.

Basurto, X. (2005). How locally designed access and use controls can prevent the tragedy of the commons in a Mexican small-scale fishing community. *Society and Natural Resources, 18*(7), 643–659.

Basurto, X. (2006). Commercial Diving and the Callo de Hacha Fishery in Seri Territory. *Journal of the Southwest, 48*(2), 189–209.

Basurto, X., Cinti, A., Bourillón, L., Rojo, M., Torre, J., & Weaver, A. H. (2012). The emergence of access controls in small-scale fishing commons: A comparative analysis of individual licenses and common property-rights in two Mexican communities. *Human Ecology, 40*(4), 597–609.

Basurto, X., & Coleman, E. (2010). Institutional and ecological interplay for successful self-governance of community-based fisheries. *Ecological Economics, 69*(5), 1094–1103.

Berkes, F. (1989). *Common Property Resources. Ecology and Community-Based Sustainable Development*. London: Belhaven Press with the International Union for Conservation of Nature and Natural Resources.

Berkes, F., Mahon, R., McConney, P., Pollnac, R., & Pomeroy, R. (2001). *Managing Small-Scale Fisheries: Alternative Directions and Methods*. Ottawa: International Development Research Center. International Development Research Centre, Canada.

Bowen, T. (2000). *Unknown Island. Seri Indians, Europeans, and San Esteban Island in the Gulf of California*. Albuquerque: University of New Mexico Press.

Bresnihan, P. (2016). *Transforming the Fisheries: Neoliberalism, Nature, and the Commons*. Lincoln: University of Nebraska Press.

Breton, Y. D., & Estrada, L. (1989). *Ciencias sociales y desarrollo de las pesquerías: modelos y métodos aplicados al caso de México*. Mexico City: Instituto National de Antropologia e Historia.

Bromley, D. W. (Ed.) (1992). *Making the Commons Work: Theory, Practice, and Policy*. San Francisco: Institute for Contemporary Studies Press.

Cariño, M. M. (1996). *Historia de las relaciones hombre naturaleza en Baja* California Sur, 1500–1940. Baja California: Universidad Autonoma de Baja California.

Cinti, A., Shaw, W., Cudney-Bueno, R., & Rojo, M. (2010). The unintended consequences of formal fisheries policies: social disparities and resource overuse in a major fishing community in the Gulf of California, Mexico. *Marine Policy, 34*(2), 328–339.

Dawney, L., Kirwan, S., & Brigstocke, J. (2015). Introduction: The promise of the commons. In: S. Kirwan, L. Dawney, J. Brigstocke (Eds.). *Space, Power and the Commons: The Struggle for Alternative Futures* (pp. 13–40): London: Routledge.

De Angelis, M. (2007). *The Beginning of History: Value Struggles and Global Capital* London. Ann Arbor: Pluto Press.

De Angelis, M. (2017). *Omnia sunt communia: On the Commons and the Transformation to Postcapitalism*. London: Zed Books Ltd.

Diario Oficial de la Federación. (1970). 28 de Noviembre de 1970. México, DF, México.

Diario Oficial de la Federación. (1975). 11 de Febrero de 1975. México, DF, México.

Diario Oficial de la Federación. (1978). 2 de Agosto de 1978. México, DF, México.

Felger, R. S., & Moser, M. B. (1985). *People of the Desert and Sea. Ethnobotany of the Seri Indians*. Tucson: University of Arizona Press.

Gibson-Graham, J., Cameron, J., & Healy, S. (2016). Commoning as a postcapitalist politics. In: A. Amin & P. Howell (Eds.), *Releasing the Commons: Rethinking the Futures of the Commons* (pp. 192–212). London: Routledge.

Johnsen, J. P. (2005). The evolution of the "harvest machinery": why capture capacity has continued to expand in Norwegian fisheries. *Marine Policy, 29*(6), 481–493.

Lansing, J. S. (2003). Complex adaptive systems. *Annual Review of Anthropology, 32*(1), 183–204.

Linebaugh, P. (2008). *The Magna Carta Manifesto: Liberties and Commons for All.* Berkeley: University of California Press.

Lobato González, P. (1996). Reflexiones en torno a la pesca ribereña. *Esfuerzo y captura: Tecnología y sobreexplotación de los recursos marinos vivos: El Colegio de México*, 301–335.

MacKenzie, D., Muniesa, F., & Siu, L. (2007). *Do Economist make Markets? On the Performativity of Economics.* Princeton: Princeton University Press.

Malkin, B. (1962). *Seri ethnozoology*. Pocatello: Idaho State College Museum.

McCay, B. J. (1987). The culture of the commoners: Historical observations on old and new world fisheries. In: B. J. McCay & J. M. Acheson (Eds.), *The Question of the Commons. The Culture and Ecology of Communal Resources* (pp. 195–216). Tucson: University of Arizona Press.

McCay, B. J. (1996). Common and private concerns. In: C. F. Susan Hanna, and Karl-Goran Maler (Eds.), *Rights to Nature: Ecological, Economic, Cultural, and Political Principles of Institutions for the Environment*. Washington, DC: Island Press.

McCay, B. J. (2002). Emergence of institutions for the commons: Contexts, situations, and events. In: E. U. Weber, S. Stonich, P. C. Stern, N. Dolsak, T. Dietz, & E. Ostrom (Eds.), *The Drama of the Commons* (pp. 361–402). Washington, DC: National Academies Press.

McCay, B. J., & Acheson, J. M. (1987). *The Question of the Commons: The Culture and Ecology of Communal Resources*. Tucson: University of Arizona Press.

Moore, J. W. (2010). 'Amsterdam is Standing on Norway' Part I: The Alchemy of Capital, Empire and Nature in the Diaspora of Silver, 1545–1648. *Journal of Agrarian Change, 10*(1), 33–68.

Moore, J. W. (2015). *Capitalism in the Web of Life: Ecology and the Accumulation of Capital.* London/New York: Verso Books.

Moser, E. (1963). Seri bands. *Kiva, 28*(3), 14–27.

National Research Council (2002). *The Drama of the Commons.* Washington, DC: The National Academies Press.

Nayak, P. K., Armitage, D., & Andrachuk, M. (2016). Power and politics of social–ecological regime shifts in the Chilika lagoon, India and Tam Giang lagoon, Vietnam. *Regional Environmental Change, 16*(2), 325–339.

Nayak, P. K., & Berkes, F. (2011). Commonisation and decommonisation: understanding the processes of change in the Chilika Lagoon, India. *Conservation and Society, 9*(2), 132.

Nenadovic, M., Basurto, X., Espinosa, M. J., Huff, S., López, J., Méndez Medina, C., … Hudson Weaver, A. (2018). *Diagnostico Nacional de las Organizaciones Pesqueras: Resumen de Resultados de las Organizaciones.* Report available through the authors.

Olson, M. (1965). *The Logic of Collective Action: Public Goods and the Theory of Groups.* Cambridge: Harvard University Press.

Ostrom, E. (1990). *Governing the Commons: The Evolution of Institutions for Collective Action.* Cambridge and New York: Cambridge University Press.

Ostrom, E. (2005). *Understanding Institutional Diversity.* Princeton: Princeton University Press.

Ostrom, E. (2007). A diagnostic approach for going beyond panaceas. *Proceedings of the National Academy of Sciences, 104*(39), 15181–15187.

Ostrom, V., Tiebout, C. M., & Warren, R. (1961). The organization of government in metropolitan areas: a theoretical inquiry. *American Political Science Review, 55*(4), 831–842.

Pagdee, A., Kim, Y.-s., & Daugherty, P. J. (2006). What makes community forest management successful: A meta-study from community forests throughout the world. *Society and Natural Resources, 19*(1), 33–52.

Persha, L., Agrawal, A., & Chhatre, A. (2011). Social and ecological synergy: Local rulemaking, forest livelihoods, and biodiversity conservation. *Science, 331*(6024), 1606–1608.

Quezada Domínguez, R. D. (1995). *Papel y transformación de las unidades de producción pesquera ejidales en el sector halieútico, Yucatán, México.* Retrieved from http://bibliotecasibe.ecosur.mx/sibe/book/000049651

Roelvink, G. (2009). Broadening the horizons of economy. *Journal of Cultural Economy, 2*(3), 325–344.

Rose, C. M. (1990). Property as storytelling: Perspectives from game theory, narrative theory, feminist theory. *Yale JL & Human., 2*, 37.

Rose, C. M. (1994). *Property and Persuasion: Essays on the History, Theory, and Rhetoric of Property.* Boulder: Westview Press.

Schlager, E. (2002). Rationality, cooperation, and common pool resources. *American Behavioral Scientist, 45*(5), 801–819.

Scott, J. C. (1998). *Seeing Like a State: How Certain Schemes to Improve the Human Condition Have Failed.* New Haven: Yale University Press.

Smith, W. N. (1954). *The Ethno-History of the Seri Indians 1890 to 1953.* (ms 316 box 3 folder 13). University of Arizona Library Special Collections, Tucson, Arizona.

Soberanes Fernández, J. L. (1994). Historia Contemporánea de la Legislación Pesquera en México. In: M. González Oropeza & M. Á. Garita Alonso (Eds.), *El regimen jurídico de la pesca en México* (Vol. Serie G: Estudios doctrinales, núm. 150, pp. 1–26). Mexico City: Instituto de Investigaciones Jurídicas.

Taylor, P. L. (2003). Reorganization or division? New strategies of community forestry in Durango, Mexico. *Society & Natural Resources, 16*(7), 643–661.

Chapter 10

Concurrent processes of commonisation and decommonisation of Guadalquivir River (south Spain)

Sherman Farhad

Introduction

Commons is understood as a dynamic process rather than a static characteristic of a resource system. Being commons or non-commons is a matter of governance configurations and social organizations, which are subject to change over time. So, which type of governance configurations and institutional arrangements facilitate long-term conservation of resources as commons? Which features of a system pave the way to convert non-commons to commons or vice versa? Commons research is mainly focused on joint use of a resource through certain activities such as fishing (Berkes, 2005; Galappaththi & Berkes, 2014), agriculture (Sang, 2008; Tatlonghari & Sumalde, 2008), tourism (Healy, 1994; Santana, Fontes Filho, & Rochas, 2015), etc. However, in many cases, one natural resource may have several uses and associated with different socio-economic activities. The objective of this chapter is to analyse Guadalquivir River (south Spain) and its three main uses (rice cultivation, fishing and tourism) in the municipality of Isla Mayor to examine how a jointly used resource can acquire both faces (commons and non-commons) simultaneously within the same system.

When we consider the commons, we are not just referring to a natural resource. Each commons represents a set of interactions, relationships and feedbacks between social and biophysical dimensions of the system. That makes the commons a social-ecological system (Berkes & Folke, 1998) with multiple dynamics, interactions and feedbacks. Commons as interconnected social-ecological systems are complex adaptive systems (Berkes, Colding, & Folke, 2003; Holling, 2001; Janssen & Ostrom, 2006; Liu et al., 2007). According to Levin (1999), self-organization characterizes the development of complex adaptive systems as all the instructions are not specified in the development of a complex system, but rather, multiple outcomes typically are possible depending on accidents of history.

Considering commons as a process, its long-term sustainability requires the ability to handle changes. Therefore, general resilience, defined as the resilience of the system as a whole to any and all kinds of disturbances (Folke et al.,

2010), becomes significant. Diversity is one of the key conditions in enabling general resilience (Carpenter et al., 2012), and it is therefore important to analyse diverse possible uses and activities associated with a commons and the possible trade-offs.

Governing the commons is always a struggle (Dietz, Ostrom, & Stern, 2003). "No single type of property regime works efficiently, fairly, and sustainably in relation to all common pool resources" (Ostrom, Burger, Field, Norgaard, & Policansky, 1999: 279). That is the reason why institutional arrangements and governance (Brondizio, Ostrom, & Young, 2009; Kooiman, 2003) become key concepts in the study of commons. In this regard and given the focus of this chapter on social-ecological systems and the governance of commons, the framework proposed by Janssen (2006) and Anderies, Janssen, and Ostrom (2004) is used to develop a case study of Isla Mayor social-ecological system and to carry out a historical institutional analysis of the commons.

Multi-level governance serves as a means for bringing diversity of interests, knowledge and information to a common forum. Effective institutional designs for commons problem solving create complex, multi-tiered systems with some levels of duplication, overlap, and contestation (Ostrom, 2005). In fact, the multi-level nature of commons problems requires multi-level solutions; i.e. the union of diverse stakeholders from different levels of governance, sharing their knowledge and power in decision-making processes. Therefore, scales, as a joint product of social and biophysical processes, and the politics of scale (Lebel, Garden, & Imamura, 2005) are crucial issues in governance analysis. It is important to determine how the political construction of scale, as an on-going dynamic, takes place (Delaney & Leitneh, 1997). Empowerment of stakeholders may necessitate acquiring the capacity to work across multiple scales (Lebel et al., 2005).

Similar to the commons, Commons governance is also dynamic by nature. It is consequently important to analyse commons governance over time as commons can become non-commons or vice versa (Galappaththi & Nayak, 2017). In dealing with commons governance, I adopt the concepts of commonisation and decommonisation (Nayak & Berkes, 2011) that provide us with the opportunity to focus on the history associated with the social-ecological system to inquire about the key factors enhancing or hampering the processes through which a commons gets converted to a non-commons and vice versa.

Undertaking an exploratory and empirical case study, this chapter aims to address how diverse uses of the Guadalquivir River in three different socio-economic areas (rice farming, tourism and fishing) of Isla Mayor (south Spain) have contributed to both processes of commonisation and decommonisation of the river at the same time. The main goal is to help shed light on the trade-offs between commonisation and decommonisation processes, and their reduction or minimisation for general resilience and long-term sustainability of the commons. I provide a glossary of terms in Table 10.1.

Table 10.1 Glossary of important terms used in this chapter

Term	Definition
Commons	Common-pool resources or commons are natural or human-made resources characterized by excludability and subtractability; i.e. those resources "in which 1) exclusion of beneficiaries through physical and institutional means is specially costly, and 2) exploitation by one user reduces resource availability for others" (Ostrom et al., 1999: 278).
Social-ecological system	A set of people, their natural and human-made resources, and the relationships among them (Anderies et al., 2004; Janssen, Anderies, & Ostrom, 2005) / "Systems, in which cultural, political, social, economic, ecological, technological, and other components interact" (Resilience Alliance, 2010: 6).
Commonisation and Decommonisation	"Commonisation is understood as a process through which a resource gets converted into a jointly used resource under commons institutions that deal with excludability and subtractability, and decommonisation refers to a process through which a jointly used resource under commons institutions loses these essential characteristics" (Nayak & Berkes, 2011: 132).
Governance	"A social function centered on steering human groups toward mutually beneficial outcomes and away from mutually harmful outcomes" (Brondizio et al., 2009: 255) "The totality of interactions, in which public as well as private actors participate, aimed at solving societal problems or creating societal opportunities" (Kooiman, 2003: 4).
Multi-level governance	"Systems of governance where there is a dispersion of authority upwards, downwards and sideways between levels of government – local, regional, national and supra-national – as well as across spheres and sectors, including states, markets and civil society" (Daniell & Kay, 2017: 4).
Politics of scale	A helpful metaphor "in drawing attention to the ways in which scale choices are constrained overtly by politics, and more subtly by choices of technologies, institutional designs, and measurements" (Lebel et al., 2005: 1).

Study area and methodology

Study area

Isla Mayor is a small municipality located in the province of Seville in southwest Spain. It covers an area of 114.4 km². It is wholly situated in a marsh ecosystem and surrounded by the Guadalquivir River, and part of its municipal district is inside Doñana Natural Park. Its particular location of being close to the mouth of the river creates increased salinity due to the Atlantic Ocean tides (Figure 10.1).

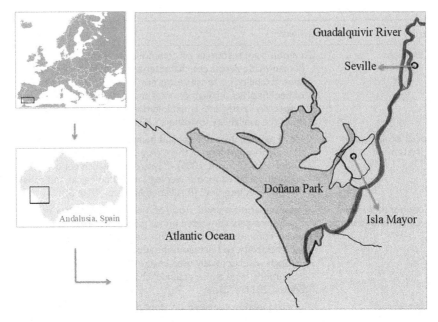

Figure 10.1 Map of the study area. A colour version of this image is downloadable as an eResource from www.routledge.com/9780367138004.

The Guadalquivir River is used for a variety of purposes such as domestic, agriculture, hydropower, industry, fishing, navigation, etc. in the region. However, a large share of the water of the river (around 87 percent) is devoted to the agriculture and livestock sectors. The river basin has a typical Mediterranean climate: temperate-warm temperatures (16.8∘C annual average) and irregular precipitation (annual average 550 l/m^2) (Confederación Hidrográfica del Guadalquivir, 2013). The physical environment provides privileged topography and climate characteristics highly suitable for rice cultivation (Del Moral, 1993; González-Arteaga, 2005). For many centuries, this marsh ecosystem was characterized by harsh natural conditions such as cycles of flood and drought, water salinity (due to its location close to the mouth of the river), soil salinity (because of being a marsh ecosystem), marsh associated human illnesses such as malaria, etc. Consequently, this territory was perceived as a distant, indomitable and demographically empty space up to the early years of the 20th century (Sabuco-Cantó, 2004).

The hydraulic constructions of this region (irrigation channels, dams, etc.) took place during Franco's regime. When the Spanish Civil War (1936–1939) was over, the National Institute of Rural Development and Colonization under de Ministry of Agriculture was established by the

Spanish State in order to increase agricultural production, to repopulate certain areas of the country, and to alleviate devastating effects of the war. The town, therefore, became known as Villafranco del Guadalquivir (later changed to Isla Mayor) and people from different regions, but especially from Valencia (already a rice-producing region), were encouraged to move to and settle in this new promising area with opportunities for better living conditions. By this means, the history of the Guadalquivir River as a commons was initiated through the habitation and the settlement of people in this area.

The region today counts a population of 5948 inhabitants. With 90 percent of its territory dedicated to rice cultivation, Isla Mayor's socio-economic fabric has essentially been shaped by the presence of the Guadalquivir River. The average rice farm in Isla Mayor is 10–20 ha. However, there are also smaller plots of less than 5 ha and bigger farms of 100 ha or more (Instituto de Estadística y Cartografía de Andalucía, 2015). This relatively large average size of rice farm made it possible to carry out intensive and highly mechanized rice farming in Isla Mayor so that several tasks such as seeding and spraying are mostly carried out by airplanes. This farming activity is managed by flood irrigation system, which allows for a continuous circulation of water during the entire vegetative cycle through a network of distribution and drainage channels. The river water is raised by powerful pumps, high enough to be introduced into the main irrigation channel.

As a secondary activity, some of the inhabitants of Isla Mayor are engaged in fishing in the river, channels and paddies. The most caught species are red crawfish, caridean shrimp, European eel, common (European) carp and liza ramada (*thinlip mullet*)[1]. In fact, fishing practices have drastically changed over time and today people mostly trap red crawfish. We rarely can find people exclusively dedicated to fishing in Isla Mayor as a primary source of occupation due to many of them being engaged in other non-fishing activities, particularly in rice farming.

Incipient tourism could be considered as a secondary activity in Isla Mayor, which is mainly based on bird watching and local gastronomy. Being on the migratory route of birds between Europe and Africa, Spanish southwest marshes are considered as Spain's most important bird area with a total of 370 registered species (Junta de Andalucía, 2008). In this special geographical context, rice fields, as human-made wetlands (Elphick, 2000), provide a crucial living and feeding space for birds. That is in fact one of the main touristic attractions of the region that brings people to watch birds in the rice fields. Moreover, rice and fish as the basic local products have provided a unique local gastronomy that could be considered as the other key touristic attraction of the town. During the weekends, some people from the neighbourhood towns and cities come here to spend the day and to have the local dish.

Research methods

Ethnographic case study was carried out in Isla Mayor from April 2010 to July 2013, in three intensive periods of four months each and extensive monitoring over the remaining time. Additional fieldwork was conducted in 2015 and 2016, undertaking several field visits to collect supplementary data. Several data collection methods were used such as semi-structured and in-depth open-ended interviews, participant observation, participatory workshop, questionnaire, and literature and document analysis (Table 10.2). Key informants and stakeholders included: rice farmers, fishers, leading local figures such as the town mayor, the rice cooperative's director, water managers, the Seville Rice

Table 10.2 Data collection methods used in the ethnographic case study

Data collection methods	Description
Literature and document analysis	Exhaustive review of policy documents, legislation, research studies and documents was carried out in order to describe and characterize the area's main social-ecological characteristics, the emergence and historical evolution of the key socio-economic activities of the area, and legislation regarding water governance, rice activity, fishing and tourism.
Semi-structured and in-depth open-ended interviews (N = 34)	Interviews were conducted with key stakeholders in order to analyse their perceptions and experiences regarding the historical evolution of the rice activity, fishing and tourism, the role of Guadalquivir River in each activity, formal and informal institutions relevant for the management of water, and the challenges in the development of fishing and tourism activities.
Participant observation	Participant observation took place in meetings, conferences, workshops, celebrations, demonstrations and informal gatherings, in which various actors including rice farmers, fishers, ecosystem managers, irrigation communities, university experts, etc. were participating, discussing and debating. This helped me to identify how local people carry out their socio-economic activities and their corresponding water managements, and how they perceive the Guadalquivir River, its values and challenges.
Participatory workshop (1 day with 19 participants)	A diverse group of rice farmers, fisherman, representatives from the rice cooperative, irrigation communities and the only tourism company of the area, and one university professional participated at the workshop. The objective of the workshop was to conduct a group discussion on their perceptions of the values, threats and potential drivers regarding the Guadalquivir River and its provided ecosystem services.
Questionnaire (N = 19)	Workshop participants were asked to answer a brief questionnaire at the beginning of the workshop with the goal of collecting their individual insights in order to compare them with their collective responses during the workshop.

Farmers Federation's director, the president of the Fishermen's Association, stakeholders in tourism, and experts at the local university.

Commonisation process of the Guadalquivir River for rice farming

Isla Mayor's current image as a social-ecological system differs significantly from what it was a few decades ago. The rice farming management has evolved towards a new governance system, which is characterized by collective action and multi-level social-ecological dynamics. This current multi-level institutional arrangement represents a type of relationship between people and the river, and a new water governance system. For a deep understanding of this process, this section analyses the historical evolution of the rice farming governance, focusing on those key elements that have strengthened the commonisation process of the Guadalquivir River for rice farming.

Background of collective irrigation water management in Spain

One of the key features that paved the way for commonisation of the river for rice farming was the tradition of collective water management in Spain. Although irrigation water management was first introduced in the Iberian Peninsula during the Roman Empire, the Arab civilization achieved an apex in irrigation technology (Nadal-Reimat, 1980). Its significant legacy is a kind of irrigation system (known as *huerta*) in Spain which is managed under a long-standing common property regime (Ostrom, 1990). Huerta irrigation system is considered as a good example of a commons as it meets the required characteristics such as locally determined rules, effective monitoring and a scale of gradually increasing punishments for rule breaking (Wall, 2014). In the ancient huerta system, irrigators were organized into *autonomous irrigation communities*, and these communities were in fact the heart of the system. The basic rules for allocating water were dependent on the decisions made by the officials of those irrigation communities concerning environmental conditions such as abundance, seasonal low water, and extraordinary drought. Moreover, the chief executives (syndics) of those communities participated in two weekly meetings of the water court (Tribuanl de las Aguas).

In spite of the relatively recent establishment of Isla Mayor and its irrigation system, its water management has adopted Spain's traditional irrigation philosophy. At the core of this water governance system lies the essential local institution (Irrigation Community), which unites several farmers in order to acquire capacity for self-management, for organizing collective use of a common water body and for distributing it in an orderly, effective and equitable way among its members.

Irrigation communities work under the supervision of the River Basin Authority, another key pillar created at the beginning of the 20th century by the central government. River basin authorities (hydrographic confederations) constitutes a great institutional heritage, and they single out the Spanish water management model by their guiding principles such as management of water through basin, comprehensive planning, interested parties' involvement, autonomy of management, etc. (Fanlo-Loras, 2010). The Guadalquivir River Basin Authority, created in 1927, corresponds to our case study.

Rice farming in Isla Mayor is managed by flood irrigation system. The water flows through a main channel and from there it branches out to the irrigation ditches, which in turn branches into smaller ditches and eventually to each paddy field. In this network of channels, the water flow is regulated by dividers or adjustable gates, which are controlled by the Irrigation Community Guards. The drainage network is organized in a similar way. At the end of the paddy field, by means of small pools or culverts, the water is discharged into a drainage ditch. Several of these ditches converge at a central drainage channel (*azarabe*), which itself leads to a general collector (Aguilar-Portero, 2010). The interconnected nature of this irrigation water body entails joint decision making and management of crucial tasks such as water salinity control at the catchment point, the amount of water to be distributed among the fields, maintenance work on the irrigation channels, etc.

Broader social-political context

The evolution of the broader social-political context in which Isla Mayor is embedded has been another pillar of the river commonisation process. The evolutionary process of both Spanish and European history during the last century has been in favor of the traditional collaborative locally based water governance. A key turning point took place in 1975 with the end of the Spanish dictatorship. The transition process and adaptation to democracy raised the necessity for changes in hydrological policy from a resource-oriented water management model (Del Moral and Saurí, 1999) or a so-called "paradigm of hydraulic works" (Ramos-Gorostiza, 2001) to a unified management of water resources (Sánchez-Martínez, Rodríguez-Ferrero, & Salas-Velasco, 2011).

The 1985 Water Act, as the cornerstone of the new water policy era, adapted water legislations to the modern democratic and decentralized framework. In this way, the River Basin Authority's functions shifted from a hydro-technical agency devoted to the construction of dams, reservoirs, and water conveyance facilities to an integrated water resource management agency at the river basin scale, holding a combined responsibility for physical infrastructure as well as water use management (Bhat & Blomquist, 2005).

This new water policy has been reinforced in 2000 by a new legislation from upper institutional level. European Union introduced a new legislative approach (2000/60/CE) called Water Framework Directive (WFD). This directive has in fact strengthened the local participation as well as the cooperation among different governance levels such as local, national and

European. River basin authorities have been given a more prominent role by this directive, and became responsible for the preparation of their own new basin hydrological plans, which include key issues such as licenses and permits for water use, general order of preferences in water allocation, water tariffs, etc. WFD has had specific emphasis on citizen participation, allowing the public to influence the outcomes of the new hydrological plans and the working process.

Multi-level governance in rice farming

Collective spirit of Spanish water management together with the socio-political evolutionary processes at both national and European levels have resulted in the creation of a participatory multi-level water governance system for rice farming in Isla Mayor. This new governance configuration has enhanced collective action and could therefore be considered as the corner stone of the river commonisation process. However, there has also been another critical element in this commonisation process called *integrated rice management*.

Integrated rice management is a farming system based on environmentally friendly techniques and limited use of chemical products and constant supervision of the paddies by specialized technicians. Integrated rice started in 1998 in Seville and today almost all the Seville rice production (98 percent) is under this farming system. The major coordination and performance of this farming system is carried out by *Seville Rice Farmers Federation*, a powerful self-organized institution, constituted in 1986 that defends the unity of the sector. At local level, this federation collaborates closely with irrigation communities.

The water management of Isla Mayor's rice farming has a multi-level configuration, and collective action is carried out through a network of linkages among different actors of diverse levels of governance (Farhad, Gual, & Ruiz-Ballesteros, 2015). As shown in Figure 10.2, irrigation communities, to which almost[2] all the rice farmers belong, form a fundamental component of this multi-layered management structure under a commons regime. Six irrigation communities correspond to this study and they cover different surface areas, from 450 to 6433 ha, according to the number of each Irrigation Community members and the size of their rice fields.

Permits for water use are generally conceded by the Guadalquivir River Basin Authority to the irrigation communities. It is the irrigation communities' responsibility to manage water supply to each farmer's plot through the network of distribution channels and ditches. In each of these irrigation communities, there is a General Assembly of Users, which is constituted by the rice farmers. The votes of the commoners in the assembly are weighted according to their cultivation areas; i.e. the larger the rice cultivation area, the more votes the commoner can have. Besides the internal meetings of the users, irrigation communities also participate in some meetings of the

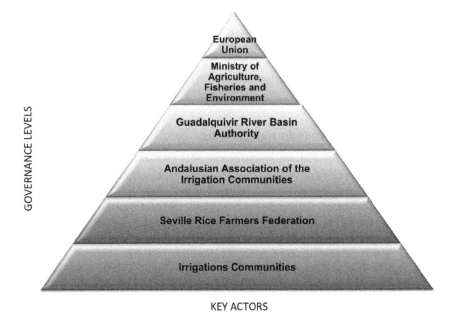

Figure 10.2 Multi-level water governance in rice farming in Isla Mayor. A colour version of this image is downloadable as an eResource from www.routledge.com/ 9780367138004.

Guadalquivir River Basin Authority and additionally collaborate with various institutions such as Seville Rice Farmers Federation, Association of the Irrigation Communities of Andalusia, Agricultural Association of the Young Farmers, etc.:

> We get involved in different organizations (such as Seville Rice Farmers Federation, Association of the Irrigation Communities of Andalusia, Agricultural Association of the Young Farmers, etc.), if and when it is convenient and useful for our Irrigation Community.
>
> (Technical director of one of the irrigation communities)

Collective action is often considered effective to deal with commons problems (Ostrom et al., 1999; Ruiz-Ballesteros & Gual, 2012; Galappaththi & Berkes, 2014; Ruiz-Ballesteros & Gálvez-García, 2014). By the same token, Isla Mayor case shows how multi-level governance has enhanced collective action, and it has thus been able to solve several commons problems, such as water salinity, challenging water allocation issues during droughts, implementation of the river dredging project, etc. The following is a detailed explanation of this multi-level governance system and its problem-solving capacity.

As mentioned above, geographical location of these rice fields on the final stretches of the Guadalquivir River makes them extremely sensitive to the Atlantic Ocean tides, and the resulting high salinity is considered as a significant problem. The multi-level water governance arrangement has been able to deal with the problem of salinity for rice cultivation in the area, and thus, the continuation of this social, cultural and economic activity. From the local perspective, irrigation communities are in charge of daily regulatory operations of salinity control for rice farming. In fact, two daily salt samples are taken from the river and sent to the Guadalquivir River Basin Authority. However, viewed from a different standpoint, the link between stakeholders and the collective negotiation power of the irrigation communities in the Guadalquivir River Basin Authority has been another key element, guaranteeing rice farmers access to maximum possible amount of irrigation water during droughts. This has been crucial in the case of rice cultivation, which requires large quantities of water, especially given its critical geographical location on the final stretches of the Guadalquivir River, which is extremely sensitive to tides.

In spite of the fact that irrigation water allocations are already defined in the basin plan, specific mechanisms exist within the participatory bodies of the Guadalquivir River Basin Authority that allow for a "certain degree of negotiation" in resource reallocation to different sectors during periods of droughts. Within the Guadalquivir River Basin Authority, the institution in charge of managing these issues is the Dam Water Release Commission. Water users have some representatives in the Dam Water Release Commission members, but the key point is that they are appointed according to used water volumes. The irrigation sector makes up the vast majority of this Commission, and therefore, together with other Dam Water Release Commission members such as Seville Rice Farmers Federation, they constitute an important force in water-related decision making.

Irrigation Communities have also served as a platform to establish informal agreements between upland and lowland rice farmers. Lowland paddies are closer to the mouth of the river and thus have a riskier position during droughts. In severe drought circumstances, there have been restrictions on the use of water, requiring the cultivation of only a certain percentage of the rice farm area. Looking back over history, key stakeholders report that during times of extreme drought, some lowland rice farmers had passed their reduced irrigation rights to the upland rice farmers, and thus divided the benefits between both of them. However, the existence of these informal agreements has been denied by some key informants during this case study research, most likely due to its illegality according to the Guadalquivir River Basin Authority.

Additionally, informal agreements exist between irrigation communities and various collaborating institutions. For example, some irrigation communities are responsible for the collection and management of the Seville Rice Farmers Federation's membership fees. According to one key informant:

It is not legal [for the Irrigation Community to collect the Seville Rice Farmers Federation's fees] but nobody has questioned it as it has been a good thing for the sector. A farmer who doesn't pay, will not receive water by the Irrigation Community, and therefore, won't be able to sow. This is a measure of pressure. It is an invented mechanism, which has guaranteed the functioning of the Seville Rice Farmers Federation.

This multi-level commons governance has also fostered adaptive capacity, preparedness and responsiveness of the system to possible emerging threats. This is the case of the Guadalquivir River dredging, a project promoted by the Seville Port Authority under the Ministry of Development, aimed at increasing the river depth to facilitate the arrival of huge cruise ships to the city of Seville for commercial and touristic purposes. The implementation of this extensive project, which is even partially financed by the European Union, has long been opposed by a coalition of a large collective composed of the WWF,[3] Ecologists in Action,[4] Rice Farmers Federation, Fishers, etc. Finally, following a 15-year battle, on March 2015, Spain's Supreme Court (fourth chamber, 5 March 2015, Madrid) ruled against the project to dredge the river, following an appeal by WWF Spain. As defended by WWF Spain in its appeal, the Supreme Court understood that the dredging would cause *modifications or alterations of the water bodies*, with the consequent *deterioration and impact* on Doñana National Park, one of the most ecologically sensitive and emblematic protected areas in Europe.

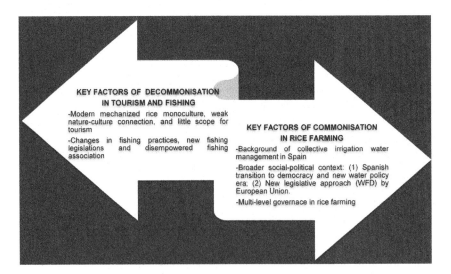

Figure 10.3 Key factors of simultaneous commonisation and decommonisation processes in Isla Mayor. A colour version of this image is downloadable as an eResource from www.routledge.com/9780367138004.

Decommonisation process of the Guadalquivir River for tourism and fishing

While the Guadalquivir River's role as a commons has been reinforced in rice farming, it has been decommonised at the same time in other socio-economic areas such as tourism and fishing. That is to say that within one social-ecological system, one sector has been commonised and the other two sectors have simultaneously been decommonised (Figure 10.3). This section consists of two parts. It first focuses on those key factors that have hindered the commonisation process of the river for tourism. Second, it discusses the central issues that have paved the way for decommonisation of the river for fishing activities.

Modern mechanized rice monoculture, weak nature-culture connection, and little scope for tourism

There are interesting examples of commonisation in tourism, where communities and cultural groups have been able to shape "new commons" (Hess, 2008) around tourism (Vail & Hultkrantz, 2000; Sharma, Nandita, Rai, & Renzino, 2002; Holden, 2005; Ruiz-Ballesteros & Gual, 2012). However, in the case of Isla Mayor, this potential for commination has not been achieved. Being an isle surrounded by the river, astonishing landscape of rice paddies, rich diversity of birds, closeness to the Doñana National Park, special gastronomy based on local products, etc., offers Isla Mayor great potential for tourism. The administration is aware of this potential and has made several attempts to promote tourism in this area. For example, several public entities (Isla Mayor Council, Puebla del Río (neighbouring village) Council, Province of Seville Council and the Andalusian Department of Tourism and Trade) collaborated and carried out a package of projects during 2004–2010 to revitalise the Guadalquivir River and to take advantage of its huge potential for touristic activity.

The tourism program consists of three projects in Isla Mayor and surrounding areas (Puebla del Río municipality). The first project is called *Isla de Pájaros* (*Birds' Island*). It is an open-air museum, where the most important Isla Mayor inhabiting birds are painted on the facades of the town's most emblematic buildings together with their names in four different languages (Spanish, English, French and Portuguese). The second one is *Dehesa de Abajo*, a Nature Reserve and protected area, where people can comfortably watch the most common birds of the area including Spain's largest breeding colony of white stork. Finally, the third project is called *Pantalán Isla Mínima*, which is a pier constructed with the main idea of giving the tourists an opportunity to come to Isla Mayor via de river and to moor their boats. Costing about €830,000 (approximately US$944,496), the mooring was officially inaugurated in 2010 but it is still out of service due to apparently some conflicts between two local villages. While Isla Mayor people have been able to solve several conflicts related to the rice activity, the absence of multi-level governance and collective action around tourism activities have made it difficult for the people to address conflicts.

Furthermore, there have been also several types of funding, mostly from the European Union, for the promotion of tourism in the area. For instance, two restaurants have received funding to develop local traditional gastronomy, and the only hotel of the town has also been opened as a result of these funding opportunities.

Unlike the above-mentioned administrative and financial supports, the tourism sector is still underdeveloped in Isla Mayor (Hernández-Ramírez, Farhad, & Gual, 2017), i.e. the potential commonisation of the river for tourism is not being achieved, and therefore, it is decommonising before being officially commonised. Looking for the reasons for this decommonisation process in tourism, surprisingly, rice activity is the main explanation.

Even though rice farming in Isla Mayor is carried out under a relatively environmentally friendly manner (*Integrated Production*), it is still an intensive and mechanized farming system. Rice farming as a daily practice of the majority of Isla Mayor inhabitants has created a peculiar social-ecological context, where common objectives do not go beyond what is required for the rice activity (Farhad, 2018). Rice production and sales process has also created a specific socio-economic context, in terms of the relationships between the Isla Mayor society members and the transactions involving rice. It is a totally paradoxical situation. On one hand, there are some powerful collective entities such as Rice Framers Federation, irrigation communities and Local Rice Cooperatives that almost all rice farmers are members of and they manage strategic requirements of the rice process such as irrigation, seeds, chemical products, European Union funding, selling, etc. Then there is the whole remaining rice practice, which is highly technological and is based on established protocols; and it therefore favors individualized management of the daily rice activity (Hernández-Ramírez et al., 2017). Moreover, it is worth mentioning that rice farming in Isla Mayor has considerable economic benefits. Farmers receive a direct subsidy of approximately €1300 (approximately US$1500)/ha (Farhad et al., 2015) from the Common Agricultural Policy (CAP) of the European Union. This adds a powerful additional incentive for rice farmers to stick with the rice farming and do not have interests in new socio-economic activities.

There is lack of actual tourism in Isla Mayor despite the extraordinary potential. In other words, there is absence of collective action to use the river as a common pool resource toward touristic endeavour. Modern agriculture, in which almost all the tasks are carried out by machines, has prevented the establishment of a deep and holistic connection between the locals and their surroundings. Instead, it is a very specific rice-centered social-ecological relationship that primarily focuses on managing and solving rice issues. So, it can be said that commonisation process in rice farming has simultaneously hindered the possible commonisation processes in other sectors such as tourism.

Changes in fishing practices, new fishing legislations and disempowered fishing association

Guadalquivir River has always provided Isla Mayor with great fishing potential. However, just like tourism, fishing sector has not been able either to develop this commonisation potential. There are three basic factors for fishing sector decommonisation in Isla Mayor.

As in the tourism sector, the key explanation for decommonisation in fishing is also the development of rice activity and its related social arrangement, which has left little scope for diversification and collective action in other sectors. Isla Mayor's fishers are not exclusively dedicated to fishing, but also to other activities, specially rice farming. So, rice activity, as an accessible source of income with decent returns has perhaps been one of the main reasons in explaining how the fishing activity and its association have waned over time. They have the safety and security of being able to count on rice!

However, in the case of fishing, there are also two additional factors. On the one hand, there are fishing legislations that have imposed excessive spatial, temporal and catchment restrictions regarding protected fish species, and this is, according to the fishers, the most critical problem for fishing activities in the entire zone. According to the President of Isla Mayor's Fishermen's Association, fishers do not find any coherent meaning in being a member of the Isla Mayor's Fishermen's Association when they are officially banned from several types of fishing. They believe that government pays very little attention and support to their needs and problems. An example of this is the case of the *European eel*, which is considered an endangered species and fishing for eel "at any stage of its development" is prohibited by the regional Andalusian government (Article 2 of Decree 396/2010) for a period of ten years. Fishers consider it as an excessive regional restriction, while, in fact, it is basically a decision taken by the European Union.

The third reason for decommonisation pertains to the modification of fishing practices over time. In the mid-1970s, 500 kg of red swamp crawfish (*Procambarus clarkia*) were brought from Louisiana (USA) and introduced in this area for commercial purposes. Considering the previously mentioned strict fishing restrictions in the area, fishers started to adapt their practices to the new situation, catching crawfish in the rice paddies and selling them to the local companies for processing and marketing. Today, Spain is the world's third (after China and the USA) largest fishing and processing area of this species. Crawfish catchment has specific features in terms of seasonality. It requires a great deal of fishers' and peelers' (mostly women) time and effort over a period of four to five months (from July to November). This partly coincides with labour work for rice (specially harvesting during October) and thus, perhaps, creates incompatibility with other activities, such as tourism and other types of fishing.

Conclusions

The majority of commons studies are focused on one specific joint use of a resource under commons institutions (Berkes, 2005; Healy, 1994; Sang, 2008). However, most of the resources can have different arrangements of joint uses at the same temporal and spatial scales and can, consequently, go under commonisation and decommonisation processes at the same time. These processes are strictly related together, and their analysis remains incomplete in commons literature. This chapter helps to address this gap and highlights how potential for commonisation could exist, but it cannot be achieved in all sectors; and how commonisation of a resource through a specific socio-economic activity and resource use may simultaneously lead to its decommonisation in other socio-economic areas. This emphasizes the need to analyse commons as a process, and with a holistic social-ecological system perspective that brings attention to all crucial elements of a system.

Commonisation and decommonisation are processes that are strongly influenced by prevailing policy and governance structures (Nayak & Berkes, 2011). The results of this study show how the evolution of rice farming governance into a multi-level system has strengthened the commonisation process in rice farming. Multi-level governance, characterized by co-existence of self-governing rules and practices at the local level with higher-level norms and institutions (Brondizio et al., 2009; Ruiz-Ballesteros & Gual, 2012), could be considered a key factor in bringing different interests together for collective action.

Despite the success achieved in rice farming, there is lack of collective power and vertical/horizontal linkages in governance structures of the other two socio-economic activities (tourism and fishing) of the area, and thus, a clear deterioration in their commonisation prospects. Having their daily practice based on a modern and highly mechanized activity, rice farmers do not generally establish a deep connection with their environment. The lack of deep nature-culture connection leaves little scope for the development of other initiatives such as locally based tourism. This is to reinforce the idea proposed by Nayak and Berkes (2011: 142) that "success of commonisation as a process depends on the close links between people and resources, not so much for economic dependence but for a more inherent and holistic relationship".

The present social-ecological structure of Isla Mayor shows traces of weak general resilience (Farhad, Gual, & Ruiz-Ballesteros, 2017). There is evidence of decommonisation in tourism and fishing. We do not know how sustainable would have been a well-developed tourism or fishing commons in Isla Mayor but their decommonisation processes mean that diversity as the main characteristic of general resilience is in danger. General resilience and long-term sustainability of a commons in all its related uses require taking into consideration the trade-offs between commonisation and decommonisation processes, and future research is needed to analyse and minimise these trade-offs.

Acknowledgements

I would like to thank the inhabitants of Isla Mayor (rice farmers, fishers, water managers, restaurants and hotel owners and workers, etc.) for their voluntary collaboration during my filed study. I gratefully acknowledge Dr. Prateep Nayak for his intellectual advice regarding the main theoretical approach of this work. I also thank Dr. Miquel A. Gual, Dr. Esteban Ruiz-Ballesteros and Dr. Macarena Hernández-Ramírez for their intellectual collaboration and support during the whole process of this research. This work was partly supported by SCARCE project (Consolider-Ingenio CSD2009-00065) and the project "Retóricas de la naturaleza y turismo de base local" (I+D CSO2012-33044), both financed by the Spanish Ministry of Economy and Competitiveness.

Notes

1 Albur in Spanish.
2 Although according to 1985 Water Act, groundwater in Spain is placed among public waters, there are still some private wells, either temporarily (until 2035 or 2038) or in perpetuity. That is the reason why a few independent farmers hold private water allocations and thus manage to get the water on their own.
3 World Wildlife Fund for Nature.
4 Confederation of over 300 Spanish ecological groups, founded 9 December 1998.

References

Aguilar-Portero, M. (2010). *Producción integrada del arroz en el sur de España.* Consejería de Agriculltura y Pesca, Servicio de Publicaciones y Divulgación, Fundación Caja Rural de Sur.

Anderies, J. M., Janssen, M. A., & Ostrom, E. (2004). A framework to analyze the robustness of social-ecological systems from an institutional perspective. *Ecology and Society*, 9, 18–34. www.ecologyandsociety.org/vol9/iss1/art18/

Berkes, F., Colding, J., & Folke, C. (2003). *Navigating social-ecological systems: Building resilience for complexity and change.* Cambridge University Press.

Berkes, F., & Folke, C. (1998). Linking social and ecological systems for resilience and sustainability. In F. Berkes, & C. Folke (Eds.), *Linking social and ecological systems: Management practices and social mechanisms for building resilience.* Cambridge University Press.

Berkes, F. (2005). Commons theory for marine resource management in a complex world. *Senri Ethnological Studies*, 67, 13–31.

Bhat, A., & Blomquist, W. (2005). Policy, politics, and water management in the Guadalquivir River Basin, Spain. *Water Resources Research*, 40, W08S07. https://doi:10.1029/2003WR002726.1

Brondizio, E. S., Ostrom, E., & Young, O. R. (2009). Connectivity and the governance of multilevel social-ecological systems: The role of social capital. *Annual Review of Environment and Resources*, 34, 253–278. http://doi:10.1146/annurev.environ.020708.100707

Carpenter, S. R., Arrow, K. J., Barrett, S., Biggs, R., Brock, W. A., Crépin, A. S., Engström, G., Folke, C., Hughes, T. P., Kautsky, N., Li, C. Z., Mccarney, G., Meng, K., Mäler, K. G., Polasky, S., Scheffer, M., Shogren, J., Sterner, T., Vincent, J. R., ... de Zeeuw, A. (2012). General resilience to cope with extreme events. *Sustainability*, 4, 3248–3259. http://doi:10.3390/su4123248

Confederación Hidrográfica del Guadalquivir. (2013, 13 January). *Memoria 2009/2011*. www.chgguadalquivir.es/

Daniell, K., & Kay, A. (2017). Multi-level governance: An introduction. In K. Daniel, & A. Kay (Eds.), *Multi-level governance: Conceptual challenges and case studies from Australia*. Australian National University Press.

Del Moral, L., & Saurí, D. (1999). Changing course: Water policy in Spain. *Environment,* 41, 12–15. http://doi:10.1080/00139159909604640

Del Moral, L. (1993). El cultivo del arroz en las marismas de Doñana: situación actual y perspectivas. *Agricultura y Sociedad*, 67, 205–233.

Delaney, D., & Leitneh, H. (1997). The political construction of scale. *Political Geography*, 16, 93–97.

Dietz, T., Ostrom, E., & Stern, P. C. (2003). The struggle to govern the commons. *Science*, 302, 1907–12. http://doi:10.1126/science.1091015.

Elphick, C. S. (2000). Functional equivalency between rice fields and seminatural wetlands habitats. *Conservation Biology*, 14, 181–191.

Fanlo-Loras, A. (2010). Las competencias del estado y el principio de unidad de gestión de cuenca a través de las confederaciones hidrográficas. *Administración Pública*, 183, 309–334.

Farhad, S., 2018. Rice production and social-ecological resilience in Isla Mayor, Andalusia, Spain. Doctoral diss., Universidad Pablo de Olavide.

Farhad, S., Gual, M. A., & Ruiz-Ballesteros, E. (2017). How does adaptive co-management relate to specified and general resilience? An approach from Isla Mayor, Andalusia, Spain. *Land Use Policy,* 67, 268–276. http://doi:10.1016/j.landusepol.2017.05.038

Farhad, S., Gual, M. A., & Ruiz-Ballesteros, E. (2015). Linking governance and ecosystem services: The case of Isla Mayor (Andalusia, Spain). *Land Use Policy*, 46, 91–102. http://doi:10.1016/j.landusepol.2015.01.019

Folke, C., Carpenter, S. R., Walker, B., Scheffer, M., Chapin, T., & Rockström, J. (2010). Resilience thinking: Integrating resilience, adaptability and transformability. *Ecology and Society*, 15(4): 20.

Galappaththi, E. K., & Berkes, F., 2014. Institutions for managing common-pool resources: the case of community-based shrimp aquaculture in northwestern Sri Lanka. *Maritime Studies*, 13, 1–16. http://doi:10.1186/s40152-014-0013-6

Galappaththi, E. K., & Nayak, P. K. (2017). Two faces of shrimp aquaculture: commonising vs. decommonising effects of a wicked driver. *Maritime Studies*, 16, 12. http://doi:10.1186/s40152-017-0066-4

González-Arteaga, J. (2005). *El arroz en las marismas del Guadalquivir: evolución y problemática actual*. Universidad de Sevilla.

Healy, R. (1994). The "common pool" problem in tourism landscapes. *Annals of Tourism Research*. 21, 596–611. https://doi.org/10.1016/0160-7383(94)90122-8

Hernández-Ramírez, M., Farhad, S., & Gual, M. A. (2017). "Selling what's yours": Nature, tourism and rice in Isla Mayor. *Gazeta de Antropología, 33*, 3.

Hess, C. (2008). *Mapping the New Commons*. Working Paper W08-21. Presented at "Governing Shared Resources: Connecting Local Experience to Global Challenges" the 12th Biennial Conference of the International Association for the Study of the Commons. University of Gloucestershire. http://dlc.dlib.indiana.edu/dlc/bitstream/handle/10535/304/Mapping_the_NewCommons.pdf

Holden, A. (2005). Achieving a sustainable relationship between common pool resources and tourism: The role of environmental ethics. *Journal of Sustainable Tourism* 13(4), 339–352. https://doi.org/10.1080/09669580508668561

Holling, C. S. (2001). Understanding the complexity of economic, ecological, and social systems. *Ecosystems*, 4, 390–405. http://doi:10.1007/s10021-001-0101-5

Janssen, M. A. (2006). Historical institutional analysis of social-ecological systems. *Journal of Institutional Economics*. 2, 127–131. https://doi.org/10.1017/S1744137406000300

Janssen, M. A., & Ostrom, E. (2006). Governing social-ecological systems. In L. Tesfatsion, K. L. Judd (Eds.), *Handbook of computational economics*. Elsevier. http://doi:10.1016/S1574-0021(05)02030-7

Janssen, M. A., Anderies, J. M., & Ostrom, E. (2005). Robustness of social-ecological systems to spatial and temporal variability. *Society and Natural Resources*, 20, 307–322. https://doi.org/10.1080/08941920601161320

Junta de Andalucía, 2008. *Guía del Espacio Natural de Doñana y su Entorno*. Consejería de Turismo, Comercio y Deporte.

Kooiman, J. (2003). *Governing as governance*. SAGE Publications.

Lebel, L., Garden, P., & Imamura, M. (2005). The politics of scale, position, and place in the governance of water resources in the Mekong region. *Ecology and Society*, 10(2): 18. [online]. www.ecologyandsociety.org/vol10/iss2/art18/

Levin, S. A. (1999). *Fragile dominion: Complexity and the commons*. Perseus Books.

Liu, J., Dietz, T., Carpenter, S. R., Alberti, M., Folke, C., Moran, E., Pell, A. N., Deadman, P., Kratz, T., Lubchenco, J., Ostrom, E., Ouyang, Z., Provencher, W., Redman, C. L., Schneider, S. H., Taylor, W. W. (2007). Complexity of coupled human and natural systems. *Science*, 317, 1513–1516. http://doi:10.1126/science.1144004

Nadal-Reimat, E. (1980). Los orígenes del regadío en España. *Revista de Estudios Agrosociales* 113, 7–37.

Nayak, P., & Berkes, F. (2011). Commonisation and decommonisation: Understanding the processes of change in the Chilika Lagoon, India. *Conservation & Society*, 9, 132–145. http://doi:10.4103/0972-4923.83723

Ostrom, E. (2005). *Understanding institutional diversity*. Princeton University Press.

Ostrom, E. (1990). *Governing the commons: The evolution of institutions for collective action*. Cambridge University Press.

Ostrom, E., Burger, J., Field, C. B., Norgaard, R. B., & Policansky, D. (1999). Revisiting the commons: Local lessons, global challenges. *Science*, 284, 278–282.

Ramos-Gorostiza, J. L. (2001). La formulación de la política hidrológica en el siglo XX: Ideas e intereses, actores y proceso político. *Ekonomiaz*, 47, 126–151.

Resilience Alliance, 2010. *Assessing Resilience in Social-Ecological Systems: Workbook for Practitioners*. Version 2.0. www.resalliance.org/3871.php

Ruiz-Ballesteros, E., & Gálvez-García, C. (2014). Community, common-pool resources and socio-ecological systems: Water management and community building in southern Spain. *Human Ecology*, 42, 847–856. http://doi:10.1007/s10745-014-9705-1

Ruiz-Ballesteros, E., & Gual, M. A. (2012). The emergence of new commons: Community and multi-level governance in the Ecuadorian coast. *Human Ecology*, 40, 847–862.

Sabuco-Cantó, A. (2004). *La isla del arroz amargo: Andaluces y Valencianos en las marismas del Guadalquivir*. Fundación Blas Infante.

Sánchez-Martínez, M. T., Rodríguez-Ferrero, N., & Salas-Velasco, M. (2011). La gestión del agua en España. La unidad de Cuenca. *Estudios Regionales*, 92, 199–220.

Sang, N. (2008). Informing common pool resource problems: A survey of preference for catchment management strategies amongst farmers and the general public in the Ythan river catchment. *Journal of Environmental Management*, 88, 1161–1174. http://DOI:10.1016/j.jenvman.2007.06.014

Santana, V. F. de., Fontes Filho, J. R., & Rochas, S. B. (2015). Gestión local de recursos de uso común en turismo: la perspectiva de Elinor Ostrom. *Estudios y Perspectivas en Turismo*, 24, 56–75.

Sharma, E., Nandita J., Rai, S. C., & Renzino L. (2002). Ecotourism in Sikkim: Contributions toward conservation of biodiversity resources. In D. K. Marothia (Ed.), *Institutionalizing common pool resources*. Concept Publishing.

Instituto de Estadística y Cartografía de Andalucía. (2015, January 13). *Sistema de Información Multiterritorial de Andalucía* www.juntadeandalucia.es/institutodeesta disticaycartografia/sima/index.htm

Tatlonghari, G., & Sumalde, Z. (2008). Formation of social capital for common pool resource management. *Asian Journal of Agriculture and Development*, 5 (2), 21–40.

Vail, D., & Hultkrantz, L. (2000). Property rights and sustainable nature tourism: Adaptation and mal-adaptation in Dalarna (Sweden) and Maine (USA). *Ecological Economics*, 35(2): 223–242. https://doi.org/10.1016/S0921-8009(00)00190-7

Wall, D. (2014). *The sustainable economics of Elinor Ostrom: Commons, contestation and craft*. Routledge.

Chapter 11

Creating a commons for global climate governance

Possibilities and perils in the Paris Climate Agreement

Craig A. Johnson

Introduction

Signed in 2015 and ratified in 2016, the Paris Climate Agreement marks an important shift in the evolution of global climate governance from what was previously a loose commitment to the principle of "common but differentiated responsibilities" to a more comprehensive and "global" effort to maintain global emissions and concentrations within 2°C (and ultimately 1.5°C) of pre-industrial levels (UNFCCC, 2015, 2.1.a).[1] Prior to Paris, the Kyoto Protocol entailed commitments only on the part of industrialized "Annex 1" countries, raising concerns that "non-Annex 1" countries (including China, India, Indonesia and Brazil) were under no obligation to reduce their own emissions.[2] Responding to pressure from industrialized countries, the Paris Agreement now entails commitments (in the form of Nationally Determined Contributions) from all of its signatories (Hohne et al., 2016; Sharma, 2017).[3] To the extent that it entailed unprecedented "North-South" cooperation, the Agreement has been deemed a diplomatic success (Kinley, 2016).

However, questions remain about the capacity and viability of the Agreement to effect changes that are equitable, sustainable and transformational for avoiding dangerous climate change (Falkner, 2016; Keohane and Victor, 2016). In the run-up to the 24th Conference of Parties (COP24) in Katowice, Poland, the Intergovernmental Panel on Climate Change (IPCC, 2018) warned that the world is still on track for a 3°C rise in global temperatures, highlighting the need to cut emissions by a further 45 percent (beyond the 20 percent target that was promised in the Agreement for achieving 2°C by 2030 (Watts, 2018). During COP24, the United States, Russia, Saudi Arabia and Kuwait responded by "watering down" the IPCC report (Harvey, 2018), leading one seasoned observer to conclude that poor and vulnerable countries had been "bullied into accepting text that is nowhere near adequate for them", (Huq, 2018).

The prospect of using multilateral agreements (such as Paris and Kyoto) to tackle global climate change is fraught with challenges. One is the "assurance dilemma" of ensuring that Parties to the Agreement are in fact living up to their end of the bargain (or in the language of the Agreement, implementing their "Intended Nationally Determined Contribution") (Keohane and Victor, 2011; 2016; Chasek et al., 2017; Held and Roger, 2018). A second is overcoming the numerous path dependencies (and related vested interests) that underlie the production and consumption of fossil fuels (Katz-Rosene and Paterson, 2018; Held and Roger, 2018). A third is the challenge of addressing an intergenerational, transboundary problem whose impacts are the result of multiple actors, decisions and feedback mechanisms that transcend any single policy or central authority (Young, 1994; Ostrom, 2010; Keohane and Victor, 2011; 2016). A fourth is the challenge of establishing a fair and equitable way of sharing the costs and burdens of mitigating and adapting to climate change (Held and Roger, 2018).

A critical question that this chapter seeks to address is whether the Paris Agreement can lay the foundations for stronger forms of cooperation by establishing a rule-based order that reduces uncertainty, offers incentives in the form of financial and technical assistance and aligns national and international interests on the goal of addressing climate change. Analytically, it draws upon two competing bodies of theory to understand the prospects for global collective action on climate change. One is the idea that repeated interaction and engagement (in the form of information sharing, developing common rules and procedures for financial and technical cooperation and aligning national and international interests) will create the conditions for more ambitious forms of cooperation (Keohane and Victor, 2011; 2016; Chasek et al., 2017; Park, 2018). A second is that global collective action is dependent upon the constellation of national and subnational political interests that manifest themselves (formally and informally) within and beyond the multilateral regime (Katz-Rosene and Paterson, 2018; Held and Roger, 2018).

As Nayak and Berkes (this volume) have observed, commons institutions undergo processes of "commonisation" and "decommonisation" that can change the rules, norms and incentives on which resource users relate to the commons, and to one another. Rules, norms and incentives are important in that they help to define the terms on which resource users may use and extract value from the commons (Ostrom, 1990). According to Ostrom (1990), local commons are more likely to thrive and survive when they are "nested" within governance structures that grant extensive rights of authority and autonomy to resource users (as opposed to absentee resource managers) in deciding local rules and norms of resource governance. In theory, the Paris Climate Agreement extends new forms of authority and autonomy to Parties that are now developing (and implementing) their own "nationally-determined contributions" (Keohane and Victor, 2016). In practice, it remains highly dependent upon the voluntary actions and evaluations of national reporting systems and the UNFCCC (Keohane and Victor, 2016; Chasek et al., 2017; Held and Roger, 2018). Drawing upon third-party evaluations and the actual text of the Agreement (UNFCCC, 2015), I make the case that the Paris

Agreement lays the foundations for stronger forms of reporting and evaluation, but fails to acknowledge (or sufficiently address) the power disparities and fossil fuel path dependencies that underlie current and future carbon trajectories. Lacking an effective means of enforcing (or even encouraging) compliance on the part of national governments, the Agreement remains highly dependent upon the contributions (and interests) of powerful states, reinforcing the fragmentation of multilateral governance on climate change.[4]

The chapter proceeds as follows. The next section first develops a theoretical framework for understanding the conditions under which multilateral actors and institutions may establish effective rules, norms and decision-making mechanisms for governing climate change. Section 3 then explores the formal mechanisms that have been put in place by the Paris Agreement for reducing uncertainty, enhancing linkages and aligning national and international interests. Section 4 concludes the chapter, highlighting questions and implications for global climate governance.

Strengthening the global climate regime

In the absence of a dominant global authority, "hard" and "soft" measures (e.g. formal treaties and less formal agreements, such as foreign aid) to establish order and predictability are often looked upon as critical factors affecting the ability of nation-states to build trust, reciprocity and cooperation with other nation-states (Young, 1994; Ostrom, 2010; Keohane and Victor, 2011; 2016; Falkner, 2016; Chasek et al., 2017; Park, 2018). Among international relations scholars, considerable attention has been paid to the role of "regimes" (defined as "... principles, norms, rules and decision-making procedures around which actors' expectations converge in a given area", (Krasner, 1982: 186) in ordering relations, expectations and cooperation in world politics (Chasek et al., 2017; Park, 2018). According to Keohane and Victor (2011), states build (and strengthen) regimes as a means of realizing the benefits of cooperation with other states and with non-state actors, such as multinational corporations and NGOs. A guiding assumption is that regimes offer benefits (e.g. predictable rules on trade, food safety, climate mitigation) that states are unable to achieve on their own.

However, regimes vary in the power, coherence and compliance they are able to achieve in relation to different (social) fields of cooperation (Keohane and Victor, 2011; O'Neill, 2016; Chasek et al., 2017). Whether regimes achieve strong integration and compliance, Keohane and Victor (2011) argue, is contingent upon (1) the interests of individual nation-states; (2) the material gains states can achieve through supporting and engaging with international regimes; and (3) their ability to manage the uncertain actions, intentions and outcomes of other states, non-state actors and events (Keohane and Victor, 2011). Compared with other international regimes (such as global telecommunications or food safety), the multilateral regime for global climate governance is considered a weakly-integrated regime (or in Keohane and Victor's terms, a "regime complex") that lacks an ability to monitor and enforce the myriad actions and decisions that affect carbon emissions and concentrations (Keohane and Victor, 2011).

An important area of interest therefore concerns the conditions under which regimes may be strengthened in relation to roles and policy commitments of nation-states. Drawing upon "institutionalist" and "neo-functionalist" thinking about rules, transnational regulations and simulated games, regime theory holds that repeated interaction and engagement (in the form of information sharing, developing shared rules, norms and incentives and aligning national and international interests) can lay the foundations for more ambitious forms of cooperation (Keohane and Victor, 2011; 2016; Chasek et al., 2017; Park, 2018). Particularly important for "regime strengthening" is the establishment of more detailed rules and procedures for reporting, monitoring and ensuring compliance on the part of nation-states (Chasek et al., 2017).

Another factor that has been instrumental in providing incentives for international cooperation is financial and technical assistance (FTA). According to Chasek et al. (2017), FTA played a critical role in expanding the scope, ambition and participation of national governments in the Basel, Rotterdam and Stockholm Conventions on hazardous waste, industrial chemicals and persistent organic pollutants (cf. O'Neill, 2016). In all of these instances, FTA (or the promise thereof) helped to structure the norms, expectations and negotiating positions of potential signatories, providing important incentives for compliance and implementation after the Conventions came into force (Chasek et al., 2017).

A third factor is the ability of powerful actors (typically states and groups of states) to influence and (ideally) align their national interests with the aims and objectives of international regimes. As a number of observers have pointed out (e.g. Chasek et al., 2017; Huq, 2018; Park, 2018), regime strengthening can occur when states or groups of powerful and/or like-minded states are able to exert pressure on the multilateral process. One important example of this kind of dynamic was the dominant role that the United States played in establishing the multilateral system (i.e. the United Nations) at the end of World War II. In this case, the US used its dominant military, economic and geopolitical power to establish a multilateral system of institutions that served its interests in containing communism, defending free markets and preventing nuclear war (Park, 2018). Within the context of multilateral climate governance, other examples of states and groups of states working together to strengthen the UNFCCC include the G77 and China forcing stronger financial commitments from Annex I countries, the Association of Small Island States pressing for greater action on Loss and Damage and, most recently, China and the United States forging a bilateral agreement that would ultimately lead to the Paris Climate Agreement in 2015 (Johnson, 2017; Sharma, 2017; Falkner, 2016; Held and Roger, 2018).

A final factor that has important bearing on the legitimacy of international regimes in the eyes of citizens, civil society organizations and other "non-Party" actors (all of whom sit outside of the official multilateral process) is the role of sub- and non-state actors and networks, including cities, Indigenous communities, NGOs and international organizations, such as the World Bank (Hale, 2016; Chan et al., 2018; Bäckstrand and Kuyper, 2017; Bäckstrand, et al., 2017; Gordon and Johnson, 2017; Van der Ven et al., 2017; Bernstein and Hoffmann, 2018). In theory, the inclusion of sub- and non-state actors and networks in multilateral processes can catalyse new forms of interaction, information sharing and innovation that occur beyond the multilateral regime (Hale, 2016; Chan et al., 2018; Bäckstrand, et al., 2017; Gordon and Johnson, 2017; Van der Ven et al., 2017; Bernstein and Hoffmann, 2018).

In short, establishing shared rules and procedures, offering incentives (in the form of financial and technical assistance), aligning national and international interests and incorporating non- and sub-state actors and networks can all play a critical role in strengthening international regimes. However, regimes are also fraught with challenges, highlighting the limitations of regime theory. First, like any collective action dilemma, international regimes are prone to free riding and defection that undermines trust, reciprocity and commitment to international agreements (Ostrom, 2010; Keohane and Victor, 2011; 2016; Chasek et al., 2017). One case in point is the ease with which member states (such as Canada) were able to pull out of or (in the case of the United States) ignore international agreements. Another is the fact that the consequences of missing one's targets have to date been effectively non-existent (see below).

A second and related problem is the challenge of implementing agreements that exceed national capacity and/or contradict the values and interests that are reflected in domestic politics, processes and institutions. Underlying the Paris Agreement is the notion that pursuing the 1.5°C target can be tailored to nationally based priorities and circumstances. However, national efforts to implement and achieve policy goals that are consistent with the Paris Agreement face the formidable challenge of managing and (in many cases) overcoming the actors whose interests lie in the extraction, processing and distribution of fossil fuels (Aykut, 2016). Moreover, national and subnational capacity for reporting and achieving emissions reductions varies enormously, raising difficult questions about the ability of the multilateral system (e.g. through the UNFCCC Secretariat and the Green Climate Fund) to build capacity for enhancing national and subnational climate governance (Aykut, 2016; Sharma, 2017; UNEP, 2017a).

A third problem stems from the normative and ethical dimensions of requiring emissions reductions from countries, regions or communities whose poverty and governance capacity make it disproportionately difficult to reduce their carbon footprint (Keohane and Victor, 2011; 2016; Johnson, 2017; Sharma, 2017). Historically, of course, these are precisely the arguments that were made in favour of exempting developing countries from past emissions reduction requirements under the Kyoto Protocol (Keohane and Victor, 2011; Hurrell and Sengupta, 2012; Hochstetler and Milkoreit, 2013; Falkner, 2016). However, as emerging economies have become increasingly affluent, their ability to resist some form of commitment has become less tenable.

A final problem stems from the realist observation that regimes are only as strong as their ability to influence (and potentially withstand) competing forms of power and authority. During and since the Kyoto period, observations have been made that global climate governance has become increasingly fragmented by "different layers and clusters of rule-making and rule implementing", (Biermann and Pattberg, 2012: 13). Whether we associate the appearance of new governance actors, layers and mechanisms with a dilution (as opposed to an augmentation) of localized power, the argument being made here is that the rise of non-state actors constitutes a significant departure from the multilateral process of central state governance (Biermann and Pattberg, 2012; Zelli and van Asselt, 2013; Bulkeley et al., 2014; Chan et al., 2016; Hsu et al., 2015; Hale, 2016; Widerberg and Stripple, 2016; Widerberg and Pattberg, 2017). In the context of multilateral climate governance, a related concern is that fossil fuel producers, processors, exporters and international organizations have exerted undue influence on the multilateral process (Bridge and Le Billon, 2017). As noted earlier, Russia, Kuwait, Saudi Arabia and the United States all refused to recognize the IPCC's latest (2018) report on the 1.5° target (Harvey, 2018). Similarly, and tellingly, the Paris Climate Agreement makes no mention of "oil", "extraction", or "fossil fuels", highlighting the limited extent to which the UNFCCC has been able to hold fossil fuel producers (including corporations, lobbyists and nation-states) to account (Bridge and Le Billon, 2017; Aykut, 2016).

In short, we have two competing perspectives on the role that international regimes may play in shaping the prospects for collective action on climate change. One is the idea that repeated interaction and engagement will enhance the prospects for more ambitious forms of international cooperation (Chasek et al., 2017; Park, 2018). A second is that collective action is dependent upon the constellation of power and political interests that underlie the production and consumption of fossil fuels.

Drawing upon regime theory, the following section explores the prospects for strengthening the Paris Agreement by reducing uncertainty, enhancing FTA and aligning national and multilateral interests on climate mitigation.

Possibilities and perils in the Paris Climate Agreement

Information sharing

In theory, disseminating information about the actions and intentions of resources and resource users can build trust, reciprocity, and predictability for stronger forms of cooperation on climate change. To what extent, then, does the Paris Agreement provide a credible means of reducing uncertainty about the state of the environment and about the commitments, actions, and intentions of Parties to the Agreement?

On this question, the Agreement has generated considerable discussion and debate about the extent to which the institutional design principles that have been put in place will frame/re-frame the expectations and actions of Parties (Falkner, 2016; Keohane and Victor, 2016; Chasek et al., 2017; Hohne et al., 2017; Sharma, 2017; UNEP, 2017a; Bernstein and Hoffmann, 2018). One issue that continues to divide analysts is the challenge of verifying emissions reductions, including the challenge of building state and non-state capacity for reporting progress on the NDCs. Given the amount of "gaming" that occurred during the Kyoto period (Ostrom, 2010; Chasek et al., 2017), concerns have been raised that verifying emissions reductions is too dependent upon the self-reporting mechanisms and criteria of the NDCs (Keohane and Victor, 2016; Hohne et al., 2017; Sharma, 2017).

At the heart of the Paris Agreement are the 5-year reporting cycles that form the basis upon which the Nationally Determined Contributions (NDCs) will be communicated with the Conference of the Parties and the UNFCCC Secretariat. According to the Agreement, a Party can enhance its NDC at any time (UNFCCC, 2015, Article 4.11), thereby "ratcheting up" national efforts for limiting temperature increases to "well below 2°C above pre-industrial levels and to pursue efforts to limit the temperature increase to 1.5°C above pre-industrial levels", (UNFCCC, 2015: Art.2.1 (a)).

On the question of reporting and capacity building, Article 11 of the Agreement outlines a number of aspirational statements for building capacity in developing countries, including "technology development, dissemination and deployment, access to climate finance, relevant aspects of education, training and public awareness, and the transparent, timely and accurate communication of information", (UNFCCC, 2015: Art. 11:1). Parties to the Agreement are also bound to provide an "enhanced transparency framework for action and support" (UNFCCC, 2015: Art. 13, 1) that includes "national communications, biennial reports and biennial update reports, international assessment and review and international consultation and analysis", (UNFCCC, 2015: Art. 13, 4).

In terms of verification, the first major assessment comes in the form of a "global stocktake" which occurs in 2023 and every 5 years thereafter. According to the Agreement, the stocktake will provide an opportunity to review "collective progress towards achieving the purpose of the Agreement and its long-term goals", (UNFCCC, 2015: Art. 14, 1). Each successive NDC will reflect a country's "highest possible ambition, reflecting its common but differentiated responsibilities and respective capabilities, in the light of different national circumstances", (UNFCCC, 2015: Art. 4.3).

Beyond the NDCs, the Agreement offers other institutional mechanisms for disseminating information about current and future climate scenarios. Particularly important in this regard is the IPCC, whose periodic (typically 5-year) and special ad hoc assessments (e.g. IPCC, 2018) provide a critical source of data and analysis on climate, vulnerability and mitigation. Also important are the transnational networks documenting and disseminating information about climate change actions and commitments, including NAZCA (Non-State Actor Zone for Climate Action), an online registry that was launched by COP20 in 2014 to track the commitments and actions of "companies, cities, subnational regions, investors and civil society organizations",[5] the carbon*n* registry, the CDP (formerly the Carbon Disclosure Project), and the Initiative for Climate Action Transparency (www.climateactiontransparency.org). (Hale, 2016; Chan et al., 2018; Bäckstrand and Kuyper, 2017; Van der Ven et al., 2017; Bernstein and Hoffmann, 2018).

Multilateral and independent reporting platforms such as these provide an important means of compiling and comparing national and subnational actions and commitments on climate change. However, as has been noted elsewhere, NAZCA and other information-sharing platforms capture only a small percentage of climate action (Hsu et al., 2016; Widerberg and Stripple 2016), highlighting the methodological and financial challenges of documenting mitigation activities in cities, regions and countries where the capacity for reporting and evaluating climate policy actions is poor. Notwithstanding the introduction of a substantially more formidable verification regime, the ability of the Paris Agreement and the UNFCCC more generally to monitor national and subnational emissions reductions remains highly dependent upon the self-reporting of Parties to the Agreement (cf. Hsu et al., 2016; Widerberg and Stripple, 2016).

The role of incentives: Financial and technical assistance

FTA is assumed to play a critical role in establishing the trust and reciprocity that can lay the foundations for stronger forms of cooperation. Compared to the Montreal Protocol (which is often considered one of the world's most successful international environmental agreements), meeting the 1.5°C target implies significant transformational costs (e.g. de-linking food, transportation and energy systems from the production and consumption of fossil fuels) for which substitutes are not easily or readily available (Chasek et al., 2017). Correspondingly, the ability of state and non-state actors to strengthen the climate regime remains highly dependent upon the financial and technical inducements that may be used in bringing otherwise "reluctant partners" into a global agreement.

In the run-up to Paris, developing countries were adamant that future commitments to reduce emissions be tied to stronger forms of climate finance from industrialized countries (Falkner, 2016; Chasek et al., 2017; Hilton and Kerr, 2017; Sharma, 2017). Particularly important in this context was the insistence that financial and technical assistance be "new and additional" to official development assistance, reiterating the commitment that was first agreed upon at the Rio Summit in 1992 (Sharma, 2017; UNEP, 2017b). In contrast to the most recent (2018) round of negotiations in Katowice, developing countries were able to act collectively and effectively in this instance because they had the support of the United States and China (Huq, 2018).

According to the Paris Agreement, Parties have "common but differentiated responsibilities and respective capabilities" for reducing emissions, adding that contributions and future ambitions be assessed "in light of different national circumstances", (UNFCCC, 2015: Art. 4, 3). However, as Sharma (2017: 38) has pointed out:

> The Agreement does not link a country's level of responsibility for causing climate change with a responsibility to pay for the impacts – therefore countries can continue to emit, confident that they cannot be held individually responsible or made to pay in proportion to their emissions.

In theory, the Green Climate Fund (GCF) is meant to provide a critical source of financial and technical support for climate adaptation and mitigation in the Global South (Keohane and Victor, 2016; Shi et al., 2016; UNEP, 2017b; Sharma, 2017). In practice, it faces a number of significant hurdles. First, the pledge to provide an additional $US100 billion per year appears only in the (non-legally-binding) preamble of the Paris Agreement (Chasek et al., 2017). Second, and related, the funds that have thus far been allocated to the GCF have been well below $100 billion per year (UNEP, 2017b). Third, there is little consensus on the kinds of funding modalities that will be used in meeting the $100 billion goal (UNEP, 2017b; Sharma, 2017). Fourth, concerns have been raised that the shortfall will be met by drawing upon private sources, whose terms will very likely be less forgiving than grants and concessional loans (UNEP, 2017b; Sharma, 2017). Fifth, the vast majority of climate finance has been spent on mitigation – as opposed to adaptation, which is arguably of higher priority for countries whose poverty and limited adaptive capacity make them particularly vulnerable to climate change (Sharma, 2017). Finally, concerns have been raised that in the absence of effective safeguards, climate finance will take the place of official development assistance, reiterating long-standing concerns about the lack of additionality in international climate finance (UNEP, 2017b; Sharma, 2017).

According to Climate Funds Update, the GCF allocated "just over USD 1 billion for projects that have a focus on mitigation, with half of this amount as concessional loans" between 2014 and 2017.[6] By comparison, GCF funding for nine adaptation-focused projects in 2017 was USD 400 million.[7] However, the vast majority of (pre- and post-GCF) funding has thus far gone to relatively wealthy middle-income countries. According to Climate Funds

Update, ten countries (including India, Morocco, Mexico, South Africa, and Indonesia) have accounted for 57 percent of total mitigation funding since 2003 (i.e. before the creation of the GCF).[8] The largest donors to date have been the United States, the United Kingdom, Japan, Germany and France.[9] While Parties are still developing norms and criteria for allocating climate finance under the Paris Agreement, the actual disbursement of GCF and other multilateral funds remains vague and imprecise (Schalatek and Bird, 2018).

In the absence of clear and transparent criteria for allocating climate finance,[10] developing countries have in recent years pushed for a more precise reckoning of the possible losses and damages incurred as a result of climate change. Formally established at COP19 in 2013, the Loss and Damage Mechanism represents an important effort on the part of low-income countries (particularly the small island developing states) to address the gap between the (modest) climate finances being provided by the wealthier countries and the needs of the Global South (Johnson, 2017; Sharma, 2017). However, the Preamble of the Agreement also states that Article 8 "does not involve or provide a basis for any liability or compensation", (UNFCCC, 2015: Para. 52), suggesting that the ability of the Mechanism to influence national or international cases will be limited.[11]

In short, the financial, technological and legal mechanisms that have been put in place during and since the Paris Agreement provide little for building trust, reciprocity and further cooperation among Parties to the Agreement, particularly those in the Global South.

Aligning national and international interests

A final and crucial factor that has important bearing on whether states will support and abide by the rules and norms of international regimes is the extent to which they represent and reflect the interests of powerful nation-states. As noted earlier, the principal point of interest for regime theory is the role of inter-state dynamics (as opposed to domestic factors and processes) in driving and explaining international cooperation on climate change.

To what extent, then, are states and groups of states realigning themselves in support of the Paris Climate Agreement?

On this question, considerable attention has been paid to the real/material and imagined/constructed stakes of sustaining, questioning or moving away from a carbon economy, including the effects that proposed changes and cuts in emissions will have on lifestyles, livelihoods and prevailing patterns of consumption (Aykut, 2016; Bernstein and Hoffmann, 2018; Held and Roger, 2018; Katz-Rosene and Paterson, 2018). Whether states lead, support or resist international climate agreements depends on many factors, including the size and strength of "green" political parties, the political mobilization of environmental NGOs, the political rules of the game (e.g. whether the state in question is a liberal democracy and, crucially, whether it uses some form of proportional representation to elect its representatives),[12] the perceived costs and benefits of implementing the proposed agreement and the role that international actors (e.g. international NGOs, transnational networks and the UNFCCC) can bring to bear on domestic actors and interests (Chasek et al., 2017).

To date, the principal actors that have taken the lead in supporting ambitious action on climate change have been the *green states* of Western and Northern Europe (e.g. Norway, Sweden, Germany, the EU), Northeast Asia and North America, whose national, transnational and subnational governments have used a combination of regulatory and economic policy instruments (e.g. fines, phase-outs, subsidies and varieties of carbon pricing) to promote low-carbon pathways (Betsill and Stevis, 2016; Chasek et al., 2017; Bernstein and Hoffmann, 2018; Schmidt and Fleig, 2018; Tobin et al., 2018). At the other extreme are the *extractivist states* (e.g. Saudi Arabia) and substates (e.g. Alberta and Canada when the federal government acts on behalf of Alberta's extractive industries), whose economies remain highly dependent on the extraction, production and processing of fossil fuels. Historically, extractivist states have resisted all but the most rudimentary forms of international action on climate change (Bridge and Le Billon, 2017; Chasek et al., 2017, Huq, 2018).

Taking a more proactive stand in promoting ambitious climate action are vulnerable states, such as Thailand, Bangladesh, Vietnam and the Maldives, whose economies, populations and infrastructure are highly exposed to the impacts of climate change (Sharma, 2017; Tobin et al., 2018). In recent years, vulnerable states and coalitions (e.g. SIDS, AOSIS) have played a critical role in pushing for more ambitious agendas (e.g. Loss and Damage) (Chasek et al., 2017; Johnson, 2017; Sharma, 2017). However, their ability to sustain this pressure has been limited by the fragmentation of inter-state coalitions, which reflects the diversity of developing country interests and agendas (Falkner, 2016; Chasek et al., 2017; Sharma, 2017), and the "bullying" tactics of powerful extractivist states (Huq, 2018).

In the absence of American leadership, more recent attention has been paid to the role of "emerging powers" (e.g. China, India, Brazil) and UN voting blocs (e.g. the G77+China) in leading, supporting, and swinging international agreements on climate change (Chasek et al., 2017; Falkner, 2016; Hilton and Kerr, 2017). Here the ability of emerging economies to pursue an ambitious mitigation agenda is also highly dependent upon the economic, military and geopolitical linkages that connect them with international regimes (including trade and military cooperation). In China's case, the "soft power" gains of committing to (or appearing to commit to) future emissions reductions help to explain its actions since 2014, as do domestic concerns about ambient air quality and respiratory health (Hilton and Kerr, 2017). However, questions remain about whether and in what form China's historic commitment will lead to more ambitious forms of action and whether it will encourage other countries to do the same (Hilton and Kerr, 2017; Chasek et al., 2017). According to Climate Action Tracker:

China's climate commitment for post-2020 is not consistent with holding warming to below 2°C, let alone limiting it to 1.5°C as required under the Paris Agreement, and is instead consistent with warming between 3°C and 4°C: if all countries were to follow China's approach, warming could reach over 3°C and up to 4°C.[13]

Skepticism about China's ability to meet its emission targets reflects the ambiguous language that has been used to articulate national climate policy (see below) and the structural challenges of reducing dependency on fossil fuels. Although it is falling (partly as a result of the government's efforts to improve ambient air quality), China's demand for coal accounts for over half of the world's coal consumption.[14] By comparison, India's demand is projected to grow by another 4 percent per year, making it 70 percent dependent on coal, oil and gas by the year 2040.[15]

Structural path dependencies such as these help to explain the ambiguous terms on which many national governments have articulated their NDCs. According to one recent survey (Tobin et al., 2018), 11 out of 162 NDCs (including India, Mexico, Chile, Malaysia and Vietnam) submitted targets that were based on "carbon intensity" (i.e. emissions as a proportion of population), which could conceivably allow them to increase their emissions if their domestic populations continue to grow. China too aims to reduce its carbon intensity in relation to GDP by 60–65 percent from 2005 levels by 2030.[16] Another 30 countries (including Kuwait, Qatar, Saudi Arabia, and the United Arab Emirates) had no explicit targets at all (Tobin et al., 2018).

Conclusions

In the words of the Nobel Prize–winning economist Douglass North (1990: 89), "effective institutions raise the benefits of cooperative solutions, or the costs of defection". This chapter has explored the ability of the Paris Climate Agreement (as a set of "rules, norms and humanly-devised constraints") to lay the foundations for stronger forms of cooperation on climate change. By examining the institutional mechanisms that have been put in place for sharing information, providing financial and technical assistance and aligning national and international interests, it makes the case that Paris has laid the foundations for stronger forms of reporting and evaluation, but fails to acknowledge (or sufficiently address) the power disparities and path dependencies that underlie current and future carbon trajectories. The Agreement expands the number of players (which of course was one of its primary objectives), but thus far the financial, technological and legal mechanisms that have been used to build trust and support for the multilateral process have been limited (Chasek et al., 2017; Johnson, 2017; Sharma, 2017; Huq, 2018).

Moving forward, a key question is whether the Agreement can institutionalize stronger forms of cooperation and commitment from nation-states. According to regime theory, disseminating information and improving transparency reduce the uncertainty that leads to non-cooperation. On this front, the UNFCCC Secretariat and the COPs have clearly developed (and at the time of writing, are still developing) new rules and mechanisms (or in the language of COP24, a "Paris rulebook") for communicating and evaluating progress on the 1.5°C target and the NDCs (Held and Roger, 2018). Alongside the large number of independent reporting mechanisms that have been established in recent years (e.g. CDP, carbon*n*), new rules and procedures will help to address the aforementioned methodological and empirical challenges, as will the growing number of sub- and non-state actors that are catalysing and documenting actions outside of the multilateral regime (Bulkeley et al., 2014; Van der Ven et al., 2017; Bernstein and Hoffmann, 2018). At the same time, national and subnational capacity for implementing, documenting, reporting and evaluating progress remains a significant challenge.

A second and related issue concerns the role of financial and technical assistance. According to regime theory, FTA provides an important incentive for supporting international regimes. Moving forward, FTA will need to be much more than this. Developing national and subnational capacity for implementing, documenting, reporting and (crucially) evaluating the NDCs is a challenge that far exceeds the current capacity of the multilateral climate regime. Like the aid industry more generally, existing flows of climate finance have by and large been inadequate, *ad hoc*, and primarily aimed at the larger middle-income countries, whose governments, consumers, and private sectors are deemed more suitable for public and private investment. Moving forward, the UNFCCC (and international organizations working outside of the multilateral regime) will need to clarify the terms on which it allocates FTA, emphasizing far more effectively the countries and regions that are least able to mitigate and adapt to climate change.

A third issue concerns the constellation of national and international interests that are driving contemporary climate politics. From the preceding, we can infer that the current constellation of national and international interests is not particularly favourable for mobilizing ambitious action on climate change. Two of the principal players (China and the United States) have changed their domestic policies in ways that cast serious doubt on their ability to lead on climate change. Outside of China and the United States, the states that could conceivably – or collectively – make a difference (e.g. India, Brazil, Indonesia, Turkey, etc.) are either structurally constrained or compromised by the influence of fossil fuel interests and extractivist states. Others, such as the vulnerable states, are either too weak, fragmented or "bullied" to make a discernible difference.

A final (and somewhat more encouraging) factor that has bearing on whether emerging economies will enhance their ambition for acting on climate change is their role in the green economy (Burns and Nicholson, 2016; Keohane and Victor, 2016; Dubash, 2016; Chasek et al., 2017; Hohne et al., 2017). Beyond the (still controversial) idea that geoengineering (Burns and Nicholson, 2016) may play a role in reducing emissions and concentrations is the growing role that emerging economies (like India and China) are playing in green energy technology. China now represents the largest producer and consumer of solar energy,[17] a factor that helps to explain its historic commitment in 2014 (Hilton and Kerr, 2017). Assuming that demand for wind and solar remains strong, emerging economies stand to benefit from developing alternative energy, creating further incentives to push for more action on climate change (Dubash, 2016). However, questions remain about the extent to which growing demand for green energy is dependent upon subsidies[18] and whether the social, economic and environmental costs of extracting the raw materials that go into green energy (e.g. copper, coltan, lithium and rare earth metals) are reinforcing old patterns of dependency and "underdevelopment" in extractivist states (Revette, 2017; Bridge and Le Billon, 2017).

Notes

1   The official text of the agreement is to (hold) "the increase in the global average temperature to well below 2°C above pre-industrial levels and pursuing efforts to limit the temperature increase to 1.5°C above pre-industrial levels", (UNFCCC, 2015: Article 2.1.a).

2   The Kyoto Protocol had been widely criticized for lacking a credible compliance mechanism for verifying emissions reductions; for failing to incorporate some of the world's largest emitters (e.g. China and the United States); for being too dependent upon economic instruments, such as carbon offsets and emissions trading schemes; and for providing too little in the way of stable and secure financing for adaptation and mitigation efforts in the Global South (cf. Keohane and Victor, 2011; 2016; Hurrell and Sengupta, 2012; Hochstetler and Milkoreit, 2013).

3   As of May 2018, 176 of the 196 Parties that had signed the agreement in December 2015 had ratified the agreement. For the purposes of this paper, "Parties" refer to the national governments that have signed and ratified the Paris Agreement.

4   For the purposes of this chapter, "multilateral" implies the existence of a rule-based order that is established and agreed upon by nation-states (Chasek et al., 2017; Park, 2018). "Institutions" are the rules, norms and other "humanly devised constraints that structure political, economic, and social interactions", (North, 1990: 97).

5   http://climateaction.unfccc.int/about (accessed 12 June 2018).

6   www.odi.org/sites/odi.org.uk/files/resource-documents/12076.pdf (accessed 20 December 2018).

7   www.odi.org/sites/odi.org.uk/files/resource-documents/12073.pdf (accessed 20 December 2018).

8   www.odi.org/sites/odi.org.uk/files/resource-documents/12076.pdf (accessed 20 December 2018).
9   www.odi.org/sites/odi.org.uk/files/resource-documents/12076.pdf (accessed 20 December 2018).
10 One possible exception is the use of "carbon budgets" which are used in framing and evaluating national and international commitments and trajectories (Hohne et al., 2017; UNEP, 2017a). Identifying and staying within one's carbon budget is not formally a part of the Paris Agreement, but the concept has been widely used as a means of tracking emissions and responsibilities for mitigation over time (Hohne et al., 2017).
11 According to Sharma (2017: 39), the decision to include the proviso was the result of a "closed-door deal" involving the United States, the EU and five small-island developing states, in which "the waiver was included in exchange for the separate Article on loss and damage and the inclusion of the 1.5°C aim".
12 Historically, green political parties have been more successful in countries (e.g. Sweden, Germany) with PR systems (Dryzek, 2013).
13 www.climateactiontracker.org/China (accessed 19 December 2018).
14 www.iea.org/coal2017/ (accessed 19 December 2018).
15 www.iea.org/countries/India/ (accessed 19 December 2018).
16 www.climateactiontracker.org/China (accessed 19 December 2018).
17 www.reuters.com/article/us-china-solar-idUSKBN15J0G7 (accessed 22 June 2018).
18 www.forbes.com/sites/michaellynch/2015/12/02/energy-subsidies-2-real-numbers/#6a9f0e991cbf (accessed 22 June 2018).

References

Aykut, S. C. (2016) "Taking a wider view on climate governance: Moving beyond the 'iceberg,' the 'elephant,' and the 'forest'", *Wiley Interdisciplinary Reviews: Climate Change* 7(3), 318–328.

Bäckstrand, K., and Kuyper, J. W. (2017). "The democratic legitimacy of orchestration: The UNFCCC, non-state actors, and transnational climate governance", *Environmental Politics* 26(4), 764–788.

Bäckstrand, Karin, Jonathan W. Kuyper, Björn-Ola Linnér, and Eva Lövbrand (2017) "Non-state actors in global climate governance: From Copenhagen to Paris and beyond", *Environmental Politics* 26(4), 561–579.

Bernstein, S., and M. Hoffmann (2018) "The politics of decarbonization and the catalytic impact of subnational climate experiments" *Policy Sciences* 51(2), 189–211.

Betsill M., Dubash N. K., and Paterson M. et al. (2015) "Building productive links between the UNFCCC and the broader global climate governance landscape", *Global Environmental Politics* 15(2): 1–10.

Betsill, M., and Stevis, D. (2016). "The politics and dynamics of energy transitions: Lessons from Colorado's (USA) "New Energy Economy", *Environment and Planning C: Government and Policy*, 34(2), 381–396.

Biermann, F., and P. Pattberg (Eds.) (2012) *Global Environmental Governance Reconsidered* Cambridge, MA: MIT Press.

Bridge, G., and P. Le Billon (2017) *Oil Second Edition*. London: Polity Press.

Bulkeley, H., Andonova, L. B., Betsill, M. M., Compagnon, D., Hale, T., Hoffman, M. J., ... Roger, C. (2014) *Transnational Climate Change Governance* Cambridge: Cambridge University Press.

Burns, W. and S. Nicholson (2016) "Governing climate engineering", in S. Nicholson and S. Jinnah (Eds.) *New Earth Politics: Essays from the Anthropocene.* Cambridge, MA: MIT Press, pp. 343–366.

Chan, S., C. Brandi and S. Bauer (2016) "Aligning transnational climate action with international climate governance: The road from Paris", *Review of European Community and International Environmental Law* 25(2), 238–247.

Chan, S., Falkner, R., Goldberg, M., and van Asselt, H. (2018) "Effective and geographically balanced? An output-based assessment of non-state climate actions", *Climate Policy*, 18(1), 1–12, DOI: 10.1080/14693062.2016.1248343.

Chasek, P. S., Downie, D. L., and Brown, J. W. (2017) *Global Environmental Politics*, 7th edn. Boulder, CO: Westview Press.

Dryzek, J. (2013) *The Politics of the Earth: Environmental Discourses.* Oxford: Oxford University Press.

Dubash, N. K. (2016) "Climate change through the lens of energy transformation", in S. Nicholson and S. Jinnah (Eds.) *New Earth Politics: Essays from the Anthropocene* Cambridge, MA: MIT Press, pp. 315–342.

Falkner, R. (2016) "The Paris Agreement and the new logic of international climate politics", *International Affairs* 92(5), 1107–1125.

Gordon, D. J., and Johnson, C. A. (2017) "The orchestration of global urban climate governance: conducting power in the post-Paris climate regime", *Environmental Politics* 26(4), 694–714.

Hale, T. (2016) ""All hands on deck": The Paris Agreement and Nonstate Climate Action", *Global Environmental Politics* 16(3), 12–22.

Hale, T., and Roger, C. (2014) "Orchestration and transnational climate governance", *The Review of International Organizations* 9(1), 59–82.

Harvey, F. (2018) "What was agreed at COP24 in Poland and why did it take so long?", *The Guardian* 16 December 2018 www.theguardian.com/environment/2018/dec/16/what-was-agreed-at-cop24-in-poland-and-why-did-it-take-so-long last downloaded (accessed 17 December 2018).

Held, D., and C. Roger (2018) "Three models of global climate governance: From Kyoto to Paris and beyond", *Global Policy* (9)4, 527–537.

Hilton, I., and Kerr, O. (2017) "The Paris Agreement: China's 'New Normal' role in international climate negotiations", *Climate Policy* 17(1), 48–58, DOI: 10.1080/14693062.2016.1228521

Hochstetler, K., and Milkoreit, M. (2013). "Emerging powers in the climate negotiations: shifting identity conceptions", *Political Research Quarterly.* 67(1), 224–235, DOI: 10.1177/1065912913510609

Hohne, N., Kuramochi, T., Warnecke, C., Rö"ser, F., Fekete, H., Hagemann, M., ... Gonzales, S. (2016). "The Paris agreement: Resolving the inconsistency between global goals and national contributions", *Climate Policy* 17(1), 16–32. doi: 10.1080/14693062.2016.1218320

Höhne, N., Fekete, H., den Elzen, M. G. J., Hof, A. F. and Kuramochi, T. (2017) "Assessing the ambition of post-2020 climate targets : A comprehensive framework", *Climate Policy*, 18:4, 425–441, DOI : 10.1080/14693062.2017.1294046

Hsu, A., Moffat, A. S., Weinfurter, A. J., and Schwartz, J. D. (2015) "Towards a new climate diplomacy", *Nature Climate Change 5*(6), 501–503.

Hsu, A., Cheng, Y., Weinfurter, A., Xu, K. and Yick, C. (2016) "Track climate pledges of cities and companies", *Nature* 532: 303–306. doi:10.1038/532303a

Hurrell, A., and Sengupta, S. (2012) "Emerging powers, North–South relations and global climate politics", *International Affairs* 88(3), 463–484.

Huq, S. (2018) "Poor and vulnerable countries were bullied at UN climate talks", *Thomson Reuters News Trust* 17 December 2018 http://news.trust.org/item/20181217110553-tyg87/ (accessed 17 December 2018).

IPCC, 2018 *Summary for Policymakers. In: Global warming of 1.5°C. An IPCC Special Report on the impacts of global warming of 1.5°C above pre-industrial levels and related global greenhouse gas emission pathways, in the context of strengthening the global response to the threat of climate change, sustainable development, and efforts to eradicate poverty* [V. Masson-Delmotte, P. Zhai, H. O. Pörtner, D. Roberts, J. Skea, P. R. Shukla, A. Pirani, W. Moufouma-Okia, C. Péan, R. Pidcock, S. Connors, J. B. R. Matthews, Y. Chen, X. Zhou, M. I. Gomis, E. Lonnoy, T. Maycock, M. Tignor, T. Waterfield (eds.)]. World Meteorological Organization, Geneva, Switzerland www.ipcc.ch/site/assets/uploads/sites/2/2018/07/SR15_SPM_High_Res.pdf (accessed 17 December 2018).

Johnson, C. A. (2017) "Holding polluting countries to account for climate change: Is "loss and damage" up to the task?", *Review of Policy Research* 34(1), 50–67.

Jenkins, R., and J. Manor (2017) *Politics and the Right to Work: India's National Rural Employment Guarantee Act* Oxford: Oxford University Press.

Katz-Rosene, R., and M. Paterson (2018) *Thinking Ecologically about the Global Political Economy* New York and London: Routledge Press.

Keohane, R., and D. Victor. (2011) "The regime complex for climate change", *Perspective on Politics* 9: 7–23.

Keohane, Robert and David Victor (2016) "Cooperation and discord in global climate policy", *Nature Climate Change* 9 May 2016 | DOI: 10.1038/NCLIMATE2937

Kinley, R. (2016) "Climate change after Paris: From turning point to transformation", *Climate Policy* 17(1), 9–15.doi: 10.1080/14693062.2016.1191009

Krasner, S. (1982) "Structural causes and regime consequences: Regimes as intervening variables", *International Organization* 36(2), 185–205.

Newell, P., and M. Paterson (2010) *Climate Capitalism: Global Warming and the Transformation of the Global Economy.* Cambridge: Cambridge University Press.

North, D. (1990) *Institutions, Institutional Change and Economic Performance.* Cambridge: Cambridge University Press.

O'Neill, K. (2016) "Institutional politics and reform", in S. Nicholson and S. Jinnah (Eds.) *New Earth Politics: Essays from the Anthropocene.* Cambridge, MA: MIT Press, pp. 157–181.

Ostrom, E. (1990) *Governing the Commons: The Evolution of Institutions for Collective Action.* Cambridge: Cambridge University Press.

Ostrom, E. (2010) "Polycentric systems for coping with collective action and global environmental change", *Global Environmental Change* 20, 550–557.

Pahl-Wostl, C. (2009) "A conceptual framework for analysing adaptive capacity and multi-level learning processes in resource governance regimes", *Global Environmental Change* 19, 354–365.

Paterson, M. (2000) *Understanding Global Environmental Politics: Domination, Accumulation, Resistance.* London: Macmillan Press.

Paterson, M., Hoffman, M., Betsill, M., and S. Bernstein (2014) "Micro foundations of policy diffusion toward complex global governance: An analysis of the transnational carbon emission trading network", *Comparative Political Studies* 47(3): pp. 420–449.

Park, S. (2018) *International Organisations and Global Problems: Theories and Explanations.* Cambridge: Cambridge University Press.

Revette, A. C. (2017) "This time it's different: Lithium extraction, cultural politics and development in Bolivia", *Third World Quarterly* 38(1), 149–168.

Schmidt, N., and A. Fleig (2018) "Global patterns of national climate policies: Analyzing 171 country portfolios on climate policy integration", *Environmental Science and Policy* 84, 177–185. https://doi.org/10.1016/j.envsci.2018.03.003

Schalatek, H., and N. Bird (2018) "The principles and criteria of public climate finance – a normative framework", *Climate Funds Update* November 2018 https://climatefundsupdate.org/wp-content/uploads/2018/11/CFF1-2018-ENG-DIGITAL.pdf (accessed 20 December 2018).

Sharma, A. (2017) "Precaution and post-caution in the Paris Agreement: Adaptation, loss and damage and finance", *Climate Policy* 17(1), 33–47, DOI: 10.1080/14693062.2016.1213697

Shi, L., Chu, E., Anguelovski, I., Aylett, A., Debats, J., Goh, K., … and Roberts, J. T. (2016) "Roadmap towards justice in urban climate adaptation research", *Nature Climate Change* 6(2), 131–137.

Tobin, P., N. Schmidt, J. Tosun, C. Burns (2018)" "Mapping states' Paris climate pledges: Analysing targets and groups at COP21", *Global Environmental Change* 48, 11–21. https://doi.org/10.1016/j.gloenvcha.2017.11.002

UNEP (2017a) *Emissions Gap Report 2017* United Nations Environment Programme www.unenvironment.org/resources/emissions-gap-report (accessed 25 May 2018).

UNEP (2017b) *The Adaptation Finance Gap Report.* United Nations Environment Programme. http://wedocs.unep.org/bitstream/handle/20.500.11822/22172/adaptation_gap_2017.pdf?sequence=1&isAllowed=y (accessed 21 June 2018).

UNFCCC (2015) *Adoption of the Paris Agreement.* https://unfccc.int/process-and-meetings/the-paris-agreement/the-paris-agreement (accessed 21 June 2018).

van der Ven, H., Bernstein, S., Hoffmann, M. (2017) "Valuing the contributions of nonstate and subnational actors to climate governance", *Global Env Politics*, 17(1): 1–20.

Watts, J. (2018) "We have 12 years to limit climate change catastrophe, warns UN", *The Guardian* 8 October 2018. www.theguardian.com/environment/2018/oct/08/global-warming-must-not-exceed-15c-warns-landmark-un-report last downloaded (accessed 17 December 2018).

Widerberg, O., and Stripple, J. (2016) "The expanding field of cooperative initiatives for decarbonization: A review of five databases", *Wiley Interdisciplinary Reviews: Climate Change* 7, 486–500.

Widerberg, O. (2017) "The 'Black Box' problem of orchestration: How to evaluate the performance of the Lima-Paris Action Agenda", *Environmental Politics* 26(4), 715–737, DOI: 10.1080/09644016.2017.1319660

Young, O. (1994) *International Governance: Protecting the Environment in a Stateless Society* Ithaca, NY: Cornell University Press.

Zelli, F., and H. van Asselt (2013) "The institutional fragmentation of global environmental governance: Causes, consequences, and responses", *Global Environmental Politics* 13(3), 1–13.

Chapter 12

Migration and the commons
Recommonisation in Indigenous Mexico

Daniel Klooster and James Robson

Introduction

Rural commons around the world face at least three interlocking social trans-formations. First, traditional agriculture is declining, rural-urban linkages are increasing, and rural livelihoods are becoming less territorially based (Berdegué, Bebbington, and Rosada 2014; Fairbairn et al. 2014; Kay 2015; Kay 2008; Haggblade, Hazell, and Reardon 2007). Second, as fertility levels fall and life expectancies rise, families are becoming smaller, rural populations are shrinking, and rural communities are becoming disproportionately eld-erly (UN 2017; Anríquez and Stloukal 2008). Third, migration is exacer-bating these trends, bringing in remittances to supplement and even replace farm income and taking working-age people away from their communities.

Demographic and cultural change, as well as the economic opportun-ities related to migration, can all be expected to alter the way rural people work together to manage their commons (Ribot, Chhatre and Lankina 2008; Ostrom 1990; Baker 2005). Migration distances commoners from rural lands and territories, complicating the social interactions that main-tain commons institutions and enable community members to reaffirm their shared norms of trust and reciprocity (Klooster 2013; Ostrom and Ahn 2009; Agrawal 2005; Baker 2005). Migration may also create space for new commons configurations to emerge (Robson et al. 2018; Robson, Klooster, and Hernández-Díaz 2019). In Mexico, studies show how migration expands the social boundaries or social field of the commons, as active migrants create trans-local linkages back to their communities of origin (Fox and Rivera-Salgado 2004; Stephen 2007). Although the *resident* populations of rural communities can decline, when the migrants who maintain a level of connection to their original communities are considered, the total number of commoners may be growing. If enough migrants stay connected, a form of trans-local commons governance may result, such that the residents of a rural village become the visible tip of an iceberg-like trans-border commu-nity (Klooster 2013, 2019). This could breathe new life into a system other-wise faltering under the strain of depopulation and become the catalyst for organisational and institutional renewal.

In this chapter, we investigate the implications of migration for traditional communal territories in Oaxaca, southern Mexico. First, we review some key elements of commons theory to guide our analysis of change in the commons. Second, we present field observations to demonstrate how migration affects the costs and benefits of maintaining the social practices which embed commons management and would seem to encourage an erosion of commons management. Third, we note the many ways that commoners are working to defend, re-shape, and re-build their commons-managing social practices in the face of migration and parallel economic and demographic change.

Studying the changing commons

An influential schema (Ostrom 1990; Schlager and Ostrom 1992) identified discrete property rights, clarified different ways they can be bundled together, and permitted rigorous comparisons of the effectiveness of different property rights arrangements. This work: (1) established the importance of locally-accepted rules and procedures (known as *institutions*) in managing the relationships between people using a common resource; and (2) noted the frequent ability of resource users to craft the institutions that govern them, usually through some form of *collective action* among users (Ostrom 1990, 2005). Such work demonstrated both theoretically and empirically that neither privatization nor government control is required for sound resource management (Agrawal 2005; Ostrom 2012), and permitted researchers to conduct nuanced work identifying varieties of and rationales for common resource management (see Euler 2018) and comparing their performance.

Building on categories established by this foundational work, commons scholars now consider the ways in which commons arrangements change over time (Berkes 2009). They identify indirect benefits such as Payment for Environmental Services and tourism for commons management and point out the profound influence on rule-making exercised by governmental, non-governmental, financial, urban, and other social actors far beyond the membership of resource-using communities (Sikor, He and Lestrelin 2017; Punjabi and Johnson 2019). For Nayak and Berkes (2011), the commons are dynamic and frequently change under broad social, political, economic, and ecological influences. Under the process of *commonisation*, collective action leads to a resource being used jointly under a set of institutions that specify who can use the resource and how it can be used. Under the process of *decommonisation*, such social practices break down; the collective action of resource users can no longer define who can and cannot use the resource nor can they determine how it can be used. The key criteria they identify are *excludability*, which encompasses the institutions defining who can and cannot use the resource and participate in crafting the rules for its use, and *subtractability,* which involves the institutions through which users coordinate the way people make use of the resource in question. Commonisation adds such institutions. Decommonisation removes them.

Village governance and the commons in Mexico and Oaxaca

Within Latin America, Mexico is furthest along a demographic transition that other countries are expected to follow (Saad 2010) – characterized by a growing, urbanizing, and rapidly aging population (Pew Research Centre 2014). Limited livelihood opportunities in communities of origin or the lure of work and life elsewhere have encouraged many Mexicans to leave their homes permanently or for an extended period of time (Bada and Feldmann 2016). An emptying out of the Mexican countryside presents significant challenges to local commons. And what happens to these regimes matters. More than a third of the country's land base and two-thirds of its forests are community-owned and managed (Sarukhán and Jiménez 2016); commons in Mexico shelter resources vital for local livelihoods, regionally important ecosystem services, and globally important biodiversity and carbon (Sarukhán and Jiménez 2016; Boege 2008).

Our work focuses on Indigenous commons in Mexico's southern state of Oaxaca, where most land is under community control and migration is an established rural livelihood strategy (Cohen 2004; Hernández-Díaz and Robson 2019a, 2019b). At 94,000 km², Oaxaca is about the size of the US State of Indiana and a bit larger than Portugal. Approximately two-thirds of its 3.9 million inhabitants self-identify as Indigenous, and around one-third speak an Indigenous language (INEGI 2015). It retains a strong rural character, with 570 municipalities and 12,000+ localities evidence of a widely dispersed population (INEGI 2017). Despite holding secure rights to lands and resources, a "culture of migration" established itself across the region during the second half of the twentieth century (Cohen 2004). By the mid-2000s, close to half of the state's population were believed to be semi-permanent or permanent residents of the Mexico City metropolitan area, the northern states of Mexico, or the United States (Bezaury 2007; Cohen and Ramirez Rios 2016).

In rural Oaxaca, most communities organise themselves under a system of semi-autonomous governance called *usos y costumbres*, which encompasses a complex mix of institutional and moral relationships that define the obligations, rights, identity, and sense of belonging of its members (see Hernández-Díaz and Robson 2019a). These institutions reflect an amalgam of institutional supply and community-level institutional evolution. The basic structures of *usos y costumbres* are detailed in the Mexican constitution and affirmed through regular and structured interactions with government and civil society (Bray 2013). Each community, however, has had its own evolutionary trajectory adapting these institutions for local governance.

Communities vary in their institutions and specific rules over usufruct of agricultural land, grazing rights, forest access, and – as we shall see – the rights and obligations of commoners who migrate.

We look at how these structures can realign in the context of a depopulated countryside. In particular, migration challenges the three main social institutions – *cargos, tequios,* and the *asamblea* – that structure and organise territorial governance and collective work and decision-making in these places. A *cargo* is an unpaid, elected post (12–36 months in duration) governing religious, civic and communal aspects of village life. *Tequio* is unpaid labour on community projects. In the *asamblea* (community assembly), community members invest time in debating courses of action, adopting rules governing their commons, and electing members to perform cargos.

Study sites and methods

We conducted ethnographic fieldwork in two Zapotec and three Chinantec Indigenous communities (Table 12.1), located in Oaxaca's Sierra Norte (northern highlands) region (Figure 12.1), and with migrants from these communities living in Mexican and US destination centres.

Multiple methods – participant observation, household surveys, informal and semi-structured interviews, territorial mapping exercises – were used to identify the impacts of migration on the institutions and structures of self-governance, and on territorial resource practices and associated knowledge in these places. All five community case studies touch on the theme of *migration and institutional change*, to show how migration impinges upon village governance systems, how institutional adaptations are diverse, unstable, and vary in outcome, and how migrants create the conditions for trans-local commons governance to emerge. Four of the five cases provide additional insights on

Table 12.1 Study communities' resident population, territorial size, and migration streams

COMMUNITY	Resident Pop. Size (INEGI 2010)	No. of Resident Commoners (estimate, 2014)	Territorial Size (ha)	Principal Migrant Destinations
Comaltepec	1115	205	18,300	Los Angeles, Mexico City, Oaxaca City
Analco	404	90	1,650	Mexico City, Oaxaca City, Los Angeles, Las Vegas
Yavesia	448	95	9,147	Mexico City, Oaxaca City, Tijuana, Los Angeles, Chicago
Tepetotutla	429	-	11,248	Los Angeles, New Jersey
Maninaltepec	347	-	13,746	Los Angeles

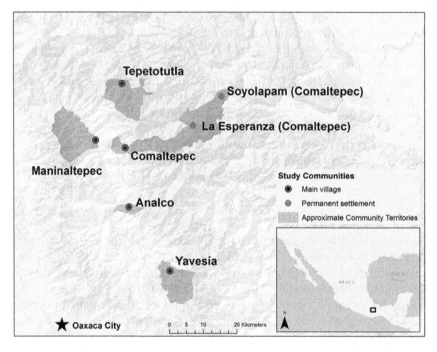

Figure 12.1 Location of study communities and their territories in northern Oaxaca.
Source: Map produced by Lisa Benvenuti, Center for Spatial Studies-University of Redlands.

the theme of *migration and environmental change*, to show how agricultural decline and forest transitions prompt changes in how territorial commons are used and perceived, including the dilemma of managing commons with fewer commoners.

Data were collected in Analco and Comaltepec during the period 2007–2010, and in Analco, Comaltepec, Yavesía, Maninaltepec and Tepetotutla during the period 2013–2016. Study participants included village authorities and residents living in the five communities in Oaxaca, and migrants from these communities residing in Oaxaca City, Mexico City, Los Angeles, Las Vegas, and Chicago. Migrants were contacted via recommendations from family members living in the home village in Oaxaca and letters of introduction from communal authorities in Mexico. All interviews were either audio-recorded or jot-noted and transcribed shortly thereafter. Transcriptions were coded to allow themes to be read across interviews, for associations to be identified between such themes, and for insights to be refined based on those relationships (Bernard 2017). To maintain anonymity, direct quotes used here are not credited to identifiable individuals.

Empirical insights and reflections

Migration dynamics in the study communities

Migration is a complex social phenomenon. It can be permanent and one-way, when individuals and families relocate permanently. It can also be temporary and circular, when a family member seeks brief employment elsewhere to raise funds that supplement a village-based livelihood. Among the five study communities, migration has been dynamic and varied, involving both temporary and permanent migration internally (within Mexico) and internationally (to the United States). In Yavesía and Analco, initial experiences with labour migration to areas of plantation agriculture on the Oaxaca-Veracruz border (1930s–1950s), were followed by temporary migration to the United States under the Bracero Program (1940s–1960s), and intense periods of wage labour migration to Oaxaca City and Mexico City (1950s–1970s) and to the United States (late 1970s–mid-2000s). In the case of Comaltepec and Maninaltepec, internal migration to Oaxaca City and Mexico City was limited, with migration taking hold in the 1980s, almost exclusively to southern California. Yavesía has additional participation (since the mid-1990s) in seasonal, guest worker migration (H-2B program) to the United States. A few Maninaltepec residents obtained similar worker visas starting about 2014. In Tepetotutla, migration exploded in the mid-1990s (predominantly to the United States), when coffee prices collapsed at the same time that the community was demanding many days of unpaid labour to build a road, a health clinic, and a powerline (Mutersbaugh 2002).

Across multiple cases, the relative importance of specific migration streams has shifted over time. Internal migration to Mexican urban centres (especially Mexico City) – a key stream from the 1950s to the 1970s – lost prominence once US-bound migration came on line. US-bound streams, in turn, have seen a previous pattern of circular migration (1970–1990s) change to one in which migrants in the United States more often remain there, returned migrants and deportees are unlikely to attempt to cross back into the United States, and young people are increasingly reluctant to incur the risks and costs of a migration attempt that their parents and older siblings would have undertaken.

Changes in village demographics

In all five study communities, rural out-migration has had a significant impact on village populations (Figure 12.2) and contributed – in tandem with declining fertility rates – to a slimming and aging of age-sex structures.

Nevertheless, it is important to note that none of these communities has emptied completely. In addition, declines in wage labour migration over the past decade, particularly to the United States, have contributed to a stabilising of village populations since the late 2000s. The latest government census data

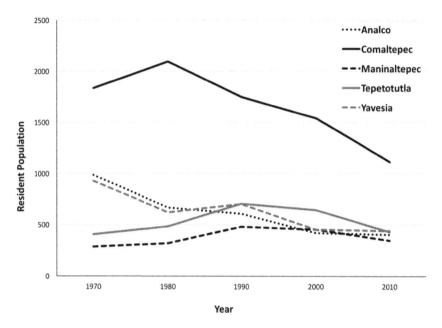

Figure 12.2 Population change in study communities' resident populations (1970–2010). *Source:* INEGI Census data, www.beta.inegi.org.mx/programas/ccpv.

confirm this (INEGI 2015). Migration may have now entered a qualitatively different phase, to revolve more around the education-inspired movement of young people.

A respatialised geography of the commons

Migration expands the social field of the commons (see Stephen 2007). When migrants look to remain active and self-organise in support of their communities of origin (Orozco and Rouse 2007; Fitzgerald 2008; Hernández-Díaz and Robson 2019b), commons regimes are opened up to encompass trans-local institutional links (Fox 2007; Greiner and Sakdapolrak 2013) and, with them, new forms of commoner profile, membership and voice (Stephen 2007; Robson 2010; Klooster 2013). Our study communities no longer comprise solely a territorially (spatially) bounded population, but rather constitute multiple populations often involved in a diversity of livelihood activities, with only a proportion residing in the "community of origin" and only some of these individuals making a living from the natural resources of the home territory.

In other words, migration has caused these commons to respatialise – to undergo a process that alters the spatial relationships between resources and resource users (see Giordano 2003; Moss 2014), and the nature of social relationships between community members and rights-holders (see Sosa Pérez and Robson 2019).

The deterritorialisation of livelihood

Migration in these places is strongly associated with changes in land use and resource practice. Traditional agricultural, pastoral, and subsistence forest activities are on the decline, but not disappearing. Over the past 40 years, households have significantly reduced their reliance on agriculture in favour of off-land activities. Even as populations have declined and land is available, the average area under cultivation per farming household has decreased, with survey data showing that households in Analco and Comaltepec were working less than half the area in 2009 that they were in 1995 (see Robson 2010). As a La Esperanza farmer explained, *'people no longer work in the countryside, there are fewer every year'*. Production has tended to decline further as the pool of available labour dwindles.

Patterns of agricultural abandonment and contraction reduce the territorial mobility of community members. This is most apparent in extensive territories, such as Comaltepec and Maninaltepec, where informants told us that seasonal settlements in different microclimates are no longer used. Farmers now carry out land-based activities much closer to their homes, abandoning more distant cultivation zones. For commons management, a reduced daily presence in areas where people used to commonly farm, graze animals, hunt or gather, complicates local monitoring of densely forested, mountainous territories.

Agricultural abandonment has led to significant forest regeneration, confirmed by our interviews and walking tours with land users, and direct landscape observations compared to historic aerial photographs and satellite imagery. In temperate-cold and temperate-dry zones, new stands of pine have colonised former corn and bean fields. On the windward side of the Sierra Norte, fewer areas of cloud forest are opened up for long-fallow agriculture, or thinned out to establish small-scale coffee and banana plantations. In Tepetotutla, community members described their land-use plan that stabilises agroforestry and slash-and-burn-and-fallow hillside *milpas* (traditional corn-bean-squash agriculture) in discrete zones. These processes are described in greater detail in Robson and Klooster (2018) and Robson and Berkes (2011).

There have been declines in several long-standing resource harvesting practices, with fewer people accessing foods and materials opportunistically as they travel to and from their plots or pastures. Declines are also attributable to the fall in average household size, a preference for modern building materials, a switch from firewood to gas for cooking, and the advanced age of many community members (see also Robson 2010; Robson and Berkes 2011). Forestry, conservation, and ecotourism activities, however, have emerged or increased in importance. Community land use planning now places greater emphasis on non-extractive and non-agricultural uses, supported by the explicit protection of high conservation-value forest lands (see Robson and Klooster 2018).

Tepetotutla, Comaltepec, Analco and Yavesía invest in physical infrastructure designed to generate revenue from domestic and international tourists. Payment for Environmental Services (PES) schemes in Tepetotutla and Maninaltepec generate funds used to address employment, infrastructure, and health service shortfalls, and to discourage young people from migrating. In some communities, the trend towards formalized conservation accompanies commercial forest use. Comaltepec and Maninaltepec have long-established logging operations that provide work for community members and funds for community projects. In Analco, secondary pine forests on abandoned agricultural fields have allowed the community to establish, for the first time, a commercial forestry operation.

The local burden of collective action

Commons management in Oaxaca derives from the local governance structures of *usos y costumbres* and, in particular, the cargo and the tequio. Migration removes working-age commoners, effectively increasing these costs for those who remain. As a resident of Analco explained, "*we suffer from a lack of people ... there are no citizens, no people to carry out cargos ... those that are here are older people, there are few youngsters, and it is the same group of citizens that have to do all the work*".

Depopulation has produced marked declines in local citizen:cargo ratios (Table 12.2), with lower ratios equating to a reduced pool of active resident labour and an increased collective workload for remaining villagers.

A dwindling pool of labour to adequately cover collective work and communal service obligations have increased tensions between village residents, who shoulder the burden of such activities, and migrant members who remain (physically) absent from the village. Labour deficits are felt most acutely in communities (Analco, Yavesía) and localities (La Esperanza and San Martin Soyolapam) with smaller populations, and can cause collectives to struggle to maintain customary standards in civic and communal governance – impacting the work they can carry out within their territories, and reducing the pool of qualified people to hold positions in the communal authorities. In several of our case communities, new or expanded land uses (e.g. forestry, ecotourism) have led to additional committees and an increase in the overall number of cargos, thereby exacerbating the overall burden.

Fewer residents also means fewer people attending asambleas (community assemblies), a critical decision-making space that underpins effective self-governance (Hernández-Díaz and Robson 2019a). Reduced participation

Table 12.2 Estimated citizen: cargo ratios in 2015 and late 1970s

Community/Locality	No. of cargos	Number of active resident citizens	Citizen: cargo ratio in 2015	Citizen: cargo ratio in late 1970s
Analco	79	81	1.02	4.25
Yavesía	77	90	1.16	no data
Tepetotutla	74	190	2.57	no data
Maninaltepec	26	65	2.5	no data
Comaltepec (total)	83	225	2.71	5.51
Santiago Comaltepec	52	165	3.02	5.08
La Esperanza	17	34	2.00	5.50
San Martin Soyolapam	14	26	1.85	no data

Figure 12.3 Community members in conversation, San Juan Evangelista Analco.
Photo credit: Jim Robson.

translates into less insights and opinions to help members draft good policies and rules, and too few candidates to choose from when electing members to perform cargos. This has become a particular concern in Yavesía, especially during the six months of the year when an additional 30–40 men are working as under H-2B visas in the US (see Ramos Morales and Robson 2019).

In essence, as the burden of commons management falls on fewer people, the costs of commons management increases for commoners resident in the village. The difficulties of communicating with migrants in far-off cities and countries adds to these costs.

A respatialised community of commoners

Migrants can and do remain active members of their communities, maintaining civic and communal rights despite being physically absent from their home villages. In all study communities, active first-generation migrants have (at some time) established migrant organisations in particular Mexican or US destination centres. This mirrors a trend evident among Oaxacan communities more broadly, where hometown associations in the United States link migrant communities to their villages of origin (Figure 12.4).

These trans-local or trans-border community structures provide an opportunity for migrant (non-resident) commoners to participate in managing their commons from afar. In other words, communities can look to integrate the labour and resources of community members living in the home village in Oaxaca with those of community members living in US and Mexican destination centres. Commons management depends directly on resident commoners interacting with each other and with government and NGO co-managers, but residents can themselves be supported and influenced by a migrant community of absent commoners (Figure 12.5).

Non-residents who remain active community members fall into two main categories. There are those who live in a regional urban centre (i.e. Oaxaca City), or who migrate temporarily, and thus can return periodically or frequently to their home village, where they can participate in person in collective work and communal governance obligations. Then there are those migrants who settle permanently outside of the home village and region, but who support the community in what way they can (or are asked to) so as to maintain their rights, and/or retain hopes to retire to or be buried in their place of origin.

However, as Figures 12.5, 12.6 and 12.7 show, not all migrants fall into these "active" categories. Many are "inactive", having cut off all ties to the community/territory of origin. As one US-based informant noted, *"there are a lot of non-active people here, the moment that they get settled they no longer have any interest in the village or its problems"*. Others are more appropriately termed "semi-active"; they may participate in migrant organising activities but do so on an occasional and limited basis (for more details, see Robson 2019a).

The ability of migrants to continue to support their home community is uncertain. Household survey data from residents of Analco and Comaltepec

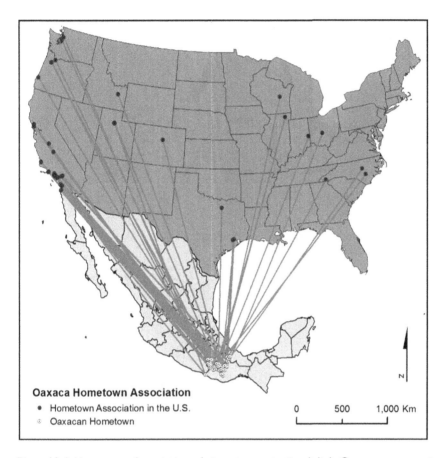

Figure 12.4 Hometown Associations (migrant organisations) link Oaxacan communities to migrant communities in the United States.

Source: Klooster 2013.

point to two main remittance trends: most money is spent on house construction, emergency medical care, or to cover daily household and school
expenses (rather than community-level investments); and the amount
remitted has dropped significantly over the past 5–10 years, as migration
rates to the United States have fallen, economic opportunities have declined,
and long-term absentees have seen their own family needs take precedence.
Money remitted back to Comaltepec, for example, showed a 50 percent
decrease during the period 2004–2014. As a migrant from Analco living in
Los Angeles explained "*things were better before, everyone had more to give,
now there isn't as much work, household expenses are really high and it's difficult*

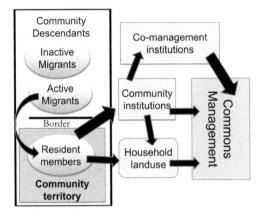

Figure 12.5 Trans-border commons management.
Source: Klooster 2013.

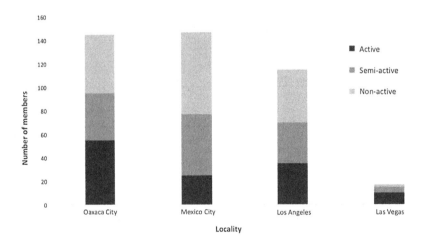

Figure 12.6 Status of first-generation migrants from Analco in US and Mexican destination centres (2015).
Source: Robson 2019a.

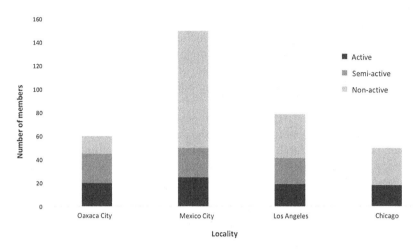

Figure 12.7 Status of first-generation migrants from Yavesía in US and Mexican destination centres (2015).

Source: Robson 2019a.

to contribute funds". Migrants also spoke of communication challenges with village authorities that further reduce their ability to participate in the governance of a community far away.

Our work suggests that migrants' willingness to provide support is less than it used to be or may lessen over time as more migrants settle permanently in destination centres. In some cases, as highlighted by the experience of Analco and Yavesía (Figures 12.6 and 12.7), the numbers of active first-generation migrants are low enough to place the future of migrant organisations in doubt. In other cases, organisations look likely to endure but migrants report a re-direction of resources away from collective remittances to the village of origin and towards meeting the needs of the migrant community.

Decommonisation pressures?

To summarize these observations, we can see that migration severely complicates the ability of commoners to maintain institutions of excludability and subtractability, the two main facets of the commonisation process. First, de-territorialised livelihoods reduce traditional ways of using the land and decrease the shared value of the commons. This erodes the incentives for commoners to maintain the rules governing resource use. At the same time, the burden of commons management falls to a smaller population of older resident commoners. These phenomena put pressure on the institutions governing subtractability. Second, the respatialised community of commoners complicates previous understandings of community membership, raising the question of who is "in" and who is "out" of the community of resource users and managers. It places resident commoners overburdened with the direct costs of commons governance into conflict with absent community members who may also claim rights to community resources. This pressures the institutions governing excludability.

Under these pressures, it is easy to imagine decommonisation by institutional decay, as a jointly managed territory transitions to a "no-man's land", where contested rules of excludability are no longer effective in defining who is "in" and who is "out" and where the rules of managing once-valuable resources are no longer enforced. Alternatively, this potential decommonisation could take the form of a "one-man's land", where joint management succumbs to appropriation by individuals specializing in using previously-common resources which are now of little interest to others.

The recommonisation response

Despite the pressures driven or exacerbated by migration, Oaxacan commons continue to function. Indigenous collectivities do adapt to potentially transformative demographic, cultural, and environmental change. As we have observed in the cases analyzed here and more widely in Oaxaca, Mexico (see Robson, Klooster, and Hernández-Díaz, 2019), affected communities develop local economies based on new forms of territorial use, rather than simply abandoning land-based activities altogether. They struggle to limit the erosion of communal norms, they adapt and reconstruct existing governance structures, developing new institutions to govern a mobile, migrant, membership. To avoid the threat of decommonisation, they have adopted a strategy of recommonisation.

Re-newed territorial use

Agricultural crisis, migration, and the de-territorialisation of rural livelihood have not de-commonised the landscape of forest and farm-based livelihoods. Instead, it delivers a changed suite of people-environment interactions, where forest transitions open up new spaces for territorial use and economic opportunities around both extractive and non-extractive activities, including government programs promoting Payment for Environmental Services schemes, ecotourism, and biodiversity conservation in community-controlled territories (see Robson and Klooster 2018). For communities, the offer of financial support in return for zoning lands for non-consumptive uses can be an attractive one given the realities of increased forest cover and small, aging village populations. And, in their own way, such government-sponsored programs help to reaffirm the collective ownership (aka commons) of

Indigenous communities at a time when communities have been made to feel vulnerable by the cumulative, negative impacts of migration.

Re-worked membership rules

The burden of managing their territorial commons in a depopulated countryside has prompted communities to experiment with significant adaptations to customary principles of collective work and communal service, in order to enable continued autonomy in the management of village affairs. Communities have responded in a variety of ways to labour shortfalls. A number have chosen to forgo less urgent collective tasks and dedicate tequio to more urgent activities, which now take longer due to the shortage of labour. Communities have also called on migrants to fulfil duties to the community, with different strategies adopted (Table 12.3). Most constitute a kind of coercive appeal to the norms of a community moral economy, in which communities develop formal rules to deny migrants access to communal resources if they do not comply with communal obligations. This is most clearly illustrated in Tepetotutla, where migrants are expected to return after a set period of time and meet community obligations in person. Three communities (Maninaltepec, Comaltepec, Analco) have rules to encourage migrants to comply with their communal service obligations but allow migrants to pay a resident to serve cargos in their place. Yavesía is the one community yet to institute changes to its statute to make these rules "legal", opting instead for a "freedom of choice" approach.

Allowing migrants to fulfil obligations to cargos and tequios through payments to substitute cargo holders departs from a strict custom of communal service being non-renumerated service to one's community. A particularly drastic form of "monetising" community institutions is evolving in Comaltepec, where municipal funds have been used since 2013 to pay cargos that used to be unpaid contributions to community self-governance (Robson 2019b). Some community members have been critical, believing that this fundamentally alters the social contract between members and their community – since doing unpaid tequios, serving non-salaried cargos, and attending asambleas has long been considered non-negotiable in order to receive the rights and benefits of community membership. Others are less beholden to past traditions, saying that such change is inevitable and necessary if collectives are to maintain control over civic and communal governance. Especially in communities and municipalities with small resident populations, fewer cargos and more paid cargos is being increasingly seen as the only way to continue under *usos y costumbres*.

In summary, Oaxacan commons are in a process of change we will term recommonisation. Commoners redefine the rights and obligations of membership when they create new rules to encourage the participation of members who no longer reside within the bounded space of a home territory and

Table 12.3 Current village rights, obligations, and restrictions for migrants

Migrant-related obligations and rights	Yavesia	Analco	Comaltepec	Tepetotutla	Maninaltepec
Time limit on absence	NO	NO	NO	YES 3 years, then fines levied	NO
Legally obligated to serve cargos (as codified in written statutes)	NO (for long-term migrants) Yes (for temporary H-2B migrants)	YES Established for migrants in Oaxaca City. In negotiation with Mexico City and US migrants. Can be through paying a surrogate. Fines and separation from communal resources and exile may result from failure to comply.	YES Obligations established by village statute in 2004–2005. Can be through paying a surrogate.	YES Fines and separation from communal resources and exile may result from failure to comply.	YES Paying a surrogate is accepted for most cargos. Increasingly difficult to enforce. Returned migrants, especially young men, preferred for major cargos.
Legally obligated to serve tequios	NO (long-term migrants) Yes (for temporary H-2B migrants)	NO But migrants expected to pay for missed tequios upon return.	NO	YES Fines and – in aggravated circumstances – separation from communal resources and exile may result from failure to comply.	YES Fines imposed for missed tequios.
Rights maintained in absentia	YES Through payment of annual community taxes, with service to migrant organisation noted. Fines levied on return for non-payment and immediate cargo service	YES Through payment of annual community taxes, with service to migrant organisation noted. Fines levied on return for non-payment and immediate cargo service. Rules set to change as new legal obligations are enforced.	YES Through payment of annual community taxes, with service to migrant organisation noted. Fines levied on return for non-payment and immediate cargo service	YES Rights maintained for three years. After that, returnees must pay fines to recognize the labour of the residents.	YES
Voice and vote in community assembly	NO (long-term migrants) Yes (for temporary H-2B migrants)	NO	NO	NO	NO But under debate as means to strengthen communal institutions.

village. As communities experiment with new institutions governing the rights and obligations of migrants, they are re-defining the terms of excludability. Commoners successfully interact with government and NGO initiatives to create new rules governing novel territorial uses such as commercial forestry, tourism, and Payment for Environmental Services. As communities come up with new institutions governing the new uses of their territories, they are re-configuring the institutions governing subtractability. Oaxacan commoners adjust the rules governing *excludability* and *subtractability* (see Nayak and Berkes 2011) to adapt to a new reality brought on by migration and associated change (Robson et al. 2018).

Looking ahead

Re-considered norms

Recommonisation both resists and adapts to changing norms. By strategising to protect what is important to them, Oaxacan community members are simultaneously questioning the relevancy and practicality of a system that demands all right-holders to serve their community equally, and asking whether the introduction of paid cargos and the removal of tequio constitutes an acceptable deviation from traditional, communalist ideologies. In all five case studies, changes following migration have chipped away at several long-standing norms and customs, particularly the principles of reciprocity upon which collective work and community membership are based. Reciprocal ties are hard to maintain in the context of de-territorialized livelihoods and a geographically dispersed membership.

Migration shows us that long-standing norms, which originated in a context when most if not all members lived and worked the land in the same "home village", can make less sense to a group of commoners now living in different places (after Stephen 2007). Migrant commoners can be torn between solidarity with those living in the village of origin, and the feeling that resident commoners do not understand or appreciate their own lived realities. Meanwhile, perspectives can diverge over time as migrants become long-term absentees, establish families in the diaspora, and a younger generation expresses a reduced commitment to communitarian values. In other words, migrants may continue to provide moral support to their communities of origin, but formal linkages will likely weaken.

In creating policies to better manage the debilitating impacts of migration, communities find themselves in a process of internal negotiation, in which they attempt to create forms of "service" in which members can participate, and exercise citizenship, regardless of where they live. These communities are thus challenged to develop a set of internal normative structures that can provide meaning across member profiles – not just village residents vs. non-residents but also returnees/deportees and youngsters, who may slip away if communities continue with traditional expectations of community membership rights and obligations and remain closed to "other kinds of being" (Dietz 2010). This suggests that Oaxacan commons will inevitably move towards a more balanced reciprocity that demands support from all but allows members to contribute in different ways based on their specific situations and capacities. Such a multi-tiered, multi-rights membership system would constitute a new social order in these places.

Continued stress from continued change

Many of the changes to institutional arrangements governing migration emerged during a time of a relatively open border to the United States. People could come and go, even returning to fulfil community obligations in person. These migration dynamics have shifted towards long-term and more permanent forms of absence (Cornelius and Lewis 2007; Jones 2009, 2014), which holds implications for the relevancy of customary institutions, as well as the institutional adaptations that encourage migrants to fulfil obligations back home. Longer absences, the dynamics of US- or Mexico City–raised families, and a persistent lack of rural economic opportunities all potentially affect ties to communities of origin and willingness or continued propensity to invest in the commons. Recommonisation mitigates, but does not eliminate, the pressures that communities face.

Baker (2005: 34) points out that under "conditions of rapid political, economic or social change, [commons] regimes are better able to persist when the change does not diversify members' opportunity costs or when it affects their interests in the same manner". This may be more readily expected in villages where migration is largely temporary or circular, but less so once migrant communities mature (Smith 2006; Portes, Escobar, and Radford 2007) and more members become long-term absentees (Jones 2009). Over time, such migrants can be less inclined to meet the customary labour obligations that underpin village life and identity, or to meet community requests for support. Such a scenario may pose particular challenges for communities with small home village populations – and more dependent on continued support from non-residents – which could struggle to maintain local structures of government (Kearney and Besserer 2004). For example, members in Analco and Yavesía expressed concern about losing municipal status and thus their highly valued autonomy to manage their own civic and communal affairs.

Conclusion

Indigenous commons in Mexico, Latin America, and other global regions are critical for conservation and sustainable development (Boillat et al. 2017; Garnett et al. 2018), but rural out-migration, together with demographic change, and the diversification of rural livelihood affects the role that Indigenous commoners can play as land managers in such places. In Oaxaca,

Mexico, migration has driven far-reaching changes, transforming both local uses and local institutions governing the commons (Robson et al. 2018). The uses of common lands and territories are shifting. Novel conservation initiatives, Payment for Ecosystem Services programs, ecotourism activities, and commercial forestry are increasing at the same time that traditional agricultural and pastoral activities decline. Meanwhile, the experience of migration reframes excludability and subtractability in a context of community members scattered across the continent, and of imaginations of future livelihoods that give less and less weight to the territorial resources of a village commons. Communal norms are up for debate; communities grapple over what rights are held by whom and what it means to be a commoner *and* a migrant. Re-configured communities debate how their landscapes should be managed for novel uses.

Yet the experience of Oaxaca also shows that individuals and groups will make significant investments to defend or hold onto values and norms that they consider important (Gavrilets and Richerson 2017). Rather than decommonising (after Nayak and Berkes 2011) under pressures from migration and associated rural change, communities are actively shaping migration's impacts through institutional adaptations and cultural resilience. These experiences suggest that commons regimes can have the institutional flexibility (Daniels 2007), legitimacy across memberships (Armitage et al. 2012), and capacity to learn (Gavin et al. 2018; Berkes 2017) to survive through times of rapid change and upheaval. They re-new territorial uses, they re-work their institutions, they re-consider their communal norms, and they re-commonise their territories and governance structures.

References

Agrawal, A. (2005). *Environmentality: Technologies of Government and the Making of Subject*. Durham, NC: Duke University Press.

Anríquez, G. and L. Stloukal. (2008). Rural population change in developing countries: Lessons for policymaking. *European View*, 7(2), 309–317.

Armitage, D., de Loë, R. and Plummer, R. (2012). Environmental governance and its implications for conservation practice. *Conservation Letters*, 5(4), 245–255.

Bada, X., and Feldmann, A. (2016). New challenges for migration studies in the Western Hemisphere. *Practicing Anthropology*, 38(1), 33–34.

Baker, M. J. (2005). *The Kuhls of Kangra: Community-Managed Irrigation in the Western Himalaya*. Seattle and London: University of Washington Press.

Berkes, F. (2009). Revising the commons paradigm. *Journal of Natural Resources Policy Research*, 1(3), 261–264.

Berkes, F. (2017). Environmental governance for the Anthropocene? Social-ecological systems, resilience, and collaborative learning. *Sustainability*, 9(7), 1232.

Berdegué, J. A., Bebbington, A. J. and Rosada, T. (2014). The rural transformation. In: B Currie-Alder, R. Kanbur, D. M. Malone, and R. Medhora (eds), *International Development: Ideas, Experience, and Prospects*. Oxford: Oxford University Press.

Bernard, H. R. (2017). *Research Methods in Anthropology: Qualitative and Quantitative Approaches*. New York: Rowman & Littlefield.

Bezaury, J. A. (2007). Organized coffee producers: Mitigating negative impacts of out-migration in Oaxaca, Mexico. *Mountain Research and Development*, 27(2), 109–113.

Boege, E. (2008). *El patrimonio biocultural de los pueblos indígenas de México: hacia la conservación in situ de la biodiversidad y agrodiversidad en los territorios indígenas* (No. Sirsi i97896803854).

Boillat, S., Scarpa, F. M., Robson, J. P., Gasparri, I., Aide, T. M., Dutra Aguiar, A. P., Anderson, L. O. et al. (2017). Land system science in Latin America: Challenges and perspectives. *Current Opinion in Environmental Sustainability*, 26, 37–46.

Bray, D. B. (2013). When the state supplies the commons: Origins, changes, and design of Mexico's common property regime. *Journal of Latin American Geography*, 12(1), 33–55.

Cohen, J. H. (2004). *The Culture of Migration in Southern Mexico*. Austin: University of Texas Press.

Cohen, J. H. and Ramirez Rios, B. (2016). Internal migration in Oaxaca: Its role and value to rural movers. *International Journal of Sociology*, 46(3), 223–235.

Cornelius, W. A. and Lewis, J. M. (eds). (2007). *Impacts of Border Enforcement on Mexican Migration: The View from Sending Communities* (Vol. 3). La Jolla, CA: Center for Comparative Immigration Studies.

Daniels, B. (2007). Emerging commons and tragic institutions. *Environmental Law*, 37, 515–571.

Dietz, G., (2010). Politization of comunalidad and the demand for autonomy. In: Meyer, L (ed), *New World of Indigenous Resistance*. San Francisco, CA: City Lights Publisher.

The Economist. (2013). *Autumn of the Patriarchs*. Available online at: www.economist.com/news/americas/21578710-traditional-demographic-patterns-are-changingastonishingly-fast-autumn-patriarchs (accessed 30 November 2020).

Ellis, F. (1998). Household strategies and rural livelihood diversification. *The Journal of Development Studies*, 35(1), 1–38.

Euler, J. (2018). Conceptualizing the commons: Moving beyond the goods-based definition by introducing the social practices of commoning as vital determinant. *Ecological Economics, 143*, 10–16.

Fairbairn, M., Fox, J., Isakson, S. R., Levien, M., Peluso, N., Razavi, S., Scoones, I. and Sivaramakrishnan, K. (2014). Introduction: New directions in agrarian political economy. *The Journal of Peasant Studies*, 41(5), 653–666.

Fitzgerald, D. (2008). Colonies of the little motherland: Membership, space, and time in Mexican migrant hometown associations. *Comparative Studies in Society and History*, 50(1), 145–169.

Fox, J. and Rivera-Salgado, G. (eds). (2004). *Indigenous Mexican Migrants in the United States*. La Jolla: Center for U.S.-Mexican Studies, UCSD/Center for Comparative Immigration Studies, UCSD, p. 526.

Fox, J., (2007). *Accountability Politics: Power and Voice in Rural Mexico*. Oxford: Oxford University Press.

Freire, G., O. Schwartz, S. Daniel et al. (2015). *Indigenous Latin America in the Twenty-First Century: The First Decade*. Washington, DC: World Bank Group. http://documents.worldbank.org/curated/en/145891467991974540/Indigenous-Latin-America-in-the twenty-first-century-the-first-decade (accessed 30 November 2020).

Garnett, S. T., Burgess, N. D., Fa, J. E., Fernández-Llamazares, Á., Molnár, Z., Robinson, C. J., Watson, J. E., Zander, K. K., Austin, B., Brondizio, E. S. and Collier, N. F. (2018). A spatial overview of the global importance of Indigenous lands for conservation. *Nature Sustainability*, 1(7), 369.

Gavin, M., McCarter, J., Berkes, F., Mead, A., Sterling, E., Tang, R. and Turner, N. (2018). Effective biodiversity conservation requires dynamic, pluralistic, partnership-based approaches. *Sustainability*, 10(6), 1846.

Gavrilets, S. and Richerson, P. J. (2017). Collective action and the evolution of social norm internalization. *Proceedings of the National Academy of Sciences*. https://doi.org/10.1073/pnas.1703857114

Giordano, M. (2003). The geography of the commons: The role of scale and space. *Annals of the American Association of Geographers,* 93(2), 365–375.

Greiner, C. and P. Sakdapolrak. (2013). Translocality: Concepts, applications, and emerging research perspectives. *Geography Compass*, 7, 373–384.

Haggblade, S., Hazell, P. B. and Reardon, T. (eds). (2007). *Transforming the Rural Nonfarm Economy: Opportunities and Threats in the Developing World.* Washington, DC: International Food Policy Research Institute.

Hernandez-Diaz, J. and Robson, J. P. (2019a). Population, territory, and governance in rural Oaxaca. In Robson, J. P., D. Klooster, and J. Hernandez-Diaz (eds), *Communities Surviving Migration: Village Governance, Environment, and Cultural Survival.* Abingdon, UK: Routledge/Earthscan.

Hernandez-Diaz, J. and Robson, J. P. (2019b). Migration dynamics and migrant organising in rural Oaxaca. In Robson, J. P., D. Klooster, and J. Hernandez-Diaz (eds), *Communities Surviving Migration: Village Governance, Environment, and Cultural Survival.* Abingdon, UK: Routledge/Earthscan.

INEGI. (n.d.). Censos y Conteos de Población y Vivienda (1970-1980-1990-1995-2000-2005-2010). Available online at: www.beta.inegi.org.mx/programas/ccpv/2010/ (accessed 30 November 2020).

INEGI. (2015). *Principales resultados de la Encuesta Intercensal 2015: Oaxaca.* Aguascalientes, Mexico: Instituto Nacional de Estadística y Geografía (INEGI).

INEGI 2017. Catálogo Único de Claves de Áreas Geoestadísticas Estatales, Municipales y Localidades. Available online at: www.inegi.org.mx/geo/contenidos/geoestadistica/CatalogoClaves.aspx (accessed 13 May 2017).

Jones, R. C. (2009). Migration permanence and village decline in Zacatecas: When you can't go home again. *The Professional Geographer*, 61(3), 382–399.

Jones, R. C. (2014). The decline of international migration as an economic force in rural areas: A Mexican case study. *International Migration Review*, 48(3), 728–761.

Kay, C. (2008). Reflections on Latin American rural studies in the neoliberal globalization period: A new rurality? *Development and Change*, 39(6), 915–943.

Kay, C. (2015). The agrarian question and the neoliberal rural transformation in Latin America. *European Review of Latin American and Caribbean Studies*, 100, 73–83.

Kearney, Michael, and Federico Besserer. 2004. "Oaxacan Municipal Governance in Transnational Context." In: J. Fox and G. Rivera-Salgado (eds), *Indigenous Mexican Migrants in the United States*, 449–466. La Jolla: Center for U.S.-Mexican Studies, University of California San Diego.

Klooster, D. (2013). The impact of transnational migration on commons management among Mexican Indigenous Communities. *Journal of Latin American Geography,* 12(1), 57–86.

Klooster, D. (2019). Santa Maria Tindu: The tip of a melting iceberg. In: Robson, J. P., D. Klooster, and J. Hernandez-Diaz (eds), *Communities Surviving Migration: Village Governance, Environment, and Cultural Survival.* Abingdon, UK: Routledge/ Earthscan.

Massey, D. S., Durand, J. and Pren, K. A. (2015). Border enforcement and return migration by documented and undocumented Mexicans. *Journal of Ethnic and Migration Studies,* 41(7), 1015–1040.

Moctezuma, M. (2000). La organización de migrantes Zacatecanos en Estados Unidos. *Cuadernos Agrarios,* 19(20), 81–104.

Moss, T. (2014). Spatiality of the commons. *International Journal of the Commons,* 8(2), 457–471.

Mutersbaugh, T. (2002). Migration, common property, and communal labor: Cultural politics and agency in a Mexican village. *Political Geography, 21*(4), 473–494.

Nayak, P. K. and Berkes, F. (2011). Commonisation and decommonisation: Understanding the processes of change in Chilika Lagoon, India. *Conservation & Society,* 9, 132–145.

Orozco, M. and Rouse, R. (2007). *Migrant Hometown Associations and Opportunities for Development: A Global Perspective.* Washington, DC: Migration Information Source.

Ostrom, E. (1990). *Governing the Commons: The Evolution of Institutions for Collective Action.* Cambridge: Cambridge University Press.

Ostrom, E. (2005). *Understanding Institutional Diversity.* Princeton, NJ: Princeton University Press.

Ostrom, E. (2012). *The Future of the Commons: Beyond Market Failure and Government Regulation.* London: Institute of Economic Affairs.

Ostrom, E. and Ahn, T. K. (2009). The meaning of social capital and its link to collective action, in G.T. Svendsen and G.L.H. Svendsen (eds), *Handbook of Social Capital: The Troika of Sociology, Political Science and Economics,* Northampton: Edward Elgar Publishing, pp. 17–35.

Otero, G. (1999). *Farewell to the Peasantry? Political Class Formation in Rural Mexico.* Boulder, CO: Westview Press.

Passel, J., Cohn, D. and Gonzalez-Barrera, A. (2012). *Net Migration from Mexico Falls to Zero and Perhaps Less.* Washington, DC: Pew Hispanic Center.

Pew Research Centre. (2014). *Attitudes about Aging: A Global Perspective.* Available online at: http://assets.pewresearch.org/wp-content/uploads/sites/2/2014/01/Pew-Research-Center-GlobalAging-Report-FINAL-January-30-20141.pdf (accessed 30 November 2020).

Porter-Bolland, L., Ellis, E. A., Guariguata, M. R., Ruiz-Mallén, I., Negrete-Yankelevich, S. and Reyes-García, V. (2012). Community managed forests and forest protected areas: An assessment of their conservation effectiveness across the tropics. *Forest Ecology and Management, 268,* 6–17.

Portes, A., Escobar, C. and Radford, A. W. (2007). Immigrant transnational organizations and development: A comparative study. *International Migration Review,* 41(1), 242–281.

Punjabi, B. and Johnson, C. (2019). The politics of rural-urban water conflict in India: Untapping the power of institutional reform. *World Development*, 120, 182–192. corrected proof available April 2. https://doi.org/10.1016/j.worlddev. 2018.03.021

Ramos Morales, M. F. and J. P. Robson. (2019). Children of the wind: Migration and change in Santa María Yavesia. In: Robson, J. P., D. Klooster, and J. Hernandez-Diaz (eds), *Communities Surviving Migration: Village Governance, Environment, and Cultural Survival.* Abingdon, UK: Routledge/Earthscan.

Ribot, J. C., Chhatre, A. and Lankina, T. (2008). Introduction: Institutional choice and recognition in the formation and consolidation of local democracy. *Conservation and Society*, 6(1), 1.

Robson, J. P. (2019a). Indigenous communities, migrant organizations, and the ephemeral nature of translocality. *Latin American Research Review*, 54(1).

Robson, J. P. (2019b). Adaptive governance or cultural transformation? The monetization of usos y costumbres in Santiago Comaltepec. In: Robson, J. P., D. Klooster, and J. Hernandez-Diaz (eds), *Communities Surviving Migration: Village Governance, Environment, and Cultural Survival.* Abingdon, UK: Routledge/Earthscan.

Robson, J. P. (2010). *The Impact of Rural to Urban Migration on Forest Commons in Oaxaca, Mexico.* Unpublished PhD Thesis, University of Manitoba. Winnipeg, Canada.

Robson, J. P. and Berkes, F. (2011). Exploring some of the myths of land use change: Can rural to urban migration drive declines in biodiversity? *Global Environmental Change*, 21(3), 844–854.

Robson, J. P., Klooster, D. J., Worthen, H. and Hernández-Díaz, J. (2018). Migration and agrarian transformation in Indigenous Mexico. *Journal of Agrarian Change* 18(2), 299–323.

Robson, J. P. and Klooster, D. (2018). Migration and a new landscape of forest use and conservation. *Environmental Conservation.* https://doi.org/10.1017/S0376892918000218.

Robson, J. P., D. Klooster, and J. Hernandez-Diaz. (2019). *Communities Surviving Migration: Village Governance, Environment, and Cultural Survival.* Abingdon, UK: Routledge/Earthscan.

Rights and Resources Initiative (RRI). (2015). *Who Owns the World's Land? A Global Baseline of Formally Recognized Indigenous and Community Land Rights.* Washington, DC: Rights and Resources Initiative.

Saad, P. (2010). Demographic trends in Latin America and the Caribbean. In Cotlear, D. (ed.), *Population Aging: Is Latin America Ready?* Washington, DC: World Bank. 43–77.

Sarukhán, J. and Jiménez, R. (2016). Generating intelligence for decision making and sustainable use of natural capital in Mexico. *Current Opinion in Environmental Sustainability* 19, 153–159.

Schlager, E. and Ostrom, E. (1992). Property-rights regimes and natural resources: A conceptual analysis. *Land Economics*, 68(3), 249–262.

Sikor, T., He, J. and Lestrelin, G. (2017). Property rights regimes and natural resources: a conceptual analysis revisited. *World Development*, *93*, 337–349.

Sosa Perez, F. and Robson, J. P. (2019). Migration, community, and land use in San Juan Evangelista Analco. In Robson, J. P., D. Klooster, and J. Hernandez-Diaz (eds), *Communities Surviving Migration: Village Governance, Environment, and Cultural Survival*. Abingdon, UK: Routledge/Earthscan.

Smith, R. (2006). *Mexican New York: Transnational Lives of New Immigrants*. Berkeley: University of California Press.

Stephen, L. (2007). *Transborder Lives: Indigenous Oaxacans in Mexico, California and Oregon*. Durham, NC: Duke University Press.

United Nations. (2017). *World Population Prospects: The 2017 Revision*. Available online at: https://esa.un.org/unpd/wpp/ (accessed 30 November 2020).

Chapter 13

Decommonisation–commonisation dynamics and social movements

Insights from a meta-analysis of case studies

Sergio Villamayor-Tomás and Gustavo García-López

Introduction

International research on the benefits of community-based natural resource management (CBNRM) regimes to achieve sustainable development lists several concerns about the vulnerability of these regimes to globalization, shortsighted government regulations, marginalisation, intensified land competition from commercial interests for resource extraction, and other political economic threats (Baynes, Herbohn, Smith, Fisher, & Bray, 2015; Blaikie, 2006; Dressler et al., 2010; Notess et al., 2018). Increasing attention has been paid to the participation of local communities in social movements against those threats (Anguelovski & Martínez Alier, 2014). Communities' capacity to manage natural resources via CBRNM regimes and mobilise for their promotion or defense are two sides of the same collective action phenomenon (Scholtens, 2016; Villamayor-Tomas, García-López, & Scholtens, 2020). However, these have so far been studied separately by scholars. Little is known, therefore, about whether and how social mobilisation contributes to better CBNRM. In this chapter, we address this question via a meta-analysis of 81 cases around the world. The key research questions we examine include: Which threats jeopardise the sustainability of CBNRM regimes and how? How do social movements and related forms of mobilisation contribute in turn to the sustainability of said regimes?

Some scholars have highlighted the intricate connections between social movements (such as those against extractive industries or large conservation areas) and the formalisation of customary community-based management regimes (Alcorn, Bamba, Masiun, Natalia, & Royo, 2003; Gerber, 2011; Kashwan, 2017; Perreault, 2001; Veuthey & Gerber, 2012); the recognition of collective territorial rights (Conde & Kallis, 2012; Kurien, 2013); and the reinvigoration of local Indigenous practices and knowledge (Armitage, 2005; Poole, 2005). Underlying these research is the understanding that local resource-dependent communities may "organise and fight for preserving their means of livelihood in the name of social justice, defence of customary territorial rights, health, or sacredness", a process which could "eventually allow them to renegotiate power distribution" (Veuthey & Gerber, 2012: 612). Apart from defending existing CBNRM initiatives, the struggles can also lead to the creation and formalisation of new community initiatives. That is precisely the case of landless peasant movements and the creation of self-organised communities for the management of newly-acquired lands (Diegues, 1998; Lynn, 1998), or the activities carried by irrigation, fishery and forest users movements to create co-management agreements (García-López & Antinori, 2018; John Kurien, 1991; Paudel, Monterroso, & Cronkleton, 2010; Verzijl, Hoogesteger, & Boelens, 2017).

This chapter focuses on social movements as drivers of commonisation processes. We broadly define social movements as "processes of collective action that are sustained across space and time, that reflect grievances around perceived injustices, and that constitute a pursuit of alternative agendas" (Bebbington et al., 2008: 2892). Most of the movements studied here correspond to environmental justice movements in rural, Global South contexts, which centre around the resistance of local resource users and Indigenous populations against the actions of large extractive activities, the government or other actors (Anguelovski & Martínez Alier, 2014; Goldman, 1997; Peet & Watts, 1996; Scheidel, Temper, Demaria, & Martínez Alier, 2017).

Commonisation and decommonisation can be understood as two opposing processes shaping the viability of CBNRM. Commonisation is understood as a "process through which a resource gets converted into a jointly used resource under commons institutions that deal with excludability and subtractability, and 'decommonisation' refers to a process through which a jointly used resource under commons institutions loses these essential characteristics" (Nayak & Berkes 2011: 133). From this perspective, CBNRM regimes can be understood as outcomes/manifestations of commonisation processes, and vulnerable to decommonisation processes. Both processes reoccur over time simultaneously as they are influenced by the prevalent social, economic, political and ecological drivers (Nayak & Berkes, 2011).

Decommonisation processes can be associated with the constraints imposed onto local CBNRM regimes by states' enclosure and recentralisation policies (De Angelis, 2012; Ribot, Agrawal, & Larson, 2006), 'fortress' conservation policies (Brockington, 2002), or elite capture and inequalities (Blaikie, 2006; Persha & Andersson, 2014). Commonisation processes, on the other hand, can be associated with certain institutional design principles (Cox, Arnold, & Villamayor-Tomas, 2010; Ostrom, 1990), devolution of management rights and co-management (Moreno-Sánchez & Maldonado, 2010; Pomeroy & Berkes, 1997), and participatory/collaborative processes (Koontz et al., 2004; Lubell, 2005).

The study of social movements contributes to the understanding of the dynamic connections between decommonisation and commonisation. As illustrated above, the very impact of decommonisation drivers constitute in many cases the motivation for communities to mobilise and participate in social movements. The rest of the chapter presents results of the meta-analysis in detail.

Methods

Methodologically, the study consists of a meta-analysis of case studies following protocols used in similar research projects (Cox et al., 2010; Hartberg, Cox, & Villamayor-Tomas, 2016). Case studies were first searched, then screened, and finally content-analysed to explore the drivers, threats and aspects through which social mobilisation can have an impact on CBNRM institutions (Villamayor-Tomas & García-López, 2018).

An initial list of potential case studies was first identified via a keyword search in Google Scholar. A case study qualified for coding if: it reported information about a specific rural community (or communities) that managed shared resources collectively (i.e., via a formal or customary common property regime), and got involved in social movements to defend its rights, interests or values concerning those resources. As a result of this process 150 studies were selected, out of which 32 were finally coded for having sufficient information. These studies also referred to other potentially relevant studies, a good number of which were also coded. The final list of studies coded was 78, which reported information about 81 cases. The dates of the selected studies ranged from 1989 to 2017.

The coding of drivers and threats was inductive, i.e., the classification emerged from the data after several iterations of coding and interpretation. The coding of the aspects through which movements can have an impact on community-based institutions was initially based on Ostrom's institutional design principles for long-lasting community-based commons governance (Cox et al., 2010). The goal was first to identify whether the movement had a positive impact on the principles, i.e., whether "collective mobilisation undermined or prevented the implementation of the design principle" (Villamayor-Tomas & García-López, 2018: 117). This was followed by an identification of the different pathways (i.e., commonisation pathways) through which movements have an impact.

Decommonisation drivers

The content analysis identified 16 different drivers of decommonisation, which can be classified into five groups: natural resource management policies, economic policies, encroachment by large and small users, and political rights policies (Figure 13.1).

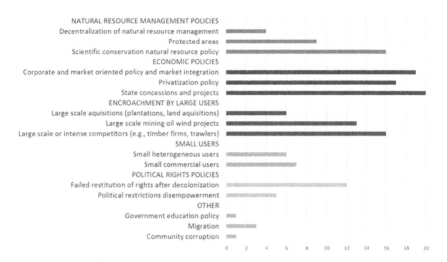

Figure 13.1 Frequency of decommonisation drivers. A colour version of this image is downloadable as an eResource from www.routledge.com/9780367138004.

Natural resource management policies

An important driver, although not particularly frequent in the data, is *recentralisation of natural resource management*. This is illustrated mostly by forest cases where decentralisation policies by central governments are used to restrict local autonomy (see similar findings in Ribot et al., 2006; Sahide et al., 2016). As per our data, this occurs via the imposition of institutions, organisations and programmatic priorities that structure or preempt local institutions and decision making (Alcorn, 2003, Springate et al., 2008, García-López & Antinori, 2018). As pointed by Alcorn for the case of *adat* communities in Indonesia, the approval of regulations to ostensibly empower *adat* institutions in local governments, translated into new institutions and a changed national discourse which undermined Indigenous *adat* autonomy and authority (Alcorn, 2003). In Mexico, a new program to strengthen self-governance by forest communities (PROFAS) in 2004 forced communities to adopt a specific institutional structure provided by the government, often supplanting or duplicating existing self-organised associations (García-López & Antinori, 2018). In the case of India's Joint Forest Management program, developed "to induce local people to help in the forest departments' regeneration efforts...rights were not provided and forest departments have often used the programme as an instrument to extend their authority structures to the village, generate funds from donors to expand their staffing and even take more lands from local people through enforcing no cultivation on JFM plots." (Springate et al., 2008: 10).[1]

The *scientific conservation policy* driver is particularly frequent in the data and relates to governments' tendency to design policies that draw exclusively on formal science-based knowledge while ignoring local worldviews, knowledge and practices (Agrawal, 1995; Berkes, 1999; Sletto, 2008). This can occur in post-colonial contexts because of the formation of new governments or in the aftermath of political transitions. In Alaska, the state "assumed jurisdiction over all marine mammal species not covered by international treaties (...) by establishing and enforcing seasons, bag limits, and methods (...) and (...) programs of scientific research...". This was done without any consideration of the existing Alaskan Native hunting and fishing rights (Langdon 1989: 156). These policies can be motivated by economic concerns, similar to the case of lobster regulations in Southwest Nova Scotia, where standard trap limits were established by the federal government to reduce "the total cost of fishing efforts and hence increasing the net incomes of fishermen" (Kearney 1989: 90).

A paradigmatic example of resource management policies that can negatively affect local communities are *protected areas*.[2] In some cases, good intentions to conserve resources are offset by the failure to recognise the complexity of the local socio-ecological environment. In Guatemala, the design of the Mayan Biosphere Reserve "did not adequately take into account the complexity of the region's pre-existing diverse population and natural resource use patterns. On the contrary, bans and other restrictions on usage were originally imposed on populations both within the reserve and in its surrounding buffer zones" (Cronkleton, 2008: 6). In other cases, lack of appropriate resources for implementation created 'paper parks', protected only in statute but not on the ground. In Honduras, the government-promoted Cayo Cochinos Protected Area lacked the personnel and resources in government agencies and ended up auctioning off the management to private enterprises and NGOs "diverting profits from natural resources away from local communities and towards elite and foreign interests" (Brondo & Brown, 2011: 95).

Economic policies

The data showed that economic policies were the most frequent drivers of community threats. *Privatisation policy* reflects the numerous initiatives carried out by governments to allocate community rights to private corporations, including not only use rights but also exclusion and alienation rights – i.e. the rights to exclude others from using the resources and to fully privatise them (Schlager & Ostrom 1992). This has been frequently done under the (incorrect) assumptions that customary land is being used in unproductive and/or unsustainable ways (e.g. Hardin's 'tragedy of the commons' myth), or not used at all; and that private property regimes can promote increased efficiency, productivity and capital investments (and therefore economic growth), as well as sustainable management. In Malawi, the official policy on land tenure issues since colonial rule has been that private ownership and statutory security are desirable for rural development. Consequently, customary land is perceived as a reserve from which private and public land ownership should be created (Chinsinga et al., 2013; Chirwa et al., 2004). The state thus actively promotes land leases: between 1991 and 1997, 1.20 million hectares of customary land were transferred to private and public land ownership following this approval process (Chinsinga et al., 2013: 1070). In cases like these, privatisation is done ex-ante via changes in property law, while in others it is done ex-post via the legalisation of illegal enclosures. In Mexico, in the 1990s, the government implemented a neoliberal reform of the Constitution and agrarian laws which allowed for the partial or full privatisation of communal lands (García-López & Antinori, 2018). Additionally, the government proposed to amend the law to "allow confiscation of land by the state on behalf of private industries and to introduce only cash compensation instead of providing new land ..." (Randeria, 2003: 48). In Ecuador, the Correa government revised the Constitution and signed a decree to authorize the legalisation of illegally established ponds for shrimp farming in community coastal mangroves (Veuthey & Gerber 2012: 616).

On many occasions, privatisation also includes the transferability of rights via markets. The underlying assumption is that this can contribute to efficient allocation of the resources (i.e., diverting their uses to make the most value out of them) under changing conditions. In New Zealand, one of the results for fisheries management of the new Labour government reform in the mid-1980s was:

> the privatisation of natural resources, particularly forests and fisheries. This led to the creation of the Quota Management System (QMS) and the allocation of Individual Transferable Quotas (ITQs) to those who could demonstrate recent commercial participation in a fishery. Ownership of ITQs granted a share in an annually determined total catch for each fishery. Under the QMS, anyone who wanted to fish commercially had to own or lease quota, as well as a fishing boat.
>
> (De Alessi 2012, 400)

Corporate and market-oriented policy is strongly linked to the global neoliberal policy shift in the 1980s and 1990s. One example is the use of governmental reforms to "open" the economies to foreign capital investments. In Mexico, the signature in the 1994 North American Free Trade Agreement (NAFTA) "eliminated commercial tariffs for timber such that Mexican timber faced stiffer competition from plantation-style" multinational corporations, affecting many communal forestry and agriculture enterprises, and impacting rural livelihoods in general (García-López & Antinori, 2018: 198–199).[3] Also, paradigmatic are the use of government subsidies and programs to promote intensive, market-oriented resource use by large corporations. In Chile, the forestry industry expanded notably after the approval of a decree through which the state subsidised 75 percent and up to 90 percent of the cost of plantations on certain lands. Similarly, in India, the "Indo-Norwegian Project for Fisheries and Fishermen Community Development (INP)" introduced new fishing technologies (mainly trawlers and purse-seine nets), built onshore infrastructure such as fish landing centres, curing yards, ice plant and cold storage, and a trawler repair workshops, and organised fishers into cooperatives, which also disbursed loans and conducted trainings" (Sinha, 2012: 374).

State concessions and projects are another important type of economic policy driver. State concessions are usually designed to incentivise large-scale investors. In Mexico, the Forest Law prior to 1986 gave public and private forestry industries monopsonistic rights over extensive areas by forcing communities to sell timber only to those industries (Klooster, 2000). Meanwhile, the neoliberal 1992 Fisheries Law "eliminated cooperatives' exclusive fishing rights and provided greater security for investors by extending the aquaculture concession period from 25 to 50 years, openly encouraging private investment" (Altamirano-Jiménez, 2017: 3). State projects are branded as measures to increase resource productivity, in many cases resulting in the benefit of powerful interest groups or industries. The Independencia Aqueduct project in Northern Mexico, for example, transferred water from the Yaqui Valley to the coastal city of Hermosillo, reflecting a shift in the regional axis of power from the agroindustry to urban and industrial water users (Radonic, 2015).

Encroachment by large-scale users

Large-scale competitors, such as timber firms and fishing trawlers, and *large-scale acquisitions and projects* such as plantations, and mining, oil and other energy ventures, are also quite important threats. In a few cases, the presence of large companies can be traced back to colonial times or authoritarian governments (Pinkerton, 1993; Brownhill, 2007; Powell, 2017), but in the majority cases it is linked to governmental reforms and economic policies that precisely support these kind of initiatives, i.e. market and corporate-oriented (Alburo-Cañete & Cañete 2013; Altamirano-Jiménez, 2017; García-López & Antinori, 2018).

In some cases, the intrusion of large-scale users is promoted by the government on the basis that they make efficient use of the resources. That is the case, for example, of the Limpasa Sugar Company in Mankhambira, Malawi, where "national level government officials particularly argue that the company is one way of productively utilizing the idle land that will help address critical foreign exchange shortages" (Chinsinga et al., 2013: 1076). In other cases, encroachment by large users just responds to short-term rent-seeking. The progressive concentration of land in the hands of a few large cattle ranchers in Acre, the Amazon (Diegues, 1998) is a good example. Other examples are the intrusion by Indian trawlers into Northern Sri Lankan marine borders (Scholtens, 2016); or the development of the prawn industry in Lake Chilika, India, featured by "unscrupulous traders and middlemen (...) politicians with their musclemen, a handful of big business families of Orissa and their local middlemen termed as "mafia", and finally, the big industrial houses" (Pattanaik, 2003: 57).

Finally, it is important to note the association of the large-scale users to issues of elite capture and corruption. In Nigeria, "the state received oil revenues, which were massively channeled to corrupt politicians, civil servants, intermediaries, contractors and motley hanger" (Turner & Brownhill, 2004: pp. 32–33). In Canada of the 1990s, "the major multinational timber companies, which leased Crown forests under long-term license agreements, played a major role in the development of forest policy and guidelines for forest practices" (Pinkerton, 1993)

Encroachment by small commercial users

A less visible but still important impact is the arrival of small, heterogeneous users in large numbers. These are in most cases *non-subsistence users (i.e. commercial or recreational users)* who reside outside of the communities. As pointed by Nguiffo (1998) with regard to the Southern Cameroon forest sector: "Poachers are professional hunters who live on selling their catch; they are not natives of the hunting grounds and have no obligation of respect to the hunting grounds or to the rules for the hunting period or local hunting taboos. They hunt to satisfy the ever-growing demand from urban centres, not the limited demand of forest inhabitants" (p. 109). As with large users, small users are motivated by short-term rent-seeking; however, they count on the favor of governments as much as large users do, and just reflect gaps and contradictions in the implementation of development and conservation policies. In Ecuador, the growth of farmed shrimp over mangroves all across Ecuador reflected "a blatant contradiction between the laws protecting the mangroves, and the practices on the ground. As a result, shrimp farming developed illegally with the implicit approval of the government as it would have been impossible to produce so much shrimp with so few concessions granted" (Veuthey & Gerber, 2012: 614).

Political rights policy

This driver relates to *inheritances from colonial and/or autocratic governments* in newly independent or democratized countries. Those inheritances mean the perpetuation of certain stereotypes about rural, resource-dependent communities. In Indonesia, the fall of Suharto's regime barely changed the colonial-inspired designation of rural communities as "isolated native groups" that need to be pushed from primitive livelihoods into civilization (Li, 2004). The new government's "official program designed to civilize such people views them as generic primitives, occupants of a tribal slot which is negatively construed. Their ethnic or tribal identities, cultural distinctiveness, livelihood practices, and ancient ties to the places they inhabit are presented in program documents as problems, evidence of closed minds and a developmental deficit that a well-meaning government must help them to overcome." (p. 344). Inheritances also can mean the continuation of certain understandings of what the "public domain" is, and certain modes of socio-economic organisation. In Colombia, the central government considered the extensive mangrove areas in the southern part of the Pacific coast as 'areas of public interest' rather than community territory (Oslender, 2004). In the El Tule village and many other rural areas in Mexico, the "Hacienda" model of agricultural exploitation (large-scale, private plantation that provides employment to members of surrounding communities) has become socially accepted over time despite its colonial foundations (Lynn, 1998).

The driver also manifests itself in the *failed restitution of political rights* in post-colonial democracies. In Peru, "successive democratic governments have failed to make progress in respecting and promoting the rights of Indigenous peoples, especially the rights of the Mapuche. Under the Indigenous Pact (adopted in 1989), they have committed themselves to recognising Indigenous peoples, (but) the government's core policy has amounted to an ill-defined land restitution plan, combined with development programs and monetary compensation, the overall goal being to prevent an Indigenous insurgency." (p. 3). In New Zealand, the 150-year plus effort of the Maori community "has resulted in limited Crown attempts to address historical grievances. There has also been limited recognition, in law, that the unique and valuable knowledge of Maori and their rights to self-determination must be protected." (Rixecker & Tipene-Matua, 2003: 256)

Decommonisation impacts and the motivation for social mobilisation

The above decommonisation drivers have different impacts on resource-dependent communities. Impacts can be classified into four groups, including livelihood impacts, resource right loses, externalities, and erosion of community assets (see Figure 13.2).

Livelihood impacts

An expected livelihood impact, although not particularly frequent in the data, is *displacement* (i.e., resettlement) of population. Mostly occurring in the forest conservation context, where the "notion that forests and people cannot coexist implies that forest dwellers must be evicted in order to protect forested areas" (Roberts, 2016: 54). Even if resettled communities are granted access

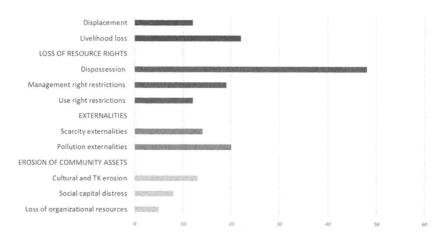

Figure 13.2 Frequency of cases per type of impact. A colour version of this image is downloadable as an eResource from www.routledge.com/9780367138004.

to new resources, promised support for resettlement projects often proves inadequate (Cronkleton, 2008, Montalba et al., 2005). This is particularly clear in colonial contexts, like that affecting the Mapuche in Chile, where the communities have tended to be confined within "small spaces with marginal productive potential and ecologically of extreme fragility" (Montalba et al., 2005: 19). In other cases, such as the riverine communities in the Amazon, the families are just forced out of their lands and left to live on their own (Schwartzman et al., 2010).

Livelihood loss, or the loss of subsistence means for community households, is the second most frequently reported impact, and closely associated to displacements. This refers mostly to the loss of access to food, fodder for livestock, construction materials, and energy sources for heating or cooking (Brownhill, 2007; Klooster, 2000; Sinha, 2012). This can be particularly damaging for already marginalised communities because of their high dependence on the commons (Martiniello, 2015; Lynn, 1998). As put by Kenney-Lazar (2012), "for a number of poorer households, the loss of forest resources was devastating because one of their only sources of income was logging timber from forested areas to build houses for wealthier families in the village". In Bolivia, nut gatherers remain some of the region's poorest residents (Paudel, 2010). Women are a particularly vulnerable due to their traditional central role in subsistence rural economies (Turner & Brownhill, 2004).

The impact also relates to health issues (Rixecker & Tipene-Matua, 2003; Powell, 2017). As pointed by Powell (2017) about the Navajo community in North America, "the accumulated risks of environmental contamination from the extractive industry became increasingly evident. Asthma from airborne pollution, cancer from residual radiation, and vanishing aquifers and tributaries reshaped Dine landscapes and bodies into a sacrifice zone of the Southwest" (p. 214).

These two drivers are closely related: displacement (and legal restrictions in access and use rights – discussed below) are the most evident ways through which the loss of livelihood happens. As pointed by Brownhill (2007), "where industrial logging, mining, plantation agriculture, ranching, real estate development, manufacturing and private 'game parks' monopolise large areas of arable land, that land is no longer available for the production of food for local consumption" (p. 3). Two other less evident mechanisms are the conversion of community members into wage-labourers and their introduction through government or NGO programs to new resource use activities. The first mechanism precludes the community from capturing the full value of its members' labour (Kenney-Lazar, 2012). The second runs the risk of failure due to the difficulties encountered by users to adapt to the new activity. In India, an "attempt to turn pastoralists into farmers failed due to the poor quality of land made available to families who had no knowledge of agriculture and no access to the inputs required for cultivation. Within a few years, many successful pastoralists, who had been selling milk and milk products over long period of time, were reduced to wage labor" (Randeria, 2003: 43).

Loss of resource rights (access, use and management)

The most frequent impact faced by communities is the *total loss of access to the resource*. The resource may be enclosed by individuals or granted in concession to the highest bidder (Montalba et al., 2005; Correia, 2010; Turner & Brownhill, 2004); encroached by competing users like large timber companies or fishing trawlers (Cronkleton, 2008; De Alessi, 2012; Diegues, 1998); devoted to new uses like in the transformation of forest land to large plantations (Alcorn, 2003; Alonso-Fradejas, 2015; Chinsinga et al., 2013), energy and transport projects (Altamirano-Jiménez, 2017; Correia, 2010; Topatimasang 2005) or conservation areas (Randeria, 2003; Paudel, 2010; Roberts, 2016); transferred from one territory to another, like in the case of water transfers (Radonic, 2015); or become unusable due to flooding (Colchester, 2005).

This process of dispossession comes with violations of political (e.g., consultation) rights, and sometimes also violence. In Uganda, the Amuru Sugar project was possible, thanks to the government's "usual arsenal of violence and bribery, in an effort to evict local inhabitants and secure land for the company" (Martiniello, 2015: 660). In India, the *Adviasi* (tribal people) have been precluded from accessing their lands by more powerful groups and corporations, which use "a combination of cunningness, corruption, and violence to alienate people from the land" (Schock, 2009: 190).

Another set of important impacts are *restrictions on the communities' use of resources*. These can take the form of elimination of exclusive use rights, like in Mexico with the 1992 Fisheries Law that eliminated cooperatives' exclusive fishing rights (Altamirano-Jiménez, 2017); or in New Zealand, where the establishment of a Quota Management System served the purpose of formalising but also limiting Maori's traditional use rights (De Alessi, 2012). Many restrictions are justified by governments and international organisations through conservation goals imposed by way of disregarding local communities' customs and potential to act as stewards of the resource (Brondo & Brown 2011; Cohen, 1989; Cronkleton, 2008; Poole, 2005).

Finally, in some cases use rights are respected but communities' *management rights* are still vulnerated. This manifests through different ways. One is the formal subordination of local authorities to higher level authorities (Alcorn, 2003; Brondo & Brown, 2011). In Indonesia, village governance law had priority over *adat* rule; district governments had to give "their approval to the appointment of any new *adat* chief, whose powers have been restricted because the village group headman and the district head can intervene in his decisions" (Alcorn, 2003: 331). Similarly, the Joint Forest Management program has been used by forest departments as an instrument to extend their authority structures to the village, generate funds from donors to expand their staffing (Springate et al., 2008). Another way is the enactment of plans or rules that constrain communities' management operations. The 1967 Maori Affairs Bill, for example, purported to improve conditions for Maori but maintained the compulsory sale of land owned by multiple Maori owners (De Alessi, 2012). In Mexico, for several decades, forest-owning communities maintained nominal control over forest land in these concessions, but they could only sell logging rights to the big industrial entities and they could not convert forests to other uses (Klooster, 2000). Finally, violations of community control rights also manifest in the tendency of governments not to consult communities when granting use rights to large infrastructure or extractive projects even if they should by law (Escobar, 1998; Nguiffo, 1998; Ohja, 2011; Paudel, 2010).

Externalities

Other important impacts include externalities that occur usually in the form of reduced resource availability and/or quality. *Scarcity externalities* (e.g., decreased resource availability) typically results from the actions of large-scale industrial firms which overexploit the stock and undermine its regeneration capacity, as seen often in fisheries (e.g., Jordan, 1989; Kurien, 1991; Morrell, 1989; Scholtens, 2016; Sinha, 2012; Somayaji & Coelho, 2017). As pointed out by Morrell (1989) with regard to the Seekena River, Canada: "Most stocks of Skeena salmon and steelhead are depressed below historical levels of abundance due primarily to overharvest in the industrial fisheries", and this increases the vulnerability of the system to fail (pp. 241–242). Scarcity externalities may occur despite the state recognition of community rights. As pointed by Scholtens (2016) in the case of fisheries in North Sri Lanka,

"North Sri Lankans now live in the ironic situation, that while enjoying fishing rights after 30 years of war, they are unable to really benefit from the Palk Bay resources in the face of a powerful trawler fleet" from Indian firms. Some externalities also result from the aggressive harvest techniques of small-scale non-subsistence users, like recreational and small commercial fishers (Langdon, 1989; Cohen, 1989), or the "silent" impact of illegal forest poachers (Nguiffo, 1998).

Degradation externalities (e.g., decreased resource quality) frequently occur at the interface between hydrological and aquatic systems, and other resource systems that are polluted by substances from mining and oil extraction (Byambajav, 2012; Hafild, 2005; Stoltenborg & Boelens, 2016; Turner and Brownhill 2004; Urkidi 2010), massive deforestation (Peña, 2003), or large-scale cultivations (Montalba et al., 2005; Alonso-Fradejas, 2015). In Mongolia, "the environmental impact of placer gold mining in Orhon was deleterious. Many mines illegally diverted river streams and released dirty water into a river system. This caused extensive damage to local rivers such as the depletion and pollution of rivers (presence of sediment particles and nutrients)" (Byambajav, 2012: 18). That is also the case of aquatic habitats impacted by soil erosion connected to forestry activities (Palmer, 2017; Pinkerton, 1993). Although less frequent, the destruction and loss of species diversity due to aggressive harvesting technologies in the context of large-scale logging (Ribot 2000) and fishing (Sinha 2012; Tang & Tang, 2001) is also significant. As described by Sinha (2012) in the case of fishing in Kerala, India, "trawlers … drag their nets along the seafloor", resulting in the destruction of all vegetation, rocky formations, sand towers and coral formations which contribute to fish reproduction (p. 377).

Erosion of community assets

A final set of impacts have to do with the erosion of communities' *cultural traits*, social capital and organisational resources. Several cases illustrate how colonization and certain government policies (e.g., conservation programs) undermine communities' cultural traits, such as collective identities, values, customs, and knowledge related to the environment (Cohen, 1989; Alcorn, 2003). As expressed by a Q'eqchi peasant regarding the consolidation of large oil palm cultivations in the Sayaxché municipality (Guatemala), "our thinking is being dominated as well as our beliefs. This is the result of the way the powerful and rich people think. Of those who want to dispossess us from our lands once again." (in Alonso-Fradejas, 2015: 498).

Communities can also suffer from *leadership corruption, gender inequality, illegal resource use, and conflict,* all of which can contribute to erosion of social capital. In San Martin, Mexico, timber smuggling "was just one minor symptom of an increasingly dysfunctional forest management system (…) concessions marginalized peasants from control over forests and from the benefits of forestry, and so the forest became, from their perspective, marginal. Alienated from their resources, they often resisted the system with tree theft, clearing, and burning" (p. 291). In Makacoulibantang, Senegal most villagers do not want wood fuel being cut from surrounding forests but, "despite their objections, some village chiefs, who are usually hereditary power centres appointed for life, allow production of wood fuel in village forests. Their decision is based partly on payoffs from merchants, and partly on the social status of merchants, which makes it difficult for chiefs to turn them down" (Ribot, 2000: 134). A final impact related to loss of social capital is the *loss of organisational resources* to operate, due to the elimination or reduction of government subsidies (De Alessi, 2012), community development programs (García-López & Antinori, 2018), and technical support for resource management planning (Stevens et al., 2014).

There are patterns in the ways specific drivers are linked to various types of impacts, as shown in Figure 13.3. We observe for instance that economic policy drivers are more frequently associated to community resource right losses, livelihood impacts and erosion of community assets, than to externalities. Meanwhile, encroachments by large-scale users tend to generate externalities and livelihood impacts.

Table 13.1 shows the variation in frequency of impacts in relation to each other. As we observe, some impacts are more frequent than others across the board. That is clearly the case of dispossession, which is present in 60 percent of the cases (i.e., in 48 cases); and livelihood loss, which, although not as frequent as dispossession, tends to occur together with most of the other impacts (see column b of Table 13.1). As repeatedly illustrated by the authors of the studies, there is a strong connection between the decommonisation impacts and the emergence of movements. Also, studies included in this analysis were elected based on the presence of movements, which suggests that the most frequent impacts are strongly associate with the emergency of movements. That said, one should not assume a direct relationship between impacts and movement emergence. First, impacts tended to manifest in bundles. None of the 81 cases reflected just one of the impacts. On the contrary, each of them reflected around three impacts on average. One case reflected six different impacts (Klooster 2000), and four cases reflected five impacts. Also, some impacts tended to align with each other more frequently than others (see Table 13.1). For example, dispossession is linked to displacement, cultural erosion and livelihood losses in 92 percent, 69 percent and 55 percent of its cases (12 cases) respectively, while pollution externalities come with scarcity and livelihood losses in 33 percent of its cases (20 cases).

Second, as pointed out in social movement studies, the ability to translate grievances into mobilisation is influenced by a fair number of factors, including the availability of organisational resources, the degree of repression by governments, or the ability of leaders to use appealing discourses, amongst others (Scheidel et al., 2017; Snow, Soule, & Kriesi, 2004). Answering

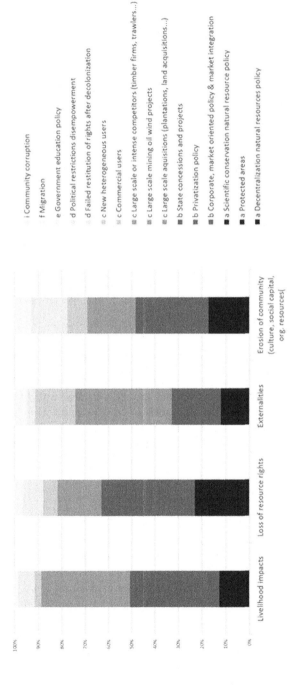

Figure 13.3 Drivers of decommonisation across types of impacts. A colour version of this image is downloadable as an eResource from www.routledge.com/9780367138004.

Table 13.1 Cross-tabulated frequencies of impacts (in percentages)

	a.	b.	c.	d.	e.	f.	g.	h.	i.	j.
a. Displacement (12)		25	92	0	0	0	8	17	0	0
b. Livelihood loss (22)	14		55	9	5	9	27	18	14	5
c. Dispossession (48)	23	25		17	8	6	8	19	4	2
d. Management rights restrict. (19)	0	11	42		21	16	11	11	16	16
e. Use right restrict. (12)	0	8	33	33		17	8	17	0	8
f. Scarcity externalities (14)	0	14	21	14	14		29	7	7	7
g. Pollution externalities (20)	5	30	20	10	5	30		15	10	5
h. Cultural-TK erosion (13)	15	31	69	15	15	8	23		8	0
i. Social capital distress (8)	0	38	25	38	0	25	25	13		0
j. Loss of org. resources (5)	0	20	20	60	20	20	20	0	0	

Note: number of cases in parenthesis

appropriately the question of emergence goes beyond the purpose of this study and would have required including cases which have presence of impacts but absence of mobilisation.

Commonisation pathways though social movements

According to our findings, social movements also contribute to commonisation through a number of pathways, which can be clustered into five groups: the defense of communal rights and territories; the promotion of economic autonomy; the promotion of community human capital; the improvement of community decision making; the enhancement of community litigation capacities; and the promotion of community organisation (see Figure 13.4) (see also Villamayor-Tomas & García-López, 2018).

Defense of communal rights and territories

By far, the most frequent pathway through which movements contribute to the commonisation is defending *community resource use and management rights*. The defense of rights is indeed one of the main reasons behind the mobilisation of communities and their participation in movements. By claiming their resource use rights, the movements defend also the collective nature of such rights. In the Yaqui Valley, Mexico, the opposition to the *Independencia* water transfer has been a defense of the access to a resource on which people's livelihoods depend as much as "a fight over historical recognition of collective Indigenous water rights" (Radonic, 2015: 37). Many of the cases related to

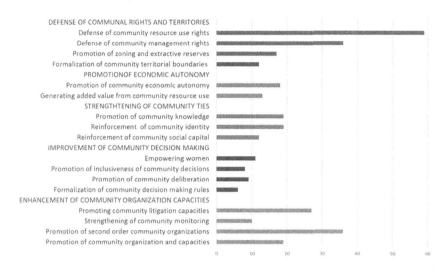

Figure 13.4 Frequency of commonisation pathways promoted by social movements. A colour version of this image is downloadable as an eResource from www. routledge.com/9780367138004.

the defense of management rights are from Indigenous communities, which often mobilise discourses of "self-determination" and autonomy (Escobar, 1998; Hoogesteger & Verzijl, 2015).

The above tends to align with efforts to *formalise rights in laws or constitutions*. For instance, in Mexico the struggles of forest communities against state and private timber concessions on their lands led to the passage of the 1986 Forest Law, which recognises communities' forest management rights (García-López & Antinori, 2018; Klooster, 2000).

Another recurrent pathway is the creation and defense of *exclusive use zones*, such as the "extractive forest reserves" promoted by the rubber tappers movement in the Brazilian Amazon, and local forest communities in Petén, Guatemala (Cronkleton, Taylor, Barry, Stone-Jovicich, & Schmink, 2008; Paudel et al., 2010); or the "trawler-free coastal fishing zones" reserved for artisanal fishing communities in Kerala and Goa, India (John Kurien, 1991; Sinha, 2012). Finally, movements also contribute to the *formalisation of boundaries*, which takes place via the elaboration of maps (Alcorn, et al. 2003; Diegues, 1998; Roberts, 2016), and the legal registration of the boundaries.

Promotion of economic autonomy

Movements also promote economic autonomy, through two mechanisms. First, they *add value to the participation of community members in CBNRM* regimes. This is accomplished by lobbying for tax benefits (Paudel et al., 2010) and attracting subsidies and development funds (Diegues 1998; García-López & Antinori 2018; Perreault, 2001), as well as by exploring new production options (Cronkleton et al., 2008), and facilitating access to markets and credit via information, diversification strategies and collective bargaining (Lynn 1998). Second, movements promote and support *community-based/grassroots development ventures*. Development ventures include community forestry enterprises for timber and non-timber products and ecotourism (Cronkleton et al., 2008; Diegues, 1998; García-López & Antinori, 2018; Klooster, 2000); agricultural cooperatives (Diniz & Gilbert, 2013a); seed exchange networks and peasant-to-peasant market exchanges (Alonso-Fradejas 2015; Turner & Brownhill, 2004); production plans (Diniz & Gilbert, 2013b); credit unions (Hafild, 2005); or certification labels (Paudel et al., 2010).

Strengthening of community ties

Community organisation is strengthened by movements through their influence on *social capital, community identity* and *community knowledge*, as reported in a fair number of cases. The reinforcement of community identity owes to an intrinsic linkage between resource use rights and political-cultural rights in many of the cases reviewed, especially in cases involving Indigenous communities. In the case of the "Pacific North Coast black communities" (PCN), much of the movement's success and impact on self-organisation had to do with the elaboration of a discourse that mobilised critical elements of the communities' "place based" identity (Escobar, 1998).

The participation of community members in movements and social mobilisation actions can also reinforce solidarity ties and trust (i.e. social capital). In the case of the mobilisations against water privatisation and the referendum promoted by community aqueduct activists in Colombia, Perera (2015) concludes that the referendum failed, but the "community water activists learned about each other, inspired each other, and developed trust" (p. 205), creating social capital for further collaboration in mobilisations and in commons management.

Movements can also build on and promote local traditional knowledge. As per the case studied, traditional knowledge is reproduced through at least three processes: (1) actual practices, like in the case of women's Green Belt Movement in Kenya (Brownhill, 2007; Turner & Brownhill, 2004); (2) educational and research campaigns, like in the case of the Dayak of Indonesia (Alcorn et al., 2003) and the *acequias* of the Rio Culebra in the United States (Peña, 2003); and (3) frames or narratives that legitimise existing knowledge, like in the case of the PCN movement in Colombia (Escobar, 1998).

Improvement of community decision making

Social movements also contribute to the implementation and quality of collective decision making in CBNRM processes. First and foremost, they can *empower women*. In Bolivia, land reform movements incorporated the recognition of women's land rights as one of their central demands, which led to legal prohibition of gender discriminations in access, tenancy, and inheritance of land, and a guarantee to women's access to land in the titling and redistribution process, irrespective of their marital status (Deere, 2017). It also led to women achieving key leading political and elected positions and the creation of a legislative commission on women. Second, movements can *lead or promote deliberation* and self-reflective discussions (i.e., beyond just voting) about everyday issues as well as legal aspects, community production practices and organisational capacity, as happened with the Dayak movement in Indonesia (Alcorn et al., 2003), the Afro-Colombian communities of the Pacific Coast (Escobar, 1998), and the community forestry network in Nepal (Ohja, 2011, Paudel et al., 2010). Third, and closely related to the above, movements can *enhance the inclusiveness of decision making* by opening spaces that give voice to the different social groups within the communities (Diniz & Gilbert, 2013a; Kenney-Lazar, 2012; Martiniello, 2015; Ojha, 2011). Fourth, movements can support and promote the *formalisation of previously informal decision-making processes* into collective-choice rules, through for instance the creation of community councils, community assemblies and other decision-making bodies (De Alessi, 2012; Oslender, 2004).

Enhancement of community organisation capacities

Lastly, CBNRM initiatives are often developed by movements in conjunction with the *promotion of community organisations and capacities*. For instance, the creation of extractive rubber-tapping reserves in Brazil was also based on the local organisation of rubber tappers and on education, health, cooperativism, and resource management research programs (Diegues, 1998). Movements can also strengthen local organisation through pedagogical strategies to educate about the meaning of new laws, founding concepts such as territory, development, traditional production, and use of natural resources (Alcorn et al., 2003; Escobar, 1998; Wouters, 2001); and promoting collaborations and exchanges of experiences among communities (Alcorn et al., 2003; Ojha, 2011).

A related strategy fostered by movements is the *creation of second-order community organisations* for multi-level resource governance. For instance, the Colorado Acequia Association (CAA) in the Culebra watershed, U.S. was created to contest the enclosure of the commons and as well as to find ways to guarantee the long-range viability of *acequia* farming. Accordingly, "the CAA defined its mission as to organise and conduct scientific and legal research to empower the *acequias* to manage and protect" said commons (Peña, 2003: 163). The Federation of Indigenous Organizations of Napo (FOIN), in the Ecuadorian Amazon, emerged as an effort by the movement to consolidate community rights and then evolved to integrate also forest management services for the communities (Cronkleton et al., 2008; Paudel, 2010; García-López & Antinori, 2018). In the case of fisheries, the Goenchea Ramponkarsancho Ekvott organisation (GRE) was formed to protect the interests of traditional fishing communities in Goa, India. Afterwards, aware of the powerful opponents they faced and the similar threats faced by the millions of traditional fishermen in other parts of coastal India, the GRE promoted the creation of the National Forum for Catamaran and Country Boat Fishermen Rights and Marine Life (Somayaji & Coelho 2017).

Finally, movements assist the communities with *litigation resources*. These resources, which include expertise and legal training, as well as economic resources and coordination, allow the communities to address courts at governance levels otherwise inaccessible to them (Brondo & Bown, 2011; Byambajav, 2012).

Conclusions

In this chapter, we have addressed, through a meta-analysis of case studies, the question of whether and how community-based natural resource management (CBRNM) regimes are jeopardised by decommonisation drivers and impacts, and the extent to which social movements contribute in turn to commonisation in affected communities.

The evidence points to the notable impact of certain drivers such as government policy (natural resource management and economic) and large-scale firms (e.g., mining, cultivations). Expectedly, these drivers impact the communities via resource externalities such as scarcity, pollution, and resource use and management right restrictions. The decommonisation drivers also affect less tangible and resource-related "community essentials" such as cultural traits, social capital, and livelihoods. As pointed elsewhere, disconnection of people from their resources is indeed a major driver of decommonisation (Nayak & Berkes, 2011). That said, in none of the cases impacts happened in isolation from each other, and hence, we argue that impacts shall be better understood by looking at bundles of them.

Also, the evidence points to the positive effect of the movements on the emergence and strengthening of CBNRM. In this regard, we show that these effects can occur through various pathways, enriching our understanding of commonisation processes. Additionally, we illustrate that movements can also generate positive spillovers beyond the specific grievances and injustices that motivate their emergence. Those "commonisation spillovers" include the promotion of economic autonomy and development, the reinvigoration of community identity ties and social capital, the improvement of community decision making, and the enhancement of community organisational capacity. Exploring whether these "commonisation spillovers" involve longer-term effects is a promising question for further research.

Notes

1 Similar findings are reported for Indonesia's community forestry program in a case outside the database (Sahide et al., 2016).
2 These initiatives have been labelled by some as "fortress conservation" (Brockington, 2002) given the tendency to exclude locals from use and decision-making in the reserves.
3 Through cases outside our database, we know that in the last decade, NAFTA has also facilitated a new influx of investments in mining and energy projects which, coupled with the communal land reforms discussed above, threaten indigenous and peasant communities (Avila-Calero, 2017; Tetreault, 2015), as has happened with neoliberal reforms elsewhere in Latin America (Hindery, 2013).

References

Agrawal, A. (1995). Dismantling the divide between indigenous and scientific knowledge. *Development and Change*, *26*(3), 413–439. https://doi.org/10.1111/j.1467-7660.1995.tb00560.x

Alburo-Cañete, K. Z. K., & Cañete, A. M. L. (2013). Towards a new social movement? Environmental conservation, livelihood, and the struggle for the protection of Tañon Strait against oil exploration in Central Philippines. *Philippine Quarterly of Culture and Society*, *41*(3/4), 252–272.

Alcorn, J. B., Bamba, J., Masiun, S., Natalia, I., & Royo, A. G. (2003). Keeping ecological resilience afloat in cross-scale turbulence: An Indigenous social movement navigates change in Indonesia. In: F. Berkes, J. Colding, & C. Folke (Eds.), *Navigating Social-Ecological Systems: Building Resilience for Complexity and Change*. London: Cambridge University Press, pp. 299–327. https://doi.org/10.1017/CBO9780511541957

Alonso-Fradejas, A. (2015). Anything but a story foretold: Multiple politics of resistance to the agrarian extractivist project in Guatemala. *The Journal of Peasant Studies*, *42*(3–4), 489–515. https://doi.org/10.1080/03066150.2015.1013468

Altamirano-Jiménez, I. (2017). "The sea is our bread": Interrupting green neoliberalism in Mexico. *Marine Policy*, *80*, 28–34.

Anguelovski, I., & Martínez Alier, J. (2014). The 'Environmentalism of the Poor' revisited: Territory and place in disconnected glocal struggles. *Ecological Economics*, *102*, 167–176. https://doi.org/http://dx.doi.org/10.1016/j.ecolecon.2014.04.005

Armitage, D. (2005). Adaptive capacity and community-based natural resource management. *Environmental Management*, *35*(6), 703–715.

Avila-Calero, S. (2017). Contesting energy transitions: Wind power and conflicts in the Isthmus of Tehuantepec. *Journal of Political Ecology 24*(1), 992–1012.

Baynes, J., Herbohn, J., Smith, C., Fisher, R., & Bray, D. (2015). Key factors which influence the success of community forestry in developing countries. *Global Environmental Change*, *35*, 226–238.

Bebbington, Anthony, Humphreys Bebbington, D., Bury, J., Lingan, J., Muñoz, J. P., & Scurrah, M. (2008). Mining and Social Movements: Struggles Over Livelihood and Rural Territorial Development in the Andes. *World Development, 36*(12), 2888–2905. https://doi.org/http://dx.doi.org/10.1016/j.worlddev.2007.11.016

Berkes, F. (1999). *Sacred Ecology: Traditional Ecological Knowledge and Resource Management.* Philadelphia: Taylor & Francis.

Blaikie, P. (2006). Is small really beautiful? Community-based natural resource management in Malawi and Botswana. *World Development, 34*(11), 1942–1957.

Brockington, D. (2002). *Fortress Conservation: The Preservation of the Mkomazi Game Reserve, Tanzania.* Bloomington: Indiana University Press.

Brondo, K., & Brown, N. (2011). Neoliberal conservation, garifuna territorial rights and resource management in the Cayos Cochinos marine protected area. *Conservation and Society, 9*(2), 91–105. https://doi.org/10.4103/0972-4923.83720

Brownhill, L. (2007). Gendered struggles for the commons-food sovereignty, tree-planting and climate change. *Women and Environments International Magazine, 74*, 34.

Byambajav, D. (2012). Mobilizing against dispossession: Gold mining and a local resistance movement in Mongolia. 北方人文研究= *Journal of the Center for Northern Humanities, 5*, 13–32.

Chinsinga, B., Chasukwa, M., & Zuka, S. P. (2013). The political economy of land grabs in Malawi: Investigating the contribution of Limphasa Sugar Corporation to rural development. *Journal of Agricultural and Environmental Ethics, 26*(6), 1065–1084.

Chirwa T. S., Mafongoya P. L., Mbewe D. N. M., & Chishala B. H. 2004. Changes in soil properties and their effects on maize productivity following Sesbania sesban and Cajanus cajan improved fallow systems in eastern Zambia. *Biology and Fertility of Soils, 40*, 20–27.

Cohen, F. (1989). Treaty Indian tribes and Washington state: The evolution of tribal involvement in fisheries management in the US Pacific Northwest. In E. Pinkerton, (Ed.) *Co-Operative Management of Local Fisheries New Directions for Improved Management and Community Development* (pp. 37–48). Vancouver: University of British Columbia Press.

Colchester, M. (2005). Maps, power, and the defense of territory: The upper Mazaruni land claim in Guyana. In J. P. Brosius, A. Lowenhaupt Tsing, & C. Zerner (Eds.), *Communities and Conservation. Histories and politics of Community-Based Natural Resource Management* (pp. 271–303). New York: AltaMira Press.

Conde, M., & Kallis, G. (2012). The global uranium rush and its Africa frontier. Effects, reactions and social movements in Namibia. *Global Environmental Change, 22*(3), 596–610.

Cox, M., Arnold, G., & Villamayor-Tomás, S. (2010). A review of design principles for community-based natural resource management. *Ecology and Society, 15*(4), 38. Retrieved from http://www.ecologyandsociety.org/vol15/iss4/art38/

Cronkleton, P., Taylor, P. L., Barry, D., Stone-Jovicich, S., & Schmink, M. (2008). *Environmental Governance and the Emergence of Forest-Based Social Movements.* CIFOR, Bogor, Indonesia.

Correia, D. (2010). "Retribution will be their reward": New Mexico's Las Gorras Blancas and the fight for the Las Vegas land grant commons. *Radical History Review, 2010*(108), 49–72.

De Alessi, M. (2012). The Political Economy of Fishing Rights and Claims: The Maori Experience in New Zealand. *Journal of Agrarian Change*, *12*(2–3), 390–412. https://doi.org/10.1111/j.1471-0366.2011.00346.x

De Angelis, M. (2012). Crises, movements and commons. *Borderlands E-Journal: New Spaces in the Humanities*, *11*(2), 4.

Deere, C. D. (2017). Women's land rights, rural social movements, and the state in the 21st-century Latin American agrarian reforms. *Journal of Agrarian Change*, *17*(2), 258–278.

Diegues, A. C. (1998). Social movements and the remaking of the commons in the Brazilian Amazon. In M. Goldman (Ed.), *Privatizing Nature: Political Struggles for the Global Commons* (pp. 54–75). London: Pluto Press.

Diniz, A. S., & Gilbert, B. (2013a). Socialist values and cooperation in Brazil's landless rural workers' movement. *Latin American Perspectives*, 0094582X13484290.

Diniz, A. S., & Gilbert, B. (2013b). Socialist values and cooperation in Brazil's landless rural workers' movement. *Latin American Perspectives*, 0094582X13484290.

Dressler, W., Büscher, B., Schoon, M., Brockington, D., Hayes, T., Kull, C. A., … Shrestha, K. (2010, March 14). From hope to crisis and back again? A critical history of the global CBNRM narrative. *Environmental Conservation*. Cambridge University Press. https://doi.org/10.1017/S0376892910000044

Escobar, A. (1998). Whose knowledge, whose nature? Biodiversity, conservation, and the political ecology of social movements. *Journal of Political Ecology*, *5*(1), 53–82.

García-López, G. A., & Antinori, C. (2018). Between grassroots collective action and state mandates: The hybridity of multi-level forest associations in Mexico. *Conservation and Society*, *16*(2), 193–204.

Gerber, J.-F. (2011). Conflicts over industrial tree plantations in the South: Who, how and why? *Global Environmental Change*, *21*(1), 165–176. https://doi.org/http://dx.doi.org/10.1016/j.gloenvcha.2010.09.005

Goldman, M. (1997). 'Customs in common": The epistemic world of the commons scholars.' *Theory and Society*, *26*(1), 1–37.

Hafild, E. (2005). Social movements, community-based natural resource management, and the struggle for democracy: Experiences from Indonesia. In J. P. Brosius, A. Lowenhaupt Tsing, & C. Zerner (Eds.), *Communities and Conservation. Histories and Politics of Community-Based Natural Resource Management* (pp. 257–268). New York: AltaMira Press.

Hartberg, Y., Cox, M., & Villamayor-Tomas, S. (2016). Supernatural monitoring and sanctioning in community-based resource management. *Religion, Brain & Behavior*, *6*(2), 95–111. doi:10.1080/2153599X.2014.959547

Hindery, D. (2013). Synergistic impacts of gas and mining development in Bolivia's Chiquitanía: The significance of analytical scale. In A. Bebbington & J. Bury (Eds.), *Subterranean Struggles: New Dynamics of Mining, Oil, and Gas in Latin America*. Austin: University of Texas Press.

Hoogesteger, J., & Verzijl, A. (2015). Grassroots scalar politics: Insights from peasant water struggles in the Ecuadorian and Peruvian Andes. *Geoforum*, *62*, 13–23.

Jordan, D. (1989). Negotiating salmon management on the Klamath River. In E. Pinkerton, *Co-Operative Management of Local Fisheries New Directions for Improved Management and Community Development* (pp. 73–81). Vancouver: University of British Columbia Press.

Kashwan, P. (2017). *Democracy in the Woods: Environmental Conservation and Social Justice in India, Tanzania, and Mexico*. London: Oxford University Press.

Kearney, J. F. (1989). Co-management or co-optation?: The ambiguities of lobster fishery management in southwest Nova Scotia, in E. Pinkerton, *Co-Operative Management of Local Fisheries New Directions for Improved Management and Community Development* (pp. 85–102). Vancouver: University of British Columbia Press.

Kenney-Lazar, M. (2012). Plantation rubber, land grabbing and social-property transformation in southern Laos. *The Journal of Peasant Studies, 39*(3–4), 1017–1037.

Klooster, D. (2000). Community forestry and tree theft in Mexico: Resistance or complicity in conservation? *Development and Change, 31*(1), 281–305.

Koontz, T. M., Steelman, T. A., Carmin, J., Korfmacher, K. S., Moseley, C., & Thomas, C. W. (2004). *Collaborative Environmental Management: What Roles for Government?* New York: Resources for the Future.

Kurien, J. (2013). Assessing the evolution of collective action and organisations. In D. C. Kalikoski (Ed.), *Collective Action and Organizations in Small-Scale Fisheries*. Rome: FAO.

Kurien, J. (1991). *Ruining the Commons and Responses of the Commoners: Coastal Overfishing and Fishermen's Actions in Kerala State, Indian*. Discussion Paper No. 23. Geneva: United Nations Research Institute for Social Development, p. 46. Retrieved from https://www.unrisd.org/unrisd/website/document.nsf/ (httpPublications)/43A54CA8B79607D480256B67005B61F8?OpenDocument.

Langdon, S. (1989). Prospects for co-management of marine mammals in Alaska. In E. Pinkerton, *Co-Operative Management of Local Fisheries New Directions for Improved Management and Community Development* (pp. 154–169). Vancouver: University of British Columbia Press.

Li, T. M. (2004). Environment, indigeneity and transnationalism. In: R. Peet & M. Watts (Eds.), *Liberation Ecologies: Environment, Development, Social Movements* (pp. 339–370). London; New York: Routledge.

Lubell, M. (2005). Do Watershed Partnerships Enhance Beliefs Conducive to Collective Action? In P. A. Sabatier, W. Focht, M. Lubell, Z. Trachtenberg, A. Vedlitz, & M. Matlock (Eds.), *Swimming Upstream: Collaborative Approaches to Watershed Management* (pp. 201–232). Cambridge, MA: MIT Press.

Lynn, S. (1998). Between NAFTA and Zapata: Responses to restructuring the commons in Chiapas and Oaxaca, Mexico. In M. Goldman (Ed.), *Privatizing nature: political struggles for the global commons*. London: Pluto Press.

Montalba, N.R., Henríquez, N.C., & Cornejo, J. A. (2005). *The economic and social context of monoculture tree plantations in Chile: The case of the commune of Lumaco, Araucania Region*. Montevideo, Uruguay: World Rainforest Movement. Retrieved from https://wrm.org.uy/wp-content/uploads/2013/03/The_Economic_and_Social_Context_of_Monoculture_Tree_Plantations_in_Chile_ch.pdf

Morrell, M. (1989). The struggle to integrate traditional Indian systems and state management in the salmon fisheries of the Skeena River, British Columbia. In *Co-Operative Management of Local Fisheries: New Directions for Improved Management and Community Development* (pp. 231–248). Vancouver: University of British Columbia Press.

Martiniello, G. (2015). Social struggles in Uganda's Acholiland: Understanding responses and resistance to Amuru sugar works. *The Journal of Peasant Studies, 42*(3–4), 653–669. https://doi.org/10.1080/03066150.2015.1032269

Moreno-Sánchez, R. del P., & Maldonado, J. H. (2010). Evaluating the role of co-management in improving governance of marine protected areas: An experimental approach in the Colombian Caribbean. *Ecological Economics*, *69*(12), 2557–2567. Retrieved from www.sciencedirect.com/science/article/B6VDY-50SBVC2-2/2/17b1f 9924eea3aa9aae51e8080200bed

Nayak, P. K., & Berkes, F. (2011). Commonisation and decommonisation: Understanding the processes of change in the Chilika Lagoon, India. *Conservation and Society*, *9*(2), 132.

Nguiffo, S.-A. (1998). In defence of the commons: Forest battles in Southern Cameroon. In M. Goldman (Ed.), *Privatizing Nature: Political Struggles for the Global Commons* (pp. 103–119). London: Pluto Press.

Notess, L., Veit, P., Monterroso, I., Emmanuel Sulle, A., Larson, A. M., Gindroz, A.-S., … Williams, A. (2018). *The Scramble for Land Rights Reducing Inequity between Communities and Companies*. Washington, DC. Retrieved from http://wriorg. s3.amazonaws.com/s3fs-public/scramble-land-rights.pdf

Ojha, H. R. (2011). The evolution of institutions for multi-level governance of forest commons: The case of community forest user groups federation in Nepal. *Sustaining Commons: Sustaining Our Future*. The thirteenth Biennial conference of the International Association for the Study of Commons, Hyderabad, India.

Oslender, U. (2004). Fleshing out the geographies of social movements: Colombia's Pacific coast black communities and the "aquatic space". *Political Geography*, *23*(8), 957–985.

Ostrom, E. (1990). *Governing the Commons: The Evolution of Institutions for Collective Action*. Cambridge, MA: Cambridge University Press.

Palmer, A. D. (2017). Contingent legal futures does the ability to exercise aboriginal rights and title turn. In K. Jalbert, A. Willow, D. Casagrande, & S. Paladino (Eds.), *ExtrACTION: Impacts, Engagements, and Alternative Futures* (pp. 93–107). London and New York: Routledge.

Pattanaik, S. (2003). Tradition, development and environmental movement of the marginalised: A study of fishing community's resistance in Orissa. *Indian Anthropologist*, *33*(1), 55–70.

Paudel, N. S., Monterroso, I., & Cronkleton, P. (2010). Community networks, collective action and forest management benefits. In *Forests for People: Community Rights and Forest Tenure Reform*. London: Earthscan.

Peet, R., & Watts, M. (1996). *Liberation Ecologies: Environment, Development, Social Movements*. New York: Routledge.

Peña, D. (2003). Identity, place and communities of resistance. In: J. Agyeman, R. D. Bullard and B. Evans (Eds.). *Just Sustainabilities: Development in an Unequal World* (pp. 146–167). Cambridge: MIT Press,.

Perera, V. (2015). Engaged universals and community economies: The (human) right to water in Colombia. *Antipode*, *47*(1), 197–215.

Perreault, T. (2001). Developing identities: Indigenous mobilisation, rural livelihoods, and resource access in Ecuadorian Amazonia. *Ecumene*, *8*(4), 381–413.

Persha, L., & Andersson, K. (2014). Elite capture risk and mitigation in decentralized forest governance regimes. *Global Environmental Change*, *24*, 265–276.

Pinkerton, E. (1993). Co-management efforts as social movements: The Tin Wis coalition and the drive for forest practices legislation in British Columbia. *Alternatives*, *19*, 33.

Pomeroy, R. S., & Berkes, F. (1997). Two to tango: The role of government in fisheries co-management. *Marine Policy, 21*(5), 465–480. Retrieved from www. sciencedirect.com/science/article/B6VCD-3SX1JFM-5/2/5ba65e7ab2157126a607 dc162b9d298f

Poole, P. (2005). Te'kuana mapping project. In J. P. Brosius, A. Lowenhaupt Tsing, & C. Zerner (Eds.), *Communities and Conservation. Histories and Politics of Community-Based Natural Resource Management* (pp. 305–325). New York: AltaMira Press.

Powell, D. E. (2017). Toward transition? challenging extractivism and the politics of the inevitable on the Navajo nation. In K. Jalbert, A. Willow, D. Casagrande, & S. Paladino (Eds.), *ExtrACTION: Impacts, engagements, and alternative futures*. New York: Routledge.

Radonic, L. (2015). Environmental violence, water rights, and (un) due process in Northwestern Mexico. *Latin American Perspectives, 42*(5), 27–47.

Randeria, S. (2003). Cunning states and unaccountable international institutions: Legal plurality, social movements and rights of local communities to common property resources. *European Journal of Sociology, 44*(01), 27–60.

Ribot, J. C. (2000). Rebellion, representation, and enfranchisement in the forest villages of Makacoulibantang, Eastern Senegal. In C. Zerner (Ed.), *People, Plants, and Justice: The Politics of Nature Conservation* (pp. 134–157). New York: Columbia University Press.

Ribot, J. C., Agrawal, A., & Larson, A. M. (2006). Recentralizing while decentralizing: How national governments reappropriate forest resources. *World Development, 34*(11), 1864–1886. https://doi.org/http://dx.doi.org/10.1016/j.worlddev.2005.11.020

Rixecker, S. S., & Tipene-Matua, B. (2003). Maori Kaupapa and the inseparability of social and environmental justice: An analysis of bioprospecting and a people's resistance to (bio) cultural assimilation. In: J. Agyeman, R.D. Bullard, & Bob Evans (Eds.), *Just Sustainabilities: Development in an Unequal World* (pp. 252–268). Cambridge: The MIT Press.

Roberts, K. (2016). It takes a rooted village: Networked resistance, connected communities, and adaptive responses to forest tenure reform in Northern Thailand. *Austrian Journal of South-East Asian Studies, 9*(1), 53.

Sahide, M. A. K., Supratman, S., Maryudi, A., Kim, Y.-S., & Giessen, L. (2016). Decentralisation policy as recentralisation strategy: Forest management units and community forestry in Indonesia. *International Forestry Review, 18*(1), 78–95. https://doi.org/10.1505/146554816818206168

Schlager, E., & Ostrom, E. (1992). Property-rights regimes and natural resources: A conceptual analysis. *Land Economics, 68*(3), 249–262. Retrieved from www.jstor.org/stable/3146375

Scheidel, A., Temper, L., Demaria, F., & Martínez-Alier, J. (2017). Ecological distribution conflicts as forces for sustainability: An overview and conceptual framework. *Sustainability Science.* https://doi.org/10.1007/s11625-017-0519-0

Schock, K. (2009). Defending and reclaiming the commons through nonviolent struggle. In: R.V. Summy (Ed.) *Nonviolent Alternatives for Social Change* (pp. 183–201). Oxford: Encyclopedia of Life Support Systems (EOLSS), UNESCO.

Scholtens, J. (2016). The elusive quest for access and collective action: North Sri Lankan fishers' thwarted struggles against a foreign trawler fleet. *International Journal of the Commons, 10*(2).

Schwartzman, S., Alencar, A., Zarin, H., & Santos Souza, A. P. (2010). Social movements and large-scale tropical forest protection on the Amazon frontier: Conservation from chaos. *The Journal of Environment & Development, 19*(3), 274–299.

Sinha, S. (2012). Transnationality and the Indian Fishworkers' Movement, 1960s–2000. *Journal of Agrarian Change, 12*(2–3), 364–389. https://doi.org/10.1111/j.1471-0366.2011.00349.x

Sletto, B. (2008). The knowledge that counts: Institutional identities, policy science, and the conflict over fire management in the Gran Sabana, Venezuela. *World Development, 36*(10), 1938–1955. https://doi.org/10.1016/J.WORLDDEV.2008.02.008

Snow, D. A., Soule, S. A., & Kriesi, H. (2004). *The Blackwell Companion to Social Movements*. Oxford: Blackwell.

Somayaji, G., & Coelho, J. P. (2017). Fissures of a blue revolution: The Ramponkars' response to mechanised fishing in Goa. *Social Change, 47*(2), 200–213.

Springate-Baginski, O., Sarin, M., Ghosh, S., Dasgupta, P., Bose, I., Banerjee, A., Sarap, K. Misra P., Behera, S., Reddy, M. G., Rao, P. T. (2008). The Indian Forest Rights Act 2006: Commoning Enclosures. *Working Paper. Norwich: Overseas Development Group, University of East Anglia*.

Stevens, C., Winterbottom, R., Springer, J., & Reytar, K. (2014). Securing rights, combating climate change: How strengthening community forest rights mitigates climate change. *World Resources Institute: Washington, DC, USA*, 56, pp. 64. ISBN: 978-1-56973-829-0. https://files.wri.org/s3fs-public/securingrights-full-report-english.pdf.

Stoltenborg, D., & Boelens, R. (2016). Disputes over land and water rights in gold mining: The case of Cerro de San Pedro, Mexico. *Water International, 41*(3), 447–467.

Tang, C.-P., & Tang, S.-Y. (2001). Negotiated autonomy: Transforming self-governing institutions for local common-pool resources in two tribal villages in Taiwan. *Human Ecology, 29*(1), 49–67.

Tetreault, D. (2015). Social environmental mining conflicts in Mexico. *Latin American Perspectives, 42*(5), 48–66.

Topatimasang, R. (2005). Mapping as a tool for community organizing against power: A Moluccas experience. In J. P. Brosius, A. Lowenhaupt Tsing, & C. Zerner (Eds.), *Communities and Conservation. Histories and politics of Community-Based Natural Resource Management* (pp. 363–390). New York: AltaMira Press.

Turner, T. E., & Brownhill, L. S. (2004). We want our land back: Gendered class analysis, the second contradiction of capitalism and social movement theory. *Capitalism Nature Socialism, 15*(4), 21–40.

Urkidi, L. (2010). A glocal environmental movement against gold mining: Pascua–Lama in Chile. *Ecological Economics, 70*(2), 219–227.

Verzijl, A., Hoogesteger, J., & Boelens, R. (2017). Grassroots scalar politics in the Peruvian Andes. In D. Suhardiman, A. Nicol, & E. Mapedza (Eds.), *Water Governance and Collective Action* (pp. 35–45). New York: Routledge.

Veuthey, S., & Gerber, J.-F. (2012). Accumulation by dispossession in coastal Ecuador: Shrimp farming, local resistance and the gender structure of mobilisations. *Global Environmental Change, 22*(3), 611–622.

Villamayor-Tomas, S., & García-López, G. (2018). Social movements as key actors in governing the commons: Evidence from community-based resource management cases across the world. *Global Environmental Change, 53*, 114–126. https://doi.org/10.1016/J.GLOENVCHA.2018.09.005

Villamayor-Tomas, S., García-López, G., & Scholtens, J. (2020). Do commons management and movements reinforce each other? Comparative insights from Mexico and Sri Lanka. *Ecological Economics, 173,* 106627. https://doi.org/10.1016/j.ecolecon.2020.106627

Wouters, M. (2001). Ethnic rights under threat: The black peasant movement against armed groups' pressure in the Chocó, Colombia. *Bulletin of Latin American Research, 20*(4), 498–519.

Chapter 14

Decommonisation and new-commonisation of mountain commons in northern Pakistan

Shah Raees Khan and C. Emdad Haque

Introduction

The chapter seeks the answer the question of "how to retain commons as commons" at a time when they are being decommonised (state-controlled protected areas – PAs from here onward) due to increasing challenges from external drivers. The main focus is to analyse transformations of the mountain commons in northern Pakistan due to the establishment of a PA system. The study investigates how mountain communities were able to formalise their traditional informal institutions and defend the community's rights on commons. We determine the various contributing factors and dynamics associated with the conversion of commons to PAs and new-commons. Changes in commons status may result from shifts in policies towards more economic gains. In some cases, the conversion of commons to state property may take place as a result of influences from external drivers. The analysis of the commons which captures changes in the economic, social, and political spheres has been conceptualised as processes of commonisation, new-commonisation and decommonisation (Nayak and Berkes, 2011; Khan, 2012). The concept of decommonisation (Nayak & Berkes, 2011) was used to analyse the processes and key factors that have contributed to the loss of commons rights of mountain communities. Here, the term decommonisation refers to a process through which jointly used resources under commons institutions lose the essential characteristics of commons (Nayak & Berkes, 2011). The term new-commonisation refers to a process through which resources get reconverted into a jointly used resource or transform into a new arrangement of creating "conservancies"; that is, with more refined rules and a management system, complementing the resource use and protection, as well as complementing the traditional practices and values (Khan, 2012).

Perspective on commons processes in northern Pakistan

In northern Pakistan, two categories of commons exist to varying degrees. First, "managed common property" – a category where established communities have control over excludability and subtractability rules, such as the pastures in Shimshal in Hunza Valley (Khan et al., 2011). For example, communities formed local institutions, such as a *Jirga* or village committee, to manage the commons and implement management rules. Second, "unmanaged common property" – a category in which an identifiable community has no proper management strategy but the access to resources is not yet open to everyone. For example, access rights were given to communities who moved to the settled village (e.g., the Gujars) but these newcomers have no rights to exclude others from accessing pastures in Naltar Valley. In such cases, newcomers remain powerless but retain a share in resource use. However, they do not have an assured share in the benefits and revenues generated from community-based conservation projects. Both the categories have undergone shifts from one regime to another and, therefore, it is important to view commons as a process to analyse these shifts and understand the factors associated with them. We use the concepts of decommonisation (Nayak & Berkes, 2011) and new-commonisation (Khan, 2012) to examine the governance of mountain commons in northern Pakistan.

In analysing these concepts, we specifically focused on determining the following:

i)   social costs (loss of rights, access, subtractability, excludability), loss of ecological resource, pastoral land and cultural amenities (affiliation to the hereditary herding practice), enhanced inequity, and disconnection of the community from the commons (Narayan et al., 2000);
ii) the power of external drivers in the conversion process;
iii) the significance of power relations; and
iv) options for retaining commons characteristics in protected areas (state property).

Research methods

The research was conducted in the Naltar and Shimshal valleys of northern Pakistan (Figure 14.1). Qualitative and quantitative methods were used to collect primary data. First, a village-based case study was conducted to collect data on how these villagers are connected with the forests and pastures. Research objectives were explored through the following participatory approaches (Chambers, 1983): semi-structured interviews, focus group discussions, resource mapping exercises, a seasonal calendar, participant observations, and a trend analysis (Pido et al., 1996). Seasonality was captured through quarterly field surveys and focus group discussions.

Individual interviews were conducted through a random sampling method to cover a sample size of ≥ 30 households in each study site. A total of 110 households, included 45 households in Naltar Bala and 65 households in Naltar Payeen, were interviewed – out of 353 households in the Naltar Valley. Two focus group discussions, one in each site, were conducted. The data were compiled and analysed using statistical analysis software Stata.

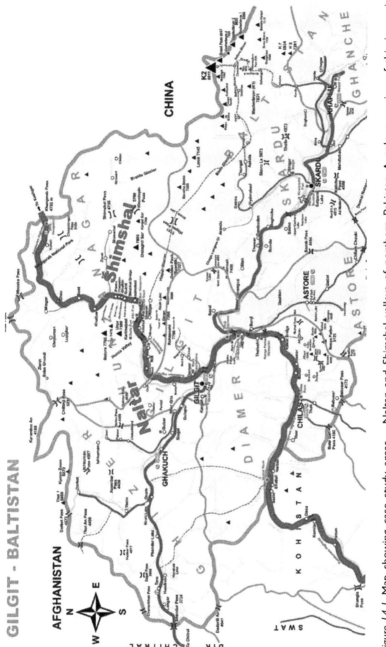

Figure 14.1 Map showing case study areas – Naltar and Shimshal valleys of northern Pakistan. A colour version of this image is downloadable as an eResource from www.routledge.com/9780367138004.

Key factors of decommonisation and loss of collective rights

Protected areas as a major driver of decommonisation

In the context of mountain areas, commons were converted by a major shift in government policy on PAs (i.e., state property), mainly to conserve the quality of wilderness and their biodiversity values (IUCN, 2003). In doing so, PAs truncated local resource-use systems and excluded Indigenous peoples from their legacies associated with natural resources, contributing to the impoverishment of local communities, and also building antipathies between parks and people (Hoole, 2008). This system has largely neglected the communities who are dependent on these common resources. Communities have traditionally been able to restrict outsiders from access to the resources and established rules among themselves for their sustainable use (Berkes, 1989; McCay & Acheson, 1987; Berkes et al., 1989; Ostrom, 1990; Cronkleton et al., 2008, Agrawal, 2014).

In most cases, communities' responses have been to "resist" such a policy shift and disregard PA provisions. This has led to the failure of the PA, and in some cases where those provisions are enforced strictly, conflicts have arisen between local communities and PA authorities. These situations threaten both biodiversity and cultural diversity in PAs. The Khunjerab National Park (KNP), in northern Pakistan, is a notable example of the conversion of a common resource to a PA replacing century-old herding practices by the local communities along with customary rights under local institutions (Butz, 1996; Knudsen, 1999; Khan et al., 2011; Khan, 2012).

As per focus group discussions in the community of Shimshal, the establishment of a PA was a plan of the national government of Pakistan to take their pasture land, rights of access and resource use away through restrictions that resulted in reduced grazing areas, confined traditional yak-herding practices to smaller areas and impacted the traditional grazing routes. One of the community members explained:

> Our traditional routes are now in the hand of the government. If we are confined to a few pastures, we won't have enough pastures to feed our livestock. Where will we take our livestock? The pastures in these areas have low productivity and if we keep our livestock longer then we won't be able to graze our livestock in these pastures next year. We will have to reduce our livestock because we cannot afford it anymore because there are no other options of livelihood in this area
>
> (anonymous, Shimshal)

These responses were clearly against the government's decision and they were unwilling to quit their rights to the resources. Whether government restrictions in the newly created PA will bring "conservation" and benefits to the communities is questionable. In reality, government control means disconnecting people from their resource. In remote areas, the government lacks proper human resources, infrastructure, and other associated instruments to manage natural resources, which contributes to the misuse of resources. In these remote areas, if the resource rights do not belong to the local community, the resource would become open access, and finally overexploited.

Case study 1: Decommonised forests and community rights in northern Pakistan

Commons management in northern Pakistan has undergone significant alterations since the Mir's (rulers) control during the pre-British and British colonial periods to state control after the abolition of the princely states in 1974. One such major shift was the introduction of the so-called centrally controlling mechanism of the commons – centralized agencies of the national government of Pakistan, forest and wildlife departments replacing the authority of local institutions. Until 1967, in the Naltar area, local tribes were free to sell their forest products to contractors, but the sales agreements had to be attested by the assistant political agent. In return, the forest department received royalties – a portion of the revenue from the sale of forests. In the early 1970s, with the abolition of the Mir's regime by, the principalities were declared state property, while in areas such as Darel and Tangir within the Diamer district, where there was a tribal system, the tribal councils negotiated with the government to retain their ownership rights (Bilal et al., 2003).

After the abolition of the principalities, Gilgit Private Forests Regulation was enacted in the early 1970s for the protection and scientific management of forests, as well as for forest conservation, and this was applied to the forests of Naltar. Rules under the Gilgit Private Forest Regulation of 1970 made provisions for access to the forest resources by the communities residing in the vicinity of the forest. These rights included the free grant of trees on permission, grazing, and the collection of dead or dry trees. Grazing was allowed only in those areas that were not closed for regeneration. However, with the regulations that were enacted in the 1970s, every outsider received access to retrieve forest resources under the statutory laws, and as a result, most of the outsiders included contractors who obtained the benefits. Despite the local communities' strong resistance, roads were constructed using public funds, and forest resources were harvested commercially by the government to earn revenues. With this change of control and the construction of Karakorum Highway (KKH), exploitation of the resources became easier for non-locals. Ironically, the state authorities blamed the local people for overexploitation of forest resources (Bilal et al., 2003).

Our investigation revealed that community acceptance of government rules was negligible, and it was evident that the illegal resource extraction by outsiders, particularly logging, remained high in areas where government control was lacking. In Naltar Valley, illegal timber harvest by outsiders was relatively higher than in other villages where community control was relatively stricter. In the Naltar Valley area, a forest control group used to manage access and the appropriation of forest resources. With the introduction of government control of the forests, their role diminished. As a result, village-level cooperatives became either dormant or dysfunctional or, in exceptional cases, newer forms of local institutions emerged. There were many other non-local actors involved in such exploitation of forests that include military authorities who used forest products extensively for constructing buildings and bridges (anonymous respondent, Naltar Payeen).

As one community member commented that:

> It is not in our hands to control the illegal cutting of the forests, and even if I resist them and stop them, government agencies would blame me rather than trying to catch the offender. These are illegal activities, and unfortunately, government people are directly involved. If it were in our control, our forest would not have disappeared.
>
> (anonymous respondent, Naltar Payeen)

Muhammad Yar (consent is given) said:

> The forest has been depleted so much that soon there may be no forest left and our valley will be a barren land. People have encroached the forest and developed patches of agriculture fields in the middle of the forest, and the Gujar community is involved in the encroachment in forest land. It is very common that people come from Gilgit town, fill up their tractors and take the timber out. The threat is that our villages will be swiped away if the forest is gone.
>
> (Muhammad Yar, 34, teacher, Naltar Payeen)

During the household interviews, respondents stated that communities were stripped of their rights to access forest resources. When they applied for fuel wood permits to the forest departmental authorities, the forest officer subjectively decided to accept or reject the request. There was no transparency in fuel wood distribution by the local government.

One of the respondents expressed that:

> I have forest around me but others enjoying the benefit from it. The forest is not in our hands; the government decides whom to give. As a result, deserving people are not getting it. Why they will give it to us when they get more money from those illegal operators?
>
> (Interview with an anonymous resident, Naltar Payeen)

It is very difficult for the poor to acquire fuel wood. A local resident narrated: "Only those people are getting fuelwood who have links with the government officials. Only a few people have access to those permits, and these include people working for the government and contractors, but not us" (interview with an anonymous resident, Naltar Payeen).

Field survey results suggested that not all community members collected fuelwood from the forest. The reasons for their reluctance were related to several factors, which included:

i) time-consuming endeavour to move deep into the forest;
ii) non-cooperation of government officials with the use of community rights to collect fuel wood; and
iii) difficult to obtain a permit for locals; only those who had a strong personal network with government officials receive such permits.

Conflicts in Naltar Valley are mainly between the locals and non-locals and pertain to rights over fuelwood and grazing between the communities of Naltar Bala, who are mainly the Gujars, and those of Naltar Payeen, who are early settlers of Naltar Valley. During the last 30–40 years, the Gujar community immigrated to Naltar to graze their animals during the summer season and eventually made permanent and semi-permanent settlements in Naltar Bala. They continued to avail the rights to graze and collect fuelwood. However, the early settlers were unclear about how this acquisition of rights of the newly settled Gujar ethnic groups was decided by the government without consultation. In turn, such lack of clarity and the entry of new settlers has led to ethnic conflicts and rivalry. However, there are military resorts, a ski slope, and government guest houses in this reserve forest; they fulfill their fuelwood requirements from the same forest. These facilities are not open to the public and no opportunities are given to locals in these resorts.

The rules under the Forest Act of 1927 describe the access rights to forest resources for communities residing in the vicinity of the forest. In reality, such access of the community members to forest resources is very limited; local communities are not involved or consulted in the management of the forest. There is now no such allocation of free grants of trees.

As one of the residents said during focus group discussions:

> The Government is neither sincere with us nor with the matter of forest management. We used to have dense forests. It was under government control, and now, only patches left as most of the forest got extracted illegally with the help of the forest department. The forest resources were given to the outsiders and we do not get dead trees to use as fuelwood. If you look at the houses of these forest department people, their walls are covered with deodar, the expensive timber. What do you think? Are they protecting the forest?
>
> (anonymous resident, Naltar Payeen)

Another resident added:

> We used to bring the dead fallen trees, and we would go up to Naltar
> Lake. The forest was dense, but gradually, it started depleting. We used
> to value our forest because we were part of it. Since the intervention of
> government, taking over of our forest, we have been separated from our
> forests.
>
> (Shafa Ali, 54, Naltar Payeen)

The key point in the conceptualisation and implementation of decommonisation was the failure of the government to recognise the interconnectedness between local communities and the conservation of forests or pasture lands. There was a clear deficiency in understanding the dependency of the local community on the commons, which are endowed with natural resources. The cases of Shimshal and Naltar provide a clear illustration of disconnecting people from their resource base as a result of external institutional intervention through a top-down state-controlled approach. They also depict the ground realities of the mismanagement of the forests and pasture resources. The imposition of rules and regulations through decommonisation has resulted in the loss of local rights and ownership of local communities. Thus, the survival and sustainability of the forest resources come under question under the state control. Table 14.1 lists the key factors of decommonisation processes.

The inertia in creating PAs with a national vision for conservation has resulted in changing the characteristics of commons from being an entity of natural resource endowment to support local livelihoods to an entity disconnected from local communities. Consequently, the conflict between the local communities and the national government has risen astronomically over rights, exclusion and subtraction.

Case study 2: Local management of the pasture commons in Shimshal

In the context of northern Pakistan, common resources have remained under community control, traditional management system and customary laws (Bilal et al., 2003). Communities regulate their rights and access to the resources in an effective manner at the local level through a set of customary rules, allocation of resource-use right, enforcement of sanctions, and compliance (Agrawal, 2014). In the following section, we analyse the commons under different regimes and the current system of yak herding in Shimshal as examples of the traditional sustainable way of governing commons. To make our argument, we attempt to highlight how communities have governed the commons and sustained the resources for centuries, and how they have used traditional institutions to control the commons.

Table 14.1 Key factors of the decommonisation process in the study area

Key factors	Indicators
International initiatives	• International conventions and treaties as drivers of change
Change in national government policies	• Shift in focus from community managed to centralized control • Interference of government • Focus on "conservation" strict in protected areas
Creation of protected areas by national governments	• Protected Areas superimposed in commons, which used to be managed effectively under customary rules to exclude others
Loss of rights of local communities	• Loss of access rights and institutional base resulted in conflicts and issues of access, loss of grazing lands
Erosion of traditional local institutions and emergence of new local institutions	• Centralized agencies such as forest and wildlife departments replaced local institutions or tried to replace them. • Decision-making control moved from the local community to a centralized administrative control • Village-level cooperatives became either dormant or dysfunctional or new forms of local institution emerged
Change in grazing practices	• Collective method of pasturing was reduced or traditional practice of Shimshali yak herding restricted • Keeping of small livestock reduced, as in Naltar Bala • Shift from livestock rearing to agriculture-oriented activities
Sense of disconnect from pasture and forest resources	• Imposition of political decisions initiated a process of disconnect, ecological, social and economic disintegration • Growing resource degradation (loss of forest in Naltar); loss of sense of belongingness with forest • Aggravation and resistance of Shimshal community • Disconnect between the government and the local communities

Source: Focus Group Discussions, Naltar Payeen and Naltar Bala

Yak-herding practice in Shimshal

Shimshal herding practice is used as a tool to manage pastures by harvesting forage to produce livestock and maintain plant composition (NASSD, 2003). Livestock is central to the Shimshal livelihood, contributing a total of 38 percent of the total economy, and they play a vital role in the region's food security (Ali & Butz, 2003). Shimshal herding practice follows a traditional pattern, profoundly influenced by climate and seasonality, by the topography of the land, and by social and cultural influences. Their traditional herding system relies on centuries of experience, knowledge of the productivity of pastures, the availability of water during summer and winter seasons, accessibility, and vulnerability to predators. An important aspect is the socio-cultural features that are embedded in their self-identity as "Shimshali". It is a community that is highly devoted to maintaining their culture, rituals and hereditary resources, as these are interwoven with the livestock herding system (Butz, 1996; Ali & Butz, 2003; Butz, 2006; Khan et al. 2011; Khan, 2012).

Decision-making in the herding system takes place at three levels: (i) household, (ii) community, and (iii) pasture-cycle (Butz, 1996). During the focus group discussion phases of decision-making were discussed. The initial decision process starts at the household level, where the household members get together to plan how many livestock need to be sent to the pastures. Decision is made by considering several factors: (a) the available number of persons (labour); (b) the affordability of the cost in terms of cash or in-kind (material); and (c) the number of milking animals available. At the community level, important considerations include the appropriateness of pasture for the specific number of livestock, the mapping of pastoral movements based on their years of experience, cultural festivals, and the timing of rituals and ceremonies.

The community-level decisions ensure that all households get an equal opportunity in the shared resource. It is important to note that the community motivation for conserving their resources is the main priority, and it is reflected in their resource-use activities. An important element is the selection of people that will accompany the livestock. In the case of yak herding, at least two people are selected based on their awareness of the pastures and knowledge of the routes. The third level of decision-making takes place at the herdsman level (pasture level). Herdsmen make decisions based on their past experience of weather and regional climatic conditions, the status of the pasture, access to pasture during winter, and availability of water. The herdsmen intend to ensure that the livestock is safe from predators and that there is enough fodder to feed on. They also need to ensure that the water requirement of the herd is fulfilled. They are responsible for the timely departure to other pastures as well as to the village prior to the celebration of "Kutch" – an event to offer gratitude to the creator for his blessings for their safe return with animals and wealth (Khan, 2012).

In achieving these goals, community members practice primarily two kinds of herding system: (i) summer pasturing, and (ii) winter pasturing. During both summer and winter pasturing times, caring for their ancestral resources, which they affiliate with Mamu Singh, the founder of Shimshal, is common. According to one popular legend, Mamu Singh – a Burusho (brushski speaking) from Baltit (Central Hunza) – discovered the Shimshal region about four centuries ago. His son, Sher, discovered all other territories, including Pamir. The lineage of Shimshal – Gazikator, Bakhtikator, and Baqikator – claims it as their ancestral land (SNT 2007).

Summer pasturing system

Summer pasturing requires a combination of ecological knowledge and climate, vegetation and carrying capacity, as they play a key role in the success of this endeavour. This arrangement is made based on two criteria: first, the availability of new vegetation in pastures for livestock, and second, community needs to cultivate agricultural products within a short season since afterward agricultural fields are required to be closed for grazing. Upon the completion of village-level decision-making about who will be going with the livestock, the herders are required to leave the village by the first week of May to Shujerab, the nearest pasture (Figure 14.2 and 14.3).

Before moving the livestock to the pastures, a selected team of villagers repair the treks and the cattle and shepherd sheds in places where damage from heavy snow and landslides has taken place. A group of herders, which includes elderly women with experience of the pastures, leads in summer pasturing (Abidi-Habib & Lawrence, 2007). The move to the next pasture is determined by weather conditions and the availability of new vegetation in the pasture. At the community level, limits are placed in terms of the total duration of grazing on each pasture, with a grace period of three to four days.

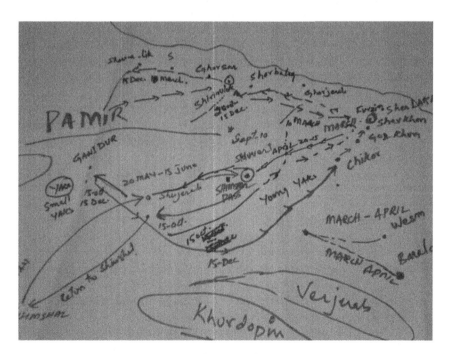

Figure 14.2 Summer and winter herding routes. A colour version of this image is downloadable as an eResource from www.routledge.com/9780367138004.

Figure 14.3 Women milking livestock in summer pastures. A colour version of this image is downloadable as an eResource from www.routledge.com/9780367138004.

The pasture-cycle continues, and several periodic stays are made at different pastures, Sher Lakhsh, Furzin-i-Dasht, Gorjerav, Sher Bulak, Ghrsar and Sher-a-lik, until they reach their final destination, Pamir, where they spend two and half months.

Most of the production of butter and other animal products take place in Pamir. In Pamir, women play a pivotal role; their prime responsibilities include milking, butter-making, and qurut-making. The main rituals are performed here in Pamir. From the perspective of herder women, Pamir pastures are mystical and pure, and purity is an important attribute to gain the blessings from "God". As Musk (a female herder who gave consent to use the name) described:

> Several of our rituals are associated with herding in Pamir. On arrival to Pamir pasture, we (women) perform a number of rituals: *Mirgichig (puri-fication) before starting any activities and then the first product of the new season is sent to our families in the village, which is consumed in a special festival with thanksgiving prayers. We* have these rituals that connect us with "God" for his creation and his blessings through the wealth in the form of the products we gather from our pastures.
>
> (Musk, female, 57, herder, Shimshal)

This expression reflects the affiliation of herders with nature and their struggle for survival in these pastures. After completing their summer pasturing, spending over five months in pastures, herders prepare for their return home. At the end of the summer period, by September 10, herders are required to leave Pamir pasture, and delays or an early return would put the livestock at risk. Delays in the return would make them end up facing cold temperatures or snow on high altitudes. Similarly, an early return would put the livestock at risk because they would have to cross several water routes. At peak water flows, it is difficult to cross these routes. As stated earlier, the arrival of herdsmen to the village from the pastures is celebrated with an event called "Kutch". This is a special occasion to thank God for their safe return with the accumulated wealth – butter, qurut (a milk product), cheese, and many other products. The celebration continues for a week, with friends and families invited to their homes. Similar type of summer pasturing is done by other herders in different pastures such as Gujerab, Lupgar, and Yazghel.

Winter pasturing system

Winter pasturing is carried out predominantly with yaks. Yak herders stay with the yaks to protect them from attacks by wolves or snow leopards, especially at the time of calving, and to prevent the herd from straying. Yak herding in Shimshal is practiced with a specific purpose of utilizing and managing pastures. Although it is very difficult to graze their yaks in winter, the community has been practicing winter pasturing for centuries to maintain the pasture resource. The community's experience and knowledge have revealed that after grazing their livestock in the summer, certain pastures remain untouched, and if those parts have not been grazed, then those pastures become less productive in the following year.

Yak herds are moved periodically based on weather conditions and the availability of food and water (Figure 14.4). There have been several incidents when the yak herds were killed due to heavy snow. Given the fact that the Shimshal community has limited land available in the village to feed their livestock, especially yaks, the pasture resource is crucial for their livelihoods.

Reflecting upon the challenges herders face, Majidullah said:

> Winter yak herding is not an easy task. We move yaks from one pasture to another so that we can maintain the pasture condition, as well as food for the yak, so we can sustain both. We cannot afford degrading the pasture and starving the yak. Thus, we have to struggle to do this, but we do it because yaks are important for our survival and it's our tradition.
>
> (Majidullah, herder, 49, Shimshal)

During the group discussion in Shimshal, communities defined the mechanism of the herding practice and the management of the resource as described in Table 14.2.

Figure 14.4 Herdsmen moving yak herds during winter. Photo by Pamir Times. A colour version of this image is downloadable as an eResource from www.routledge. com/9780367138004.

Table 14.2 Key mechanisms of pasture resources management in Shimshal

Mechanism	Purpose
Village-level decisions: all village heads and household heads have a role in the decision-making process. The village elder (lumberdar) makes the decision.	Involve all village heads and household heads in decision-making. To provide equal opportunity to every household and to bound every individual to abide by collective decisions and the regulations made by the community.
Household level decisions: all members of the household have a role in household level decisions.	Involve all household members in decision-making process and provide equal opportunity to every household member. To ensure their commitment, availability, contribution in labour work.
Pasture-cycle level decisions: all herders have a role in these decisions.	Informed decision based on climate conditions, accessibility, availability of fodder and safety of the livestock.
Pasture management: a series of pasturing decisions on the specific pastures, pasturing cycles, and times of pasturing to determine duration and livestock numbers.	To attain maximum benefit from the resource; to maintain pasture quality; and to ensure the continuous supply of fodder for the livestock in different seasons and facilitate new growth of vegetation. To retain their tradition and heritage, a symbol of their pride.

Source: Focus Group Discussion with Shimshal Community

New-commonisation

It is defined as a process through which resources get converted into a jointly used resource, as in the case of northern Pakistan, where the commons get converted to "conservancies" (Khan, 2012). These commons do not revert back to its original state (ownership) rather, they get transformed into a new arrangement, that is, with more refined rules and a management system, complementing the resource use and protection, as well as complementing the traditional practices and values (Khan, 2012). Following Nayak and Berkes (2011) we prefer to use the term new-commonisation because this is a new arrangement in which commons get converted to conservancies under a new arrangement for resource management. For examining mountain commons, it is important to understand the categories of commons as described earlier: managed commons and unmanaged commons. In this process there are two main variants: (1) NGO-led new-commonisation; (2) community-led new-commonisation. If new-commonisation happens through external forces and interventions then it could be termed as NGO-led new-commonisation and if the process resulted through inner dynamism to bring the change in the system through the formalisation of the traditional institutions, it would be termed as a community-led new-commonisation. To analyse new-commonisation process, we refer to the example of unmanaged commons (pasture resources) with no proper commons management system as a point to illustrate new-commonisation facilitated by international organisations.

Efforts towards new-commonisation

The two cases presented above demonstrate the negative outcomes of a state-controlled resources. As in the forest case, state control has led to occupation by non-locals, illegal timber harvest and degradation. In the case of pastures, conflicts have arisen between communities and governments over resource-use rights. It is apparent that the strict PA approach – which views human agents and nature as separate entities, asserts the presence of communities as a concern and incompatible with conservation, and requires the exclusion of communities from the PAs – has resulted in failure to achieve the conservation objectives not only in northern Pakistan but also in many other parts of the world (Borrini-Feyerabend et al., 2004; Hansen & DeFries, 2007). Studies show that PAs have not succeeded in meeting their management objectives, chiefly because of conflicting views of nature, different definitions of conservation, and a profound misunderstanding of the communities (WWF, 2004). The state institutions have undertaken the conservationist point of view on the understanding of nature and on the practices of Indigenous communities, and they have made ineffective decisions that have resulted in separating humans from nature (Hough, 1988, 1994; Hoole, 2008).

In the face of stern criticism and in recognition of the failure of a strict conservationist approach, new initiatives were taken to build collective action in managing the common resources that were under pressure for sustainable use; this can be termed the "new-commonisation" process. The purpose of these new initiatives was to conserve resources and biodiversity values, and simultaneously provide livelihood security to local communities (IUCN 2006). New-commonisation initiatives have focused on marginalised and resource deficient communities that desire to have common resources for their livelihood security. The key purpose in the new-commonisation process was to reverse the failure of the government to recognise the complexities of the local community, the linkages of livelihood with the commons and natural resources, and the welfare of the local communities. The establishment of traditional PAs was not an effective measure to conserve biodiversity because the local communities relied on these resources for their survival and grazing seemed to increase the productivity of pastures. These conventional PAs have led to severe social conflicts in Pakistan and other parts of the world.

Thus, there was a call for achieving a balance between conservation and the resource-use needs and practices of local communities. In response to a call to adopt an approach that would bring the local communities back to managing the commons, PAs, and other natural resources, many new experiments or pilot projects were undertaken. Pakistan was no exception, where several community-focused conservation projects were developed as experiments. One such experiment was the Mountain Area Conservancy Project (MACP) which focused on building capacities of local communities to negotiate their rights to natural resources. However, the major drawbacks of this project was that the project fostered dependencies on external funding and revenues from trophy hunting rather than making communities self-reliant. Further, it created a dependency on government subsidies and compensations. However, the potential in MACP included promotion of natural resources as a basis for community economic and human development by strengthening existing institutions and promoting self-reliance. Such a process potentially makes the communities strong allies in conservation programs that can promote commons-based livelihood security.

Local institutions and new partnerships in commons management: A way forward

In an earlier section, we explained the traditional mechanisms of pasture management in Shimshal as a prime example of a local informal institution for managing commons. This informal institution evolved over centuries and maintained its rules and regulations. However, in response to the emerging loss of control over natural resources and the commons by the local communities, and as a method of "self-organization" (Berkes, 2006), some local institutions have attempted to take on new roles under reformed mandates.

The local informal institution of Shimshal felt it was losing the power to defend the community against the state. With this concern, they formulated a plan to formalise the traditional institution. This resulted in the Shimshal Natural Trust (SNT), which is a newly formed institution, but grounded in the principles of traditional informal institutions. This transition can be recognised as evidence of the adaptive capacity of local-level institutions to learn, adapt, and self-organise under uncertainties and changes in social-ecological systems (Berkes, 2006; Abidi-Habibi & Lawrence, 2007).

The birth of the Shimshal Nature Trust (SNT) is an example of the evolution of an informal institution to recognise its power of self-governance and self-organisation during time of adversity (Ostrom, 1990, 2005, Agrawal, 2014), especially in response to the establishment of the Khunjerab National Park. The initial resistance of Shimshal communities, expressed through a collective voice by informal institutions to defend Shimshali's rights and ownership over the park, was not respected by the government policy. Local resistance through the informal institution did not accomplish success in protecting their self-governance over the resources, and the conflict over the Park and PAs and their resources remained unresolved.

The transformation of the traditional institution was obviously a result of a new way of thinking about how to defend local interests with a view to a "more intellectual and formalised engagement" with the state (Abidi-Habib & Lawrence, 2007, p. 35). The aim was to receive recognition of the common voices in the community, to retain all aspects of the informal community institution, and to manage the natural resources through traditional rules and regulations, but in a formalised way. It was, indeed, a strategy adopted by the local community to maintain their self-control over their own resources and to respond to the emerging situation (Khan, 2012).

The community transferred the entire pasture commons to Shimshal Nature Trust as *Waqf* (given away), which was inalienable under Islamic law. The SNT held the common territories of Shimshal under a legal trust against national park paradigms (Abidi-Habib & Lawrence, 2007). In this case, Shimshal Nature Trust earned its recognition, with the power and authority of the local community. In terms of its functional role, SNT transformed itself into a more formalised institution. The institution was in the process of gaining political and legal recognition to supplement other partners in the ongoing conservation activities. The governance structure of SNT validated their efforts in both horizontal and vertical integration towards achieving its goals (Figure 14.5).

In this governance model, which Khan (2012) termed as re-commonisation, Shimshal Nature Trust has all the authority to make decisions at the village level based on a mutual consensus of the advisory committee (Figure 14.2). The advisory committee includes the village heads from all five villages and members selected by each village as representatives to discuss their villages' point of view. These members are elected by the village through an annual

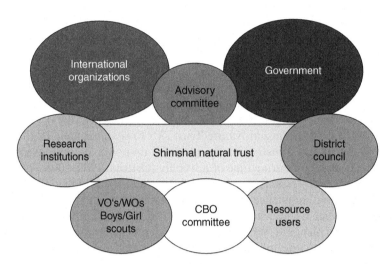

Figure 14.5 Governance model and cross-scale linkages. A colour version of this image is downloadable as an eResource from www.routledge.com/9780367138004.

election process. The nominations are based on the proposed representatives' ability to lead the village in the conservation and development work.

A task force exists in Shimshal Valley, comprised of a Village Organization (VO), established by the Aga Khan Rural Support Program, a Women's Organization (WO), the Boy Scouts, and Girl Guides. These teams are volunteer groups that perform certain tasks to help the village community. As no government body exists within the village, these volunteer groups facilitate the community during cultural ceremonies and events. The community as a whole represents a "Resource User Group" which follows the rules and regulations defined and implemented by SNT (the institution). SNT has developed linkages with a number of international organisations such as the International Union for Conservation (IUCN), World Wide Fund for Nature-Pakistan (WWF-P), and researchers like David Butz, Abidi-Habibi, and others who are contributing to the community through their research work (SNT, 2005).

Currently, there is very little involvement of the government in conservation efforts, except for the issuance of trophy hunting licenses. However, state involvement is needed to generate opportunities and to facilitate the communities' efforts to conserve local resources and sustaining the livelihoods through building eco-tourism in the region. This will involve conservation of resources and sustaining local livelihoods through focus on both biological resources as well local culture and traditions. The outcomes of the FGDs in Shimshal clearly illustrated that SNT is deeply involved in strengthening

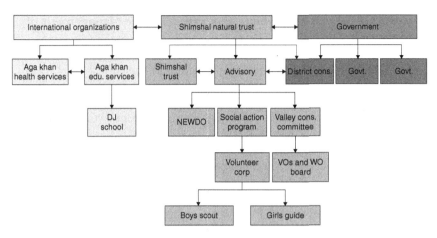

Figure 14.6 Formal and informal institutions in Shimshal. A colour version of this image is downloadable as an eResource from www.routledge.com/9780367138004.

cross-scale linkages (Figure 14.2). SNT is working together with other formal and informal institutions to protect the natural resources and to share the benefits received by the local community for conservation activities through the following initiatives (Figure 14.6):

- Obtain recognition of the institution at the regional, national and international levels
- Ensure economic benefits for the village from the sustainable use (trophy hunting) of wildlife
- Provide training to the local communities in wildlife survey
- Introduce environmental education programs for the schools
- Formulate and implement the management of pasture resources with sustainability goals.

Other organisations with which the community has linkages are involved in the development of the village. For example, these include formal institutions like Aga Khan Education Service (AKES), Social Action Program (provides supply of drinking water), volunteer corps (discussed earlier), Naunihal Education Welfare and Development Organization (NEWDO) (English medium school established by the community with the help of various donors), and Shimshal Trust Fund. All these institutions are working under the umbrella of Shimshal Nature Trust (SNT). Box 14.1 outlines the outcomes of the focus group discussions in Shimshal concerning revenue generation for the management of the park.

Box 14.1 Details on revenue generation for the management of the park in Shimshal

- Development of a detailed map (features of the park)
- Designation of park features (declaring core zones for the breeding of wildlife, site-seeing, wildlife watching, and camping)
- Levy of entry fee for vehicles passing through the park on Karakoram Highway (KKH)
- Levy of a fee on vehicles, which will generate an estimated annual income of Rs. 3,60,000 per annum based on Rs. 100 per vehicle and an average of 100 vehicles per day. With the expansion of KKH and travel between China and Pakistan, the number may go up
- Levy of an entry fee for visitors entering the park for pleasure or hiking
- Trophy hunting (sustainable harvest) of ibex and Blue sheep
- Establishment of trails to site-seeing areas
- Annual census of wildlife (ungulates) as well as other animals
- Summer eco-tourism to pastures (showing the traditional way of yak herding and the traditional pastoral system for education and learning)
- Identification of important plants (medicinal and other important plants)
- Conservation and maintenance of soil and water resources
- Developing criteria and indicators for the conservation and maintenance of biodiversity and ecosystem functions

---

Is new-commonisation a right strategy for sustainability of commons?

The key argument in the conceptualisation and implementation of new-commonisation is that the communities' role in the management of the resource is vital for its protection and sustainability. It also takes into consideration the role of the international community to intervene and facilitate the process when local communities are lacking in financial as well as technical resources for the conservation of forests or pasture lands. There is a clear understanding of the connections between the communities and the resource, and their dependence for livelihoods. The case of Naltar provides a clear illustration of disconnection of the community their resource base as a result of external institutional intervention through a state-controlled approach. It also depicts the ground realities of mismanagement of the forest and pasture resources. In other cases, due to lack of protection and control, the reserve forests are facing the threats of depletion. Thus, the survival and sustainability of forest resources become questionable under state control. It is important to initiate the process of new-commonisation, not only for the commons but also in the PAs that are considered no one's property, as in the case of the reserve forest in Naltar. The key factors of the new-commonisation processes are summarised in the Table 14.3.

Conclusions

The chapter offers an insight into the conversion and transformation of the commons and factors influencing the processes. First, it discussed the

Table 14.3 Key factors of the new-commonisation process in northern Pakistan

Key Factors	Indicators
Favorable resource conditions	• A good resource base and sound ecological health • Better ecological condition of the resource and regulated grazing practices for maintaining pasture productivity • Shared benefit for everyone • Low conflict
Rules about inclusion and exclusion (under customary rights)	• Only selected villages have the rights for grazing in selected pastures • Outsiders from the village are not allowed for any extraction of resources except those who have acquired permission from the community to graze livestock for one season, based on the productivity of the pastures
Strong local institutions	• Village-level local institutions for resource management • Distribution of functional responsibilities amongst institutions • Community-based institutions in command
Relatively low population densities	• Sparsely distributed populations • Difficult for grazers to form more cohesive and manageable groups
Clear rights and entitlements	• Customary practices established specific rights of villagers with regard to access, use, management • Resource rights mutually sanctioned by community and recognised through legal arrangements
Government policies	• No interference • Recognised local management of resource through Jirga system
Grazing practices	• Season-based, specific pastures • Focused on resource sustainability • Based on collective action involving village groups or the entire village
Sense of connection to High pastures	• Social and economic benefits, ecological and political advantages, cultural practices kept the communities connected to the high mountain pastures • Living within mountains with livestock a "way of life" and sense of belonging

Source: Focus Group Discussions

property regimes and conceptualised two new categories based on the management practices: (i) "managed common property", which has an identifiable community with control of exclusion, and (ii) "unmanaged common property", which is the category that has an identifiable community without a proper management strategy, but access to resources is not open to all. Our study also examined the issues of combined property regimes under a co-management arrangement. We argued that property rights cannot be held only as exclusive rights; rather, they need to be shared. This kind of conceptualisation of property rights is important especially within the context of a co-management arrangement because such an arrangement cannot be clearly defined either as state or common property regimes.

Following Nayak and Berkes (2011), we investigated: (i) the case of the Shimshal herding system and the impact of the establishment of Khunjerab National Park; and (ii) the traditional rights of the Naltar community and the impacts under state-controlled reserve forest regulations. We used the concept of new-commonisation to understand the emerging trend of involving local communities and the government in a joint venture in commons management in northern Pakistan. The Mountain Areas Conservancy Project (MACP), its impacts, and the lessons learned from it were assessed. Finally, we illustrated the case of Shimshal Nature Trust (SNT), a transformation of a traditional institute to a formalised institution, as well as the best practices on how to sustain the commons through conservation and the preservation of local livelihood values and culture within the existing PAs framework and ongoing transformations.

In the context of property rights, it appears that property rights regimes are stable. However, a close examination of them provides a different perspective; that is, that characteristically, they are dynamic and change from one regime to another. These dynamic property rights regimes are responding to several factors and drivers both at the local level as well as the international level (Nayak & Berkes, 2011). In property regimes, shifts may occur in response to various internal and external forces, power and policies, and mechanism need to be put in place to be in place to protect the property rights of local communities.

In the context of Khunjerab National Park (KNP), the Shimshal community's involvement in yak herding has been a century-old traditional livelihood activity, but in the eyes of park management, it is considered detrimental to ecological stability. This contradiction needs to be resolved on the basis of logic, equity, and fairness, and more importantly by putting the very question of survival of the local communities at the forefront. The role of the local community in the park management has been neglected by the state; empowering the local community would build a sense of ownership, enable them to care for their resources, and eventually help conserve the resources. Forest depletion cannot be controlled by a single authority (such as the state). Transferring ownership of pastures and giving up control to the revitalised and newly formalised local institutions would establish a new regime based on shared principles of multi-level partnership. It is critical to recognise here that the role of the state would not be eliminated at all under the new regime, but the state would serve in an advisory and regulatory role.

We conclude by highlighting that the commons are changing and processes of new-commonisation are taking shape in the face of external drivers. The onset of new-commonisation, new initiatives to build communities for collective action in managing the commons that were under pressure for sustainable use, has brought in hopes of the forest and pasture commons in northern Pakistan. Here, commonisation or re-commonisation illustrates a shift in the processes of resource use. The transformation of a traditional institution to a formalised institution in the case of Shimshal depicts a process of attainment of community power in self-governance and self-organisation during times of adversity – expressed through a collective voice by informal institutions to defend their rights over common resources. In our case study, the Shimshal community re-organised themselves to take control of the common resources and exercise their customary laws. This process of new-commonisation is indicative of an empowering process that promises to bring sustainable management of the forest and pasture commons in northern Pakistan.

References

Abidi-Habib, M., & Lawrence, A. (2007). Revolt and remember: How the Shimshal Nature Trust develops and sustains social-ecological resilience in northern Pakistan. *Ecology and Society, 12*(2), 35. Retrieved from www.ecologyandsociety.org/vol12/iss2/art35/

Agrawal, A. (2014). Studying the commons, governing common-pool resource outcomes: Some concluding thoughts. *Environmental Science and Policy 36*, 86–91.

Agrawal, A. (2002). Common resources and institutional sustainability. In E. Ostrom, T. Dietz, N. Dolsak, P. C. Stern, S. Stonich, & E. U. Weber (Eds.), *The drama of the commons* (pp. 41–86). Washington, DC: National Academy Press.

Ali, I., & Butz, D. (2003). The Shimshal governance model – a CCA, a sense of cultural identity, a way of life. *Policy Matters, 12*, 111–120.

Berkes, F. (1986). Local-level management and the commons problem: A comparative study of Turkish coastal fisheries. *Marine Policy, 10*, 215–229.

Berkes, F. (Ed.). (1989). *Common property resources: Ecology and community-based sustainable development*. London, UK: Belhaven Press.

Berkes, F. (2002). Cross-scale institutional linkages: Perspective from the bottom up. In E. Ostrom, T. Dietz, N. Dolsak, P. C. Stern, S. Stonich, & E. U. Weber (Eds.), *The drama of the commons* (pp. 293–321). Washington, DC: National Academy Press.

Berkes, F. (2006). From community-based resources management to complex systems: The scale issues and marine commons. *Ecology and Society, 11*(1), 45. Retrieved from www.ecologyandsociety.org/vol11/iss1/art45/

Berkes, F. (2007). Adaptive co-management and complexity: Exploring the many faces of co-management. In D. Armitage, F. Berkes, & N. Doubleday (Eds.), *Adaptive co-management* (pp. 19–37). Vancouver: University of British Columbia Press.

Berkes, F., Colding, J., & Folke, C. (2000). Rediscovery of traditional ecological knowledge as adaptive management. *Ecological Applications, 10*(5), 1251–1262.

Berkes, F., Colding, J., & Folke, C. (Eds.). (2003). *Navigating social-ecological systems, building resilience for complexity and change.* Cambridge: Cambridge University Press.

Berkes, F., Davidson-Hunt, I., & Davidson-Hunt, K. (1998b). Diversity of common property resource use and diversity of social interests in the western Indian Himalaya. *Mountain Research and Development, 18*, 19–33.

Berkes, F., & Farvar, M. T. (1989). Introduction and overview. In F. Berkes (Ed.), *Common property resources: Ecology and community-based sustainable development* (pp. 1–17). London: Belhaven Press.

Berkes, F., Feeny, D., McCay, B. J., & Acheson, J. M. (1989). The benefits of commons. *Nature, 340*, 91–93.

Berkes, F., & Folke, C. (1993). A system perspective on the interrelationships between natural, human-made and cultural capital. *Ecological Economics, 5*(1), 1–8.

Berkes, F., & Folke, C. (1994). Investing in cultural capital for the sustainable use of natural capital. In A. M. Janson et al. (Ed.), *Investing in national capital: The ecological economics approach to sustainability* (pp. 128–149). Washington, DC: Island Press.

Berkes, F., & Folke, C. (Eds.). (1998). *Linking social and ecological systems, management practices and social mechanisms for building resilience.* Cambridge: Cambridge University Press.

Berkes, F., & Gardner, J. (Eds.). (1997). Mountain environments and sustainability. In *Sustainability of mountain environments in India and Canada* (pp. 1–18), Winnipeg, MB: University of Manitoba.

Bilal, A., Haque, H., & Moore, P. (2003). *Customary Laws, IUCN.* Pakistan: The World Conservation Union.

Borrini-Feyerabend, G., Kothari, A., & Oviedo, G. (2004). *Indigenous and local communities and Protected Areas: Towards equity and enhanced conservation.* Gland, Switzerland, and Cambridge, UK: IUCN.

Bromley, D. W., Feeuy, D., McKean, M., E Peters, Gilles, J., Oakerson, R., Runge, C. E., & Thomson, J. (Eds.). (1992). *Making the commons work: Theory, practice, and policy.* San Francisco, CA: Institute for Contemporary Studies Press.

Brosius, J. P., Tsing A. L., & Zerner, C. (1998). Representing communities: Histories and politics of community-based natural resource management. *Society and Natural Resources, 11*, 157–168.

Butz, D. (1992). *Developing sustainable communities: Community development and modernity in Shimshal* (Doctoral Thesis). McMaster University, Hamilton, ON, Canada.

Butz, D. (1996). Sustaining indigenous communities: Symbolic and instrumental dimensions of pastoral resource use in Shimshal, Pakistan. *The Canadian Geographer, 40*(1), 36–53.

Butz, D. (2006). Tourism and portering labour relations in Shimshal, Gojal Hunza. In H. Kreutzmann (Ed.), *Karakoram in transition: The Hunza Valley* (pp. 394–403). Oxford and Karachi: Oxford University Press.

Chambers, R. (1983). *Rural development: Putting the last first.* London: Longman.

Chambers, R., & Conway, G. (1992). *Sustainable rural livelihoods: Practical concepts for the 21st Century* (Discussion Paper 296, Institute of Development Studies, Sussex). Brighton: University of Sussex.

Cronkleton, P., Taylor, P. L., Barry, D., Stone-Jovicich, S., & Schmink, M. (2008). *Environmental governance and the emergence of forest-based social movements.*

Occasional Paper 49. Bogor, Indonesia: Center for International Forestry Research.

Hansen, A. J., & DeFries, R. (2007). Ecological mechanisms linking protected areas to surrounding lands. *Ecological Applications, 17*, 974–988. Retrieved from http://dx.doi.org/10.1890/05-1098

Hardin, G. (1968). The tragedy of commons. *Science, 162*, 1243–1248.

Hardin, J. L. (1988). Obstacles to effective management of conflicts between national parks and surrounding human communities in developing countries. *Environmental Conservation, 15*(2), 129–136.

Hoole, A. (2008). *Community-based conservation and Protected Areas in Namibia: Social-ecological, linkages for biodiversity* (PhD Thesis). University of Manitoba, Winnipeg, Canada.

Hough, J. L. (1988). Obstacles to effective management of conflicts between national parks and surrounding human communities in developing countries. *Environmental Conservation, 15*(2), 129–136.

Hough, J. L. (1994). Institutional constraints to the integration of conservation and development: A case study of Madagascar. *Society and Natural Resources, 7*, 119–124.

IUCN. (1994). *Guidelines for Protected Area management categories (CNPPA with the assistance of WCMC)*. Gland, Switzerland, and Cambridge, UK: IUCN.

IUCN. (1996). Resolutions and recommendations, World Conservation Congress, Montreal (Canada), 13–23 October, 1996. *Management, 24*(4), 449–465. Retrieved on 14 February 2003 from http://iucn.org/ wcc/resolutions/resrecen.pdf

IUCN. (1999). *Biodiversity action plan for Pakistan*. Islamabad, Pakistan: IUCN-Pakistan.

IUCN. (2000). Linking people with nature: Biodiversity conservation strategy. In *Linking people with nature: Biodiversity conservation strategy for the Himal Region. IUCN Conference Proceedings, Rajendrapur 24–25 January 2000* (pp. 12–14).

IUCN. (2003). *Strategy for sustainable development* (Background paper). Islamabad, Pakistan: IUCN-Pakistan.

IUCN. (2005). *Regional mountain program in Asia*. Retrieved in August 2005 from www.iucn.org/places/asia/pdf/fact_sheets/Mountains.pdf

IUCN. (2006). *Mountain areas conservancy project document*. Islamabad, Pakistan: IUCN-Pakistan. Retrieved from http://iucn.org/about/union/secretariat/offices/asia/asia_where_work/

Khan, S. (2012). Linking conservation with sustainable mountain livelihoods: A Case study of northern Pakistan (Ph.D. dissertation). University of Manitoba, Winnipeg, Canada.

Khan, S., Rehman, S., & Sunderland, T. (2011). Commons becoming non-commons in the efforts for reconciliation between conservation and livelihoods: A case study of northern Pakistan. *Journal of Horticulture and Forestry, 3*(3), 63–71. Retrieved in March 2011 from www.academicjournals.org/jhf

Knudsen, A. (1999). Conservation and controversy in the Karakoram: Khunjerab National Park Pakistan. *Journal of Political Ecology, 56*, 1–29. Retrieved in June 2009 from http://dizzy.library.arizona.edu/ej/jpe/vol6~1.htm.

MACP. (1999). *Mountain area conservancy project document*. Islamabad, Pakistan: IUCN-Pakistan. Retrieved in June 2009 from www.macp-pk.org/docs/Project percent20Document.PDF

McCay, B. J., & Acheson, J. M. (1987). *The question of the commons: The culture and ecology of communal resource*. Tucson: University of Arizona Press.

McKay, L. (2001). *Cross-scale issues in the management of protected areas in India: The case study of Great Himalayan National Park and Manali Sanctuary* (Master's Thesis). Winnipeg, MB: University of Manitoba.

NASSD. (2003). *Northern areas conservation strategy*. Islamabad, Pakistan: IUCN-Pakistan.

Narayan, D, Patel, R., Schafft, K., Rademacher, A., & Koch-Schulte, S. (2000). *Voices of the poor: Can anyone hear us?* New York: Oxford University Press for the World Bank.

Nayak, P., & Berkes, F. (2008). Politics of co-optation: Community forest management versus joint forest management in Orissa, India. *Environmental Management, 90*, 70–88.

Nayak, P. K., & Berkes, F. (2010). Whose marginalization? Politics around environmental injustices in India's Chilika Lagoon. *Local Environment, 15*, 553–567.

Nayak, P. K., & Berkes, F. (2011). Commonisation and decommonisation: Understanding the processes of change in Chilika Lagoon, India. *Conservation and Society* (in press, accepted 19 August 2010).

Nuding M. A. (2000) Wildlife management in Namibia: The conservancy approach. In T. O' Riordan, and S. Stoll- Kleemann, (eds.). *Biodiversity, sustainability and human communities*, London: Cambridge University Press.

Ostrom, E. (1987). Institutional arrangements for resolving the commons dilemma: Some contending approaches. In B. J. McCay & J. M. Acheson (Eds.), *The question of the commons* (pp. 250–265). Tucson: University of Arizona Press.

Ostrom, E. (1990). *Governing the commons: The evolution of institutions for collective action*. London: Cambridge University Press.

Ostrom, E. (2005). *Understanding institutional diversity*. Princeton, NJ: Princeton University Press.

Ostrom, E., Burger, J., Field, C. B., Norgaard, R. B., & Policansky, D. (1999). Revisiting the commons: Local lessons, global challenges. *Science, 284*(5412), 278–282.

Ostrom, E., & Schlager, E. (1996). The formation of property rights. In S. S. Hanna, C. Folke, & K. Maler (Eds.), *Rights to nature: Ecological, cultural, and political principles of institutions for the environment* (pp. 127–156). Washington, DC: Island Press.

Ostrom, V., Fenny, D., & Pitch, H. (1988). *Rethinking institutional analysis development: Issues, alternatives and choices*. Panama: ICEG. Retrieved in December 2011 from pakistan/projects/archived_projects/proj_arc_macp.cfm

Pido, M.D., Pomeroy, R.S., Carlos, M.B., & Garces, L.R. (1996). *A handbook for rapid appraisal of fisheries management systems*. ICLARM Education Series 16, ICLARM, Manila, Philippines.

SNT. (2005). *Shimshal Nature Trust (SNT)*. Retrieved in October 2005 from www.snt.org.pk/aboutus.html

SNT. (2007). *Shimshal History*. Retrieved in October 2008 from www.snt.org.pk/aboutus.html

WWF. (2004). *Are protected areas working? Analysis of forest protected areas by WWF*. Gland, Switzerland: WWF International.

Part V

Closing

Chapter 15

Governance and the process of (de)commonisation

Derek Armitage, Evan J. Andrews, Jessica Blythe, Ana Carolina E. Dias, Prateep Kumar Nayak, Jeremy Pittman and Sajida Sultana

Introduction

This chapter considers how "governance" contributes to the processes of commonisation and decommonisation in coastal systems. Nayak and Berkes (2011) define commonisation as a process in which resources (e.g., lagoons, fisheries, forests) are "converted" through time and space into jointly used systems via institutions (e.g., rules or access) and collective action. In turn, these institutions and collective action provide the foundation to address the classic commons problems of excludability and subtractability (see Chapter 1). No resource commons exist in a vacuum, however, and because of changes in social and ecological conditions, processes of commonisation and decommonisation (i.e., the loss of jointly used resource under commons institutions) are dynamic. Central to this dynamic feedback process, and the focus of this chapter, is the role of governance.

Governance refers to the processes (e.g., decision making, planning, political alliances) and institutions (e.g., rules, rule-making, rights, practices) through which societies make decisions. Governance is thus already a part of the processes we refer to here as commonisation and decommonisation. Indeed, oscillations among centralized and more decentralized governance regimes reflect important shifts in how we govern the commons, the role of the state relative to other actors, and the institutions that societies have in order to sustain just and equitable coastal commons (Ayers et al. 2018). In many jurisdictions, there has been a push to privatise the commons and off-load state responsibility (Ribot et al. 2006; Larson and Soto 2008; Berkes 2010), while in other contexts, hybrid models of governance involving state and non-state actors cooperating to achieve shared goals have also emerged (Lemos and Agrawal 2006; Bridge and Perreault 2009). Ultimately, pathways to commonisation – of which there might be many – are likely to require the co-production of accountable and collaborative actor networks across levels of decision making, legitimate institutions, rules and rule-making systems that clarify rights, and sensitivity to the effects of power (material and discursive) and environmental change that influence how societies make decisions that affect the coastal commons (Lebel 2012).

The chapter is organised as follows. First, we briefly synthesise concepts from the commons literature to develop a working framework to understand processes of commonisation and decommonisation through a governance lens. Second, we apply this framework to four commons cases featuring coastal systems, including cases from Brazil, Mozambique, Dominica and Pakistan. Third, we distill lessons from these cases to anticipate and highlight some of the governance-related drivers that catalyse processes of decommonisation and a return to commonisation. Our intent is not to "separate" governance from the processes and social–ecological systems in which it is a part. Rather, we treat governance as an analytical unit to consider its influence and implications, and to examine the combinations of governing features that help to shape (de)commonisation processes. Pathways for transformative change and sustainable social-ecological outcomes in coastal commons are more likely to emerge with this understanding.

A framework to connect governance and (de)commonisation

Biermann et al. (2009) define governance as the "... system of formal and informal rules, rule-making systems, and actor networks at all levels of human society (from local to global) ... set up to steer societies towards preventing, mitigating, and adapting to global and local environmental change". This definition is helpful because it is action-oriented and draws attention to the potential of governance to "steer" societies along particular trajectories or pathways. Indeed, as a key driver of the commonisation process, governance can result in dramatic shifts in property rights regimes, such as the emergence of enclosures through protected areas or privatisation, or transformations in how decisions are made (i.e., from a centralized to more decentralized model). Importantly, processes and institutions of governance co-evolve, emerge and at times collapse, reflecting a need to understand their role – positive and negative, and at different scales – in processes of commonisation and decommonisation.

Efforts to bring change in a complex resource commons will inevitably intersect with the concept of governance, both as the institutions and processes through which decisions are made, or as an analytical lens through which to understand how and why a particular situation has emerged. For instance, significant attention has been directed at understanding what arrangements can yield sustainable social and ecological outcomes in the commons (Ostrom 2000). Command and control, or state-centered approaches to decision making have been criticised for their failure to reflect the complexity and multiscale reality of most commons (Holling and Meffe 1996). Instead, hybrid governance arrangements (see Lemos and Agrawal 2006) have emerged because they support a diversity of views and understandings that can yield better outcomes, but these too have limitations (e.g., high transaction costs).

In this chapter, our concern with the processes of commonisation is normative. The process of commonisation is theorised to yield better social and ecological outcomes, and this may often be the case (Fabricius et al. 2004). In contrast, certain circumstances of decommonisation may be linked to aims of conserving biodiversity *in-situ*. The ecological benefits in this case may be positive, but the social legacy of such processes has often been negative (Holt et al. 2005). Here, we are primarily concerned with the governance pathways that transform (Blythe et al. 2018) commons in ways that yield positive social and ecological outcomes. In many circumstances, such transformations are linked to the re-emergence and strengthening of community institutions, assertion of access rights and decision making by local groups, shifts in the effects of power (material and discursive), and the formation of durable and meaningful networks of actors engaged in collective action to sustain commons resources and institutions (Armitage et al. 2017).

Governance pathways that support transformative changes and process of commonisation are linked to diverse dimensions and related circumstances. Here we focus on three as an initial entrée to this analytical challenge (Figure 15.1). First, networks of actors across scales are theorised to enhance coordination among different actors, improve information and resource flows, and foster knowledge sharing and learning (Folke et al. 2005). The presence and efficacy of collaborative networks may thus play an important role in processes of commonisation. Second, the "bundles of rights" (Schlager and Ostrom 1992) and hybrid property regimes that exist in different commons reflect a level of social complexity that intersects directly with collective action efforts and governance processes. Rights of access, withdrawal, management, exclusion and alienation of resources, or parts of a resource, through time and space (see Barry and Meinzen-Dick 2008) are also part of the commonisation narrative, and are reflected in formal and informal or customary laws, regulations, cultural norms, social values and social relationships or property practices (Ribot and Peluso 2003; Sikor and Lund 2009). Third, how governance is perceived and constructed through relations of power – material and discursive – is also important. Our focus on discourse practices is limited in our analysis, but we note that narratives (see Roe 1991) about governance (e.g., the benefits of privatisation, increased efficiency) also reflect material relations of power (whose narrative takes hold) with direct implications for processes of decommonisation and commonisation.

Figure 15.1 provides a working framework through which we can consider the connected processes of commonisation and decommonisation across scales. We recognise that no single framework can fully address the confounding diversity of institutions, arrangements and the discourse that influence the role of governance and the commons. However, we build on the commons and governance literatures here and draw attention in this framework to several important dimensions relevant to the cases we explore in more depth below.

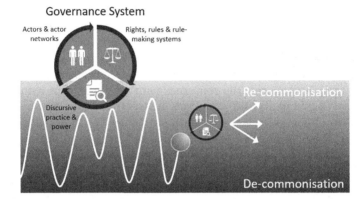

Figure 15.1 The role of governance in shaping processes of commonisation and decommonisation in social–ecological systems (social–ecological system represented here by the grey sphere). A colour version of this image is downloadable as an eResource from www.routledge.com/9780367138004.

The three governance dimensions are considered in different bodies of scholarship and can be interpreted through different theoretical perspectives. Here, we draw principally on two of these perspectives, noting they are not entirely distinct. For example, Ostrom's (1990) original principles for governance of the commons (e.g., dealing with group size and homogeneity, benefit and cost distribution mechanisms, the existence of monitoring systems, and clearly defined resource system boundaries) highlight a suite of institutional conditions for collective action. Such *institutionalist* perspectives have been instrumental in advancing commons theory and concepts of governance (North 1990). Institutions, rules and rule-making systems are indeed means through which governance takes place, especially when considered through the lens of rational choice.

Yet, institutions *per se* are not the only crucial attribute of governance (Hall and Taylor 1996). Complex and dynamic contexts and messy "social" conditions have also been recognised as determining in significant ways how institutions and governance structures manifest and yield particular outcomes (Edwards and Steins 1999). In this regard, *political ecological* perspectives have been particularly valuable in drawing attention to social power and politics, the mediating influence of identity, class, gender and knowledge, and the material and non-material dimensions (i.e., discourse) of governance in commons situations. Indeed, traditional concerns of political ecological theory of particular utility here include: (a) the role of power, scale and levels of organisation; (b) the positioning of social actors; and (c) social constructions of nature and the policy narratives that shape governance (Armitage 2008).

Lessons from experience: Governance pathways and processes of (de)commonisation

We apply our working framework to structure an analysis of several cases that reflect in different ways processes of commonisation and decommonisation. These cases are chosen purposively and reflect the coastal commons in which we have worked. We do not claim these cases represent an easily comparable set of conditions or experiences, yet each case does offer evidence of commonisation and decommonisation amenable to our analysis. Therefore, our aim in learning exploratory lessons from these cases is to highlight the influence of governance in commonisation, and specifically, those issues related to actor networks, institutions and rules, and relationships of power.

Tarituba community and Tamoios protected area, Paraty, Brazil

Along the coast of Rio de Janeiro state, the mountains of the Atlantic Forest meet the seascape, creating both inland and marine hotspots of biodiversity (Creed et al. 2007). Known as "the green coast", this setting is the most developed region of Brazil and is also home to several coastal communities that depend upon the direct use of natural resources to sustain their livelihoods (Hanazaki et al. 2013). Intertwined with natural areas and traditional fishing territories, industrial poles, energy production plants (e.g., nuclear and hydroelectric), and oil extraction platforms are installed along the coast (Dias 2015).

Until 2006, before the implementation of a marine protected area (MPA) in the region, the coast was characterised as "open access". However, informal agreements between small-scale fishers who used the area were in place. These agreements characterised the informal commonisation of the area and included the banishment of trawl fisheries in shallow areas around the islands and avoiding catching juveniles – before reproductive maturation (Dias 2015). A period of decommonisation occurred with the creation of a no-take zone, restricting traditional activities in the area. It was followed by a formal commonisation period two decades later with a Commitment Term between fishers and the protected area that allowed for traditional fishing. A significant catalyst of decommonisation began in 1987, when a nuclear power plant was implemented along the coast of Angra dos Reis, and close to the municipality of Paraty. In keeping with the Federal Decree 84.973/80, which stipulates that nuclear power plants must be co-located in the areas defined as ecological stations, MPA was also created between Paraty and Angra dos Reis in 1990. Tamoios is a no-take MPA under the most restrictive category of protected areas established by the national system of protected areas (Federal Law 9.985/2000), also known as "Ecological Station" (Decree 98.864/90). Tamoios Ecological Station only allows for scientific research and environmental interpretation activities. Tourism and other sources of public use are not permitted. The MPA encompasses 29 islands and a surrounding marine area of one kilometer, with a total area of 8,700 hectares. Tamoios Ecological Station was created in 1990 with no local participation and only *de facto* implementation in 2006, when enforcement operations begun. Locals disagreed with the top-down approach of MPA implementation and with the restrictions imposed, arguing their traditional fishing spots were included in the delimitation of the MPA without consultation and their participation, restricting local access to resources (e.g., seafood and fish) (Bavinck et al. 2017). This situation led to negative impacts on food security, local identity and collective interactions. Although several coastal communities traditionally used the area, this was especially relevant to the community of Tarituba (located in Paraty) given its dependence on fisheries and because the entire surrounding marine area was set aside for conservation.

Local fishers are represented by the City Council of Paraty. In 2009, they formally requested the manager of Tamoios Ecological Station to authorize small-scale fishing inside this protected area. Since this request, the management council of Tamoios Ecological Station has discussed potential solutions. In 2012, a "Commitment Term" was proposed and a working group created under the Thematic Chamber of Aquaculture and Fisheries, within the management council, to negotiate the terms and agreements to be included (Seixas et al. 2017). In 2013, an initial version of the Term established specific marine areas and fishing gears Tarituba small-scale fishers were allowed to use, in addition to rights and commitments of both parties (fishers and managers). The validity of the Commitment Term was set for one year, with the possibility renewal for an additional year. It was agreed that during its period of validity, the fishing activities performed should be monitored, including both socioeconomic (e.g., income generation) and ecological (e.g., amount and type of species caught) aspects. The Commitment Term was approved in 2017, after several attempts. Setbacks included divergent interpretations of rules, lack of political will, changes in the tool used (e.g., Commitment Term, Behaviour Adjustment Term), inclusion of other actors during the process (e.g., Federal Public Prosecution Office), and changes in the agreements requested by the President of the Conservation Agency who was responsible for final approval (Seixas et al. 2017).

During this process, it was clear that within the same institution, rules and regulations were interpreted in different ways according to the point of view of each stakeholder. Rules were not straightforward and remained subject to be interpreted in different ways according to actors' backgrounds and worldviews (Dias 2015), and the actors themselves were far from being homogeneous in their views.

Privatisation, resources rights, and aquaculture in Mozambique

Mozambique's recent history is characterised by a brief period of commonisation followed by a steady shift towards decommonisation. In

1975, Mozambique gained independence from Portugal and the new government (led by the FRELIMO party) developed collective forms of production inspired by Julius Nyerere's African socialism. FRELIMO's reforms focused on the "socialization of countryside" through the creation of the state farms and factories, communal villages, and cooperatives (Pitcher 2002). The socialist period following independence can be characterised as commonisation, where common resources were reallocated from colonial ownerships for the exclusive use of communities. However, decision-making power was concentrated within the central state, with little input from community or private sector stakeholders.

Two years after independence, Mozambique descended into civil war. During the war, millions of people were displaced and were forced to settle on new land or moved to urban areas (Pitcher 2002). Weakened by the war and a faltering economy, the new government turned to the World Bank and the International Monetary Fund. The World Bank implemented a structural adjustment programme and its associated regulations including smaller government, market liberalization, and privatisation. State farms were converted to private enterprises. The government also began leasing large expanses of apparently vacant land to commercial investors. The process of privatisation did not include recognition of local customary rights and shifted land ownership and economic control to the private sector (Pitcher 2002).

A peace agreement was signed in 1992. However, the wave of decommonisation continued. While internally displaced Mozambicans began to return to their homes, seemingly unused land was allocated to foreign investors by government agencies (Pitcher 2002). Former colonial landholders were also reclaiming their rights, in most cases over land that was concurrently claimed by local communities. As the country began post-war reconstruction, the government recognised two potentially competing needs: (1) securing land rights for Mozambique's rural population and (2) creating a welcoming environment for foreign investment (Kanji et al. 2002). To meet both objectives, the government created a hybrid system of rights allocation. The resulting Land Law of 1997 specifies that land is the property of the state, but local communities can be collective holders of land rights and can apply for "land use and benefit rights" (Chilundo et al. 2005). Importantly, local people can offer proof of land rights through oral testimony, which lowers the financial barriers of registration that often block poor or marginalized people from establishing their rights (Nielsen et al. 2011). Yet, foreign firms can also apply for land use and benefits rights (Chilundo et al. 2005). Thus, in practice the Land Law seeks to secure smallholder rights and also creates an enabling environment for private investors.

Given the creation of an enabling environment, the first private shrimp farm was established by a French company in 1994. By 2010, the farm employed 400 full-time workers and consisted of 340 ha of ponds. As with most private ventures, the farm redefined access to commons in the area. For example, residents of the nearby community reported that prior to the

shrimp farm, the land was used as a commons to support subsistence livelihood activities, such as salt making and fishing, by the surrounding villages
(Blythe et al. 2015). After the opening of the farm, they were excluded and
physically blocked from accessing this previously held common land. In addition, farm employees were exposed to the volatile nature of high density
export-oriented aquaculture during an outbreak of the white spot syndrome
virus (WSSV) in 2011 which closed the farm for one year (FAO 2013). Yet, the
impacts of this decommonisation process have not been entirely negative for
the local community. The farm provided an important source of income for
some households (Blythe et al. 2015). In a largely subsistence economy, cash
can be critical for covering basic expenses such as school fees. Like many cases
of decommonisation, commercial aquaculture development in Mozambique
has been shaped by conflicts of interest between different actors, changing
property rights and access, and issues relating to smallholder power.

Ocean governance and the development of pelagic fisheries in Dominica

Dominica is a Small Island State in the Eastern Caribbean. Small-scale fisheries are an important component of coastal community livelihoods and
local food security for the island. Recently, the use of small-scale moored
fish aggregating device (FADs) technology has allowed fishers to more efficiently target offshore pelagic fish species, which potentially enhance local
livelihoods and food security. However, the use of FADs has also sparked
important questions regarding commonisation and decommonisation of offshore pelagic fisheries resources. The development and placement of FADs
transforms offshore marine space from an open access to public good, but
the direction of transformation is partially determined by processes of
institution-crafting. If individual fishers are left to their own to develop and
place FADs, the emerging institutions and rules shift offshore marine space,
and the fisheries resources found there, towards private property, which has
caused significant conflict among fishers as they struggle to protect what they
see as theirs. However, with the development of new rules at the national-
level, offshore marine space is being commonised again, which has reduced
the conflict between fishers, but possibly introduces problems of free-riding,
as individual fishers no longer see value in working to maintain the FADs.
These processes have led to a suite of diverse actors becoming involved at
multiple levels.

   The main actors involved in the commonisation/decommonisation
processes are the Government of Domnica's Fisheries Division, the Japanese
International Cooperation Agency (JICA), the local fisheries cooperatives,
and the fishers themselves. The Fisheries Division is responsible for developing
and enforcing fisheries legislation and regulations. They recently partnered
with JICA on programs related to the expansion of the FADs fishing practices

through training programs and resource provision for FADs construction. Local fisheries cooperatives serve as community hubs for organising local fishers, and they serve as an entry point for the distribution of resources and capacity to pursue FADs fishing. Fishers control the day-to-day operation of the FADs fishery, and they make operational decisions regarding the type of fishing employed, locations, etc.

When the FADs technology was originally introduced to Dominica, few rules existed in offshore areas to guide fishing practices. Furthermore, there were limited rules around FADs' ownership, placement, access, etc. As fishers saw the benefits of FAD fishing, they began to finance and place their own FADs in the absence of broader rules governing the fishery. Furthermore, they treated privately owned FADs as personal property and acted to exclude other fishers who had not contributed to the development of individual FADs. Essentially, the fishers were shifting offshore commons from a state of being a public good (i.e., low subtractability and excludability) to private property (i.e., high subtractability and excludability).

This shift produced a significant amount of conflict in local communities, as fishers struggled to obtain access to FADs, secure and exclude access to their own FADs, and compete over prime locations for FADs placement. Recognising the challenges, the Fisheries Division stepped in to develop FADs fishing rules, which governed all aspects of FADs ownership, use, development, and access. They devised rules to control access to FADs. Essentially, only registered and licensed fishers could fish around the FADs, and licensed and registered fishers could access any FADs found in Dominica's waters – even those placed by private individuals. These new rules once again shifted offshore commons, but this time from private property to a common pool resource (i.e., high subtractability, low excludability) by removing access barriers to the FADs for fishing purposes.

The discourse around FADs largely promotes FADs as a "good thing" for livelihoods, wellbeing, food security, etc. Additionally, much of the discourse about FADs in the Caribbean in general promotes them as a means of improving nearshore resource conservation by shifting fishing pressure to offshore resources. While the debate continues about the value of FADs in this sense, an often over-looked element in the current discourse is the potential impacts to offshore pelagic ecosystems. Nonetheless, the discourse centering on the benefits of FADs was largely used to justify the commonisation of the resource. FADs were considered good for the fishers, good for the public, and good for Dominica on a whole, which is why FADs fishery development was pursued and the barriers to accessing the FADs were removed. Furthermore, this discourse was used to justify the appropriation of privately owned FADs from fishers who had taken the initiative to place their own FADs and advance the industry in the first place. These fishers lose exclusive access to their own FADs but gain access to the suite of other FADs in Dominica's waters. However, there are still power issues at play, and in some ways, these fishers – who were usually quite successful and considered as serious fishers in their communities – were somewhat punished for their ingenuity and initiative.

Shifts in property rights in Nurreri and Jabho Lagoon, Pakistan

The Nurreri and Jubho lagoons (both are Ramsar sites under the Ramsar Convention) in southeast Pakistan are part of a lagoon complex that also consist of Pateji and Cholri lagoons. Both Nurerri and Jubho lagoons are shallow, brackish with barren mudflats and are temporary home to several migratory birds. Here, experiences with decommonisation and commonisation are reflected in four distinct shifts in the property rights system, including free hold, a license system, a period of ranger control, and finally, a contract system.

During the "free hold" stage, when there was no rule or policies from the state, these lagoons were perceived as "open access", although, local communities were managing both Nurreri and Jabho lagoons as de facto commons. These lagoons were used as a source of drinking water as well as to irrigate agriculture lands in the surrounding areas by the local communities. There used to be an informal understanding on how much water to use, when to use it, and which area of the lagoons were to be used for drinking and irrigation purposes. Because of the small number of users in the fisher and non-fisher communities, the rules for access, use and management of lagoon resources were relatively straightforward. However, these informal arrangements proved less successful when the population increased and income from fishery activities intensified in-migration.

In response to emerging challenges (i.e. increasing population, pollution and overuse), the Nurreri and Jubho lagoons transitioned from an informal to a formal management arrangement through the introduction of a license by the provincial wildlife department. Under the "license system", access and withdrawal rights were only given to Indigenous fishing communities. People without a license were not allowed to access or use the two lagoons. Management rights were given to local fishing community leaders and later on transferred to the local fisheries department to ensure sustainable use and control overexploitation. Similarly, rights of exclusion and alienation were held with the local government and state. As a result, there was no overexploitation and fishing communities were happy with the license system. However, this system did not survive for a long time.

With the establishment of the Sindh Fisheries Department in 1980, the national government replaced the license system with a "contract system". This was the time when many companies started formal fisheries business in the coastal areas of Sindh. These lagoons were in the center of the Economic Zone of Sindh and were thus exploited for fish. This "contract system" gave the rights of access, withdrawal, and management to the contract holders only. Contracts were issued to both fisher and non-fisher communities, but this system was also manipulated through forged bidding processes. Most contracts were issued to powerful people including landlords and large firms and majority of the Indigenous fisher communities were excluded. Fishers were not allowed to access fishing grounds without the permission of the contract holder and they were punished for raising their voice (and in some cases they were even killed) (Wasim 2007).

The contract system was further entrenched when the government allowed the "Pakistan Rangers" (paramilitary forces) to take control of coastal areas, including Nurreri and Jabho lagoons. The primary mission of the Pakistan Rangers is to secure strategic sites such as Pakistan's International Border, including water bodies (i.e. lagoons closer to the border). Rangers were allowed by the government to access and use these lagoons for fishing to meet their food requirement. Subsequently, the Rangers expanded their control to take over management and exclusion rights of the lagoons.

However, the Nurreri and Jabho lagoons can also be taken as a classic example where civil society organisations and NGOs created awareness in the local fisher communities resulting in the communities voicing their concerns against existing government policy for lagoon management. They continued their struggle until the government restored turned community rights to the lagoon through the reinstation of the license system.

The case of the Nurreri and Jabho lagoons clearly reflects a decommonisation process in which the outcomes have been largely negative for local people and the ecosystem of Nurreri and Jabho lagoons. While transitions in property rights are a clear reflection of decommonisation, a process of commonisation has slowly started to take hold through the restoration of the license system. However, a number of other factors such as unequal social power, the broader economic situation, ineffective policies, lack of coordination and poor governance remain unaddressed. While commonisation took significant efforts by the local users to regain their access, such efforts have compelled the government to re-introduce the license system.

Lessons learned: Governance and the pathways of commonisation

Each of the cases we cover in this chapter offers insights on the influence of governance in the context of dynamic processes of commonisation. In this section, we distil some main lessons from these cases, organised around the core themes of our framework. In doing so, we seek to consider the similarities and differences across the cases, and start first with some general observations about our entry point into an understanding of the processes of commonisation experienced in these cases.

As is likely reflected in most contexts, historical events provide a useful starting point (e.g., the temporal and spatial entrée) for analysis of commonisation and decommonisation. Choosing where to start, however, influences what gets told about these cases and how we interpret them. For example, Brazil, Dominica, and Pakistan show similar patterns of "decommonisation" and back to processes of commonisation but that may be because our starting points in each of these cases is a policy or institutional change that undermined access of local people to the resources to which they historically had some control (e.g., MPAs in Brazil, FADs in Dominica). Mozambique offers an interesting counter-example, however, because of progressive land laws enacted in the 1970s have given way to land privatisation. Beyond the dynamic processes of commonisation, we are interested in longer-term social and ecological outcomes, and in the ways in which governance has mediated the commonisation experience in different cases. In this regard, we turn next to a discussion of actor and actor roles in commonisation, consideration of rules and rights, and subsequently the implications of power and discursive practices on commonisation processes.

Actors

Actors and actor networks play an important role in advancing commonisation and decommonisation. In three cases, different levels governments exercised decision-making authority that functioned as a driver of commonisation. In other words, while governance was broadly defined, government actors had considerable roles to play, as decision-makers, interveners, and change-makers. For example, in the Brazil case, the nuclear power plant and "ecological station" were connected through state-level regulation. Implementation involved no participation from affected local populations. Similarly, in the Pakistan case, transitions among property rights systems (i.e., license, contract, and ranger systems) were driven initially by actor networks with centralized authority, although subsequent transfer of rights to various groups created alternative networks with authority over management, alienation, and excludability rights. In addition, the creation of the Fisheries Act and exploitation of oil and gas resources Paraty were done without direct consultation with those most affected.

Importantly, decision making at various levels initiated and advanced commonisation processes to satisfy actor interests. In three cases, for example, state-level decisions-making initiated decommonisation to promote the "national interest". The Dominican case offers an interesting example, where decommonisation was used to support local-level interests and a return to processes of commonisation involved efforts to rebalance those interests. In Mozambique, state-level decisions created regulatory space for future commonisation, while in Brazil, lower-level government representation pushed negotiation with state for redress of local interests.

Rules and rights

Property regimes reflect a level of social complexity that intersects directly with rules around collective action and the governance processes that give rise to those property rights regimes. In all four cases, the implementation of rules were key drivers of commonisation by reshaping rights. In Mozambique, for instance, the Land Law created hybridized rights system that recognised competing economic and local interests. Paradoxically, this set the conditions that enabled decommonisation and created regulatory space for future commonisation. Similarly, in Pakistan, the rules around contracts for lagoon access drove decommonisation but then the return to the license system catalysed commonisation with legislation developed to protect rights of Indigenous communities.

In all four cases, rights were highly dynamic social elements during commonisation processes. The experience in Pakistan is a particularly clear example of how, during commonisation, bundles of rights are separated, shifted, and reconfigured. Here, the earlier licensing system included access and withdrawal rights for Indigenous fishing communities, management rights to local fishing cooperatives, while retaining rights of alienation with local and state governments. The emergence of the contract system, however, transferred the rights of access, withdrawal, and management to the contract holders only, creating significant negative externalities on local users, particularly when these were consolidated in the hands of the Rangers.

The same dynamic social elements largely hold true in the other cases as well. For example, in Mozambique, commonisation involved collective land rights in the context of the socialist political and economic regime pre-civil war. However, decommonisation involved concurrent claims over property and private ownership which reduced access to a wide range of small farmers, reconfiguring the original rights regime in significant ways. Finally, in the Brazil case, the traditional resource use and withdrawal rights that associated with the emergence of the MPA were lost through processes of decommonisation. Through the establishment of the "Commitment Term", some of those rights were returned, illustrating a partial reversal.

Power and discursive practices

The influence of power in shaping commonisation and decommonisation processes are reflected throughout different aspects of the cases, and the implications are often significant. In Dominica, for example, privately owned FADs not only excluded other fishers, but conversely in the process of commonisation, the source of this economic power was reduced and perceived as punishment for local ingenuity and initiative. And in Mozambique, while the Land Law was originally established to support local communities, private investors became more powerful and influenced access and use of common resource. Investors with capital were privileged by government. Ultimately, the effect of these decommonisation processes is often to weaken the capacity for future commonisation efforts (even as windows of opportunity arise to do so), and to influence the perceived legitimacy of governance arrangements and actors that have catalysed or augmented these processes.

Manifestations of visible power (Raik et al. 2008) and its effects on commonisation are evident in each of the cases. Indeed, the positioning of new actors with capacity, status and power catalysed and shaped new commonisation processes where actors with financial capacity shaped particular economic interests and in so doing became catalysts for decommonisation. For example, in Mozambique, this includes the World Bank and International Monetary Fund with structural adjustment programs (SAPs) that create the institutional and regulatory conditions that catalyse decommonisation through the privatisation of resources. In Dominica, agent-centered power is visible in the form of a partnership with the Japanese International Cooperation Agency (JICA) that had a significant influence on the delivery and programming associated with the implementation of FADs. In the absence of clear rules of access, withdrawal and management, as well as collaborative actor networks, this situation contributed to decommonisation. As a counter-example, in Pakistan, the position of civil society groups with status and power advanced local interests in a process of commonisation, and in Brazil, new actors (i.e., federal prosecutors) became involved as a part of conditional commonisation associated with the Commitment Term.

Discursive practices reflect a less visible form of power that shape conditions for commonisation, and the motivations for particular initiatives. Discourse about governance has direct implications for processes of decommonisation and commonisation (e.g., privatisation, efficiency) and can be used to justify or promote certain interventions. Discursive power likely has a role in shaping commonisation, although we have not specifically undertaken an analysis of the discursive practices in each case. For example, in Mozambique the discourse around private investors has played a role in privileging certain actions that have contributed to decommonisation, while in Pakistan, the discourse around the Rangers accords them certain rights and privileges not granted to other less prestigious actors.

Conclusion

This chapter developed and applied an initial framework to consider the role of governance in the commonisation processes in coastal systems. Cases from Brazil, Mozambique, Dominica and Pakistan have provided the empirical context for our analysis. Drawing on these diverse cases, we have highlighted some of the features of governance that shape the pathways of commonisation and their implications for people and ecosystems.

There are challenges, however, when seeking to understand commonisation across these cases. For example, it is hard to explicitly characterise and compare the commonisation processes involved because the historical antecedents and contexts of each case are unique. As well, we have made specific choices about our temporal and spatial point of entry for analysis in each case, and those choices influence how we interpret governance events and their outcomes. Other entry points (e.g., a different institutional change or natural event) would influence what insights we gain from these cases.

Nevertheless, there are some broad observations that we can develop about the influence of governance on commonisation and decommonisation processes. As noted above, the cases do not share the same pattern of change. Yet, in all four cases commonisation involved disruptive periods with new forms of governance characterised by expanded networks of actors. The outcome was more complicated social processes and "messier" contexts. For example, in three cases (Mozambique, Dominica, and Pakistan), commonisation co-emerged with new institutions, sometimes replacing customary ones or strengthening weak ones. This expansion exists when commonisation involved attempts to return to old institutions. This is most distinct in the Brazilian case, in which commonisation involved an attempt to return to an institutional context that existed before de-commonisation. However, the social context in governance had changed and old institutions came with new and contradictory interpretations, suggesting that commonisation cannot be used to turn back time and it often comes with transaction costs. Once rights are lost through decommonisation, getting them back is challenging. In all four cases, then, we observed that "rights" (i.e., property rights) were the currency around which, and from which, power was expressed. The struggle for rights and by extension, access to natural resources and traditional livelihoods represented a difficult reality in processes of commonisation. As these insights reveal, governance emerges in the process of commonisation in two important ways. The first is when governance involves unorganised networks of diverse actors that can exert power to enjoy rights in the absence of strong rules. The second is when governance involves the coordination of actor networks, strategies and power to bring about change, typically during rule-making processes that shape the distribution of rights.

Our analysis here has been normative, and we are interested in understanding the governance attributes that support pathways for transformative change and sustainable social-ecological outcomes in coastal commons. As reflected in these cases, those pathways must be informed by the dynamic experiences with commonisation specific to each case. However, by focusing on the actors, rights and rules, and the practices that shape power, a better understanding of the role of governance in commonisation is possible. Commonisation is a process and periods of decommonisation and commonisation are inevitable. However, by understanding the role of actors, rights, rules and power, we can begin to better interpret these processes and their implications for people and their environments.

References

Ayers, A. L., J. N. Kittinger, and M. B. Vaughan. (2018). Whose right to manage? Distribution of property rights affects equity and power dynamics in comanagement. *Ecology and Society*, 23(2), 37. https://doi.org/10.5751/ES-10124-230237

Armitage, D. (2008). Governance and the commons in a multi-level world. *International Journal of the Commons*, 2(1), 7–32.

Armitage D., Charles T., Berkes F. (Eds.) (2017) Governing the Coastal Commons: Communities, Resilience and Transformation. New York: Routledge.

Barry, D. and Meinzen-Dick, R. (2008). The Invisible Map: Community Tenure Rights. Paper presented at the 12th Conference of the International Association for the Study of the Commons (IASC), Cheltenham, UK, 27 pages.

Bavinck, M., Berkes, F., Charles, A., Dias, A. C. E., Doubleday, N., Nayak, P. and Sowman, M. (2017). The impact of coastal grabbing on community conservation – a global reconnaissance. *Maritime Studies*, 16(1), 8.

Berkes, F. (2010). Devolution of environment and resources governance: Trends and future. *Environmental Conservation*, 37(4), 489–500. http://dx.doi.org/10.1017/S037689291000072X

Biermann, F., Betsill M. M., Gupta, J. et al. (2009). Earth system governance: People, places and the planet. Science and implementation plan of the earth system governance project, ESG Report No. 1. Bonn, IHDP: The Earth System Governance Project.

Blythe, J., Flaherty, M. and Murray, G. (2015). Vulnerability of coastal livelihoods to shrimp farming: Insights from Mozambique. *Ambio*, 44, 275–284.

Blythe, J., Silver, J., Evans, L., Armitage, D., Bennett, N. J., Moore, M. L., ... & Brown, K. (2018). The dark side of transformation: Latent risks in contemporary sustainability discourse. *Antipode*, 50(5), 1206–1223.

Bridge, G. and Perreault, T. (2009). Environmental governance. In: N. Castree, D. Demeritt, D. Liverman, B. Rhoads (eds.) *A Companion to Environmental Geography*. Hoboken, NJ: Blackwell. 475–497.

Chilundo, A., Cau, M. B., Malauene, D. and Muchanga, V. (2005). Land registration in Nampula and Zambezia provinces (Research Report 6). London: International Institute for Environment and Development.

Creed, J. C., Pires, D. O. and Figueiredo, M. A. O. (Org.) (2007). Biodiversidade marinha da Baía da Ilha Grande. Biodiversidade 23, Brasília: MMA / SBF 417p.

Dias, A. C. E. (2015). Fisheries participatory monitoring at Tarituba Community, Paraty (Brazil): Reconciling conservation and small-scale fisheries (Masters Dissertation), University of Campinas, Brazil. Retrieved from: http://repositorio.unicamp.br/bitstream/REPOSIP/315833/1/Dias_AnaCarolinaEstevesM.pdf

Edwards, V. M. and Steins, N. A. (1999). A framework for analyzing contextual factors in common pool resource research. *Journal of Environmental Policy and Planning*, 1, 205–221.

Fabricius, C., Koch, E., Magome, H. and Turner, S., (eds.). (2004). *Rights, Resources and Rural Development: Community-Based Natural Resource Management in Southern Africa*. London: Earthscan.

FAO. (2013). *Development of a Sub-Regional Strategy for Improving Biosecurity in the Sub-Regional Countries of the Mozambique Channel.* Rome. Food and Agricultural Organization.

Folke, C., Hahn, T., Olsson, P. and Norberg, J. (2005). Adaptive governance of social-ecological systems. *Annual Review of Environment and Resources*, 30, 441–473.

Hall, P. A. and Taylor, R. C. R. (1996). Political science and the three institutionalisms. *Political Studies*, XLIV, 936–957.

Hanazaki, N., Berkes, F., Seixas, C. S. and Peroni, N. (2013). Livelihood diversity, food security and resilience among the Caiçara of coastal Brazil. *Human Ecology*, 41, 152–164.

Holling, C. S. and Meffe, G. K. 1996. Command and control and the pathology of natural resource management. Conservation Biology, 10(2), 328–337.

Holt, F. L. (2005). The catch-22 of conservation: Indigenous peoples, biologists and cultural change. *Human Ecology*, 33, 199–215.

Kanji, N., Braga, C. and Mitullah, W. (2002). *Promoting Land Rights in Africa: How do NGOs make a difference?* London: IIED.

Larson, A. M. and Soto, F. (2008). Decentralization of natural resource governance regimes. *Annual Review of Environment and Resources*, 33, 213–239.

Lemos, M. C. and Agrawal A. (2006). Environmental governance. *Annual Review of Environment and Resources*, 31, 297–325.

Lebel, L. (2012). Governance and coastal boundaries in the tropics. *Current Opinion in Environmental Sustainability*, 4(2), 243–251.

Nayak, P. K. and F. Berkes. (2011). Commonisation and decommonisation: Understanding the processes of change in Chilika Lagoon, India. *Conservation and Society*, 9, 132–145.

Nielsen, R. L., Tanner, C. and Knox, A. (2011). Mozambique's innovative land law. Focus on Land in Africa, Program Brief.

North, D. C. (1990). Institutions, Institutional Change and Economic Performance. Cambridge: Cambridge University Press.

Ostrom, E. (1990). *Governing the Commons: The Evolution of Institutions for Collective Action.* Cambridge: Cambridge University Press.

Ostrom, E. 2000. Collective action and the evolution of social norms. The Journal of Economic Perspectives. 14(3): 137–158. www.jstor.org/stable/2646923

Pitcher, M. A. (2002). *Transforming Mozambique: The Politics of Privatisation, 1975–2000.* Cambridge: Cambridge University Press.

Raik, D. B., Wilson, A. L., Decker, D. J. 2008. Power in natural resources management: An application of theory. *Society and Natural Resource*, 21, 729–739.

Ribot, J. C. and Peluso, N. L. (2003). *A theory of access. Rural Sociology*, 68(2), 153–181. http://dx.doi.org/10.1111/j.1549-0831.2003.tb00133.x

Ribot, J. C., Agrawal, A. and Larson, A. M. (2006). Recentralizing while decentralizing: How national governments reappropriate forest resources. *World Development*, 34, 1864–1886.

Roe, E. M. 1991. Development narratives, or making the best of blueprint development. World Development 19(4), 287–300. https://doi.org/10.1016/0305-750X(91)90177-J

Schlager, E. and E. Ostrom. (1992). Property-rights regimes and natural resources: A conceptual analysis. *Land Economics*, 68(3), 249–262. http://dx.doi.org/10.2307/3146375

Seixas, C. S., Dias, A. C. E. and De Freitas, R. R. (2017). Navigating adaptive co-management in Paraty, Brazil: Winds, turbulence, and progress. In: D. Armitage, A. Charles and F. Berkes (eds.). *Governing the Coastal Commons: Communities, Resilience and Transformations* (pp. 157–180). London: Routledge/Earthscan.

Sikor, T. and C. Lund. (2009). Access and property: A question of power and authority. *Development and Change*, 40(1), 1–22.

Wasim, M. P. (2007). Issues, growth and instability of inland fish production in Sindh (Pakistan): Spatial–temporal analysis. *Pakistan Economic and Social Review*, 45(2), 203–230.

Young, O. R., King, L. A. and Schroeder, H. (2008). *Institutions and Environmental Change*. Cambridge, MA, and London, UK: MIT Press.

Chapter 16

Commonisation–decommonisation perspective

Lessons for practice, policy and theory

Prateep Kumar Nayak

Introduction

The individual chapter contributions in this book focus on various issues and dynamics associated with the processes of commonisation and decommonisation. Some focus more on commonisation trends while a few others talk about the drivers and outcomes of decommonisation. A number of chapters provide hope by outlining novel ways to respond to decommonisation, and to engage in a process of commonisation, suggesting that these processes can be parallel. The authors use a variety of terms to articulate these processes of reengaging in commonisation, discussed further later in this chapter.

The next section provides an analytical summary of each chapter and draws important lessons for our understanding of commonisation and decommonisation processes in a wide variety of commons contexts. The lessons are based on the chapter authors' attempt to respond to the five questions set out in Chapter 1: (1) What factors cause or contribute to the processes of commonisation and decommonisation? (2) What are some of the impacts and major trends emerging from these processes? (3) What is being done by the communities and the governments to sustain commonisation and respond to decommonisation? (4) What lessons for practice, policy and theory of commons governance can be learnt from our experience with commonisation and decommonisation, with particular reference to resulting threats from the privatisation of commons (enclosures) (5) How can these lessons be used to maintain "commons as commons" in the face of growing challenges from extreme social and environmental changes, with particular attention to strengthening community-based commons governance.

Synthesis and key insights

What do the chapters say about commonisation-decommonisation?

Each chapter summary and the key insights resulting from it are presented by section. Three chapters focus on *decommonisation* to provide details on processes through which a jointly used resource under commons institutions loses their essential characteristics of excludability and subtractability. Four chapters take on the theme of *commonisation* to explore processes through which a resource gets converted into a jointly used resource under commons institutions and collective action that deal with excludability and subtractability, building on the Chapter 1 discussion of these concepts. The original definitions, conceptual framing and essential characteristics of commonisation and decommonisation have been outlined in Nayak and Berkes (2011). Six chapters exclusively focus on the *commonisation and decommonisation as two-way feedback and parallel processes*, with multiple possibilities around either making or breaking the commons. These chapters engage in a thorough examination of how it is possible that some elements of the commons can undergo commonisation whereas other aspects of the same commons may remain subject to decommonisation challenges. Two chapters, including this one, offer *governance perspectives and lessons* on managing commons as a dynamic process and the ingredients required to promote commonisation and ward off the challenges posed by decommonisation.

All chapters in the book respond, in some form or other, to the complexity linked to how commoners continuously grapple with excludability and subtractability challenges (Ostrom 1990). Questions about who is included and who is excluded from the commons, especially given the historical connections of potential users, is not easy to determine. Similarly, maintaining a set of rules around distribution and allocation of benefits, while ensuring that use by one user does not affect resource availability for others, is often equally perplexing. Therefore, in dealing with the two characteristics of excludability and subtractability, the chapters respond to the core challenge of maintaining commons as a commons, which is understood as "those resources in which exclusion of beneficiaries through physical and institutional means is especially costly, and exploitation by one user reduces resource availability for others" (Ostrom et al. 1999: 278).

The chapters aim to provide clarity on the excludability/subtractability conundrum (see Chapter 1) by offering empirical evidence on the perspective of commons as a process. Both commonisation and decommonisation are discussed as processes along a continuum that is potentially two-way and iterative due to the influence of the prevailing social, cultural, economic, ecological and political histories and traditions shaping the context and the influences of various drivers of change (Nayak and Berkes 2014). The chapters expose multiple possible scenarios with regard to commonisation-decommonisation processes. First, any resource can enter into a process of commonisation. Second, established commons, or resources that have been commonised, could also revert back to decommonisation. Third, commons can go through a parallel process of commonisation and decommonisation. Fourth, commonisation-decommonisation challenges can be talked through appropriate governance mechanisms that are reflected in the principles, institutions and interactions pertaining to how decisions are made about the commons.

Chapters focusing on the roots of decommonisation

Patricia Dorn and Simron Jit Singh (Chapter 2 on *The Dynamics and Performance of Marine Tourism Commons (MTC) in the Karimunjawa Island Marine National Park, Indonesia*) provide a social-ecological systems perspective of commonisation and decommonisation processes linked to marine tourism based on their thorough study of the Karimunjawa Island Marine National Park, Indonesia. Marine tourism commons (MTC) have been referred to as a "new common-pool resource" which, therefore, help extend the analysis of commonisation and decommonisation to novel domains, both conceptually and in reality. Dorn and Singh's work in Karimunjawa has two thrusts. First, they engage in identifying the institutional and resource dynamics shaping Karimunjawa Marine Tourism Commons over a period of three decades (1982–2014). The processes of commonisation and decommonisation around the coral reef ecosystem of Karimunjawa are seen unfolding through four phases: Open-access and state property; Starting commonisation and privatisation; Struggling commonisation; and Decommonisation. Second, the authors conduct a detailed analysis of the fourth phase focusing on decommonisation (2012–ongoing), using Ostrom's social-ecological systems framework. This revealed that out of the more than 50 multitier variables, 30 pointed to weak institutional performance in the management of the coral reef, combined with the failing governance system, contributed to low commonisation and high decommonisation of the Karimunjawa marine tourism commons.

It is evident from the chapter that just within four decades, commons in Karimunjawa have gone from a centralised state-controlled regime to varying experiences of commonisation before quickly falling into the trap of decommonisation. Such a complex process, which we call commons, warrants an integrated analysis justified by a social-ecological systems approach that bring to treatment the resource units, resource system, users and governance system, all on the same platform.

Jeremy Pittman (Chapter 3 on *The Cascading Effects of Coastal Commonisation and Decommonisation*) introduces moving changes in the nature of coastal commons – sandy beaches and its use as tourist attractions – that is heavily influenced by competing demands on a single object (i.e., sand). While one set of interests pulls it towards being more of a commons through imposing principles of excludability and subtractability, an opposing set of interests pushes it towards a different type of use that suggests decommonisation. Pittman engages with this riddle through an exploratory case study of the Lesser Antilles – a group of islands in the Eastern Caribbean – that focuses on the (de)commonisation processes in the otherwise commonising sandy beaches. The first part of the story is about the desire and attempt by tourists and the tour operators to add exclusivity to the sandy beaches (historically known as public resources under collective use) by changing them to club resources that inhibits local access. The second part of the story brings in the booming construction industry, often linked to the increasing need for infrastructure support for the tourism sector, which promotes sand mining in the same beaches and riverbanks of the Islands. This tussle between competing interests for the sandy beaches in the Lesser Antilles adds to the already complex processes of commonisation, triggers decommonisation and exposes numerous governance challenges. One party values the "space" (and aesthetics) within the coastal commons, sandy beaches in this case, and the other sees the "object" (i.e., sand) within the same space. One is focused on the intangible, non-material benefits of a collective space, while the other is hooked on to the benefits that lie in its material and tangible outcomes. How do we tackle this "looming tragedy"?

Coastal commons around the world are undergoing transformations in the face of pressures and change. We learn from the analysis by Pittman that the pressures experienced by these commons or collective spaces would benefit from creative adjustments to the governance regimes and prepare them to manage potentially deleterious effects, as well as taking advantage of opportunities. Points to highlight include a thorough understanding of what makes these spaces a commons in the first place, followed by a systematic understanding of the forces that drive decommonisation, the nitty-gritty about how decommonisation actually progresses once it sets in, the varying levels of impact, and prospects of multi level and multisectoral governance in responding to challenges.

Vipul Singh (Chapter 4 on *Governing Fluvial Commons in Colonial Bihar: Alluvion and Diluvion Regulation and Decommonisation*) alerts us to the crude politics that onsets and perpetuates decommonisation over centuries. His historical analysis of fluvial commons in the colonial Bihar of Eastern India known as *diara* land (i.e., seasonal cutting and deposition of soil in the riverbed customarily used as commons by local communities) provides a glimpse at the extremely long processes of commonisation and decommonisation that spans several centuries. Singh prefers to call the *diara* land "ephemeral commons" due to the frequent process of their seasonal disappearance and reappearance that had created equally transient dependencies by local communities. Consequently, these commons remained outside of any government and institutional control but also without any permanent land tenure system recognising local rights until the 1770 great famine in Bengal. This is when the colonial government of the British East India Company realised the huge loss of revenue from these hitherto unclaimed territories. By early 19th century, a centralised land revenue system was put in place through the Alluvion and Diluvion Regulation of 1825 in order to bring the fluvial *diara* land under permanent revenue settlement. This introduced decommonisation processes to the traditional management of these fluvial river commons. However, the ecological challenges associated with the ephemeral nature of these *diara* commons led to disputes and lawsuits related to land and fishing rights that were considered unprofitable by the colonial government. This brought a second wave of decommonisation as *diara* lands were leased out to the highest bidder, often being the Zamindars (i.e., feudal landlords) that continues to date in some form or the other.

What happens at a point of extreme decommonisation? What does a commons become at this stage? Singh's historical narratives suggest that life of commons, after the critical threshold of extreme decommonisation, often flips into a new regime characterised by centralisation, rent-seeking attitude, exploitation of the resource as well as the local people, through the mechanism of either state control or privatisation (de facto or de jure) or both. However, a way out of this mess may simply require legal restoration of the ephemeral land-river commons, along with recognition of customary rights through a bold reformulation of governance mechanisms. Such recognition is not necessarily problematic; it is not unfounded, given two centuries of historical evidence to support a vibrant process of commonisation in the *diara* lands (fluvial commons) of colonial Bihar in India. Singh warns that steps to recommonise are essential and in fact unavoidable.

What enables commonisation?

Eranga Kokila Galappaththi and Iroshani Madu Galappaththi (Chapter 5 on *Five Key Characteristics that Drive Commonisation: Empirical Evidence from Sri Lankan Shrimp Aquaculture*) take us to a new area of commons discussion by introducing the concept of aquaculture commons and providing concrete guidelines of what constitutes the key conditions for successful commonisation. Their case study is based in the interconnected Chilaw, Mundal, and Puttalam lagoon system in northwestern Sri Lanka which has a rich history of persistent aquaculture over a period of five decades. Following a detailed historical account of aquaculture development, Galappaththi and Galappaththi explain the root cause of strong commonisation in Sri Lankan shrimp aquaculture sector, i.e., collective response of the shrimp farmers to address challenges from shrimp disease by managing the interconnected lagoon system as a commons. It is important to note here that prior to this effort, shrimp aquaculture was conducted primarily as an individual ownership-based private business enterprise. Two measures were notable in contributing to implementing shrimp aquaculture commonisation in Sri Lanka. The first was the development of zonal crop calendar to manage shrimp diseases and its legalisation by the Ministry of Fisheries and Aquatic Resources Development in Sri Lanka. The crop calendar's main objective was to minimise the damage caused by shrimp diseases and to increase shrimp production. The second was the creation of a multi-layered institutional structure to manage a private-communal-state mixed management aquaculture regime but with the community-based institutions (known as Samithiya) at the core.

As explained elsewhere, commonisation and decommonisation are two faces of shrimp aquaculture management processes (Galappaththi and Nayak 2017). To better understand these processes, it is important to understand the conditions, characteristics and aspects that drive each face. Galappaththi and Galappaththi conclude with a set of five key characteristics of community-based shrimp aquaculture that can drive commonisation. They include (1) the existence of bottom-up multi-level institutions and a mixed commons governance regime, (2) collaboration and collective action among shrimp farmers who face uncertainty and share challenges, (3) partnerships and government support for the commons governance system, (4) adaptiveness throughout the commons governance process, and (5) effective networking and information sharing through community cooperatives. We learn from this chapter that adaptive variations of these conditions and characteristics can significantly contribute to commonisation and respond to decommonisation processes in similar contexts elsewhere.

Gabriela Lichtenstein and Carlos Cowan Ros (Chapter 6 on *Vicuña Conservation and the Reinvigoration of Indigenous Communities in the Andes*) apply the commonisation and decommonisation approach to the "herds of the Gods" – vicuñas, *Vicugna vicugna*, in the Puna and Altiplano high Andean ecoregions in Argentina, Bolivia, Chile, Ecuador and Peru, and turn our attention to the less-explored concept of wildlife commons. The authors clarify that "although vicuñas can be considered an 'uncommon' common-pool resource (CPR), they do exhibit the two principal commons characteristics of subtractability and excludability". From a rich history of communal management, vicuña commons of the Andes experienced piercing decommonisation verging near extinction following the Spanish Conquest in the Andean Region. However, subsequent commonisation efforts led by the indigenous communities have helped vicuña population to bounce back. Lichtenstein and Cowan Ros detail these processes of commonisation and (re)commonisation though, first, providing a historical background on the decommonisation process of vicuñas and their near extinction, and second, analysing their recent commonisation led by Indigenous communities and state agents at different levels of government in the province of Jujuy, Argentina. (Re)commonisation was achieved through a vicuña management programme developed in the Andes based on the key principles of community-based wildlife management and strong focus on local community institutions (i.e., cooperatives).

What are some of the enabling conditions to reverse decommonisation and put vicuña management in the Andes on the path of (re)commonisation? Lichtenstein and Cowan Ros identify a number of such enabling conditions linked to resource system characteristics, relatively low human population density, rules about inclusion and exclusion, social and economic factors, enabling legislation, land tenure, supportive government policies, strong cross-scale institutional linkages, and technological innovation. Vicuña (re)commonisation has created combined positive impacts through generating local income and local/regional development, ecosystem services via species and biodiversity conservation, and reinforced the opportunity to rearticulate ongoing Andean ethnic identities and to strengthen local cultural values.

Patricia E. (Ellie) Perkins (Chapter 7 on *Commoning and Climate Justice*) takes decommonisation and commonisation debate to the domain of global commons by focusing on climate and justice. Perkins elaborates on the possibility of replacing the notion of centralised, top-down, state-oriented and market-driven systems affecting the global climate through collective responses across local to global scales. Quoting Indigenous economist Ronald Trosper, Perkins argues that climate change touches every material and human element in this world and provides evidence that every life on this planet depends on a common-pool resource (the atmosphere) but in tandem with many other common-pool resources, such as freshwater, fisheries, and forests. It is evident that people depend upon these common-pool resources more than they think. Thus, Perkins examines two related questions in this chapter: How should people organise themselves when they depend upon a common-pool resource? How do we study examples where people have developed complex and productive systems around the commons?

This chapter uses several international examples of traditional and new forms of commons as responses to climate-related threats that are collective in nature. It provides preliminary empirical evidence about how and in what circumstances people may develop equitable communal institutions, rather than ones that cause community fragmentation. Perkins explains that commoning represents a dynamic and emergent means of risk-reduction and livelihood provision which can address the shortcomings of both market and state-oriented economic systems. Such an analysis is increasingly relevant as climate change threatens human subsistence worldwide. The indicators of commoning involves the communities' openness/boundaries, historical experiences and aptitudes with collective governance, social networks and social learning, political and economic interdependence, diversity, income distribution, and cultural factors. Perkins' chapter helps to explore indicators, preconditions, or opportunities for commoning processes with regard to climate justice and engages in exploring ways to reduce climate change fairly. A process of commoning involves building fair institutions that can help to "bring out the best in people".

Yolanda Lopez-Maldonado (Chapter 8 on *Understanding Groundwater Common Pool Resources: Commonisation and Decommonisation of Cenotes in Yucatan, Mexico*) examines the commons that lie beneath the earth – the groundwater commons. Lopez-Maldonado argues in favour of a move from hydrological sciences to integrated social-ecological perspectives to study how groundwater interacts with the social system in a dynamic manner.

There is a gap in the information about how societies develop and follow rules, norms and actions to access these hidden commons. A case study based on the Maya people of Yucatan is used as the foundation to provide social, ecological and management insights on groundwater over different time scales. Lopez-Maldonado uses the social-ecological systems framework by Ostrom to present a three-step analysis: First, she examines the groundwater social-ecological system in the Maya lands of Yucatan by focusing on the biophysical conditions of the groundwater basin, along with the social system including resource user dynamics. Second, she analyses the knowledge systems of groundwater users to explore values, beliefs and practices, along with processes of cultural transmission and the relationships between the users and their natural environment. Third, she applies the concepts of commonisation and decommonisation to make sense of the ongoing changes in the Yucatan groundwater social-ecological system.

The chapter suggests that decommonisation studies need to deal with at least three core challenges, including the task of combining the analysis of both historical and current management processes; use of a robust analytical framework to decipher the appropriate variables; and the integrative analysis of methods and tools to reverse the process of decommonisation.

Commonisation and decommonisation as parallel processes

Xavier Basurto and **Alejandro García Lozano** (Chapter 9 on *Commoning and the Commons as More-than-Resources: A Historical Perspective on Comcáac or Seri Fishing*) engage in a systematic re-thinking of the commons as commoning – a process and praxis that is embodied, ongoing and historically situated sets of relations between humans and nonhumans. The focus of this chapter is to outline the processes through which commons emerge, and factors that influence their formation and dissolution with specific reference to the Seri or Comcáac people in the Sonoran Desert of northwest Mexico. Basurto and Lozano skillfully document the dynamic and often contradictory processes that characterise the fishing commons in Comcáac territory, where ongoing processes of (de)commonisation are inevitably entangled with the material and non-material realities inherently related to the commons.

Using the case of the Comcáac, the chapter applies the concept of commoning (i.e., emphasis on relational understandings of commons with explicit focus on the commons as process and praxis) to reveal a diverse set of interrelated insights relevant to commonisation and decommonisation: First, creation of discrete conceptual categories are not a useful proposition if commons are to be seen as a process which is influenced by multiple tensions and complex socio-historical processes. Second, importance of scale that emphasise on the understanding of how processes of commonisation, decommonisation and commoning are embedded in broader contexts of national policies, discourses, and worldviews. Specific attention needs to be paid to the inherent contradictions resulting from the outcomes of collective action across multiple scales. Third, understanding commons as a process and praxis requires strong linkages with stories, narratives and verbal and non-verbal expressions that often shape collective action. Who is telling the story is important, so does the recognition that such discursive and symbolic dimensions are helpful in obtaining a deeper understanding of commons as ongoing process. Fourth, an emphasis on diverse relationships that captures both human and non human engagements in the commons space and processes. This will require an understanding of the ways in which commons institutions are embedded in and constituted through the evolving relations comprising human and non human entities.

In highlighting the process and practice oriented focus of commonisation and decommonisation, Basurto and Lozano argue that a real understanding of the commons starts with praxis being at the forefront of the analysis, and recognising the view that a commons needs to be practiced in order to become one.

Sherman Farhad (Chapter 10 on *Concurrent Processes of Commonisation and Decommonisation of Guadalquivir River South Spain*) brings an emphasis to the understanding of commonisation and decommonisation as parallel processes in which each one can influence how the other unfolds. The larger commons in this case is the Guadalquivir River in south-west Spain where Isla Mayor social-ecological system was studied. Key tenets of commonisation and decommonisation were observed in three interrelated activities that are dependent on the Guadalquivir River commons: rice cultivation, fishing, and tourism. While it is our general understanding that if commonisation and decommonisation are to happen, they would take place at the level of the entire Guadalquivir River commons. Farhad's findings point to different conclusions. In the case of Isla Mayor social-ecological system, improved multi-level governance strengthened commonisation of the river for rice cultivation. However, rice farming has created obstacles for the commonisation of the river for tourism. Further, adoption of new technology for rice cultivation along with multiple policy changes, government restrictions and modifications in fishing practices have created a pathway for decommonisation of the Guadalquivir River for fishing. As a result, part of the river commons is able to undergo a process of commonisation, while other aspects or activities based on the river became vulnerable to decommonisation. This suggests that commonisation in a particular area of the commons in question may simultaneously lead to decommonisation in its other aspects.

Learning from the experiences of rice farming in the Guadalquivir River commons, what will it take to create similar success in the tourism and fishing sectors to achieve an inclusive process of commonisation? The chapter highlights that the multiple faces of the commons require specific scholarly attention in order to understand conditions that push commons towards becoming "non-commons". In this unique case study, Farhad's analysis shows how commonisation and decommonisation can act as drivers for each other and contribute significantly to the shaping up of these processes. The many trade-offs and complementarities between commonisation and decommonisation processes need further examination. It is futile to study commonisation and decommonisation at the level of the entire commons system such as the Guadalquivir River because these processes run through the different commons in the same geographic area – rice cultivation, fishing, and tourism. A holistic and inclusive approach that pays equal attention to all aspects of a commons is necessary to understand commonisation and decommonisation processes. Commonisation and decommonisation analysis must include historical and current perspectives, and future directions.

Craig A. Johnson (Chapter 11 on *Creating a Commons for Global Climate Governance: Possibilities and Perils in the Paris Climate Agreement*) reflects on the likelihood of a global commons regime for collaborative climate governance related to the recent Paris Climate Agreement. The key motivation expressed by Johnson is to delve into the subject of whether the prospects created by the Agreement can be taken to its logical outcomes through a commons arrangement for governing global climate. He notes the significant shifts in the evolution of global climate governance from what was "previously a loose commitment to the principle of 'common but differentiated responsibilities' to a more comprehensive and 'global' effort ...". However, the vexed issue of excludability and subtractability raises a key question about the capacity and viability of the Agreement to create responses to climate change that are equitable, sustainable and transformational. Johnson engages in two areas of analysis including ways on how to strengthen the global climate regime, and possibilities and perils in the Paris Climate Agreement.

The chapter offers important insights on whether the Paris Agreement can lay the foundations for stronger forms of cooperation and global collective action by establishing a rule-based order that reduces uncertainty, offers diverse incentives and aligns multi-level interests to achieve the goal of addressing climate change. Two sets of competing ideas help further reflect on this topic: First, the idea that continuous interaction and engagement can create conditions for cooperation. Second, global collective action remains subject to an assemblage of multiscale political interests.

Daniel Klooster and **James Robson** (Chapter 12 on *Migration and the Commons: Re-Commonisation in Indigenous Mexico*) elaborate on the connections between migration and the commons, especially focusing on how migration creates novel opportunities for commoners to respond to the challenges posed by decommonisation. In many places migration is already intensifying the ongoing changes in the local resource base (i.e., declines in agriculture, increase in rural-urban linkages, changes in livelihoods) and demographic patterns (i.e., disproportionate change in fertility levels and life expectancy, rise in nuclear families, shrinking rural population, elderly-dominated rural communities). While the most general view has been that migration separates the commoners physically, materially and mentally from the commons, possibility of migration engaging the commoners in novel ways to maintain their previous relationships with the commons has remained largely unaddressed. Klooster and Robson untangle this particular notion through a case study of Zapotec and Chinantec Indigenous communities in Oaxaca's Sierra Norte (northern highlands) region, Mexico. They investigate key implications of migration for traditional communal territories in Oaxaca and make explicit the many ways that commoners are working to defend, re-shape, and re-build their commons.

Migration and associated rural changes create physical and mental separation between the commons and the commoners, replace their livelihood dependences, disrupt livelihoods, disorganise the place-based social relationships and shared norms, and impact the commoners' incentive to engage in the commons. These factors signify the onset of decommonisation processes. However, this chapter provides glowing evidence of how the commoners in Oaxaca have "avoided an outcome of decommonisation, and have instead engaged in a process of re-commonisation involving new uses of the commons and the crafting of novel rules establishing the rights and obligations of migrant commoners". Here, decommonisation pressures have been met with re-commonisation responses through structural, normative and functional readjustments undertaken by the actions of the commoners, i.e., renewing territorial use, re-working the membership rules, re-considering norms, and continuing to address ongoing stress from the changes in the commons. The prospect of re-commonisation creates opportunities for the commons to become an active and continuous process in the face of adverse environmental and social change.

Villamayor-Tomás and **García-López** (Chapter 13 on *Decommonisation-Commonisation Dynamics and Social Movements: Insights from a Meta-Analysis of Case Studies*) use social movements as a cause of commonisation and an effect of decommonisation in community-based natural resource management contexts. While excessive decommonisation potentially triggers social movements, commonisation can result from the mobilising effects of these movements. This particular construct is examined through a meta-analysis of case studies, i.e., 78 references from literature reporting about 81 cases, 1989–2017, where commons communities have mobilised against challenges posed by decommonisation. Three interrelated areas of analysis provide clarity on the multiple linkages between decommonisation, commonisation and social movements. First, a large set of decommonisation drivers, a total of 16 reported in the chapter, provide insights on the processes of commons disintegration. These drivers represent resource management and economic policies, encroachment and de facto privatisation by internal and external users, and entrenched legacies of historical, political and rights regimes. Second, 11 impacts of decommonisation in the areas of livelihoods, resource rights, externalities and status of community asset expose the implications of decommonisation. However, these impacts also influence the practices of commons communities and motivate them to respond through social movements. Third, the authors find 17 commonisation pathways through which social movements enable commons communities to respond to decommonisation and contribute to commonisation. The identified pathways broadly include: defense of communal rights and territories; promotion of economic autonomy; strengthening of human capital; improvement in community decision making; enhancement in community litigation response capacities; and promotion of community organisation.

Through the analytical description of the decommonisation drivers and their impacts, and commonisation pathways, the chapter provides some answers to a set of questions: (1) At what level of decommonisation communities begin to mobilise and resort to social movements. (2) What are the key elements of commonisation that signify a reversal in the ongoing decommonising effects? (3) What other factors work with social movements in addressing decommonisation and promoting commonisation? Answers to these questions help illustrate that resulting impacts of decommonisation drivers constitute, in many cases, the motivation for commons communities to mobilise and participate in social movements. It highlights that the success of commons depends on the capacity of the commoners to mobilise against external threats through participation in social movements. The continuum of commonisation-decommonisation is maintained through the invocation of social movements by the commons-dependent communities.

Shah Raees Khan and **C. Emdad Haque** (Chapter 14 on *Decommonisation and New-Commonisation of Mountain Commons in Northern Pakistan*) take us to the Shimshal and Naltar Valley in northern Pakistan to provide a snapshot of mountain community responses in the face of growing threats from decommonisation of their forest and pasture commons, primarily through imposition of state-controlled Protected Areas. They delve into the question "how to retain commons as commons at a time when they are being decommonised through top-down state control and interventions". To that effect, they focus on the process of transformations of the commons in northern Pakistan to examine the dynamic features of mountain commons, local commons management systems, use of customary norms, rules and regulations and how they were adversely impacted by the establishment of a Protected Area system. While many commons around the world have reportedly succumbed to such threats and regulatory changes, the findings from Northern Pakistan mountain commons reflect hope and promise.

The chapter provide an overview of what happens when these remote mountain commons face challenges of decommonisation. Do they survive? Or do they fall into the endless trap of losing their key characteristics of being a commons? Kahn and Haque present intriguing findings from their study to conclude that these remote mountain communities have taken recourse to a brand new approach that they call new-commonisation. They define the term new-commonisation as a process through which resources get converted into a jointly used regime or transform into a new arrangement of creating "conservancies"; that is, with more refined rules and a management system, the resource use and protection, as well as the traditional practices and values (Khan, 2012). Here, the commoners have chosen to work with the government in transforming local commons institutions into formally recognised institutions and successfully retain the traditional commons to defend their customary rights regime. Thus, new-commonisation provides new energy to the otherwise threatened commons arrangements to revive and restore but, at the same time, also strives to retain the traditional, customary and historical norms and practices in the effort to maintain commons as commons as if it is a process. This exemplifies the novelty in the ways commoners engage in the commons in nurturing commonisation and responding to decommonisation processes.

Derek Armitage and **colleagues** (Chapter 15 on *Governance and the Process of (De)Commonisation*) wrap up the discussion on commonisation and decommonisation by linking it with governance – the means through which societies make decisions about their own affairs. Whether it is about nurturing a process of active commonisation or responding to the undesirable effects of decommonisation, the role of governance has been described in this chapter as an essential element for success in the commons. Armitage and colleagues pursue this through a three-step systematic analysis. First, they construct a working framework to connect governance and (de)commonisation, and propose a pathway for transformative changes in the commons. The framework includes three dimensions: network of actors across scales; bundle of rights along with rules and rule-making system; and power and discursive practices, all drawn from broad areas of governance and commons theory. Second, the framework is applied to present four case studies from Brazil, Mozambique, Dominica and Pakistan, all representing coastal social-ecological systems (commons). Third, lessons learnt are captured as insights for possible governance pathways supporting commonisation, and their implications for people and ecosystems.

However, governance pathways to commonisation is not straightforward and cannot be considered a blueprint. There are obvious challenges based on historical influences and context specificities that can make the process of seeking commonisation dynamic and decommonisation a stark reality. Nonetheless, governance stands as an inclusive concept with its broad focus on processes, principles, institutions, and interactions that can steer societies along particular trajectories or pathways for sustaining the commons. Armitage and colleagues rightly argue that "governance is already a part of the processes we refer to here as commonisation and de-commonisation". The chapter, however, reminds us that commonisation is a process, a means, and not an end in itself. In the real world, periods of de-commonisation and commonisation are inevitable.

Many faces of commonisation and decommonisation

The processes of commonisation and decommonisation may have multiple manifestations, which motivated the chapter authors to frame these terms in different ways (Table 16.1). Commonisation and decommonisation processes are about putting in place well-defined rules around excludability and subtractability. The negotiations to address contestations happen through the coming and working together of people within the non-human context, which is defined as a process of *commoning* (Basurto and Lozano, 2021; Perkins, 2021). The human actors who actively engage in the commoning processes can be seen as the *commoners* and they also play crucial roles during pressures from decommonisation (Klooster and Robson, 2021). Extreme forms of decommonisation forces the commons to suffer significant loss of excludability and subtractability characteristics turning them into *non-commons* (Farhad, 2021). However, decommonisation is pervasive and deeply entrenched. There is no particular moment in the development of commons which can be ascribed to the triggering of decommonisation. The commoners in many places around the world have used decommonisation as opportunity to strengthen commonisation. This reinforcement of commonisation in the face of decommonisation threats has been discussed as *re-commonisation, (re)commonisation* and *new-commonisation* (Klooster and Robson, 2021; Armitage et al., 2021; Lichtenstein and Cowan Ros, 2021; Khan and Haque, 2021). Success in this type of commonisation (re- and new-commonisation) can bring in place *new common-pool resources* (Dorn and Singh, 2021).

It is important to understand the ways in which commoners respond to decommonisation challenges and impacts. Decommonisation processes can proceed in parallel with commonisation. Singh (2021) reports that in certain contexts the very resource around which commonisation and decommonisation processes revolve often remains elusive, leading to the suggestion that they are *ephemeral commons*. As an extension of the meaning of ephemeral commons, Lichtenstein and Cowan Ros (2021) use the term *"uncommon" common-pool resource* to explain unusual resources, e.g., vicuñas (*Vicugna vicugna*) that have come to be managed as commons.

Seeing the commons as a process

Commons are known as places of continuous interaction between people and nature. Elements of commons that may appear to be stable at one time and place may be subject to change at another. These changes are influenced by economic, social, ecological and political factors across multiple scales. The dynamic nature of the commons may manifest as adaptation and fine-tuning

Table 16.1 Multiple ways in which commonisation-decommonisation processes are explained

Perspectives	Description/Definition
Commoning	Describes the constant coming together of humans with(in) their broader milieu, and can be understood as a constantly changing and evolving relationality between humans, nonhumans, their territories and histories, and the forging of subjectivities that ultimately give meaning to issues such as tenure, substractability and excludability. (Basurto and Lozano, Chapter 9)
Commoning	Largely depends on sharing well-governed common-pool resources and works best when giving is respected and socially rewarded so that there can be "reciprocity between what is given and what is taken". (Perkins, Chapter 7)
Commoners/ Absent Commoners	Are users that are engaging in processes and actions to defend, re-shape, and re-build their commons by managing social practices in the face of parallel economic and demographic changes. (Klooster and Robson, Chapter 12)
Non-Commons	Distortions in governance configurations and social organisations, which are subject to change over time, leading to situations where governance and institutional arrangements are unable to facilitate long-term conservation of resources as commons. (Farhad, Chapter 10)
Re-Commonisation	Takes place where the commoners have able to avoid an outcome of de-commonisation, and have instead engaged in a process of re-commonisation involving new uses of the commons and the crafting of novel rules establishing the rights and obligations of commoners. (Klooster and Robson, Chapter 12)
Re-Commonisation	Happens when governance attributes that support pathways for transformative change and sustainable social-ecological outcomes in the commons replace features of decommonisation, i.e., when governance involves the coordination of actor networks, strategies and power to bring about change, typically during rule-making processes that shape the distribution of rights in the face of decommonisation. (Armitage et al., Chapter 15)
(Re) commonisation	A process through which the real threats of decommonisation (e.g., global market influence and commodification of the commons) are replaced by processes of commonisation through the reshaping of ancient knowledge, traditions and local forms of production, and re-connecting local communities with one another and the natural world and the life within it. (Lichtenstein and Cowan Ros, Chapter 6)

(continued)

Table 16.1 Cont.

Perspectives	Description/Definition
New-Commonisation	Refers to a process through which resources get converted into a jointly used resources or transform into a new arrangement such as creating "conservancies"; that is, with more refined rules and a management system, complementing the resource use and protection, as well as building synergy with the traditional practices and values. (Khan and Haque, Chapter 14)
New Common-Pool Resource	Refers to a process when a social-ecological system experiences a changing set of resource regimes replacing historical experiences of decommonisation and help the SES undergo a dynamic new institutional process. (Dorn and Singh, Chapter 2)
Ephemeral Commons	Situation in which the very natural process through which a resource commons is created leads to ecologically ephemeral territories and associated instabilities and uncertainties in the life of the community dependent on it.
	Ephemeral commons go through cyclical and frequent processes of creation and dissolution that devoid it of acquiring any permanent character and allows it to retain only temporary nature through frequent changes. (Singh, Chapter 4)
"Uncommon" Common-Pool Resource	Although generally not seen as commons these resources do exhibit the two principal characteristics of excludability and subtractability. (Lichtenstein and Cowan Ros, Chapter 6)

over time or may result in the replacement of one kind of rights and access regime by another. As a result, it is imperative to understand commons as a process and not as a final configuration.

The notion of commonisation and decommonisation highlights the process aspect of commons. Chapter 1 clarifies that commonisation is understood as a process through which a resource gets converted into a jointly used resource under commons institutions and collective action that deal with excludability and subtractability. Decommonisation refers to a process through which a jointly used resource under commons institutions loses these essential characteristics (Nayak and Berkes 2011). Excludability and subtractability characteristics are at the core of the commons being a dynamic and complex process. Excludability pertains to the question of who is and who is not a legitimate user of a resource (question of exclusion and inclusion). Subtractability deals with the rules of resource distribution and allocation among the users, without which exploitation by one user will reduce resource availability for others (Ostrom 1990). The kind of questions both excludability and subtractability principles seek to engage make them indisputably continuous, and force them to stay open for discussion, negotiation and possible resolution, without any definite endpoint.

As the case examples in the chapters show, there are a great variety of property-rights regimes within which commons may be held, a crucial aspect of commonisation and decommonisation processes. However, there are only four kinds of "pure" property-rights regimes – open-access, private-property, common-property, and state-property (Bromley 1992). Arguably, all different types of property regimes can provide viable conditions for commons. However, the question about which type of property regime is most viable for a given context is subject to contestations and, therefore, not easily discernible. As highlighted in Chapter 1, a given regime may provide a better match for a particular resource at a particular time and place, but none of the regimes is considered intrinsically superior to any other. In practice, many resources are held in overlapping combinations of these regimes (Bromley 1992; Dietz et al. 2003; Ostrom 2005). In many situations this is related to the ever-changing nature of commons. This leads to the necessity of a process-oriented approach.

The process dimension of commons is further emphasised through a range of interdisciplinary approaches used to analyse the processes of commonisation and decommonisation. First, the social-ecological systems perspective defines commons as complex systems of humans and nature (Berkes et al. 2003; Ostrom 2009). Second, commons are intensely contested domains and highly political spaces (Johnson 2004; Nayak and Berkes 2008). Third, commons inherently include the questions of justice, fairness and equity pertaining both to distribution of benefits and the procedures surrounding it. Fourth, commons success largely depends on institutional and governance arrangements (Ostrom 1990, 2005). Here, key principles of partnership, collaboration, trust, power-sharing, institution-building, social learning, problem-solving and good governance strongly influence commonisation and decommonisation processes and outcomes (Armitage et al. 2007; Berkes 2007). Fifth, sense of place and stewardship help build strong foundation of a commons and equip commoners to respond to commonisation and decommonisation challenges.

Commonisation and decommonisation focus primarily on processes of change in the commons, and the implications for how commons can be governed as commons in the long run. A renewed focus on understanding the process aspect of commons is novel. New approaches must be crafted to better anticipate and respond to the crisis in the commons that are linked to decommonisation and ensure their sustainability through commonisation. Even though there has been relevant literature, none explicitly dealt with commons as a process and provided a conceptual framework to examine it. The attempt in this book is to fill this gap. The challenges confronting the commons cannot be resolved through incremental change in conventional practices and approaches (Armitage et al. 2017). As a result, deliberate and novel approaches are required to govern the commons towards sustainability. *Making Commons Dynamic* addresses this gap by putting forward the commonisation-decommonisation framework as an analytical tool to examine multiple possibilities around making or breaking the commons. Novel problems require novel responses, and much remains to be done. The challenge of keeping commons as commons is real, and understanding the commons as a process through the lens of commonisation and decommonisation is only a beginning.

References

Armitage, D., Andrews, E. J., Blythe, J., Dias, A. C. E., Nayak, P. K., Pittman, J. and Sultana, S. (2021). Governance and the process of (de)commonisation. In: P. K. Nayak (Ed.). *Framing commons as a process: The rudiments of commonisation and decommonisation.* London and New York: Routledge.

Armitage, D., Berkes, F. and Doubleday, N. (2007). *Adaptive co-management: Collaboration, learning and multi-level governance.* Vancouver: University of British Columbia Press.

Armitage, D., Charles, A., Berkes, F. (Eds.) (2017). *Governing the coastal commons: Communities, resilience and transformation.* London/New York: Earthscan/ Routledge.

Basurto, X. and Lozano, A. G. (2021). Commoning and the commons as more-than-resources: A historical perspective on Comcáac or Seri fishing. In: P. K. Nayak (Ed.). *Framing commons as a process: The rudiments of commonisation and decommonisation.* London and New York: Routledge.

Berkes, F. (2007). Community-based conservation in a globalized world. *Proceedings of the National Academy of Sciences,* 104, 15188–15193.

Berkes, F., Colding, J. and Folke, C. (Eds.). (2003). *Navigating social-ecological systems: Building resilience for complexity and change.* Cambridge: Cambridge University Press.

Bromley, D. W. (Ed.) (1992). *Making the commons work: Theory, practice, and policy.* San Francisco: ICS Press.

Dietz, T., Ostrom, E. and Stern, P. (2003). The struggle to govern the commons. *Science,* 302, 1907–1912.

Dorn, P. and Singh, S. J. (2021). The dynamics and performance of Marine Tourism Commons (MTC) in the Karimunjawa Island Marine National Park, Indonesia. In: P. K. Nayak (Ed.). *Framing commons as a process: The rudiments of commonisation and decommonisation.* London and New York: Routledge.

Farhad, S. (2021). Concurrent processes of commonisation and decommonisation of Guadalquivir river (South Spain). In: P. K. Nayak (Ed.). *Framing commons as a process: The rudiments of commonisation and decommonisation.* London and New York: Routledge.

Galappaththi, E. and Nayak, P. K. (2017). Two faces of shrimp aquaculture: Commonising vs. decommonising effects of a wicked driver. *Maritime Studies* 16:12. DOI 10.1186/s40152-017-0066-4

Johnson, C. (2004). Uncommon ground: The "poverty of history" in common property discourses. *Development and Change,* 35(3), 407–433.

Khan, S. R. (2012). Linking Conservation with Sustainable Mountain Livelihoods: A Case Study of Northern Pakistan. Doctoral thesis, University of Manitoba, Canada. http://hdl.handle.net/1993/8898

Khan, S. and Haque, C. E. (2021). Decommonisation and new-commonisation of mountain commons in Northern Pakistan. In: P. K. Nayak (Ed.). *Framing commons as a process: The rudiments of commonisation and decommonisation*. London and New York: Routledge.

Klooster, D. and Robson, J. (2021). Migration and the commons: Recommonisation in Indigenous Mexico. In: P. K. Nayak (Ed.). *Framing commons as a process: The rudiments of commonisation and decommonisation*. London and New York: Routledge.

Lichtenstein, G. and Cowan Ros, C. (2021). Vicuña conservation and the reinvigoration of indigenous communities in the Andes. In: P. K. Nayak (Ed.). *Framing commons as a process: The rudiments of commonisation and decommonisation*. London and New York: Routledge.

Nayak, P. K. and Berkes, F. (2008). Politics of cooptation: Self-organized community forest management and joint forest management in Orissa, India. *Environmental Management,* 41, 707–718.

Nayak, P. K. and Berkes, F. (2011). Commonisation and decommonisation: understanding the processes of change in Chilika Lagoon, India. *Conservation and Society,* 9, 132–145. http://dx.doi.org/10.4103/0972-4923.83723

Nayak, P. K. and Berkes, F. (2014). Linking global drivers with local and regional change: A social-ecological system approach in Chilika Lagoon, Bay of Bengal. *Regional Environmental Change,* 14, 2067–2078.

Ostrom, E. (1990). *Governing the commons: The evolution of institutions for collective action*. Cambridge: Cambridge University Press.

Ostrom, E. (2005). *Understanding institutional diversity*. Princeton: Princeton University Press.

Ostrom, E. (2009). A general framework for analysing sustainability of social-ecological systems. *Science,* 325 (5939), 419–422.

Ostrom, E., J. Burger, C. B. Field, R. B. Norgaard and D. Policansky. (1999). Revisiting the commons: Local lessons, global challenges. *Science,* 284, 278–282.

Perkins, P. E. (2021). Commoning and climate justice. In: P. K. Nayak (Ed.). *Framing commons as a process: The rudiments of commonisation and decommonisation*. London and New York: Routledge.

Singh, V. (2021). Governing fluvial commons in colonial Bihar: Alluvion and Diluvion Regulation and decommonisation. In: P. K. Nayak (Ed.). *Framing commons as a process: The rudiments of commonisation and decommonisation*. London and New York: Routledge.

Index

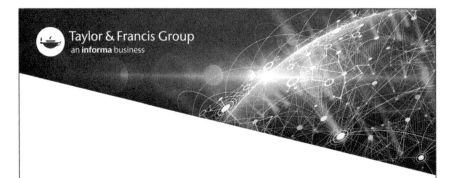